DRIVEN

DRIVEN

Inside BMW, the Most Admired Car
Company in the World

DAVID KILEY

WILEY

John Wiley & Sons, Inc.

Published by John Wiley & Sons, Inc., Hoboken, New Jersey.
Published simultaneously in Canada.

For general information on our other products and services please contact our Customer Care Department within the United States at (800) 762-2974, outside the United States at (317) 572-3993 or fax (317) 572-4002.

Wiley also publishes its books in a variety of electronic formats. Some content that appears in print may not be available in electronic books. For more information about Wiley products, visit our web site at *www.Wiley.com*.

Photo of Stefan and Johanna Quandt used with permission of AFP/Getty Images. All other photos courtesy of BMW.

Library of Congress Cataloging-in-Publication Data

Kiley, David.
    Driven : inside BMW, the most admired car company in the world / David Kiley.
        p. cm.
    Includes index.
    ISBN 0-471-26920-4 (cloth)
    1. Bayerische Motoren Werke—History.   2. Automobile industry and trade—Germany—History.   I. Title.
    HD9710.G44K55 2004
    338.7'629222'0943—dc22

                                                                    2004001538

Printed in the United States of America

10   9   8   7   6   5   4   3   2   1

To the memory of Gustav Otto, as well as to the tens of thousands of unheralded people associated with BMW over the years who have made it the company and brand it is today.

Contents

Acknowledgments   ix

Introduction   1

1   The Ultimate Cars   7

2   The Ultimate History   47

3   The Ultimate Family   81

4   The Ultimate Brand   107

5   The Ultimate Stylists   151

6   The Ultimate Blunder   195

7   The Ultimate Brand Expansion   231

8   The Ultimate Hydrogen Future   273

Epilogue: The Ultimate Outlook   293

Notes   297

Index   303

Acknowledgments

No book comes together without many people helping the author.

First on my list of thanks is my wife, Amy, who supports my life and my work every day in so many ways that it makes it difficult to ever thank her properly. Thank you.

Daniel Forbes proved again that he is a great friend, writer, and editor, saving me from too many rewritten pages. May Dan and I always be friends and mutual boosters. Elaine Catton offered invaluable friendship and assistance, including a few of the interviews in this book that are critical to telling the BMW story. Thanks to Paul Eisenstein, editor and publisher of www.thecarconnection.com, for sharing some of his articles and notes with me.

Sara Naegele proved to be a writer's dream, an editorial assistant that I hope will work with me on all my books. Paul Kiley and Gabe Williams provided valuable research and translation services. Thank you to Cordelia Wolfe, who was nice enough to let me drive her wonderful BMW 2002 so that I could see for myself why it set the industry on fire 35 years ago.

BMW's top management embraced my project from the beginning and granted me critical access to the company. I especially wish to thank Dr. Helmut Panke, Dr. Burkhard Goeschel, Dr. Michael Ganal,

Chris Bangle, Gerhard Richter, Tom Purves, Jack Pitney, Jim McDowell, and Christoph Huss. Thanks also to former BMW executives Bernd Pischetsrieder, Wolfgang Reitzle, and Victor Doolan for their time and insights.

The communication departments of BMW AG and BMW of North America made many of my tasks easy. Their professional and good-natured cooperation was invaluable. I especially want to thank Richard Gaul, Rob Mitchell, Martha McKinley, Dave Buchko, Gordon Keil, Karen Vonder Meulen, Jochen Frey, and Martina Wimmer. Thanks to all the helpful folks at Fallon Worldwide, too, for an invaluable tour around the BMW brand communication strategy. And thanks to Tony Gott, Howard Moshe, and Bob Austin of Rolls-Royce.

This is my second book for John Wiley & Sons. As with my first book, I have benefited immensely from the guidance and support of executive editor Airíe Stuart, as well as Linda Witzling. Hardworking reporters need good editors, and I have been fortunate to have two this time around. Thanks also to the work of Emily Conway.

The auto team at *USA Today*—Judith Austin, Jim Healey, Earle Eldridge, and Jayne O'Donnell—pick me up in a variety of ways every day, week in and week out. They make my day job rewarding, and their support of my book writing is evident in these pages as well. I am grateful, too, for the support of my editors at *USA Today*.

D.K.

Introduction

Safe to say, I'm not alone in calling BMW the most admired car company in the world. I venture such a bold, highly subjective statement only after numerous conversations over the years with men and women working for car companies, car magazines, and advertising agencies. It's a notion supported by my years of journalism covering the auto industry and test-driving any number of BMWs. I've driven BMWs for two decades now, judging them against vehicles built by Infiniti, Mercedes-Benz, Saab, Lexus, Acura, Jaguar, and others. Every time I slip behind the wheel, *it* leaps out at me—an *authenticity* and a sure-footedness that characterizes nearly all the vehicles BMW produces. Their design, performance under the hood, and the balance and agility of each vehicle are superb. Even when a competitor surfaces and achieves more horsepower or a faster 0- to 60-mph time, most true car aficionados sense in their gut that those other cars are trying to be *Bimmer* beaters. Nearly every time, those posers, especially those competing against the BMW 3 Series, 5 Series, and M Series cars, play a poor Jayne Mansfield to BMW's Marilyn Monroe, or an earnest Vic Damone to BMW's Frank Sinatra. Not slop, but not the top.

Overall, it's been a company grounded in nearly airtight *consistency* as well as *authenticity* when it comes to BMW-branded vehicles.

Authenticity, my research always found, is a trait bred in the bone at
BMW. Not just of product, but of brand. My years of studying, writing about, and working in marketing tell me that authenticity is perhaps the most important aspect of a successful brand, especially with
cars. The worst marketing howlers occur when companies lose sight
of what a brand stands for, trying instead to force it into some modern, ill-fitting suit to appeal to a younger, hipper audience, or hurrying
a poor specimen to market in order to fill a suddenly popular market
niche. Examples abound: the Mercedes A Class, an egg-shaped city car
that bears no relation to the Mercedes E Class or coupes; the Volkswagen Phaeton, a VW luxury sedan costing $70,000 to $80,000 and
wearing the same brand as the $16,000 Polo (a subcompact sold out-
side the United States); the Chrysler TC, a curious and laughable 1980s
exercise involving a Maserati design bum-rushed onto a Chrysler
LeBaron; the Porsche 924, a sport hatchback that was built originally
for VW but eventually sold as a Porsche; the Jaguar X-Type, a front-
drive car grafted onto the platform of a Ford Mondeo. To BMW's
credit, it has not executed a product in the past 30 years that can be
stamped as silly or unworthy of its brand character as "The Ultimate
Driving Machine." Even during the painful mid-1990s, when it lost billions on the misguided purchase of the British Rover Group, BMW
inflicted no harm on its own core marque. And early in the twenty-
first century, when BMW's American-born designer Chris Bangle
began turning out his first designs unencumbered by the reins of longtime product chief Wolfgang Reitzle, criticism of the cars focused for
the most part on some of Bangle's design choices—trunk shape, headlamps, a cut line here or there. The driving machine guts underneath
the hotly debated designs were hardly questioned for their superiority
over the competition.

General Motors product chief Bob Lutz, formerly a management
board member at BMW in charge of sales and marketing, calls BMW
the most focused brand in the industry "and a model for any company
trying to figure out what it stands for." At GM, Lutz regularly holds up
BMW brand focus as a benchmark to executives in charge of defining
GM's stable of often muddled brands.

Chrysler Group's head of sales and marketing in 2001 and 2002, Jim
Schroer, told me he was trying to bring "BMW thinking" to the reorganization of Chrysler's Chrysler, Dodge, and Jeep brands—not so

much Mercedes-Benz thinking, despite the naive slight against his parent company, but "BMW thinking." Said Schroer, "BMW is relentless in driving home a focused brand message and strategy that everyone in the company, top to bottom, understands. That's gold when you achieve that in a company."

Ron Harbour, president of Harbour & Associates, the auto industry's acknowledged expert on productivity, someone who has studied every global car company and been to most of the industry's factories, agrees that BMW is top of the industry when it comes to the combination of financial performance and the product it puts on the road. Says Harbour, "BMW has created a brand that is exclusive and exquisite. It's more than just putting nicer leather in the cars or the fit and finish. It's the total commitment in the organization to putting the best products on the road, according to the company's definition of 'best.' BMW really puts product before anything else, before productivity or ease of manufacture or anything else, and its success is rooted in that commitment."

It wasn't until a July 2002 interview with BMW chairman Dr. Helmut Panke that I realized the secret of BMW's success corresponded with some of the best advice I ever received from my own parents. On occasion, my mother told my five siblings and me, "Remember who you are." Behind that advice is the simple idea that if we would only keep in mind how she and my father wanted us to conduct ourselves, all would remain right in our world. Those words, in fact, are etched on my father's gravestone. I asked Panke, who was a consultant at McKinsey & Co. before joining BMW in 1982, what he would tell companies seeking insight from BMW if he were still charging McKinsey big bucks for his advice. Said Panke, "I would say: Focus on understanding *who you are,* what you stand for. What are the values you have in the organization? What are the values you believe in for the products and services that you sell and provide? People like to play charades when they are children. But in real life you cannot impersonate other values and characters and basic principles. There is a sentence I often use to crystallize what we are about. And I think it's important to be able to do that: to articulate the one idea in one sentence that captures the company's character so that everyone understands and believes it. 'BMW builds high-performance products because BMW is a high-performance organization.' This is an idea that speaks not just to our products. It is across seemingly unrelated fields and organizations within the company. Striving for better performance than our competitors is something that drives our controllers and our human resources people, not just our designers and engineers."

If it sounds basic, that's because it is. But it's BMW's sterling execution over the years of such a simple notion that has other car companies looking to BMW for answers. Consistency may be the most difficult and elusive target in the auto industry for the simple fact that as CEOs and designers and marketing directors play musical chairs with each other's jobs, each feels the need to pull up the stakes set by his or her predecessor and drive them home elsewhere, whether the company or brand needs it or not. Ad campaigns and marketing strategies change almost biannually in the auto business. Not at BMW. Since its American ad agency coined "The Ultimate Driving Machine" as the company's marketing and advertising theme in the mid-1970s, it hasn't wavered from that message in its communication. Its global business units have adopted their own translations of "The Ultimate Driving Machine," which doesn't always translate exactly the same. In other countries, the phrase translates roughly to "The Joy of Driving." In any case, the *idea* is the same all around the world.

The companies with the best, most valuable brands don't chase trends or bellow after customers. They remain true to what they are, and they attract people due to consistent trustworthiness and appeal. This core concept of *authenticity* is key to those of us who pay the rent as branding practitioners or are even brand conscious. There are those who think brand consciousness is a reflection of shallow character. Bunk! Think about it: Most consumers who eschew brand consciousness are actually *very* conscious of the brand they are wearing or driving. They like to think that because they don't aspire to a BMW or Rolex watch that they aren't brand conscious. But someone who chooses a Honda Civic, especially a gas-electric hybrid Civic, a Swatch, Chuck Taylor Converse sneakers, or Birkenstock shoes is just as brand conscious as the Bimmer, Rolex, and Nike consumer—and probably a lot more self-righteous to boot. It's not a stretch to say that those responsible for merchandising Honda, Swatch, and Converse have probably spent at least some bit of time examining how BMW develops and nurtures its brand.

Thus the point of this book: to look at the history of BMW, both long ago and more recently, and to tap into the thinking of the people who run BMW and have fostered its success. Luckily, my privileged peek came at an auspicious time. BMW has just fought through perhaps its most topsy-turvy period in 40 years, following a major and uncharacteristic shredding of the management ranks and at the dawn of an upheaval in its product design culture that made the company such a rock-ribbed touchstone in the first place.

Some partisans might claim Toyota or Honda as the most admired car company because of their consistent financial gains, lusty profit margins, and stellar reputation for quality. Journalists could make a case for either Japanese company as the best in the world. Certainly, as the industry is feverishly cutting costs, both companies serve as a better model than BMW for efficiency, quality, and productivity, though BMW's net profit margin has usually been better than Honda's. Besides turning in its own respectable quality and productivity scores in industry surveys and studies, BMW consistently delivers on three devilishly difficult measures of performance: high operating profit margin; product that not only sells consistently, but is consistently praised by the motoring press; and a clear and consistent aspirational marketing message. Honda and Toyota, as good as they are, are still frequently guilty of building vehicles that are mere appliances, lacking the vim and panache of real "motorcars," with all the connotation that designation implies. Consider a 2003 review of the Acura TSX in *The New York Times*. Journalist Dan Neil noted, "Agile and athletic, fuel efficient, luxuriously refined and loaded with standard features like a 360-watt sound system, leather upholstery, power moon-roof and a stability control system, the TSX undercuts a similarly equipped BMW 325i—a main rival for your affections—by $6,000." But, Neil writes, "If the 2004 TSX has a weakness, it is . . . an appliance-like vapidity, a soulessness, a gravity for which there is no center."[1] This kind of comparison between an arguably better-manufactured, higher-quality Japanese car and BMW plays out remarkably often.

BMW's status as an industry benchmark for both product development and marketing makes it unique. I know of no company in or out of the auto industry that benchmarks Toyota for its marketing strategies. I know of no company that benchmarks Toyota or Honda for artful design. Along with Mercedes-Benz, companies emulate Toyota and Honda for engineering, manufacturing process, and quality. But competitors benchmark BMW for design, engineering, quality, and marketing all at once.

As previously noted, the only loud hiccup in an otherwise admirable four-decade run was the acquisition of the Rover Group in 1994, which resulted in subsequent losses adding up to more than $8 billion over six years. Chapter 6 deals with the "The Ultimate Blunder," the acquisition and eventual disposal of the Rover Group. That was an exercise that hopefully provides a lesson or two in how *not* to make an acquisition, how *not* to manage an acquisition after it's made, and finally, how to consign a bad deal to history and get on with the next success. Even the company's one glaring misstep provides a course in moving on. Recovery was boosted by BMW's years of consistent brand focus that provided the company's leaders with a clear road map to restored pride and profitability.

One caveat for the gearheads and racing buffs: Compression ratios and engine bores are tackled only as necessary to tell the tale and hopefully convey some insight and perspective along the way. Better technical and racing journalists than I who bang around under the hood have chronicled those important aspects of BMW's history in other fine books. I introduce some of BMW's products in Chapter 1 to provide background material, and further product discussions occur in every chapter. And while racing is part of BMW's proud past, I plumb its depths only as needed since, as aficionados know, auto racing is a world unto itself and one where I'm but a tourist. Finally, fans of BMW's fine motorcycles may be disappointed that I give its small-but-storied business short treatment in these pages, but because it is such a separate business from carmaking, I discuss it mostly in historical and design terms—and only where it makes sense to do so. I devote a full chapter to the mysterious Quandt family, which has owned a controlling stake in BMW since 1959 and calls most of the shots there. Like the Ford family, the Quandts, who are much more secretive and private than the Fords, have had their tragedies, triumphs, and interesting characters.

In the end, BMW is simply the most stable, muscled, deepwater brand in the business. Cadillac, Ford, Chrysler, Mercedes-Benz, Jaguar, Saab, Acura, and Infiniti all struggle, stumble, and sometimes mire in the muck with bad advertising, bad product, bad management, or some maladroit combination of all three. A July 2002 *Forbes* article on BMW carried the appropriate headline: "The Best Driven Brand."[2]

The Ultimate Cars

ONE

There will never be a boring BMW.
—BMW CHAIRMAN DR. HELMUT PANKE

It is difficult to be completely objective when discussing motorcars produced by Bayerische Motoren Werke—Bavarian Motor Works. BMW. For people who fancy driving and do not see driving as a mere conveyance to get from here to there, no other automobile company has been as consistent as BMW in delivering top-notch motoring to driving enthusiasts. The vehicles have long been the essence of sporty driving, combining thoughtful engineering, originality, craftsmanship, speed, and handling. BMW vehicles are unique. They are the cars studied by other companies for how to build a car that is fun to drive. BMWs are built for connoisseurs of driving, just as Leica cameras are made for photographers, not just shutterbugs, and Savile Row suits are made by London's exclusive clothiers for people of means who care a great deal about their appearance. Slip behind the wheel of most any BMW and driving gloves suddenly seem very appropriate, not a silly extravagance. Drive a 325i or a 540i around an uncongested city and out on the highway, and the differences between a BMW and a Buick become crystal clear. Where the Buick feels vague, soft, and swishy, the BMW feels sharp and crisp, like it's riding on rails. Staring down at the graphically beautiful blue, white, and black BMW logo (an airplane propeller against a blue Bavarian sky) in the center of the steering wheel, the driver is greeted with a symbol of a company that for more than 80 years has largely succeeded in building and selling cars that buyers view as special, unique, and worth more money than cars built for the masses.

People who do not much value, appreciate, or especially enjoy the act of driving surely look upon the price of a BMW, versus the Buick, as an extravagance. But for those of us who enjoy driving, the difference between a BMW and a modern Buick is the difference between breathing fresh, clean air and breathing the recirculated air in a pressurized commercial jumbo jet.

It's impossible to do justice to all of the wonderful BMW vehicles developed in Bavaria over the decades, but a sampling of a few is a good way to start telling BMW's story.

The 2004 5 Series

Before delving into BMW's history, a look at its present (fall 2003) is in order. There was more anticipation surrounding the debut of the 2004 5 Series in late 2003 than there had been for any other BMW model in the previous three years. Why? Because in contrast with the long-running love affair between the motoring press and BMW, reviewers have run hot and cold with the 2002 7 Series and the 2003 Z4. Those two cars mark the start of a new era at BMW, one that reflects a dramatic change in design aesthetics and a redefinition of how big and broad the BMW brand can or should be, a change brought about by new management.

Helmut Panke took over as chairman in 2002, following the three-year run of Joachim Milberg, who took over in 1999 after BMW's supervisory board ousted chairman Bernd Pischetsrieder and long-time product development chief Wolfgang Reitzle, who had largely defined the look of BMW vehicles for 15 years. A year later, three more significant members of BMW's management board resigned over differences of opinion about strategy with Milberg and Panke. At no time in BMW's modern history, which began in 1959 when Herbert Quandt took controlling interest in the automaker, had the perennially ultrastable BMW undergone such shift and tumult.

Leading up to the debut of the 2002 7 Series, the company's flagship car, BMW had long been known and appreciated for its classically designed ultranimble and speedy vehicles. Chief designer Chris Bangle, though, with the 7 Series and 2003 Z4 roadster, introduced the start of a more avant-garde palette. The definition of *avant-garde,* of course, begs that not everyone will agree that the designs are good. But the sometimes caustic and withering criticism of the two models (see Chapter 5) by the most influential motoring magazines in the world and many of BMW's devoted customers was very different from the usual majority opinion that BMW can do no wrong when it comes to sport sedans and performance cars. The 7 Series came first, ominously shown to the public for the first time at the Frankfurt Motor Show on September 11, 2001. BMW's new flagship received some of the most scathing commentary the auto industry has witnessed in 20 years. Only the impossibly ugly and gangly Pontiac Aztek sport utility vehicle from General Motors received as much, or perhaps more, derision from auto journalists in the previous five years. The vitriol against Bangle about these models has been so pointed that *Automobile* magazine in its July 2003 issue heralding the 5 Series suggested it had been hit with "The Bangle Stick," a not too subtle play on "Ugly Stick" (many a barb about a poorly designed car or unattractive person includes a remark about having been hit with an "ugly stick"). Critics lambasted the 7 Series' balky tail end, fussy front fascia, and often confounding electronic iDrive. The iDrive is a computer-mouse-like gizmo in the center console that is meant to help the driver control more than 700 functions of the car, from air conditioners to a navigation system, though it made tuning the radio a chore in need of the owners manual. Then came the Z4 a year later at the Paris Motor Show. The rear spoiler integrated into the trunk of the Z4 roadster was compared by many writers to a duck's bill, not a typically desirable metaphor for what is supposed to be a serious open-air performance sports car. The side sheet metal of the Z4 carries eye-catching lines and creases that reflect Bangle's notion that a car should have lines and shapes found in nature, such as flames and windblown wheat fields, rather than just pleasant geometry. The aesthetic was lost on most, and too startling for a lot of BMW admirers and journalists.

The 7 Series and Z4, by Bangle's own admission, represented "bookends" of his new design scheme, the "outer limits" of what he thinks is correct for the new design direction at BMW. The 5 Series and 3 Series, which carry more than half of BMW's global sales volume and profit, he has long said, would look like logical progressions from these cars, but not as radical. Still, the anticipation of the 5 Series had been building, especially among those who have long loved BMW's classic, practically timeless designs but dislike Bangle's new, more "fashionable" direction. To be fair to Bangle, it is often lost in the scalding criticisms of the new designs that BMW's management board, the *Vorstand*, made up today of six men, vote on and finally approve a design after at least three are presented to them in full-size clay form. One of those designs presented for each model continues to be a conservative design option, very much a stepped evolution from the classic designs that made BMW successful in the 1980s and 1990s. Yes, Bangle is leading the new design direction at BMW, but he gets his power and approval from a group of men who could have chosen more evolutionary, conservative, and safe styles for the 7 Series and Z4 instead of Bangle's avant-garde choices. Dr. Burkhard Goeschel has been the management board member in charge of product development since 2000 and is thus Bangle's boss and advocate on the *Vorstand*. For reasons unclear to many, he has not received nearly as much hate mail or criticism from the motor press as Bangle.

There was a feeling among BMW followers and journalists that maybe the cooler than expected reception for the 7 Series and Z4 prompted some late changes to the 5 Series, that somehow BMW would decide to cool things down a bit and that the risks accepted for lower-volume models like the 7 Series and Z4 wouldn't be acceptable in the high-stakes 5 Series. Too, the 5 Series was looked at as the true gateway of BMW's most aggressive product onslaught in its history, as it rolls out a new or completely updated model every three months between mid-2003 and the end of 2005. While the 3 Series contributes more total sales to BMW, the 5 Series is the heart of whether BMW has true and unshakable credibility in the eyes of luxury-car buyers and the motor press.

Though BMW management appeared as confident as a hardware store owner selling hammers when it made the rounds among dealers and the media with the new 5 Series, there was good reason to fret about the reception of the 2004 5 Series, the fifth 5 Series since the car debuted in 1972. Consider the standard against which the new 5 Series will be measured. *Car and Driver,* certainly one of the best judges of automotive horseflesh in the motor media, has made the 5 Series a perennial winner in its annual top 10 list. In 2002, the magazine's editor, Csaba Csere, wrote: "There's a section of road on our 10Best loop that is heavily crowned and afflicted with a long series of severe bumps on the right side of the lane. Even well above 70 mph, the BMW 540, with its suspension pumping furiously, glided over this jangling stretch as serenely as if it were on freshly rolled pavement. Yet a mile farther down the road, when the pavement combines a diabolical series of lateral wiggles with a selection of severe dips and humpback rises, the 540 hunkered down, planted its tires, and negotiated the corners securely with no extraneous body movements."[1] A year before, the magazine extolled, "This athletic behavior is particularly gratifying because the 5-Series models deliver an absorbent, beautifully damped ride that sets the standard for controlled comfort among luxury sedans." *Consumer Reports* in 2003 called the 5 Series "one of the finest automobiles in the world."[2] The 2004 5 Series had a tough act to follow, and BMW management was right to be anxious about the reception of the car, as it accounts for nearly one-fifth of the company's annual sales and an estimated 25 percent of profits.

It's a fact of the auto business that every car company marketing a midsized luxury car is gunning for the 5 Series, and that goes for Audi, Acura, Infiniti, Lexus, Cadillac, and even Mercedes-Benz, whose 2002 E Class makeover seems closer to the BMW 5 Series than the previous-generation E Class.

The previous 5 Series introduced in late 1995 (code-named E39 inside BMW) was the fourth generation of the 5 Series. With lines and shape that today look as classic as a tuxedo, it was viewed even then as cutting-edge classy. "Conservative, yet aggressive," says BMW historian Marc Cranswick.[3] British motor magazine *Autocar,* in 1999, called the 5 Series, "Arguably the best range of cars in the real world."[4] Why have the 5 Series and many other BMWs, such as the 3 Series, been considered the best in their classes? What is it that separates the ride and handling of a BMW from a Cadillac, Lincoln, or Lexus?

- *Balance.* BMW has a canny and exacting way of distributing the weight in its cars nearly or exactly 50-50 between the front of the car and the back. Do you ever wonder why a Pontiac Grand Prix, for example, just doesn't drive like a BMW despite its faux race-track moniker? With the front-drive configuration in the Pontiac compared with BMW's rear-drive setup, the 2004 Pontiac has 63 percent of its weight riding on the front wheels. That makes cornering and braking a much different experience than in the BMW. Imagine walking or running down the street with a 20-pound weight strapped to your chest. Then imagine doing it with 10 pounds strapped to your front and 10 pounds strapped to your back. With balance comes control during movement.

- *Power-to-weight ratio.* Reducing weight and tweaking up the power output of the engine is an art at BMW. The absolute weight and the mass inertia of a car around its vertical axis are crucial to any car's lateral, vertical, and longitudinal dynamics—that is how the driver experiences the dynamic behavior of a car. This ratio literally determines how the car feels during braking, taking every turn, and accelerating from a dead stop. The balance of the car, combined with maximizing power and minimizing weight, is what makes a BMW seem so much more nimble than other cars. U.S. drivers may be surprised to learn that BMW is not all that preoccupied with achieving top 0- to 60-mph times when *Car and Driver* or *Road & Track* pit BMWs against Porsches, Acuras, Nissans, or Mercedes-Benzes. BMW is not nearly as interested in speed as it is handling and enjoyability. Thus, power-to-weight ratios are *not* that crucial if a car's performance is judged merely by 0- to 60-mph drag racing standards. Power-to-weight ratios, though, are critical for achieving the best cornering, braking, and cruising performance. An advertisement for the BMW Z3 touches on this. "Happiness isn't around the corner. Happiness *is* the corner." The higher the horsepower and the lighter the vehicle, the easier it is for the engineers to achieve better low-end torque (power at low revolutions of the engine). Take the BMW M3, for example. Peak power from the engine doesn't arrive until 7,900 rpm, but 80 percent of total torque is available at a mere 2000 rpm. With a six-speed manual gearbox, this means the car pulls away from a stop with a greater sense of urgency than almost any other street car, at less than 3,000 rpm. That low-end torque comes in handy when BMW drivers are pulling out onto the autobahn from an on-ramp or at their highest level of enjoyment on remote twisty roads where speed is limited by the drive course and frequency of turns. A BMW M5 has a power-to-weight ratio of one horsepower per 10 pounds of weight, while the 2004 5 Series ratio is 11.2 pounds per one horsepower. An Acura TL, by contrast, has a ratio of 13.2 pounds of weight to one horsepower, plus it has the disability of being front-wheel drive, thus lacking BMW's balance.

- *Brakes.* Despite all the hype about 0- to 60-mph times in the United States, braking power is more important in Germany, BMW's primary market, and likely to earn more praise in the European motor press. Indeed, the time of 150 to 0 kilometers per hour (kph) gets more press attention than 0- to 60-mph acceleration. Braking power is one of the most important aspects of giving BMW drivers the feeling of total control of the vehicle, no matter the driving condition. Drivers in the United States, for example, moving at 80 miles per hour have at their disposal brakes that were designed to stop a car going 140 miles per hour. BMW uses four sensors, one at each wheel, in its antilock braking systems rather than the three sensors that most car companies employ. Each of BMW's four sensors carries accurate feedback from a specific wheel independently, whereas a three-sensor system provides an *average* wheel speed for rear wheels. This average reading can be inaccurate when one side of the car is on dry pavement and the other is on ice. Some antilock braking systems pulsate as few as four times a second, while BMW's ABS pulsates 12 to 15 times per second. The pulsation represents a cycle in which pressure is first released from a particular wheel that has begun to lock and then allowed to resume. The faster the cycle, the closer you are to achieving maximum braking efficiency. BMW's ABS also provides yaw control, which keeps the car's back end from swinging to the side by providing the proper balance between maximum braking and stability when one side of the car is on ice and the other is on dry pavement.

It's technical stuff, but such things are the heart and soul of BMW. BMW engineers obsess about these things. Even though many BMW buyers don't understand the hardware, and don't want to, most understand that it adds up to the reason they bought the car in the first place.

———

BMW designed the 2004 5 Series under a burden of tradition and reputation much greater than was the case when bringing the redesigned 2002 7 Series or 2003 Z4 to market. The first 5 Series was originally introduced with two models around the time of the 1972 Olympic Games in Munich, built at the (then) recently refurbished Dingolfing plant acquired by BMW when it bought the facility from the defunct German automaker Glas. BMW models in the 1960s, starting with the 1500 in the early 1960s and closing with the 2002 models at the end of the decade, were called BMW's "New Class" (see Chapter 2), marking a complete transformation of the postwar BMW and signifying that the company was ready to mount a challenge to Mercedes-Benz. While BMW calls its model ranges *Series,* as in 7 Series, 5 Series, and 3 Series, Mercedes has long called its model ranges *Classes,* as in C Class, E Class, and S Class. The introduction of the 5 Series, though, was not part of BMW's New Class, but rather viewed as "The New Generation." It's an important turning point for BMW because, while the New Class put BMW on the map financially and critically for the first time after World War II, the 5 Series, it could be argued, was the first high-volume BMW car to be developed under the shelter of true financial stability combined with the top-notch know-how of BMW's engineers and designers. With sales volumes increasing worldwide to 167,000 cars sold in 1971, BMW was hardly the well-kept secret of the auto industry and a car merely for people in the know. It was becoming more familiar, and other carmakers were increasingly scrutinizing the Bavarians. With greater attention to passenger comfort, trunk space, and interior design than past models had received, the 5 Series was the first sign of the company going at least a bit mainstream in the luxury segment, with an undeniable seat at the global auto industry table.

BMW had already established a pattern, which its customers loved, of expanding a product series through a wide range of engine derivatives. The original BMW 1500 platform with its 1.5-liter engine, for example, was stretched upward, with a 1.6-liter engine, a 1.8-liter engine, and finally, a 2000 with its 2.0-liter engine. Along the way the 1600 had versions with a single carburetor, with two carburetors, and so on. But those cars were not originally designed with the strategy in mind. It just sort of happened through the ingenuity of BMW's engineers and product development executives. The marketing executives soon saw that offering numerous engine derivatives was a sound way to further differentiate BMW from its competitors and establish its credentials as a serious engineering-driven brand. Further, buyers were willing to pay a premium for a unique engine and power package as long as it came with BMW's trademark sporty driving character. BMW saw throughout the 1960s that it could achieve very strong profits by proliferating engine derivatives as well as body styles over the course of a seven- to eight-year life of a model series. By constant and annual upgrade and freshening of the model series, it could keep sales relatively strong and stable rather than endure the dramatic falloff in sales after four years in the market that other car companies took for granted. Rivals like Opel, Ford, and Audi typically launched a new vehicle and left it alone for three or four years before doing only cosmetic improvement such as grille and headlamp modifications. BMW was constantly expanding, improving, and tinkering with a series after it was launched.

The groundwork for the new 5 Series and its six-cylinder engines, which would raise the 5 Series from "very good" to "great," was laid in 1965 when BMW began developing a six-cylinder engine that would enable the company to challenge the lower end of the Mercedes-Benz lineup with cars of comparable size and power. The first cars to carry the engine were the 1968 BMW 2500 and 2800. Those top-of-the-line sedans were extremely well received despite dear price tags of 14,485 deutsche marks ($5,284) for the 2500 and 17,250 deutsche marks for the 2800. These prices matched those of Mercedes for its 250S and 250SE. *Road & Track* gushed: "The all-new six cylinder engine is a jewel. At low speeds it combines a sporting exhaust note . . . with a modest amount of BMW cam drive whine and practically no other under-hood noise; as the revs climb toward the redline of 6200 rpm it takes on a snarl delightfully like that of a Porsche 911."[5] In reference to the price of the car, *Road & Track* noted, ". . . that's the price you pay for top quality . . . and there is no doubt that its performance is faster, more sporting and longer legged than that of its nearest competitor."[6] That competitor, everyone knew without the magazine saying so, was the small Mercedes. In 1971, faced with a revalued deutsche mark that raised prices, BMW began marketing a 2500 (the "Bavaria") with a bit less content in the United States. The idea was to keep the bigger sedan at a competitive price of about $5,000, $1,200 less than the 2500, while also playing up the BMW's unique German origin. *Road & Track* was then moved to rate the Bavaria one of its "Best Buys."[7] The car got a publicity boost when Jacqueline Kennedy Onassis was photographed transporting her children in a Bavaria to and from the family's New York City apartment and a horse farm and estate in rural New Jersey. BMW's mystique, already well established in Europe, was solidly taking hold in North America.

While the 2500 and 2800 proved to be successful large cars, the new 1972 5 Series (code-named E12 inside BMW) was developed as the successor to BMW's 1800 and 2000 models, but with an engine range that began with a four-cylinder and ended with the new-generation six-cylinder engines. The engines ranged from a small 1.8-liter four-cylinder to a 220-horsepower 3.0-liter six-cylinder, a very unusual and broad range of power for one model in those days. The 5 Series also clarified BMW's numeric naming system. "Five" was the series, while the next two numbers reflected the engine size; thus the 3.0-liter 5 Series became the 530. Letters would be added to represent certain technology. For example, the 530i meant the car was fuel-*injected*. Later, the 535iX would mean the car was equipped with a 3.5-liter engine, all-wheel drive (X), and fuel injection. "It was an ingenious and most effective system and still is," says GM's Bob Lutz. Indeed, other automakers have for over 30 years tried to create a memorable alphanumeric naming system, but none has stuck to buyers' consciousness like those of BMW and Mercedes-Benz. In fact, says former Mazda North America chief executive Charlie Hughes, who took Mazda to a new alphanumeric naming system in 2003 with vehicles dubbed Mazda6 and Mazda3, "BMW is what makes going to an alphanumeric system desirable. . . . BMW made it so such names are associated with premium brands."[8]

The original 520/520i was powered by a two-liter, four-cylinder engine. The first six-cylinder version, the 525/525i, had a 2.5-liter engine. As the line matured through 1974 and 1975, a 2.8-liter six-cylinder was added, the 528, and then a two 2.0-liter small-six-cylinder engine joined the model range. A puny 1.8-liter four-cylinder was also added to help cope with the oil shortage and soaring gasoline prices, but it was not a favorite of BMW drivers. It lacked the oomph BMW buyers craved. Specifically for the U.S. market, a 530i 3.0-liter six-cylinder was introduced. All those engine configurations, says former BMW development chief Wolfgang Reitzle, gave the customer a sense that his or her car was "practically one of a kind." Indeed, if the buyer chose a 520i and then opted for one of the less frequently selected colors, it's very likely that he or she wound up with the only one in that particular county. Too, the constant freshening of the series with new engine technology or power outputs kept the motor press interested in the series over the course of a seven-year run. Motor journalists are by nature interested in power upgrades and new technology under the hood, so they have long been more apt to write about a new 2.5-liter engine in a car they already respect than to pay attention to new headlamp and grille designs on the newest Ford if it lacks substantial engine or power upgrades.

Besides the engine refinement in the 5 Series, the car's outer shell looked more sophisticated than the previous BMWs and was more economical to build. Designed by BMW's French design leader, Paul Bracq, the car had an executive look without being stodgy. A larger greenhouse than many other cars of the early 1970s, it had a mark of freshness and lightness on its feet that like-sized saloons didn't possess. *Road & Track* said of the 530i, which it compared with the Bavaria, ". . . an excellent compromise of softness and firmness. Harshness over small, sharp disturbances has been reduced to practically nil and pitching over gentle pavement undulations—our biggest criticism of previous BMW chassis behavior—is gone."[9] A heavier car than the 1800/2000 it replaced, some said the 5 Series had softened its sporting edge when it first came out, but the quick additions of the larger engines calmed down those mild criticisms. A chief rival of the day in Europe was a line of midsized cars from Ford, the Granada. While the BMW and the Ford both had front-strut suspensions and an independent semitrailing-arm rear, noted auto historian Martin Buckley, "The BMW looks neat and agile, the Ford looks gross and cumbersome." At home in Germany, BMW was being chased a bit by Audi for performance positioning. Audi, by then a unit of Volkswagen, launched the 100LS and 100GL. They were front-drive, but had a nimble, quality feel similar to BMW's. Still, BMW had the better image. Among other reasons, Audi kept its engines smaller than BMW's, so they were less powerful. BMW was viewed as a brand for up-and-coming professionals, while Audi was a car more apt to be driven by a mortgage banker or an insurance actuary. BMW, as noted previously, is a rock-solid devotee of rear-drive engineering architecture, which enables it to achieve the perfect balance of weight critical to the BMW driving experience. Nevertheless, in the 1970s the company tested front-drive, transverse-mounted 5 Series models. All were rejected by BMW's testers, who saw no advantages and many disadvantages. "Let Audi [which developed front-drive cars] be Audi, and we will be BMW," says Wolfgang Reitzle about the decision to stick with rear-drive chassis development.[10]

The original 5 Series carried through 1981 with yearly upgrades, power enhancements, and the odd body modification. A facelift in 1977 revised the hood and raised the twin-kidney grille a bit. And the fuel-filler cap was moved from the rear to the side of the car. *Consumer Guide*'s 1981 review of the 5 Series indicates that the constant tweaking was worthwhile. "A very mechanical car in overall feel . . . for those who value superior dynamic capabilities. . . . Offers meticulous craftsmanship and a good deal of practicality plus an eager, sporty character. Rather exclusive and hardly cheap [about $22,000 basic in 1981] but considering what it can do the 528i isn't outlandishly priced. Recommended for those who appreciate—and can afford—the better things in life."[11]

———

It is perhaps not surprising that BMW benchmarked its own 5 Series—but not the 5 Series that was fading into history—to determine where to take the 2004 model. Five-series product manager Martin Birkman said the 1988 5 Series, known as E34 inside BMW, was more of an inspiration for the 2004 "Fiver." "The proportions of that car were really perfect, so we started with that car and made everything about 5 percent bigger—taller, longer and wider," said Birkman.[12] Weight distribution in the front and rear of the car's center is almost a perfect 50-50, owing to some tricky engineering work done to put costly aluminum in the front end and weld it to steel, a marriage normally resisted by those two metals. It was an expensive solution to achieve incrementally better weight distribution, but it speaks to the company's obsession over balance.

While the tail end of the 5 Series looks very much related to the controversial 7 Series, Birkman nevertheless doesn't wholeheartedly agree that the Five's trunk is *based* on the debatable 7 Series tail. It seems an odd denial, though the company has clearly become defensive about the criticism of the 7 Series trunk and thus perhaps doesn't want the two to be so readily compared. To keep the car's shoulders high and square, the belt line (where the car's body meets the side windows) continues from the front of the car all the way around to the back, literally belting the car. The front headlamps have contoured eyebrows that invade the top plane of the hood. Brickman says it's to make the car look "predator-like." Perhaps, but the headlamps have a decidedly feminine appearance, like the sequined eye mask of a woman at a costume ball.

The steering wheel movement, the input required by the driver at various speeds, and the feedback from the car as felt through the steering wheel to the driver's hands are all critical ingredients to the BMW driving experience. The driving experience is why most buyers willingly pay more for a BMW than they would for a Dodge or even an Acura of similar horsepower. Traditional steering systems in most cars have limitations because companies are forced to calibrate the steering one way for every driving condition. Through a complex combination of electronic controllers, BMW set out to develop a system that changes the input required from the driver depending on the speed and conditions. The significance of a change like this can't be underestimated for a brand like BMW. Trying to reinvent the way a BMW is steered is equivalent to Coca-Cola going from bottles to cans or a wine producer changing from corks to screw caps. Some purists still won't drink Coke from a can because they insist it doesn't taste as good. Similarly, driving enthusiasts turn a skeptical eye toward the use of sensors and electronics meant to make steering easier or better for fear that the gizmos will lessen the enjoyment of driving the car. With Active Steering, the most obvious effect is that drivers don't find themselves crossing arm over arm on the steering wheel as often during sharp cornering. Parking, too, requires far fewer turns of the wheel. Active Steering varies the steering transmission ratio electronically in direct relation to the style and speed of driving and road conditions. Under normal road conditions at low and medium speeds, the steering becomes more direct, requiring less effort by the driver and increasing the car's agility in city traffic or when parking. At high speeds the steering becomes less direct, offering improved directional stability—less lane waver. When cornering at high speeds or when undertaking sudden movements, the steering stiffens up by monitoring increases in the yaw rate—the side-to-side movement of the car. Active Steering relies on the input of electronic sensors to vary the amount of front-wheel turn in relation to how much the steering wheel turns. When the system's sensors detect driver input at the steering wheel (turning motion), a computer analyzes the data and then sends the information to an electric motor and linkage. Based on this input, the front wheels are turned the appropriate amount. The system can also intervene in an instant to provide a correction if the rear end of the car starts to break away—for example, in an emergency maneuver. The system adjusts a set of gears on the lower end of the steering column to create the best steering ratio. It does this by evaluating the steering assistance provided by an electric power steering motor plus the amount that the driver turns the steering wheel. In low-speed driving and turning, the ratio is a quick 10 to 1, making parking easy. The ratio slows progressively to 18 to 1 in normal conditions and to, say, 20 to 1 on the autobahn, so that a slight twitch of the wheel while the driver dials a cell phone or lights a cigarette doesn't threaten to put the car in a ditch. The steering ratio of cars without Active Steering is set at 14 to 1.

Why all this new engineering? Does the average driver care? The quick answer is simply that BMW must continue to innovate driving dynamics in a way that other companies aren't thinking about. If it doesn't, "the brand dies," says product development chief Burkhard Goeschel. When engineers looked anew at the relationship between driver and steering as the company developed the new 5 Series, they found that most drivers handle the steering wheel too aggressively, which destabilizes the behavior and performance of the car. They concluded that the whole experience would be enhanced if the car literally helped make better drivers out of its customers. The Active Steering system works in tandem with BMW's Dynamic Stability Control system, a device BMW has long used that combines control of the car's antilock brakes and steering to stabilize the car in emergency situations or simply in challenging driving conditions. Electronics are so sophisticated, though, that the danger recognized during development was in taking too much of the control out of the driver's hands. On a slalom course, the result is that a driver not only isn't prompted to cross wrists or throw arm over arm (bad form in any case), but the driver doesn't even have to shuffle hands (the proper method if driving on a slalom course or the equivalent road condition). "BMWs aren't driving couches like some cars strive to be," says Goeschel. This is where BMW spent years perfecting the system. "It's always in the last 10 percent. . . . That's what separates companies. Any company with access to the technology could achieve 90 percent of this system. But figuring out the last 10 percent, the part where we balanced how much the system does for the driver versus how much the car does for the driver, took as long to get right as the front 90 percent of the development," he says. The result is that the 5 Series equipped with Active Steering is incredibly agile at low speeds and far more precise and stable at autobahn speeds than the previous 5 Series, which was already viewed by many motor journalists as the finest sport sedan in the world!

The experience of this system is wonderful on its own, but it shines when a driver alternates between a "Fiver" car with Active Steering and one without. Noted *Bimmer* magazine, "Through the sea of cones on the slalom course, the normal car felt like a boat, sluggish and requiring lots of wheel twirling. By comparison, Active Steering made the big and heavy BMW feel like a nimble sports car. . . . When we turned into the first bend in the stock 530i [the car without Active Steering], it felt like custard pudding. Imprecise is not a word we would ever have used to describe BMW's excellent rack-and-pinion steering before, especially when compared with its rivals."[13] Another benefit of the combined Active Steering and Stability Control, especially at highway speeds, is to make the car feel smaller to drive, which is a good thing. In a lane change maneuver on the autobahn, going over 125 miles per hour, a standard 5 Series performs well, but there is inevitable lag from the back of the car. With Active Steering, the response of the rear of the car in the same exercise was faster and cleaner, giving the car a more agile feel—indeed, making the 535 feel more like the M3.[14] Noted *Bimmer* writer Ian Kuah, "Driving the Active Steering 5er was like having a light coming on in a darkened room." Even in 300-degree turns, a driver's hands never leave the nine o'clock and three o'clock positions.[15]

———

There is plenty of tension within BMW during the development of a new vehicle. However, when the focus of the brand is so tight and the people so well steeped in the dimensions and sensibilities of the brand, the tension is dynamic rather than counterproductive, with various constituencies arguing over mission and direction even before the first lines are drawn. Says Anton Ruf, project manager on the 7 Series, 5 Series, and 6 Series introduced in 2004: "There is a deeply pragmatic and largely non-politicized approach to getting things done at BMW. The sun doesn't shine every day at BMW during a product development phase. We argue intensely about issues. However, once a decision has been taken, we all get behind it and move on with strong dedication, even if it wasn't in our favor."[16]

New product development at BMW is divided into four phases: the *strategic phase* (what the market segment is, what drives it, what BMW thinks will drive it seven years from now when the car comes out, and what will drive it 17 years from now when someone is still driving a 10-year-old BMW); the *initial phase* (design sketches and technology ideas); the *concept phase* (usually at least three concepts that have been green-lighted); and *series development* (the development of the concept voted on and approved by the management board).

New product planning and development works under a matrix structure. Each project team has representation from the various relevant areas—marketing, styling, engines, chassis, and suspension, among others—while the various departments from which the team members are drawn work across all projects with each team. Management and financial responsibility rest with the project team. This structure is, in itself, not particularly groundbreaking and can be found in one form or another in most vehicle manufacturers.

Five-Series marketing chief at BMW AG Matthias Hoffmann says that, although all other disciplines have their input during the strategic phase of product development, it is marketing that very much dominates the process. Every marketing manager draws a pyramid of priorities in which marketing is at the peak. The basis of the 7 Series, for example, was defined not in physical terms but in strategic terms, and it all rotated around the brand values of sportiness and dynamism, with reference also to BMW's historical values of agility and controlled yet exciting driving.[17] BMW has long worked this way, though it can't be stressed enough that this thinking is relatively new to most automakers, which have long treated marketing as an afterthought and very much the soft side of a masculine business. Even when General Motors decided in the early 1990s to take marketing more seriously (after all, it did have six brands to manage), it badly botched its execution by hiring a flock of cookie and soap marketers. They lacked the depth of understanding about the relationship of American consumers to their cars, and GM lost a decade while it developed bland product after bland product only loosely connected to a series of disjointed and inconsistent ad campaigns, leaving most of the company's brands in a tangle by 2002 and 2003, when it began introducing a new generation of much better and higher-quality vehicles than it had produced in the previous two decades.

Ruf doesn't see consistent global branding as unique to BMW, placing Mercedes and Porsche (and, to a lesser extent, Audi) in the same category. True, the Germans have been better focused on marketing despite being known for their engineering prowess. They point out, too, that in the premium segment, it is easier to remain focused because you're not creating something for the masses. Also true. Appealing to a smaller, more focused group of buyers helps a company focus brand communications. But they are being kind to their competitors. Having to appeal to the masses isn't an excuse for disregarding a sound and stable marketing anchor as the starting point for any worthwhile product idea. Volkswagen did it successfully for decades. Again, the German engineering culture and education system seems to have figured out a way to instill the importance of marketing, the "soft side" of the car business, even in its most technology-driven gearheads.

Says Ruf, "We don't want to fill the world with BMWs, like a mass product."[18] BMW's brand focus on sportiness and dynamism brings with it the exclusivity that makes BMW aspirational. "Increasing volume is about exploring new niches and markets, not about broadening the appeal of individual products," he says. "This is why we have entered new segments with products such as the X5 and X3 Sport Activity Vehicles. It enables us to maintain the focus of our core product strength."

One of the biggest issues facing BMW in the development of the 7 Series, as well as the 5 Series and 6 Series, was the incorporation of significantly higher levels of comfort features and gadgets, which puts enormous pressure on engineers responsible for packaging the hardware into the car while at the same time keeping down the vehicle's weight. In addition, too much featuring and gadgetry could push their cars too far into competitive territory with brands like Cadillac and Lexus, which would be in conflict with BMW's sporty brand image. An example of the differences being looked after by engineers is sound. Lexus and Cadillac strive to keep a cabin as quiet as an isolation chamber. This pleases their traditional customers and helps the brands score exceptionally well on J.D. Power and Associates' annual Initial Quality Survey, which tracks customer complaints during the first 90 days of ownership. The top complaint customers have these days is wind and engine noise. BMW reckons that its customers want to hear a bit of the engine, the sound of which it takes great pains to tune as meticulously as a harp. Another tension point in the 7 Series was the decision to offer only an automatic gearbox, which was settled on at the beginning, partially in support of the push to win space in the center of the vehicle. "By removing the center console where the gearshifter and handbrake were located in the previous 7 Series, engineers won 8 liters of space," says Ruf, "to locate the iDrive."[19] And it was this rearrangement of space that led to another contentious move, the column-mounted shift-by-wire stick. BMW removed the console gearshifter and replaced it with a smallish column shifter that is so light it can be confused with windshield-wiper controller. Though the new shifter is sufficiently robust while being technologically advanced, it has a flimsy feel compared with traditional shifters. Many BMW devotees don't like its wimpy feel.

All the major internal battles over what product is most correct for the brand, says Ruf, are fought during the initial strategic phases, at which point the styling is agreed on. According to Ruf, the styling for the controversial 2001 7 Series, for example, had already been agreed to before the departure of product chief Wolfgang Reitzle and chairman Bernd Pischetsrieder. This contradicts comments made by both men, who have said the most controversial elements, the tail-end styling and the iDrive electronics controller, were approved by them but that the final execution was changed after they departed in ways they did not think wise. Final designs are very much collective decisions by the management board, and even the three design candidates they will ultimately vote on to arrive at the winning idea are determined collectively before the final vote. Ruf forcefully makes this point as a counterpoint to those who would lay blame and credit for designs solely or predominantly on chief designer Chris Bangle. If the board didn't want the early concepts Bangle's designers brought forward to develop into full-blown concepts to be voted on, he'd be replaced, and fast. The departures of Reitzle and Pischetsrieder, says Ruf, didn't have any significant impact on the direction of the 7 Series project. Nor did their departures significantly impact the 5 and 6 Series projects that had begun during their tenures, Ruf also notes, pointing out that former chairman Joachim Milberg and his successor Helmut Panke were both *Vorstand* members at the time Reitzle and Pischetsrieder left. Too, Burkhard Goeschel, Reitzle's eventual successor on the board, was already playing a key role. Talking to people on the *Vorstand,* such as Panke, Goeschel, and sales and marketing chief Michael Ganal does not yield much in the way of anecdotes regarding the internal debate about the 7 Series. Some, though, come through from Bangle and the design team (see Chapter 5) in terms of the thinking that went into the car's final look. BMW is much happier for the world not to know its internal arguments. Ruf, in fact, refused to be drawn into revealing the nature of the internal discussions on the styling of the 7, though others acknowledged there *was* conflict over the issues that dog BMW today—the trunk and the iDrive. This, of course, is not a bad thing. Nevertheless, BMW executives are trained not to air their dirty laundry in public. Former BMW sales and marketing boss Bob Lutz, now the head of product development at GM, says, "There must be conflict for anything good to come out the other end. But it *is* important that once a decision is reached, the organization must get behind it. If you snipe at a product or design after there has been a consensus decision, it feeds the press's appetite for conflict and mistrust and the product, in the end, is written about as being disowned by its very creators, and therefore discredited, before consumers even have a chance to vote on it."

The iDrive was greatly enhanced to be made simpler in the 5 Series. BMW was convinced that journalists who spent only a few days in a 7 Series with iDrive would complain about its complexity, whereas owners would master the system, but a report by *Consumer Reports* magazine two years after it went on sale says otherwise. The 7 Series ranked sixth out of seven luxury sedans based on reliability and complaints. "Even after months of driving, our testers found the complex multi-function iDrive system confusing and difficult to master," said the magazine.[20]

The 6 Series

The 2005 6 Series coupe, a car built on some of the bones of the 5 Series, will be the first 6 Series to be sold in showrooms since 1989. Designer Chris Bangle had wanted to get a "legitimate" coupe onto the road since his arrival at BMW in 1992. Bangle uses the word *legitimate* because most of BMW's coupes since 1960 have been little more than chopped off sedans, not coupes developed as such from the ground.

By the early 1970s, BMW knew that its popular and well-regarded 3.0 CS coupe, marketed since 1968 and noteworthy for its absence of a center pillar, would not meet future federal standards for either rollover or collision protection. BMW's French design chief Paul Bracq set about to design a replacement that would retain the elegant sportiness of the CS, but with a much higher degree of driver and occupant protection than had been a part of any previous BMW coupe. The 6 Series that debuted at the 1976 Geneva Motor Show is one of the most beloved BMW models in the company's recent history. Noted by the motor press for being longer, lower, wider, and heavier than the earlier coupes, the body shell bore the unmistakable elegance of the artist who had drawn its lines. BMW installed a 185-horsepower, six-cylinder engine, slightly modified from the engine that had been in the 3.0 CS. The motoring press was delighted with the car. Typical was *Road & Track,* which reviewed the 1977 model, the first to be sold in the United States: "This engine is without a doubt the most sophisticated production in-line six [cylinder engine] in the world."[21] The magazine compared the body style to a Rodin sculpture. A year later when BMW introduced the fuel-injected 633CSi, the magazine wrote: ". . . the perfect example of engineering improvements and comfort refinements that make a great GT car even more pleasurable." The magazine also praised the car's ergonomic design, a seldom cited point of praise for sports coupes. This was BMW's strategy of constant improvement under the hood at its best, compelling motoring magazines to review the same car twice in 12 months. Six Series handling was more entertaining than the handling of Jaguars and Mercedes, and the elegant, understated styling appealed perfectly to those who were buying BMWs because they were a bit less obvious displays of wealth than Jags and Benzes. The only sore spot for the 6 Series was the price tag, which was $23,600 in 1978 and a wallet-wilting $40,000 by 1983, thanks in part to the U.S. greenback weakening against the deutsche mark. In the early 1980s, the 6 Series was at the center of an un-BMW-like race with Mercedes-Benz to produce the fastest sports coupe on the continent. Mercedes V8 450SLC was besting the BMW 6, but BMW responded by installing a 3.5-liter in-line six-cylinder engine into the 635i. BMW's engineers added speed accessories like a front air dam and rear spoiler, all of which gave the coupe a top speed of 140 miles per hour and a 0- to 62-mph (100 kph) speed of 7.3 seconds, compared with 8.9 seconds for the 630CS. The United States, always playing second fiddle to Europe, didn't see the 3.5-liter speedster until 1987. That year, too, the company decided there should be something special for the serious motor-heads. The M6, from BMW's M Series of road-going race cars, was adapted from the 6 Series with a 24-valve head on the 3.5-liter engine, creating a 256-horsepower power plant. This car, even today, is one of BMW's most collectible models.

By the end of its run in 1989, BMW had sold more than 86,000 of the 6 Series cars. Revered for its styling and power, the 6 Series was exhibited in several museums around the world as a defining piece of late-twentieth-century design. Its 13-year run without stem-to-stern redesign represents the longest run for any single model in BMW's history. The 6 Series established a supercar-slaying reputation that failed to extend to its replacement, the overweight 8 Series coupe that debuted in 1989 and was one of the company's few duds. Appreciated mainly by BMW aficionados who simply won't buy any other make, neither its design, speed, handling, or any other single aspect of the car impressed the motoring press or customers who comparison shopped. The 6 Series was the defining coupe for BMW, setting the standard for other car companies.

The first sign of a new 6 Series for a new century was the Z9 concept car shown at the 1999 Frankfurt Motor Show. The lines of the Z9's exterior design were clean, simple, and yet dramatic, with a long, sleek bonnet and short, muscular tail. The most dramatic design element of this car was the two gull-wing doors that could also be opened horizontally like conventional doors. This feature was never considered for production, but made for a dramatic splash in the show. The Z9 also featured a forerunner to the iDrive controller previously mentioned.

"We have struggled with the idea of a coupe since I have been at the company and before that," says Bangle. BMW always did coupes, but only the original 6 Series ever really "came to life" in Bangle's eyes. Even the original 6 Series looked too much like a "cut down sedan" to Bangle. There are real differences in the proper design language of roadsters, coupes, GT coupes, and touring coupes. The 2005 6 Series is meant to be a touring coupe, which means most roadster fans won't even be tempted by it until the 500-horsepower M6, expected by 2006, makes its debut. Michael Stahmer, the executive in charge of developing the 6 Series, says the hardtop coupe is a car designed with the "empty nester" in mind. Stahmer struggles over this term, because it does not exist in Germany, and he admits he learned it during the 6 Series project from his American counterparts. "The personality of this car appeals most directly to a male, educated, with grown children or no children, income of at least $200,000 or more, and who is not interested in over-stated design," says Stahmer. The most direct competitor to the new 6 Series is the Jaguar XK coupe, which, like the new Six, comes in a convertible that was designed separately from the hardtop coupe rather than by simply adding a convertible top or retracting hardtop to the existing car. Before settling on the design that is the 2005 6 Series, BMW struggled with several "GT" designs, cars whose designs were clearly influenced by race-car design. All of them, says Bangle, were just wrongheaded. Though the 6 Series is built largely off the parts of 5 Series, its design, says Bangle, is actually derived from the 7 Series. Indeed, the same designer, Adrian van Hooydonk, whose design became the 7 Series, was also a lead designer on the 6 Series.

The new 6 Series uses advanced materials to reduce weight. The front chassis, hood, and doors are aluminum; the front fenders and trunk lid are thermoplastic. The 645Ci weighs in at about 3,500 pounds, roughly 300 pounds lighter than the previous coupe sold by BMW, the 840Ci. Besides shedding weight, the hybrid construction materials help it to achieve an ideal 50-50 weight distribution. The rear-drive 6 Series launching in 2004 starts with one engine: the 4.4-liter V8 from the 745i. It delivers 333 horsepower at 6,100 rpm along with 325 lb-ft of torque at 3,700 rpm—good enough to push manual versions from 0 to 60 mph in 5.6 seconds.

————

The Z9, 5 Series, 7 Series, 6 Series, and every other car coming out of BMW for the next several years are very much influenced by Burkhard Goeschel. The *Vorstand* member in charge of product development today, Goeschel is typical of the kind of engineer and executive for which BMW hunts. He grew up in Stuttgart in the shadow of the Mercedes-Benz plant where his father was employed as an engineer. "We ate and slept cars at my house from my earliest memories," says Goeschel. One of his clearest memories was riding with his father in the famous Mercedes 300SL Gullwing in the early 1950s before it made its debut at the Geneva Motor Show in 1955. No wonder, then, that the Z9 had gull-wing doors. The first car that he owned, like every young German, was a Volkswagen Beetle. But Goeschel's Beetle was modified with special air intakes, a 1.5-liter truck engine, a front-mounted oil cooler, double carburetors, "and a great big STP sticker across the rear window," he recalls. Goeschel was tapped by chairman Joachim Milberg in 2000 after Wolfgang Ziebart resigned after just one year on the job. Goeschel had worked his way up through the engine-engineering ranks at BMW. He had a difficult act to follow. Where Reitzle was a captivating public speaker and achieved a cult of personality inside and outside BMW, covered by the German business media as though he were a rock star, Goeschel has long been a hardworking, talented, if unsung, engineer, working on some of BMW's most celebrated models, including the 3 Series, 5 Series, Z3 and Z4, Mini Cooper S, and two generations of 7 Series, as well as the company's long-running hydrogen car program. To Milberg and his successor, Helmut Panke, Goeschel was a welcome change from Reitzle who, while considered one of the most talented product development car executives in the business, could be very divisive and polarizing inside BMW.

Goeschel doesn't espouse the obsessive attention to styling or pontificate about the study and thought of "brand" for which Reitzle was famous (see Chapter 5). As an engine engineer, he is also one of those at BMW known for a "sensitive bottom." That simply means that he is good at sensing where a car's engine, chassis, brakes, and shocks need to be tuned and tweaked to achieve true "BMWness." Goeschel, who joined BMW in 1979 after leaving Mercedes-Benz, is as much a product of BMW as are the motorcars on which he works. The people BMW molds are as important as the vehicles.

———

While Goeschel is responsible for how well BMW cars move down the road, and he and Chris Bangle craft the designs voted on by the *Vorstand,* the man most responsible for product, design, brand, and profitability is the chairman, Dr. Helmut Panke, who took over as chairman in 2002 from Joachim Milberg, who held the post for just three years. Panke was Milberg's chief financial officer and the architect of BMW's rapid financial restructuring following the 2000 $3.2 billion charge against earnings taken as part of the divestiture of the Rover Group. Unlike Pischetsrieder and his predecessor, longtime chairman Eberhard von Kuenheim, Panke tends to resist the ceremonial trappings of his office. German auto chieftains such as Ferdinand Piech, who was VW's *Vorstand* chairman in the 1990s, and Daimler-Chrysler chairman Jürgen Schrempp publicly posture themselves in almost regal terms. When they are available at motor shows, they typically conduct very few interviews with journalists—and those in secluded little rooms in the bowels of the show halls, with public relations people treating the occasion like a state visit. Panke, in sharp contrast, is uncomfortable with such formalities, warmly greeting journalists and employees of far lesser rank more like a congenial college professor than head of a storied builder of high-performance vehicles. Panke stands about six foot three and weighs barely 175 pounds. Although lean, he stands strong, like a hickory stick in a perfectly tailored suit. He was born in 1946 in Storkow, in the Prussian district of Fürstenwalde, but the family soon migrated to Munich. Panke was a top student as a teenager and won a scholarship to the prestigious Phillips Exeter Academy in Exeter, New Hampshire, in the United States. That is where Panke's love of the United States started to flower. He returned to Germany in 1965 to serve in the army and then to attend the University of Munich, where he earned a masters degree in physics. In 1976, he earned his doctoral degree in physics.

After college he worked at the Swiss Institute of Nuclear Research and taught at the University of Munich. Two years of teaching led to a job at the international consulting firm, McKinsey & Co. In 1982, he left McKinsey, where he had been working on BMW business, to join the automaker as head of planning and controlling in the research and development area. As with any fast-track BMW executive, Panke churned through a series of key jobs that would make him *Vorstand* timber and a valuable addition to BMW's deep-bench approach to staffing. Like a baseball team with too many stars and sluggers on its roster, BMW has a tradition of cultivating many more top executives than it needs to fill the limited number of spots on the *Vorstand*. In 1993, Panke was sent to run BMW's U.S. division, a dream job for him. There, he began to forge and carry out a retrenching of BMW's North American operations, which had seen sales drop from 1985 to 1992. He forced Germany to adjust content in BMWs so that prices could be lowered to be more competitive with new Japanese entries Lexus and Infiniti, initiated a program to improve BMW's dealer body and emphasize less expensive service, and had cup holders, leather interiors, and stereos installed in models to appeal to American tastes.

He also oversaw the building of BMW's first U.S. assembly plant in Spartanburg, South Carolina. Fed up with the rising demands of German unions and determined to transform an essentially regional carmaker into a truly global player, then–manufacturing chief Bernd Pischetsrieder was intent on opening BMW's first full-scale foreign assembly plant in the United States. The American South was the logical region in which to locate the factory, as it had the needed coastal ports for German-imported parts and a favorable time zone for travel and phone calls to and from Germany. Too, it was far away from the organizing base of the United Auto Workers labor union. Pischetsrieder and then–planning director Panke acquired a Chrysler minivan and toured several possible locales in the former American Confederacy, adopting false names, "Pischet" and "Panic," when they checked into hotels for the night. With a map of potential plant sites to guide them, the team rolled through backwoods villages and fast-growing cities, comparing living conditions, checking transportation routes, and breakfasting at many a Waffle House. Back in Germany, they crunched their numbers and settled on Spartanburg, an area not far from the historic town and port of Charleston that had already attracted nearly 50 German companies. In November 1994, BMW's new plant formally went into operation, producing the Z3 roadster, followed by the X5 SUV in 1999 and then the Z4, successor to the Z3.

Panke is in many ways the perfectly evolved BMW chairman. Von Kuenheim was regal, aloof, and dictatorial in his style of managing the company, never getting overly familiar with most of his management board and always traveling to see his constituencies with entourage and plenty of notice of arrival. It was a style that seemed to suit the times, as BMW grew from a respectable upstart when von Kuenheim took over in 1971 to the respected, if still niche, producer of some of the world's most admired automobiles. Pischetsrieder, a protégé of von Kuenheim's, was much less formal in his movements, but nevertheless basked in the trappings of his position and ran the company like a bishop—by order rather than consensus building. When Pischetsrieder was forced to resign in 1999 by the Quandt family, weary of the billions lost in his acquisition and subsequent running of the British Rover Group, the very reluctant production chief Joachim Milberg stepped in for what would be a short and transitional three-year run as chairman. Milberg was smart and capable, but quiet, a professorial chairman who, associates say, just went about his business. "No trumpets. No fuss. Let's just get this company refocused on the core business of building BMWs and now Minis and do what we do best," said communications chief Richard Gaul to describe Milberg's style. A back ailment compelled Milberg to retire in early 2002, but in truth he was more than happy to give the job over to his chief financial officer, Panke, who was guiding the restoration of BMW's balance sheet and earnings performance after the Rover debacle and doing so superbly in the eyes of Milberg and the Quandts.

Panke, perhaps not surprisingly, is more similar to Milberg than to Pischetsrieder or von Kuenheim, but with more natural and obvious outward leadership qualities than Milberg. Nary an associate or underling would describe Panke as regal, ruthless, or rock-star-like. But while Milberg frequently seemed awkward and uncomfortable in the public role of chairman, Panke works a roomful of politicians, journalists, bankers, or car dealers better than any German corporate chairman and most American ones as well. Though he often finds himself on stages or a dais, his demeanor in public and private seems earnest, not just an act for the benefit of cameras or a print journalist's tape recorder. Whereas Pischetsrieder and Wolfgang Reitzle would hold court privately in hotel suites with invited courtiers and dealers, Panke eschews such cliquish acts and is more likely to simply head to the hotel bar to talk with the dealers or the media depending on the group.

Though any German working for BMW is steeped in automobile engineering and culture, Panke is not viewed by his peers at Volkswagen and Mercedes-Benz as a "car guy." Being a physicist and having come up in BMW ranks as an administrator, planner, controller, human resources chief, and finance guy, he doesn't have the grease under his nails or scars on the back of his hands from grazing a hot manifold or two—things that tend to make German motoring aficionados more respectful. Von Kuenheim didn't have those qualities, either, and he knew it. That may be why von Kuenheim so carefully molded his own image over two decades with limited interviews and an imperial posture. If Panke doesn't have the ability, like a Ferdinand Piech, to take apart a car and put it back together, he is nevertheless a fanatical car and driving enthusiast, often opting to drive a Mini Cooper S or BMW M5 for weekend driving trips.

While Panke can be "scary smart," says AutoPacific consultant Jim Hall, in the way he breaks down a problem or argument, Panke may have at least one flaw as chairman of a top car company known for its engineering prowess—a tendency to slip into *McKinseyspeak* when making his points. German car executives traditionally do not go in much for corporate mission statements or catchy management slogans. There is something about such devices that lacks grit or seriousness of purpose. But Panke finds the practice useful to keep people focused.

"I believe in what I call the four Ps," says Panke. "The right people; passion in the way we do our jobs and work with one another; absolute premium positioning in whatever we do from making cars to making profit; and always we are process driven, not personality driven." That last *P* may be the most important, as the fifth *P*, of course, is for *Panke*. Von Kuenheim, Pischetsrieder, and Reitzle all built cults of personality around them, and those cults competed with one another. Panke observed this from his vantage points in both Munich and the United States. Panke doesn't want people to follow *him;* he wants people to follow his program and his processes. He doesn't want people to look to *him* for answers, but rather he wants them to find the answers in the processes he leads. Underlying the cults of personality that went before him, there was always a strong corporate culture at BMW. This explains why BMW has not had to go outside its ranks to find its chairmen, and why *Vorstand* members, even after two purges in 1999 and 2000 following the Rover problems, all came from within BMW's ranks. Milberg was the closest to being an outsider, having joined the company as production chief in 1992, but even he had been at the company seven years before being tapped for the chairman's job.

During an interview at BMW's Munich headquarters, Panke chimes in with another alliterative McKinseyism. "Continuity, consensus, cooperation and cadre." It's a bit tortured, but underlying the sloganeering is his desire for steady upward growth in revenue, market share, and above all profit. Panke is obsessed with profit. Not because of his background as finance chief, but because he knows that "profit brings choice and options, and the more options you have the more successful you are and the more successful you are perceived from the outside." He believes he will accomplish this by avoiding conflict within the ranks, especially within the management board. Since Wolfgang Reitzle left in 1999 and took his obsessive and lordly control over product design with him, BMW design has added a fifth *C* to Panke's conversation, one with which he is clearly less comfortable: *controversy.*

Along with Chris Bangle, Panke is on the front line of absorbing brickbats from journalists, dealers, and customers who don't like the direction the company is taking with products like the 7 Series, 5 Series, Z4, and even concept cars that foreshadow future products. Says Panke, "We listen, and we even make some changes and improvements constantly, but we can't let our judgment be too heavily influenced by what consumers tell us today or six months ago. That is how many other car companies have gotten into trouble with boring designs. The best way to guard against developing boring vehicles, vehicles that do not match the brand promise, is by sticking to a strategy that everyone knows and understands; also, by carefully selecting the right people who understand the brand and love driving." Because of Panke's nonengineering background, many, especially in Germany, question whether he has the right sensibilities to push a poor design out of contention and elevate and promote a superior design with the *Vorstand*. "Team building is a good thing, but it helps to have someone at the top who instinctively knows the right design from the wrong design," says one Daimler-Chrysler *Vorstand* member about rival BMW.

Give Panke a chance, though, and he will wax eloquent about the connections between the legendary 2002 sport sedan of the late 1960s and early 1970s and today's 330i. "The two are absolutely connected. . . . Both make most of the torque available at lower revs. . . . The feedback to the driver in the two are quite similar," says Panke. He continues: "The key to a BMW is feeling safe and in total control whether driving at 80 kilometers per hour or 240 kilometers per hour. If you can drive at 240 and feel safe and controlled, the effect at 80 is quite special and what sets us apart. Not having to guess what the car will do when you push on the accelerator or brake." Panke seems as steeped as he needs to be in knowledge of engine bores, damping, and suspension engineering. He obsesses, though, about the BMW brand and each product's connection to it. At the 2003 New York Auto Show, discussing Saab's decision not only to adopt a car from Subaru, the WRX, and turn it into a Saab, but also to adapt a Chevrolet Trailblazer into a Saab SUV, he said, "These are decisions Saab and General Motors [GM owns Saab] are making for financial reasons because they feel they have no options with Saab's profits nonexistent. It goes back to what I said about profits creating options, and options creating strength. What will the Saab brand stand for ten years from now with products that don't match the brand? We can debate the designs of our new cars, a line here or there or the electronics system, but the fact remains that the BMW brand has stood for exactly the same principles and has delivered on the same brand promise for 40 years."

———

One of the toughest decisions BMW reckoned with in the 1990s was whether to develop a sport utility vehicle under the BMW brand. Panke, as head of corporate planning, dithered with his colleagues about whether it was appropriate or correct for BMW to have any vehicle that could loosely be termed an SUV donning the blue, white, and black BMW brand jewelry. Under product chief Wolfgang Reitzle, the exercise went on, developing a vehicle off some of the bones of the 5 Series platform that would be an all-activity vehicle. But when BMW purchased the Land Rover brand in 1994 along with the rest of the decrepit Rover Group, plans for a BMW SUV, or Sport Activity Vehicle (SAV) in the BMW lexicon, were delayed. After the Rover unit proved to be a drag on the entire BMW organization and was put up for sale in 2000 (see Chapter 6), Panke didn't need much convincing that the fastest return route to financial health was to ditch Land Rover along with the Rover brand, since it was clear that the vehicle that would become the BMW X5 was every inch a BMW and a perfectly adequate SUV to meet the American market demand for such vehicles. It was a bold stroke to sell Land Rover, a move that compelled three *Vorstand* members to resign, but one that Panke saw as strategically wise and the fastest route to financial and "cultural" health inside BMW. The move has proved wise, since BMW received $2.9 billion for Land Rover from Ford, which continues to have difficulty both rationalizing its purchase and improving Land Rover's historically poor manufacturing quality.

The idea for the X5 was vexing because many of the elements of an American sport utility vehicle seemed at odds with BMW's engineering sensibilities. Precise steering feedback from an SUV is difficult to achieve because the vehicle is engineered more for towing and potential off-roading than for road driving. A higher seating position and higher center or gravity, too, would force an "un-BMW" feel into the vehicle, despite the BMW logo in the center of the steering wheel. Argh! This is why BMW bought Land Rover! Says Goeschel, "The X5 presented quite a dilemma. We saw that the segment was growing very fast in the U.S., but it was not so easy to figure out where the opportunity was for BMW. We know BMW stood for sportiness, agility, dynamic driving. But how to make this happen in this kind of vehicle? We threw out the idea of a two-speed reduction gearbox, which is so common in SUVs in order to help them maintain high levels of power while going slow in off-road situations. We set out to make a BMW that happened to be an activity vehicle, not an SUV that had to be a BMW. This was a guiding principal." DaimlerChrysler, for example, has to design a lot of capability into a Jeep Grand Cherokee so that it can climb up the side of a mountain. Those engineering choices, though, make the Grand Cherokee a bit jouncey on the road, with vague handling characteristics. BMW reckoned correctly, though, that it would be foolish to design a vehicle to go off-roading when 99 percent of its customers using the X5 99 percent of the time wouldn't even be tempted to go off-road. So it built the X5 off parts and pieces of the 5 Series chassis, raised the seating position and ground clearance slightly, but maintained the same seating position of the driver as in the 5 Series. The X5 has independent suspension in both the front and rear, which means each wheel can react independently to the road. Trucks and SUVs, by contrast, often have the rear wheels tied together by a solid rear axle, which makes them tougher and able to tow more weight, but usually creates a crummy ride on the road. To help give the higher-riding vehicle that hunkered-down feel of a BMW car, Goeschel says the engine was forced down under the hood several centimeters lower than they thought they could achieve when they started out. The lower the center of gravity, created by the weight of the engine, the more solid and sure-footed the vehicle feels.

The X5 has proved to be the best recent example of how BMW's enormous brand equity and goodwill with its customers can make up for a vehicle that is deemed by critics as only adequate at best. Maybe people are willing to forgive BMW a bit for its SUV, sorry . . . SAV, attempt. *Car & Driver,* a perennial fan of BMWs, noted that, despite the all-wheel-drive technology meant to make up for the otherwise deficient rear-drive setup in snow and rain, ". . . customers who buy a Sport-package-equipped X5 thinking they can play mountain goat on slick roads will be disappointed, as snow-covered roads . . . had us wishing for a more sure-footed snow vehicle, such as almost any front-wheel-drive sedan on the market. . . . The traction control does what it can, but if the tires aren't getting traction, you're slipping and slid-ing."[22] The magazine also said, "So what, then, are we to make of BMW's new X5? Great looks, a nearly flawless interior, a commend-able powertrain, and exceptional build quality, combined with a rough ride, limited cargo capacity, and marginal snow and off-road capabili-ties. If you want a sport-utility vehicle that emphasizes utility, we'd recommend a Mercedes ML430 or a Jeep Grand Cherokee. If you lean more toward the 'sport,' the BMW 540i station wagon holds more than the X5 and performs much better on the road."[23] Exceptional build quality? In point of fact, the X5 was recalled more than a dozen times between 2000 and the end of 2003, a hassle for even the most dedicated BMW owner. *Consumer Reports* criticized this lack of quality performance and didn't recommend the X5. In J.D. Power's 2002 Initial Quality Survey, the X5 scored 159 problems per 100 vehicles reported by owners in the first three months, almost 50 percent more than in the 5 Series sedans. However, Strategic Vision, a California consulting firm that has its own method of measuring quality, which takes into account how "delighted" the customer is with the product, scored the X5 "top luxury SUV" in its 2003 report, tying with the Infiniti FX45 (brand new for 2003), but besting all others. In its third year of production! BMW was also the top-ranked brand overall in the firm's Total Quality Survey, meaning that BMW customers are more delighted with their vehicles on the whole than customers of any other brand. When confronted with the J.D. Power, *Consumer Reports,* and *Car and Driver* verdicts on the X5, chairman Helmut Panke and Goeschel quickly bring up the Strategic Vision verdict. Says Panke: "It's not that we don't analyze the *Consumer Reports* results and J.D. Power and listen to what those surveys show, but the Strategic Vision measure is more important to us because it takes into account how pleased our customers are with the product, the brand, and our company. It doesn't overemphasize just one issue like wind or engine noise or maybe excessive brake dust on the wheels, which can hurt performance in the J.D. Power ranking." Goeschel chimes in with his frustration regarding such surveys. "We lost a bunch of points on rear-seat cup holders, but we fixed them," says Goeschel, admitting that BMW doesn't seem to know how to make a great cup holder. "We solved the problem for all time on the rear-seat cup holders . . . we took them out, and you know we haven't received one letter complaining," chuckles Goeschel.

Goeschel, too, directs his interviewer to a line in the *Car and Driver* review cited to him earlier: "Although sport-utilities and sports sedans have about as much in common as giraffes and gazelles, I [the magazine's reviewer] have to admit that the X5 does the best job yet of blurring the boundary between the two species."[24] Says Goeschel, "That was what we set out to do from the start."

People who know what a BMW is supposed to drive like are BMW's most precious resource, says Goeschel. "We have to have people who know what a BMW is supposed to feel like in their bones, in their hands, and in their bottoms. . . . BMWs are about feel, but most people don't know why they feel it or what exactly they feel. They just feel it."

M Series

Perhaps the best expression of the way a BMW feels and why people flock to the brand even if it needs a few more trips to the repair garage than a Honda or Toyota is the M Series.

The M in BMW's celebrated M Series stands simply for *Motor*. Motor sports has been a key to BMW's marketing and product development since the 1920s. Even before BMW had its own branded cars to sell, it successfully launched its motorcycle business in the early 1920s backed by the motorcycle's stellar record on the motorbike race courses. In the 1930s, BMW and Auto Union ruled the international Grand Prix circuit. BMW Motorsports historian Alan Henry says the most significant date in BMW racing history must be June 14, 1936, when Ernst Henne gave the BMW 328 its race debut in the Eifelrennen at the Nurburgring, coming away with victory in the up-to-two-liter engine class. The 1938 Mille Miglia saw a two-liter class victory as well for the BMW 328, which was driven, ironically, not by a German, but by Englishman A. F. P. Fane, who was later killed in his Royal Air Force fighter plane in a battle against the Germans—who, ironically and tragically, were flying planes with BMW engines.

BMW competed in motorsports in the postwar period, but suspended its Formula 2 program at the end of the 1970 season. The program was scuttled by sales and marketing director Paul Hahnemann, who some say withdrew funding in an internal political power play when his job was threatened. Others say the reason was the death of the popular driver Gerhard Mitter in a 1969 practice run at the Nurburgring. The race team that won BMW's last race draped their car in a black shroud at the end of the race in a small gesture of protest that attracted much publicity in the German media and perturbed management. By 1972, the company rechartered its motorsports program as BMW Motorsport GmbH. Starting in 1975, BMW's chief motorsports engineer was Paul Rosche, who began working up a racing version of the new BMW 3 Series, which had replaced the 2002 model that had put BMW on the map in the late 1960s and early 1970s. That car proved quite successful on German and North American race-tracks and revved the whole organization, which was, not by accident, full of racing enthusiasts.

While BMW racked up wins on the track and continued to work with customizing companies Alpina and Schnitzer on engines and cars for the racing circuit, the company was receiving laurels and compliments at the auto shows starting in 1972 for its BMW Turbo concept designed by Paul Bracq and championed through the BMW system by sales and marketing chief Bob Lutz, who had succeeded the ousted Paul Hahnemann. The Turbo had gull-wing doors, a futuristic wedge shape, and, of course, a turbocharged engine. It never had any potential as a volume production car, and by 1977 the business case hadn't yet been made for producing a car based on the Turbo even on a limited-edition basis for select customers. But BMW Motorsport chief Jochen Neerpasch wanted a car to replace the celebrated BMW CSL car on the racetrack that would challenge Porsche. That year, a road-going prototype mid-engine race car based on the Turbo's looks was spotted in Italy near the Lamborghini workshops. BMW had commissioned the Italian exotic car builder to ready a small batch of cars it would come to call the M1. In order to race the car, the rules stipulated that a certain number had to be sold to the public. A year later, with Lamborghini having produced only seven hand-built Turbos after delays endemic to Italian car builders, the project was taken back by BMW and planted at German coach-builder Bauer. The road-going Turbo released in 1979 was dubbed M1 and was powered by an in-line six-cylinder 3.5-liter engine already employed in the 635CSi coupe and 735i saloon. The standard M1 engine produced 277 horsepower, while the turbocharged racetrack version produced 700 horsepower. The 0-to 60-mph time was less than six seconds, and top speed was 160 miles per hour. To accommodate the racing engine, the space-frame chassis was sturdy and rigid as a brick. The cockpit interior relied heavily on BMW bits and pieces from other cars and was trimmed in gray and black with a hooded instrument cluster displaying white-on-black circular dials. A thick leather steering wheel dominated the interior. A decade after it was introduced, the M1 was viewed as a collectible classic. Motoring writer David Vivian wrote in *Autocar & Motor* in 1991: "The M1 still gets enough things right to put many modern Ferraris and Porsches to shame. A large measure of the car's charm, of course, stems from its classic engine. A truly broad performance band is delivered without tantrums. The big six pulls cleanly from just 1,000 rpms with the kind of throttle response that can split the hairs on the back of your hand. High speeds are achieved with a sense of éffortlessness which, once experienced, you don't want to give up. . . . The abiding impression, however, is of a fine-honed repertoire of abilities that straddle that thin line between icy perfection and red-blooded entertainment without any glaring anomalies to cloud the issue."[25] BMW sold 397 road-going M1s before ceasing production.

Motor sports and developing high-performance cars are not just marketing exercises to go with the old "Win on Sunday, sell on Monday" selling principle. BMW competes in motor sports because the organization has long believed and demonstrated that engineering for race cars makes for better product for the everyday customers because its engineers have been up against fierce racetrack competition and the high standards of performance and endurance required of race cars.

The M1 was no exception, despite the low-slung, sleek appearance that made it seem to many as a mere exercise in Bavarian testesterone run amok. Eric Dymock wrote in BMW's publication *Celebration,* "Bracq's prototype had been constructed by Michelotti in Turin and was intended as a riposte to the vogue for Experimental Safety Vehicles (ESVs). Far from being tank-like, the BMW Turbo, as it was known, used a 2002 four-cylinder engine with a turbo charger, and had deformable structures and a jointed steering column, together with a strong roll-over bar to achieve what was known in the post [consumer safety advocate] Ralph Nader jargon as 'passive safety.' Yet, BMW stood out for passive safety, that is to say providing the driver with the best means of actively avoiding an accident rather than passively sitting waiting for it. Accordingly, the car was equipped with anti-lock brakes [a novelty in 1979], and its mid engine configuration, designed to provide the best possible weight distribution, gave increased safety through superior handling."

After the critical and morale-boosting success of the M1, BMW set out to develop more "M Power" cars across its model range. The first was the M535i, launched in 1985. The responsiveness of the car's engine set it apart. Between 2,000 and 6,000 rpms in any gear, wrote *Motor Sport,* there was no hesitation or drop off in speed. The car's exterior screamed, "This is something special."[26] A bit gaudy by today's standards, the red-and-blue M striping ran the length of the car at door-handle height. The striping was also carried through under the front intakes below the twin-kidney grille, as well as across the trunk lid just below the spoiler. As always, the M logo adorned the front of the car beside the right headlamp. The power plant produced 218 horsepower at 5,200 rpm. More bolstering in the special M seats was both distinctive and needed for the kind of driving M buyers encountered. By 1985, the car had been updated with a new body shell with the new-generation 5 Series, which was not terribly different from the original 5 Series.[27] But the M cars were on the minds of BMW buyers and were doing exactly the job they were meant to. Car companies often look to produce "halo" cars. Chevrolet has its Corvette. Acura has its NSX (modeled somewhat after the M1), and Dodge has its Viper. On one hand, carmakers fund these low-volume, high-performance cars to draw shoppers into the showrooms even if they aren't buying. On the other, they hope, most often in vain, that the Corvette will cast gold dust on the über–rental car Chevy Malibu and that the Viper will do the same on the humdrum Dodge Stratus family sedan. Shoppers with even a fraction of the brains they are born with, though, don't really associate the Chevy bowtie logo on the front of the Corvette too much with the bowtie on the Malibu for which they are negotiating monthly payments. BMW, on the other hand, after the M1, created an ongoing brand of special-performance cars that were completely and understandably tied to the cars they were selling to less speed-oriented customers with lighter wallets. The M535i was unmistakably the faster-footed and somewhat more garishly dressed brother of the standard 535i. Indeed, in 2002, 2003, and 2004, as Chrysler, General Motors, Mazda, Mitsubishi, and Ford all launch or expand performance brands similar to M, such as Ford SVT and MazdaSpeed, the companies most commonly refer to BMW's M brand as their planning and marketing model.

———

Gerhard Richter, the general manager of the M Series, says there is a "spirit and character" of M engines that differentiates them from other BMW engines. For BMW, M cars are the most intelligent way the company can resolve conflicting goals. The first goal is the creation of high-performance cars, which customers expect. The second goal is to create feedback and response in the car that lets the owner-driver know right away that he or she is driving a racing car. The M Power engines are based on what Richter calls "the high rev" concept. By pairing an engine that achieves high performance at high rpms with an appropriate transmission, BMW ensures what the Germans call a high *Durchzugskraft,* which gives the package a unique driving character at high and low speeds on the one hand, while making it especially efficient and highly controllable for the driver on the other. Relative to their performance output, M cars are the most efficient sedans in the category in terms of fuel economy and emissions control. Is that particularly important? To develop a lot of power without paying equal attention to emissions and crash standards is something many can do. BMW sets out to do both as a way of setting the brand apart, says Richter who calls it "socially responsible fun."

When the M5 was launched in 1984, the second M car to be derived from the 5 Series, BMW was ever more serious about its M cars, which were developing a following worldwide. For the M5, the company dropped the gaudy striping that had adorned the M1 and identified the speed demons with just the understated M5 badge on the front grille, the rear corner of the trunk lid, and on the sills of the car, so anyone who missed the exterior badges would see one upon opening the door. The steering wheel, of course, had the badge, and the seats had small M color bars on the backrests that looked a little like a military decoration. When finished in black, the car looked like just another 5 Series, and only those familiar with the M designation knew at a passing glance what drove before them—under the hood, screaming off the engine block, "M Power." M cars, especially starting with the dignified M5, are cars for driving connoisseurs. Journalist Michael Scarlett of *Autocar* wrote in 1985, ". . . there is nothing sporty, nothing crude, above all nothing to show off about this 5 Series car. Then, the 80 kilometer per hour near-city limit on the autobahn south to Garmisch Partenkirchen ends, and the new BMW-designed, Getrag-machined gearbox is double-declutched into third and the right foot flattened. Instantly, my back is shoved into the seat and I am cursing mildly as the rev limiter cuts in before the 6,900 rpm red line, at 96 mph—not that it really matters."[28] M cars perhaps more than others inspire journalists to wax poetic in their descriptions, trying more than usual to describe the experience. That is, after all, the crux of the BMW brand and the eye of the M subbrand: to turn driving into the best experience of the day . . . on most days.

In 2000, *Car and Driver* called the then-new M5 "The Most Desirable Sedan in the World."[29] That's not mincing words by a publication that, while generous with its editorial pages devoted to the Bavarians, does not automatically anoint the blue-white-and-black with top-dog status when facing off against Audi, Mercedes, Infiniti, and Acura. The magazine in 2003, for example, gave its nod to the Honda S2000 convertible roadster over the brand-new Z4 and didn't have any qualms about doing so. The 2000 M5 is a two-ton rock-ribbed joy machine for people who love to drive. The eight-cylinder, 4.9-liter engine produces 395 horsepower and enough low-end torque to make most owners always want to take the long way home. "How do you characterize a roomy four-door, leather-lined luxury capsule that can keep up with a C5 Corvette? All the way to 150 mph! With a quarter-mile performance of 13.3 seconds at 108 mph, let's just call it the fastest production sedan on the planet," wrote *Car and Driver's* editor Casba Csere.[30] Pitted against the Mercedes E55 AMG and Jaguar XJ in *Car and Driver's* test, the M5 stopped in the shortest span (156 feet) from 70 mph, and it performed the emergency-lane-change maneuver successfully at the highest speed (66.2 mph).

By 2003, when the magazine took the M5 to Arizona for a face-off against more freshly minted competitors with higher horsepower—the Audi RS6, the Mercedes E55 AMG, and the Jaguar S-Type R—the M5 was dethroned by the brand-new redesigned Audi. But the M5, built on what was in 2003 a seven-year-old 5 Series chassis, handily topped the Jag and Mercedes, both on brand-new platforms. One of the features for which BMW sets itself apart in this class, though, is in being the only entry with a manual transmission. That's knowing your audience! Though the magazine chose the Audi as number one among performance sedans, it noted that the M5 was still the best balanced of the lot, with a 52.2/47.8 percent front-to-rear weight distribution. BMW's relentless obsession for balance pays off, and its owners know it. The front-drive Audi, though outfitted with Quattro all-wheel drive (front-drive cars just can't measure up, which is why I was surprised by *Car and Driver's* conclusion), has a 59.6/40.4 percent weight distribution, enough to completely change the cornering and maneuvering dynamics for a driver whose rear end is sensitive enough to know the difference and wants to spend in excess of $70,000 for the pleasure of driving.

European Car correspondent and contributor to this book Elaine Catton says of the M5: "Ten kilometers outside Munich, the [speed] restriction lifts and my foot drops. This is what the M5 was made for. It's a mighty shove, but without the 'oh shit' factor that some lively Italian super sports cars might dish out—no jittery thoroughbred here."

———

To talk about BMW products without delving a bit into horsepower, gearboxes, and the occasional sentence on steering ratios would be like talking about Mozart or Michelangelo without discussing meter and pitch in the case of the former and brushstrokes, paint recipes, and sculpture techniques in the case of the latter. BMWs, more than any other brand of motorcar, have, for at least 40 years, been consistently fun to drive, backed by an organization that places that objective above all others. Make it fun. Whatever you do, it has to be fun. That's what makes the company so consistent and so admired; the commitment to that principle.

The Ultimate History

T W O

. . . He trusts the young force which impels him
And safely and tirelessly holds the controls,
When he finally masters the tricks of the wind
And brings the force of the air into his sway . . ."[1]
—GUSTAV OTTO

Before the 1960s, BMW's main stock-in-trade was aircraft engines, motorcycles, and short production runs of often pricey overpowered saloons (the European term for sedan) along with a handful of elegant sports cars. There was also a cheap novelty car, the Isetta "bubble car" of the 1950s. And the first big-volume BMW, the Dixi 3/15 of the late 1920s and early 1930s, was merely a car the company licensed from British car-maker Austin. Before German industrialist Herbert Quandt assumed command in 1959, BMW was a hodgepodge mix of typically missed possibilities. It was Bavaria's automaker, true, which ensured a strong allegiance among customers in that by and large still quite independent German state. But by 1959, BMW was falling apart, made up as it was of bits and pieces of the prewar company stitched together with postwar string. Bankruptcy loomed as the company poised itself to disintegrate into the arms of Daimler-Benz, parent of Mercedes-Benz, waiting ominously in the wings. It was difficult to see at that critical juncture in the company's history what BMW was worth. BMW represented a potentially unique idea about how cars should be built, but it hadn't yet figured how to build those theoretical cars consistently or profitably.

What BMW has done over the past 40 years, though, is to meld technology and design into an almost seamless dialogue. For designers and engineers confronted with that blank slate, the question is, which comes first—the elegant technical solution or one that benefits BMW overall? The answer is, neither and both. There's not a BMW engineer alive today who can separate the two goals. It all adds up to an organization that knows what it is about, run by people who deep down know that the heart and soul of its brand is always, first and last, about one thing: the pleasure of driving.

————

To fully grasp BMW's twentieth and twenty-first-century accomplishments, it pays to ponder the company's origin. BMW's modern history begins in earnest around 1960, but its travails and triumphs over the first six decades of the century are not inconsequential. The company's accumulated design and business decisions in the first 40 years of the twentieth century, before World War II, continue to influence, albeit mostly in intangible ways, recent and even current designs and decisions. Condensing that history for the general reader, one could start with the aircraft business, which got its start in Munich not far from BMW's current home base, or a small automobile factory in Eisenach, Germany, that built cars 16 years before the Archduke Ferdinand's assassination in Sarajevo let slip the dogs of World War I. Let's start with the cars.

The history of BMW as a car company unfolded in 1896 at a small factory in Eisenach, in the Thuringia province of central Germany. That's where Heinrich Ehrhardt registered the Eisenach Vehicle Factory. It employed over 600 people its first year, producing military vehicles of every stripe, bicycles, electrically powered vehicles for both military and civilian use, and gas-powered internal combustion engines. The decade following that 1896 start was a transitional decade in transportation history, as manifested by the electric vehicle built by the company between 1899 and 1902, the Wartburg Electric. Resembling a motorized carriage, it was little more than a horse carriage powered by an electric motor that could easily be hitched to a horse if the manufactured power source ran out of juice. Wartburgs were highly regarded among the early manufacturers. Racers unleashed them on the track as early as 1899, recording impressive speeds of 37 miles per hour. By 1902, the firm produced a racer that hit 75 miles per hour.

In 1903, Ehrhardt pulled out of the firm he started, giving way to an engineer named Willy Seck. Seck focused the company on the Dixi, a vehicle that might be a reliable revenue producer as military contracts ebbed and flowed. First shown at motor shows in 1904, the Dixi came in three versions—the two-cylinder, eight-horsepower S6; the one-cylinder 1,200-cc T7, which maxed out at 25 miles per hour; and the four-cylinder 3.5-liter, 16-horsepower S12/14. Production for all three models numbered just over 200.

The company puttered along in this fashion, producing low-volume, handcrafted, highly customized vehicles until 1909. That year, Eisenach produced 650 small, light, four-cylinder, 14-horsepower cars known as the R8. The R8 morphed into touring cars, two-seater sports cars, and a variety of commercial and government vehicles such as ambulances and postal vehicles.

Sales boomed as World War I lurked unseen in the horizon. But when war began in 1914, auto production stopped and the Eisenach factory was taken over for military production. It was later dismantled by the victors' Allied Control Commission.

Car production recommenced in 1919 with two prewar Dixi models. Two more years elapsed before an up-to-date vehicle was developed. The Dixi G1 was a large and pricey four-cylinder car that cranked out between 6 and 18 horsepower depending on the engine employed under the bonnet; a more powerful version flaunted itself on the German racing circuit. It was a strategy BMW employed to great success throughout the twentieth century and into the next, offering its models in numerous power configurations, all of them promoted through high-performing engines, high-recognition branding, and high-profile racing.

In 1921, as Germany plunged deeper into a postwar funk marked by high unemployment, the Eisenach plant was purchased by Gothaerwaggonfabrik, a railcar manufacturer that found Eisenach's production capacity for brake systems appealing. Running counter to the beleaguered postwar economy, the Dixi errantly emphasized large, expensive vehicles on the theory that those with money would still spend it on such premium cars. In addition, the company suffered from poor productivity—the number of worker-hours it took to build one car. The economy and logistical torque of Henry Ford's assembly line were still a foreign concept; German cars were made largely by hand, and the cost per unit remained prohibitively high.

By 1927, the company, commonly referred to as the Dixi Werke, was in dire straits. Businessman Jakob Shapiro, who had cobbled together the deal for Gothaer to take over Dixi, merged the firm with another small Gothaer vehicle producer and built a large six-cylinder Dixi. Despite a low price, it sold poorly. The Eisenach plant then seized upon a small, cheap car in the hope of bailing out the company. To do this, the company did not rely on its own engineers' and designers' ingenuity to design something from scratch, but rather chose to license a design that had already proven itself a substantial success in a market (Great Britain) similar to Germany's. Spared the costs of developing a new vehicle, Dixi could put all its limited resources into manufacturing and marketing.

A deal was struck with the British carmaker Sir Herbert Austin to build the two-seater Austin Seven (also known as the "Baby Austin") at Eisenach as a Dixi. It was a small car that ran on gasoline rather than on the more expensive diesel fuel required of many cars of the day, at a cost only slightly more than a premium-priced motorcycle. Already successful with Britain's middle and lower-middle classes, the Austin Seven was a safe bet to appeal to the same buyers in Germany.

The Seven licensing deal, though, was not enough to preserve Dixi as an independent automaker. Shapiro, whose other holdings were not thriving, put the company up for sale and found a willing buyer in motorcycle and aero-engine builder Bayerische Motoren Werke—BMW. The deal cost BMW 10 million Reichsmarks, which seemed like a fair price until BMW discovered that Dixi owner Eisenach had 7.8 million Reichsmarks of hidden debt, which BMW had to assume in a deal that perhaps foreshadowed the Rover acquisition in the mid-1990s. While Rover had no hidden debt, BMW didn't fully understand the intractable and hideously expensive infrastructure problems until after it purchased the company.

So BMW's first motorcar experience was not hatched in the workshops of its own clever engineers, but in the factories and design studios of Great Britain.

Sir Herbert Austin founded the Austin Motor Company in the summer of 1905. In November that year, he moved his factory into the former premises of White and Pike printing works at Longbridge, situated beside the Bristol Road, the River Rea, and the joint Midland and Great Western Railway line from Longbridge to Halesowen. Austin developed the idea for the Austin Seven, an elegant solution, he believed, to the challenge of providing inexpensive, fuel-efficient transportation. The Seven, first sold in 1922, quickly became the best-selling model in Great Britain, and Sir Herbert became convinced of the Seven's prospects for success in world markets. In 1928 he sent representatives to Germany, Japan, and pre-Depression America to license the design to local manufacturers. Arthur J. Brandt, a former top-shelf General Motors executive who'd left to blaze a trail with his own car company, set up the American Austin Car Company in Butler, Pennsylvania, not far from the steel mills that would supply the enterprise. Austin would also strike a deal with the Japanese company Jidosha Seizo Co., which sold the car as the Datsun. The company reorganized as Nissan in 1934, with the Seven being its only car until 1937.

Robust but almost primitive in design, the Seven was marvelously simple to manufacture. In engineering terms, it required little more than would a motorcycle with two additional wheels. Legend has it that Sir Herbert Austin literally laid out the basics of the car on the green felt of an English billiard table with a piece of cue chalk. At 1,150 pounds, with a 75-inch wheelbase, it was obviously lightweight and structurally simple, so Austin omitted such costly extravagances as shock absorbers. The brakes were barely adequate to stop a motorcycle, let alone a car, but they were up to snuff given the almost nonexistent regulatory standards at the time. Dixi, along with every other licensee, would improve the basic Seven package with better brakes and shocks, along with engines that cranked out more than the paltry 38 miles per hour of the basic Seven's 10.5-horsepower, 750-cc engine.

The widespread initial success of the Austin Seven, say some automotive historians, came from the scant competition among genuine budget-priced small cars in the 1920s and 1930s. In the late 1920s and early 1930s there was bonafide competition from the British automakers Morris, Triumph, Standard, and others, so the Austin offered something to maintain a competitive edge. That something was the engine. The car's other components were on a par with most of the competition, but no other company came close to producing a sub-1,000-cc engine as robust, reliable, and tunable as the Austin Seven's. Alternative uses quickly proliferated for an engine that ran like a clock, with a number of conversions for marine and tractor use. The Seven was such an admirable overall package that it turned up on most of the shortlists compiled at the end of the twentieth century as one of the century's top five most influential designs, along with the Volkswagen Beetle, Ford Model T, Morris Mini, and Ford Mustang.

In Germany, Shapiro had bet right by buying the Austin license. The acquisition of Dixi proved to be a critical one for BMW, not only because it then started making cars, but because Eisenach served as the headquarters for all BMW automotive operations between 1928 and 1939: The wartime production that displaced car building occupied the factory until the war's end in 1945.

———

BMW formally recognizes its birthday as March 7, 1916, the day Gustav Otto's fledgling aircraft company morphed into a new company just as he handed off ownership to others. That perhaps sounds like an inauspicious beginning, but Otto is nevertheless considered a reluctant father of the company we know today as BMW. That is because the Bavarian Aircraft Works would not have spawned the eventual BMW aircraft company, which in turn led to the auto company, without Otto's mechanical genius, love of flying, family pride, and dedication to building some of the most sought-after aircraft engines of the time.

Otto's father, Nikolaus August Otto, who died in 1891, invented the "Otto" combustion engine, which was the first viable internal combustion engine featuring the correct timing of ignition and combustion. Nikolaus Otto was, and is, lionized by German society and in the history books, and Gustav labored under the same dilemma as many scions of famous and accomplished men. He had a difficult time blazing his own path while obscured by his father's long shadow.

Otto's own letters reveal him as thoughtful, sentimental, and often melancholy—far from a surly German shop rat. In his letters to his wife, Otto gave voice to poetry to express his passion for flying and creating.

In the Name of the Pilot

The crowd rejoices, the pilot longs for fame,
He accepts the wheel of fate without fear,
Today he is the vanquished, tomorrow the victor.
In the bright sky above he blazes his trail.
He trusts the young force which impels him
And safely and tirelessly hold the controls,
When he finally masters the tricks of the wind
And brings the force of the air into his sway.
Up up and away! So that great valleys vanish
And steep slopes lie harmlessly below.
He wants to experience man's greatest desire
And fly to meet his young fortune. . . .[2]

In 1910, Otto built a biplane with an engine he designed with his partner, Gabriel Letsch, that took the nascent German flying community by storm. By 1912, he had formed the Munich Aircraft Company and sold 30 planes, some powered by Daimler engines; in 1913 he sold 47 aircraft to the Bavarian army.

Internecine military politics, especially between the Bavarian war ministry and the Prussian army, which eschewed Otto's planes, along with this visionary's inability to navigate the maze of personalities and payoffs with his integrity and pride intact, left him deeply troubled. In 1915, Otto was admitted to a Munich mental hospital with what would currently be called clinical depression; the company muddled along for a year with little help from Otto. With bankruptcy looming, Otto agreed to a buyout that would provide him with enough to cover his financial commitments and medical bills. Bavarian Airplane Works was formed with six directors: two bankers, a machine factory executive, a lawyer, and two engineers (Herman Backstein and Gustav Otto).

Though Otto would remain with the newly chartered firm for only a short time, it is worth repeating a line from the prospectus for the Gustav Otto Works, a document that elegantly captures the relationship between aircraft and auto engines in the early history of BMW. It encapsulates the brand over the next century—cars and motorcycles alike—grounded in the imagery, emotional combustion, and excitement of flight itself. As Otto put it, "The aircraft question is closely linked to the existence and development of the car industry . . . and I am here proudly able to honour the memory of my father, Dr. N. A. Otto, as the inventor of the four-stroke engine whose operating principle forms the basis of all present day car and aircraft engines."[3]

———

Starting up about the same time as the Otto aircraft firm, the Karl Rapp Motorwerke in 1913 began producing aircraft engines that could win altitude and speed competitions and therefore military contracts. The Rapp Engine Works was a subsidiary of Flugwerk, an airplane maker, and Rapp was an engineer who had come up through the Daimler system.

As the dogs of war began howling in 1914, Rapp had precious production capacity and quickly won contracts from Prussia and Austro-Hungary to produce 25 large V12 aircraft engines. Rapp's company began buying four-cylinder water-cooled aircraft engines from the Gustav Otto company whose operations it absorbed. By 1916, Rapp Motor Works was employing 370 people and more than 100 machine tools. An Austrian engineer, Franz Josef Popp, largely directed Rapp's business affairs, including securing the all-important military contracts. Popp arrived at Rapp at the direction of the Imperial Austro-Hungary War Ministry to oversee production of 10 million Reichsmarks worth of airplane engines. The Hungarians liked the idea of Popp overseeing their investment, as he was both an engineer and a lieutenant in the Austrian army reserves.

On the strength of this new business, Popp transformed the Rapp company into Bayerische Motoren Werke GmbH. Shortly after the incorporation though, Popp found the company stretched too thin trying to keep up with the war-fueled demand. He turned to a shadowy, influential financier, Camillo Castiglioni, who was head of the Wiener Bankverein and a board member of several industrial concerns. Popp and Castiglioni together recapitalized the company, and Rapp departed in 1917 none too happily. In short, Popp and his partner forced Rapp out. The company was reincorporated in 1918 as BMW AG.

In 1917, BMW brought a new product to market that would boost its aircraft reputation, the Type IIIa, water-cooled, six-cylinder engine, designed by chief engineer Max Friz—a grand engineering mind who would dominate BMW's product development culture on into the 1960s. Friz worked previously at Daimler, where he had designed engines that won Grand Prix car races and powered sport airplanes and World War I fighter planes. The squadron of Baron von Richthofen, known as the Red Baron, used the first planes with the Type IIIa. A Junkers Ju F13 with this engine set a world altitude record in 1919 with eight crew members aboard.

In 1917, Popp convinced the German government to buy the BMW IIIa engine. By mid-1918, Friz had upped the power in the Type IV to 250 horsepower, and later increased it to 320 horsepower, a level of performance that beat the vaunted Daimler. BMW began licensing the production of the engine to other manufacturers as the prestige of the blue, black, and white logo found a strong toehold. It had over 3,500 employees and was financially sound.

But after the armistice was signed in 1919, the Allies prohibited German military aircraft engine production. BMW had built up a terrific reputation for engineering prowess, but now had no product line that could exploit it, especially since civilian aircraft was a barely established business. BMW needed a transitional product strategy to get it through some undetermined period of Allied oversight, so it turned to boat and truck engines and farming equipment. It wasn't enough, though financial ruin was staved off by a fortuitous contract for 10,000 railroad brake systems. Meanwhile, Popp continued in secret to work on aircraft engines with engineering director Friz; a Friz-designed six-cylinder engine achieved an astonishing—for the time—altitude record of 31,826 feet.

Harsh business realities prompted BMW's largest stockholder, Castiglioni, to consider abandoning engine development and production in favor of producing brake systems exclusively for other vehicle manufacturers. Germany was mired in a postwar slump, as the value of the Reichsmark fell like a stone. It was all too much for Castiglioni. In 1920 he sold his holdings for 28 million Reichsmarks to the chief executive of Knorr Bremsen AG, a diversified company whose business included brake systems and components for auto, marine, and industrial engines. With few aircraft engines on order, BMW limped along by manufacturing brake systems for railway cars, office furniture, and workbenches, as well as cut-down aviation engines for marine and industrial use.

Castiglioni shrewdly bought back the company in 1922. He had bet correctly that after he sold his interest two years earlier the company's value would plummet so he could reacquire it with greatly devalued German currency and make out well. Indeed, Castiglioni was able to .buy all of BMW's shares from Knorr for far less than he sold it. He had stayed in touch with Popp during the three-year hiatus so that Popp would do what he could to keep the engineering and design talent motivated and, most important, intact. This was just the sort of thing that made Castiglioni a formidable presence in German financial markets, though he cultivated a largely anonymous public profile.

Upon Castiglioni's return, the company began producing motorcycle engines for such motorcycle makers as England's Victoria brand. BMW also produced its own motorized bicycle, called the Flink, a forerunner to the moped, which had a small two-stroke engine that riders engaged with a clutch when they needed some extra oomph. Leveraging BMW's growing reputation for speed and durability in aircraft engines into a consumer market, Popp had been eyeing the motorcycle market for some time. After all, motorcycles would excite and motivate his engineers far more than did railroad brake systems, and they'd serve as a stepping-stone to what Popp really wanted to build: cars.

In 1921, Friz developed a motorcycle engine for Victoria that turned out to be one of the great engines of the decade. Sold as the Bayern Kleinmotor (Bavarian Small Engine), it had two horizontally opposed cylinders, known as a "Boxer" engine, a unique configuration for the day. Besides Victoria-Werke, motorcycle maker Stockdorf AG and bike builder Bison GmbH of Vienna also bought these little marvels. An improved Kleinmotor would next power the first motorcycle sold under BMW's own brand. This engine, which was adapted for other uses, became a cash cow in 1922 and 1923 and enhanced the reputation for sound and superior engine design already forged in BMW's aero-engine development. The Kleinmotor's commercial success convinced BMW that it should build its own motorcycles in addition to building engines for others. First, the company built a bike, the Helios, whose design was licensed from the British manufacturer Douglas. But the first motorcycle BMW designed from the ground up was the R32.

The R32 debuted at the Paris Motor Show in 1923, and it was hailed immediately as the most elegantly designed engine of the day. BMW historian Jan P. Norbye said of the R32, "With the R32, Friz and BMW leaped into the vanguard of the motorcycle art. And, indeed, it was art." Friz's powertrain broke new ground.[4] On a rigid, tubular frame, he mounted an 8.5-horsepower, 500-cc twin-cylinder engine, with the cylinder axes set across the frame; a longitudinal crankshaft gave equal cooling to both cylinders. The gearbox pinions turned in the transverse plane. Design and motorcycle enthusiasts will recognize the elegance of this design compared with others, both then and now. Friz did not opt for the more conventional solution of beveled gears turning in the direction of rotation through a 90-degree angle, as applies to a chain drive. Friz designed a flexible coupling on the gearbox output shaft combined with a straight shaft with a pinion on its rear end to match a ring gear in the rear wheel hub—thus, the first shaft-drive motorcycle, the basic design BMW still employs today!

The R32 engine was small and light for its day. The bike had a total weight of just 264 pounds, a good 10 percent lighter than the next-lightest bike. Fuel consumption was about 80 miles per gallon, and it reached a top speed of about 60 miles per hour.[5] It wasn't too fast, but it immediately won hearts and fans for its reliability. Even with its low top speed, it began winning competitions before BMW started beefing up racing engines and subsequent production bikes; it simply outlasted less reliable bikes on the sometimes brutally rough race courses, especially those that traversed the Harz Mountains.

German historian Halwart Schrader termed the R32 "one of the most ingenious designs of the time."[6] All of the Bauhaus school's uncluttered ideals seemed represented by the BMW R32 and its artistic triangular lines dripping with elegance. It was a machine that demanded to be ridden—ridden hard and admired.

By 1923, the prohibition on German aircraft production was lifted, so BMW began hitting on all cylinders. Castiglioni had always wanted to extend BMW's brand into building cars. In 1921 he laid plans to build a design of Ferdinand Porsche's later in the decade, and he pondered manufacturing a design of the renowned engineer Wunibold Kamm. Both plans fell short.

As enticing as auto production soon became to true motoring

enthusiasts like Popp and Castiglioni, it remained an unstable financial proposition. Since each model was so costly to produce, any design became a veritable bet-the-company proposition. With new designs like Kamm's and Porsche's sometimes taking years to certify for durability and performance, bankers would get nervous. Producing engines to sell to the actual risk takers and building their own motorcycles appealed to BMW board members a lot more than building and marketing cars for themselves. In 1925, BMW sales were 15 million Reichsmarks ($3.6 million). The motorcycle product line included nine bikes. BMW won more than 100 motorcycle races that year, and boasted 573 first-place finishes by 1928. This is when BMW's brand recognition for engineering excellence took off and took hold across Europe. By 1928, BMW's fortunes looked bright, with revenues at 27 million Reischsmarks ($6.4 million), up 77 percent in just three years. Why take risks building cars?

BMW engineers chomped at the bit to design and build cars from the ground up. A good balance between cars, romance, and fiscal responsibility was the acquisition of the Dixi Werks, which was churning out the financially proven Austin Seven under license. In terms of easing the deal through and also winning the approval of BMW's board, it helped immeasurably that Dixi's major stockholder, Jakob Shapiro, also sat on BMW's board.

Hand-tooled or not, motorcycles remained the vehicle for the masses, while cars were for a more rarified class. German designers and engineers were slow to depart from the custom-coach car-building system. Some prominent men, though, wanted to bring automobiles to the masses. Knowing the need for a low-cost car for the working class, Ferdinand Porsche, for example, wore out a fair bit of shoe leather trying to get car companies to support his *Volksauto* design (which would later become the Beetle) before Adolf Hitler seized on the concept and backed it with Third Reich money in the mid-1930s. As Hitler began clawing his way to the top, he had seen as early as 1925 that German greatness would be judged not by its railroads but by its highways and the automobiles owned per capita. To justify what would become the vast autobahn system, the keys to more cars needed to nestle in many more pockets.

With the acquisition of Dixi in 1928, BMW started selling the proven Austin Seven, which it renamed as BMW 3/15. The name 3/15 indicated the car had three speeds and produced 15 horsepower. Not much more expensive than a premium-priced motorcycle and sidecar, it attracted housewives as well as professionals like lawyers and accountants. Twenty-five thousand 3/15s were sold between 1927 and 1931, with the military even rejiggering some for all sorts of work-horse army needs. In 1929, a 3/15 two-seater sports car cost 2,200 Reichsmarks ($523), and a convertible saloon cost 2,625 Reichsmarks ($625.00).

The 3/15 gave way to the BMW 3/20 in 1933, the first car to don the blue, white, and black BMW propeller roundel logo on the grille. The 3/20 was bigger than the 3/15, with a backbone rear-drive chassis similar to the one Ferdinand Porsche would eventually put into the Beetle. But unlike Porsche's car, which had swinging half-axles in the rear only, the 3/20 had them both front and rear. The six-cylinder 303, which also debuted in 1933, was the first BMW to sport the twin-kidney front grille—a BMW design signature into the twenty-first century.

In 1933, the 3/20 and its derivatives were the first homegrown BMW designs from Max Friz, who had long chafed under making the Austin-licensed 3/15. Unlike the Austin Seven, the 3/20 was more than just a car for the masses. The United States and most of western Europe were gripped by the Depression, but the German economy was looking up. As the Nazis began suppressing political opposition and asserting German nationalism, jobs proliferated, and the government intervened to rein in the inflation that had whipsawed the economy since the end of the Great War. By 1934, BMW had achieved $82 million in sales from aero engines, motorcycles, and cars, with some 13,000 people collecting BMW paychecks. Autobahns were being built, and BMW's engineers saw an emerging opportunity to build more substantial touring cars for the growing middle class.

Of modern design and proportions, the BMW 3/20 and 303 were quite a step up from the runabout stance of the Dixi-badged Austin Seven. The curves embodied the Bauhaus design of the time. The cars came in four-seaters, two-seaters, and cabriolet styles, and they started at 2,650 Reichsmarks ($1,043). The 303 was the six-cylinder model, and it sported such innovations as folding front seats to ease backseat access. In 1934, BMW introduced the 315/1, a groundbreaking, two-passenger sports car that was built on the 303 chassis, but was a different animal entirely, with far more curbside appeal. The Frazer-Nash Co. began importing 303s to the United Kingdom and sold Frazer-Nash BMWs and assorted derivative vehicles well into the 1950s!

The 326 saloon, the first BMW to challenge Mercedes-Benz in the saloon segment, debuted in 1936 and was the most successful prewar BMW despite criticism about its conservative styling and sludgy handling. In some ways it was a forerunner to the 7 Series sedans first launched in the mid-1980s. A long-distance cruiser, the 326 spawned a heavy-duty Jeep-like vehicle for the German military. Its acceleration was pedestrian, but the 1971-cc engine yielded a 70-mph cruising speed, which meant it could travel better than a mile a minute between Munich and Frankfurt without boiling over—no mean feat for a car in the mid-1930s. The 326, like the later 7 Series, was a leap up the ladder in challenging Mercedes' hold on the German premium large-car business.

Hitler had become serious about fostering the German auto industry. In 1936, the United States had 70 percent of the world's more than 40 million automobiles, or one car for every 4.5 Americans. With less than one-half the American population, Germany had just one automobile for every 49 citizens. BMW had no real interest in or connection to Hitler's concept of a people's car. BMW's Popp had, in fact, publicly declared that the bus was the best "people's car."[7] But Hitler laid his plans with the great designer and engineer Dr. Ferdinand Porsche, and he poured millions of Reichsmarks into developing the car. Where most cars cost the equivalent of well over $1,000, Hitler wanted a car that he could offer to the masses, a *Volksauto,* for an amount equal to about $400. By doing so, he would rally the hearts and minds of the working classes around the Reich with a carrot to go along with his well-known stick.

BMW's Popp and Max Friz were not outwardly supportive of Nazism. But like many industrialists of the time, they sought ways to get along with Hitler and the Reich in order to maintain their own wealth and positions and keep their factories running and their employees working. BMW was profiting greatly from the sale of aero engines to the Luftwaffe. BMW's proven water-cooled Mark IV aero engine and the new air-cooled BMW 132 became the mainstays of the Third Reich's air force. The military also bought thousands of motorbikes a year from BMW. Industrialists were willing, if not committed, cogs in the insanity that gripped Germany in the 1930s. Though the true politics and morality of people like Popp, Friz, Porsche, and members of the Quandt family during Hitler's reign are often debated and defended, it's worth noting a statement by U.S. Brigadier General Telford Taylor, a principal prosecutor of Nazi officials and leading German industrialists at the post–World War II Nuremberg war crimes trials: "Without the cooperation of German industry and the Nazi party, Hitler and his party would never have been able to assume power in Germany, and the Third Reich would never have dared to plunge the world into a war."[8] Were they guilty of being Nazis? Not really. Were they without guilt? No.

Popp wanted to give Hitler what he wanted in the way of his *Volkswagen*—as well as winning results at the racetrack, because it was expedient and wiser to do so than to disappoint the führer. Success in those days was literally defined in one way: Does it please Hitler?

As the people's car project, the *Volksauto,* unfolded, Popp and Mercedes-Benz managing director Wilhelm Kissel got credit for pointing out to Hitler and his industrial advisers that 25 to 30 percent of the price of any automobile was consumed by taxes and 20 percent fell to distribution. Though neither Mercedes nor BMW would be building the car, Hitler commended the two for figuring out some key aspects of the economics of the project, which were key to the *Volksauto*'s viability. By eliminating the tax and distributing directly to buyers by way of a subscription scheme, half of the retail costs could be shaved off the top, the two men advised Hitler. Whereas Popp had previously said it couldn't be done for less than 3,500 Reichsmarks (about $800), and the auto trade association was then working with a benchmarking price of 1,500 Reichsmarks ($600), Hitler wanted a car that would cost about 1,000 Reichsmarks ($400).

Popp and Kissel were friendly competitors who viewed Hitler's takeover of Germany in 1933 with alarm. The Nazis by the mid-1930s inserted their own men in BMW and Daimler-Benz factories to watch BMW managers like hawks as they produced engines for the Luftwaffe as well as other parts and pieces for the war machine. Popp and Kissel actually considered merging Mercedes and BMW, but such discussions went nowhere with war looming and the Third Reich calling the shots on German industry. It was another fortuitous twist of fate that would help keep BMW independent into the twenty-first century.

A stern, private man, Popp wasn't so much arrogant, according to his subordinates, as merely indifferent to the people below him. Fastidious about his appearance and obsessive about others' view of him, he was disarmingly formal most of the time, often starting conversations with underlings with what amounted to a lecture. His mantra for BMW in the late 1920s and 1930s set the course of the company: Decisions would never be made that sacrificed quality for quantity. He felt that the 320 was the best car in the world, and the R32 motorcycle and its descendants the best motorbikes in the world.

The BMW 328 was introduced in 1936 and powered by the same in-line six-cylinder engine that drove the 326. This was the car, more than any other, that defined the prewar BMW and established the company's reputation for both engineering under the hood and exterior design. The 328 even inspired some design cues for the later Z3 and Z4, the 1990s roadsters BMW made to attempt to recapture some of the roadster market. While still in prototype form, the 328 won at the famed Nurburgring racetrack, averaging 67 miles per hour over the course of a 70-mile race. The 328 ushered in a new era for sports cars, with headlights in the fenders instead of in the front fascia, small running boards, a streamlined body, and no exterior door handles. Historian Lawrence Meredith notes, "It's light weight, advanced road manners, smooth engine and graceful beauty put the 328 leagues ahead of virtually anything else produced in its class at the time. English car collector and historian Michael Barker . . . rates it above everything else, including several Ferraris he's owned."[9] A high-priced bauble, few could afford it in prewar Germany, and just 462 were produced before BMW stopped making civilian cars in 1939.

By 1937, flush with production for the Hitler war machine, sales of motorbikes and cars around western Europe, and sales of aero engines the world over, BMW's revenues were 143 million Reichsmarks ($57 million). The company, 14,000 employees strong, boasted 26 million Reichsmarks ($10.5 million) in cash reserves and just 2.4 million Reichsmarks ($1.2 million) in debt. Also that year, BMW built its 100,000th motorcycle. A year later, with war heating up, BMW's sales doubled, remarkable for a company in any circumstance, to 275 million Reichsmarks ($310 million), with reserves of 54 million Reichsmarks ($21 million). It now had 26,919 people on the payroll, but this starts to include slave labor.

The real hit of 1937 was the R35 motorcycle. The cross-country sport bike had a top speed of 62 miles per hour, and it was as sturdy as bricks. The Reich would buy 15,000 R35s over three years. The R35 was succeeded by the R75, which was designed solely for the military's use and produced at the Eisenach factory until to 1945. The bike was designed specifically for the rigors of the Russian front, as well as the North African desert. These bikes, the envy of both sides during the war, were often outfitted with machine guns mounted on a sidecar turret. The bike, not designed to be driven without a sidecar, was powerful enough to move three soldiers plus a mounted gun. The R75 used the same tires as Kubelwagens, the German jeep, which was built off the chassis of Hitler's *Volksauto*, a smart practicality of war-zone design. In war, parts are cannibalized from vehicles all the time, and there was always a shortage of tires, especially near the front. Along with the Kubelwagen, the R75 was the German military's wartime workhorse.

By the end of the 1930s, it was clear that BMW—though not well-known outside of Germany except among car cognoscenti—was beginning to hatch a credible alternative if not yet a full-blown rivalry to the much more established Mercedes. But car production stopped in 1939, as Hitler needed a first-class airplane and airplane engine manufacturer far more than a rising, second-tier automaker. Aero engines and parts supplanted cars at the Munich plant. And what planes! The BMW engines were hailed as perhaps the best on either side of the war by German, British, and American pilots alike. BMW manufactured full aero engines, as well as cylinder liners, crankshafts, valves, oil coolers, exhaust systems, engine cowlings, propeller adjustment fittings, and the like for others. Besides the production at its old Eisenach plant, BMW was turning out war matériel in Munich and Spandau, as well as at a new "shadow" factory in Allach, which used slave labor from the Dachau concentration camp.

In 1941, sales were up to 385 million Reichsmarks ($154 million), and BMW aero engineers developed the BMW 109-003 jet engine, the first production jet ever to power an aircraft. In 1942, however, friction developed between the Reich SS and BMW's management, and Popp was charged with incompetence and ousted as BMW's leader, ostensibly for keeping BMW vested in air-cooled aero engines instead of the mandated water-cooled engines. The real reasons, though, were that

Popp had refused to turn over the assembly lines entirely to aero-engine production and failed to comply with an order to transfer motorcycle production to another plant so that the motorbike plant could also be used for aero engines. Popp reckoned by 1942 that the outcome of the war was already determined, with America now fully engaged, and he felt the company's car production capacity would be necessary to rebuild.

BMW's Munich production buildings had their roofs painted to appear like rows and rows of suburban houses with quaint gardens and picturesque trees to avoid Allied bombing raids and airborne reconnaissance photographers. After Popp's departure, the SS directed BMW to begin developing and testing jet engines, which would leave Allied planes looking like they were standing still. Indeed, at the close of the war, the Allies found a complete BMW 003 jet engine hidden in a potash mine near the town of Magdeburg. It was the first time they had seen it.

————

As World War II drew to its painful close, BMW was in dire straits politically, economically, and geographically. Its plant in Munich had been destroyed by Allied bombs, and the plant in Eisenach was unfortunately in the Soviet zone. BMW's plant in Milbertshofen fell into the American zone. An order to raze the factory was staved off, and the 1,000 or so workers were set to making pots and pans (they literally hammered cylinder heads from engines into pots) and other assorted oddments for the postwar rebuilding effort.

Popp was arrested by the Allies and questioned about his role in turning BMW over to the Nazis to make war goods. He was later released and spared trial at Nuremberg. The Russians took over in Eisenach and started building prewar BMW 321 and 327 cars and R35 motorcycles for the Russian market and Russian zone of Germany. When they began building the cars and motorbikes, the Russians at first employed the blue, white, and black propeller logo, but later changed the Bavarian blue to Soviet red and the lettering to EMW, the E standing for Eisenach.

BMW's technical director, Kurt Donath, succeeded Popp in 1942 and stayed on after the war trying to salvage the company by making motorcycles. But Donath was forced to put BMW into receivership in

1948. Then the company was bailed out by bankers Hans-Karl von Mangoldt-Reiboldt who became BMW's president and Hanns Grewenig who became sales chief. That year, BMW was allowed to build motorcycles again.

———

BMW jumped—or rather, lumbered—back into the car business in 1951 when it launched the boatlike 501 model at the Frankfurt Motor Show. Anathema to BMW's latter-day nimble driving characteristics, it was a waddling, 65-horsepower four-door saloon. Disdained by the motoring press and even by those running BMW, it was also weighed down by the astronomical cost of 17,500 deutsche marks ($4,166) at a time when the average office worker earned just DM360 ($86) per month. BMW introduced a somewhat improved, V8-powered, 2.6-liter model in 1954, but its sales languished, too. BMW's comeback was going nowhere. Dwarfed by the postwar success of Volkswagen and Daimler-Benz, BMW lacked its competitors' good fortune. VW's chief executive, Heinz Nordhoff, benefited from Dr. Porsche's simple design, one that had proven itself before and during the war—all research and development lavishly financed by the Third Reich. Numerous versions of the car had been fathered by Porsche and the German army, such as the amphibious Schwimmenwagen and other derivatives, which further refined the car's reliability and versatility. The Beetle was cheap to make and sound as a brick—ideal for postwar Germans in lower- and middle-class families. Ask any German car executive today what his or her first car was and invariably the answer is the Beetle. Daimler's Sindelfingen factory had been spared the bombs, so the company was able to resume production of its finely crafted cars. While BMW was still struggling to rise anew in 1954, Daimler had the financial strength and production capability to turn out no less than the 300SL Gullwing sports car, a paragon still praised today for its innovative design and performance.

Germany's economic recovery was in full swing by the mid-1950s, yet BMW languished with the big pricey saloons. Dubbed the "Baroque Angels," the bulbous and lumbering V8 saloons that BMW was trying to sell were not taken very seriously. They were considered anathema to BMW's hard-won reputation for performance and sportiness. American car importer and dealer Max Hoffman, the "Baron of

Park Avenue," in New York City was as keen to import BMWs as he was Porsches and Volkswagens, which he had begun selling with success. Hoffman, who would play a key role in the growth of the German car industry in North America for the next quarter century, loved the prewar BMWs. He imported V8 502s to his Manhattan dealership, but they were slow to sell. Only a sports car, the fast and eye-catching 507, which Hoffman literally helped design and which was shown at the Frankfurt Motor Show in 1955, drew praise. Again, sports cars were what BMW seemed to know best. But the company still struggled with quality. The 507s were practically hand-built and cost even more to buy than the sterling Mercedes Gullwing; in fact, only 253 were even made. But the seeds were being sown for BMW's eventual core strength.

Turning a bit desperate in 1955, BMW introduced the Isetta, a microcar whose design was licensed from Italian scooter maker Iso SpA. Powered by a 247-cc motorcycle engine, the Isetta had a top speed of 55 mph—if you could stand the noise and vibration—and got 42 miles a gallon. If nothing else, the car was a nifty curiosity that arrived in time for sales to benefit from the oil shortages and high fuel prices that resulted from the crisis when Egypt closed the Suez Canal in 1955.

To get back into the "real" car business, BMW developed the 700, powered by a BMW motorcycle engine, a smart contemporary design by the Italian design house Michelotti. It was good for 80 miles per hour. Faster and more fuel efficient than the Volkswagen Beetle, it could not, alas, come near VW's price advantage. It sold a meaningful 190,000 units between 1959 and 1965, but achieved nothing like the meteoric rise of the Beetle in Europe and North America.

In 1959, BMW faced a serious financial threat. Since reentering the car business in 1952, it had failed to come up with a solid moneymaker. It limped along on motorcycles and some aero-engine sales. Lacking a clear strategic direction and casting about for a silver bullet to solve its problems, BMW had been toiling away fatally at the opposite ends of the car business, selling critically disdained yet expensive saloons and the small, cheap Isetta. BMW had no mid-market car that could compete on value when the middle class flourished in the late 1950s as the German economy kicked into gear. BMW's board, in a quandary, fell to squabbling. The Bavarian government was even considering a bailout, which would have involved selling shares to Daimler-Benz.

BMW shareholders saw this as a terrible waste, believing as most did that BMW could again rival Mercedes-Benz as it had done before the war. If Daimler-Benz got control, that would probably be the end of the BMW marque on cars; the company would probably survive only as a maker of motorcycles and engines.

But German industrialist, scion of two generations of one of Germany's most prosperous families, Herbert Quandt had other ideas. Herbert and his half-brother Harald ran the still considerable battery firm, AFA (later Varta), left to them by their father, Günther. The Quandts were a wealthy family from the Brandenburg town of Pritzwalk, where they first achieved wealth in the nineteenth century as a Dutch rope-making and textile operation. By the 1930s, the family's holdings also included chemicals, electric works, batteries, and war matériel.

At a December 1959 meeting in Munich, BMW's board recommended selling the company to Daimler—a move successfully opposed by the shareholders and labor union alike. Within three months of the meeting, Herbert and Harald Quandt acquired 30 percent of BMW's shares and began restructuring the company, giving the development engineers orders to produce a decent, reliable, midrange car that people would want at a competitive price. The only route to profitability required the Quandts to put their own money into developing such a car. That first car was the 1500, cobbled together in two years, not the usual four it took back then to develop and adequately test a new vehicle. Launched at the 1961 Frankfurt Motor Show, the 1500 was the first car from BMW to follow in the footsteps of the Dixi and then the BMW 3/15 of nearly 30 years before. It was a mass-produced three-box, practical sedan, yet with sharper lines than anything BMW had previously produced. The curvaceous, chrome-laden car bodies of the 1940s and 1950s were now kaput. The 1500 was light and had large doors for easy egress. Named for its 1,500-cc engine, it had a thoroughly modern 1960s design and definite European flavor, which was key to potential sales in the United States that BMW pined for. It could be an interesting counterpoint to the cars Detroit was making. Ford was making Fairlanes and Galaxies: long, heavy, lumbering cars with excessive rear overhangs to haul enough luggage for a family of six.

Major shareholders Herbert and Harald Quandt knew that Munich badly needed the affordable midsize sedan, a project known internally as "the family car." Engineer Alex von Falkenhausen was given a green light to upgrade one of his earlier engine designs to power the car. The resulting 80-hp, 1,500-cc, 30-degree-slant hemihead four was mated to a four-speed manual gearbox featuring Porsche synchromesh on all forward gears. A complete departure from the bigger, classically styled BMW 502 V8 "Baroque Angels," the new 1500 boasted a modern unit body/chassis and fully independent suspension with MacPherson front struts and rear semitrailing arms. The 1500's vertical kidney grilles, tall greenhouse, low belt line, slim pillars, flat hood and deck, and straight body lines were styling cues that soon became BMW hallmarks. *Car and Driver* enthused, "On fast turns, the car corners commendably . . . with very little body roll." The magazine's testers called it ". . . an extremely pleasant and sensible automobile . . . which will outperform more powerful cars including some two seaters."[10]

Market research suggested to BMW there was considerable growth potential in compact, sporty, medium-range saloons. Something was happening in music and other quadrants of pop culture, art, and design that was clearly marking a split with the prewar past. It was the dawn of a new era. By 1965, the Beatles were at the height of their career, Cassius "I am the greatest" Clay had mesmerized the sporting world, and the race was on between the Americans and Russians to land on the moon. It was the perfect time for a car with the agility and dynamism of the BMW 1500 to come onto the scene. Unlike the boat-like proportions of many sedans of the 1950s, the 1500 appeared to slope forward a bit, with the front and rear both raked at a steep angle. It gave the 1500 an aggressive, shark-like appearance, a BMW look that lasted some 20 years, with some of the "sharkish" design cues being carried forward to some models just introduced in the twenty-first century. Front-to-rear weight distribution was 53.5 to 46.5 percent, a fine ratio in those days, though BMW would later work hard to achieve almost perfect 50-50 weight distribution in most future models. The 1500's near-perfect balance set BMW on the straight and true path of emphasizing handling above all other brand characteristics. This was the beginning of the modern BMW.

That same year, 1962, Detroit began releasing some smaller sedans that, to the casual observer, looked akin to what BMW was doing in terms of small saloons, though the 1500 trumped just about all others in modernity of design: cars like the Plymouth Valiant, Studebaker Hawk, and Dodge Dart. A new car culture was emerging in America, one that was interested in speed and performance.

Chief stylist Wilhem Hofmeister gave the BMW 1500 a low waistline and a correspondingly low engine hood and rear end. This striking outline and the excellent suspension, with spring struts at the front and semitrailing arms at the rear, made the BMW 1500 a trendsetter for the entire automobile industry. While BMW had gotten the design right, the price, at DM9,500 ($2,375), was still higher than that of similar-category Fords and Opels. Nor was it yet equal to the manufacturing standards of BMW's rival to the north, Mercedes-Benz. BMW's quality control inspectors rejected faulty gearboxes and axles at an alarming rate, and even those that passed the line broke far too quickly far too often.

BMW's future formula was clear: four doors, room for five, a sporty engine, fine handling, neat styling, and high-speed autobahn capability. The performance of the 1,500-cc engine engineered by von Falkenhausen was achieved because BMW had assigned one of the leading racing car engineers in the country to the task. Von Falkenhausen's skills and desires for fast sporty driving were a perfect match for where BMW wanted to take the brand. The BMW board had originally tasked him with developing a 1300 cc engine. But von Falkenhausen felt the new engine should be 2,000 cubic centimeters. He was able to convince the BMW board to accept a 1,500-cc engine that could be easily expanded to a 2.0-liter.

Von Falkenhausen thought BMW needed to have a good two-liter engine, so when BMW agreed to build the 1500, he designed it so it could easily be made into an 1,800-cc size and then, with a new casting technique, a two-liter engine. That engine was the basis for every "New Class" model, which added up to 3.5 million units sold in the 1960s and into the 1970s. The so-called M10/12 engine would find its way into all the four-door 1500 to 2000 cars, the two-door 1600 to 2002 series, the 3 Series models of the 1970s and 1980s, and the four-cylinder 5 Series.

Said *Car and Driver* about the powertrain: "The 1500 engine has been criticized for its lack of flexibility, but we cannot agree with this. On very substantial hills we gave the car full throttle at 2000 rpm in 4th gear, and it did wonders in pulling itself out of such predicaments.

Again, this may be due at least in part to the carburetor settings employed, but as we drove the car, flexibility as such (as distinct from torque and low speed acceleration) was very near being outstanding." In tests conducted by reviewers, top speed proved even higher than BMW's numbers. *Car and Driver* continued, "Even more important in daily use is the unobtrusive way the car hangs on to its cruising speed, once it has been attained. Repeatedly, over winding roads infested with lots of traffic, we noted average speeds substantially higher than we would have guessed from the way the car handled. This feeling of always remaining at a comfortable, even leisurely, speed level was shared by our passengers in front and back, and is a tribute to the engine as well as to the running gear."[11]

———

Alex von Falkenhausen, from a famous and prestigious Bavarian military family, was one of the leading automotive engineers in Germany before and after the war, playing a leading role in developing BMW's 328 model with engineers Alfred Boning, Fritz Fiedler, and Ernst Loof, as well as BMW's best prewar motorcycles. The 328 sports car dominated races in Europe in the late 1930s and won the Mille Miglia in 1940 in Brescia.

During the war, von Falkenhausen and the rest of the product development department based themselves at Elsholz Castle at Berg on Lake Starnberg. According to an account by BMW historian Horst Monnich, after news spread in 1945 that Hitler had died in his bunker, von Falkenhausen crossed the Danube to head to Nuremberg.[12] He rode an R75 motorcycle through U.S. Air Force strafing to the village of Leonsburg, where his family was staying in safety. After avoiding the throngs of retreating German soldiers and refugees, he was surprised to find the family estate occupied by German SS officers. He was hoping to find Americans or Brits, if anyone. Von Falkenhausen hid out for days on the estate, waiting for the SS to leave. When they did, he gathered up his family and went to a barn where, under horse blankets and rusting ploughs, he had squirreled away a BMW 328. It hardly looked like it would run, but that had been done to make it look inoperable to anyone who might have stumbled on it. In fact, the master engineer had greased the rims and talcum-powdered the tires before burying them. The Americans arrived shortly afterward, and von Falkenhausen was grilled by intelligence officers. He willingly told them all he knew, including all the background on the motorcycles and one-man tank he had designed, as well as secret projects for other war machines he knew about and where the Allies might find the workshops. He also told them that he didn't believe they would encounter any army resistance between Regensburg and Munich, which is where the Americans were headed. U.S. Army General George Patton briefly took up residence in the family's estate, which was then returned to von Falkenhausen and his family.

Von Falkenhausen, with no job at the shattered BMW plant, set up shop in Munich, in part with tools he acquired at auction from the BMW factories that were now making bicycles and cookware. The engineer began tuning prewar 328s. Some were converted into single-seaters, and in 1948 von Falkenhausen decided to build racing cars under his own brand using the BMW 328 engine. After 1953, his AFM brand faded away, and von Falkenhausen went back to doing design work for BMW, handling chassis design for the 507 sports car that was met with such high praise at the 1955 Frankfurt Motor Show. The *Suddeutsche Zeitung* said the car combined the "gutsy power of an express locomotive with the playful elegance of an English greyhound," and said it was a cross between an aeroplane and a car, a "jetfighter for the motorway" and a "technological and design miracle."[13] The biggest disappointment, however, was that just as American importer Max Hoffman was supposed to make good on an order of 2,000 of the 507s, with possibly 3,000 more, he backed out. General Motors had just introduced the Chevrolet Corvette; Ford had brought out its Thunderbird, with as much power and design élan as the 507, but at a far lower price tag; and BMW had no brand yet in the United States from which it could hope to command premium prices.

Von Falkenhausen continued to work with BMW and became technical director of the company's sporting programs. "Aristocratic, inflexible, stubborn, modest, quiet" is how historian Monnich describes one of BMW's most revered design men.[14] He designed the successful engines that helped BMW to dominate touring-car racing in the 1960s and 1970s and recruited many of the engineers who went on to produce the famous BMW turbo engines in the 1980s. He retired in 1975, handing over the technical directorship of BMW Motorsport to Paul Rosche.

Developing a new car usually took at least four years (and often longer) in the early 1960s, but the 1500 had been hastily hammered and screwed together in less than 24 months. Nonetheless, the 1500 was a thoroughly modern car, a sleek Italian suit compared to the 700's raccoon overcoat. The 1500 also had some giddyap, with its in-line 4-cylinder engine. The use of in-line engines instead of V-shape engines has always been to maximize front-to-rear weight balance. Such a configuration and weight distribution helps create understeer on hard cornering and made the car more stable during high-speed driving.

In fact, the contrast between undertsteer and oversteer is a key BMW engineering principal that its buyers have long appreciated. If the rear tires of a car approach their traction limit more rapidly than do the front tires, then the rear of the car tends to steer a wider path than that traced by the front wheels. This rotates the car more than the driver intends and, if nothing is done, leads to the car turning a smaller-radius corner. When this occurs, the car is said to *oversteer.* If the front tires approach their traction limit more rapidly, the effect is that the front of the car takes a wider-radius curve than the driver intends, and the car is said to *understeer.* Understeering is considered safer than oversteering. If the car understeers and no correction is made, the car executes a wider corner than intended but remains stable. If the car oversteers, the turn in question has a smaller radius than intended; the smaller radius produces higher cornering forces that bring the required traction even closer to the limit of the rear wheels, which unfortunately leads to even more oversteer. Today, oversteer is blamed for sport utility rollovers because of the high center of gravity in SUVs relative to the length and width of their wheelbase. Understeer—a safer setup for drivers of average abilities when traveling at high speeds—is viewed by BMW as the kind of "active safety" it has long trumpeted in its marketing.

The 1500 could hit 95 miles per hour. A more powerful version that cost some DM500 ($125) more than the 1500 was introduced at the Frankfurt Motor Show in 1963 as the well-received 1800. The 1800Ti, a saloon with genuine performance attributes, was particularly praised in the press. Power was boosted to 110 horsepower at 5,800 rpm by increasing the compression ratio. A rear antiroll bar added stiffness and stability for better handling. Encouraged by the car's reception, BMW spun out 200 special editions with special equipment and engine add-ons that made them more appropriate for the racetrack than the autobahn. Indeed, nearly all were snatched up by race-car drivers, adding to BMW's mystique. *Car and Driver* noted in its review that the 1800Ti would appeal to drivers torn between a real sports car or a luxury saloon.[15] Embodying the best attributes of both, the magazines dubbed it a "super saloon." BMW replaced the base model 1500 in 1964 with a bigger engine variant, the 1600. Reaction to the more powerful and more expensive 1800 was so positive that it outsold the cheaper car two to one for the next two years. In short, after mucking around with Baroque angels and bubble cars, BMW found itself a niche (sports sedans) that it could profitably exploit—one that made its cars distinct from those of its richer rival up in Stuttgart.

Only in 1963 and 1964 did BMW start to find solid footing as a brand, and the man most responsible for establishing the brand was Paul Hahnemann, an SS officer during the war, who had come to BMW from Auto Union in 1961. He told *Der Spiegel*, "Anyone transferring from a Mercedes-Benz to another make is taking a step down, while anyone going from a Mercedes-Benz to BMW is taking a step *across*. Not a step up . . ."[16]

Almost immediately, Hahnemann emphasized a niche strategy in both marketing and product development. Having the two functions march in lockstep would underpin BMW's success for decades hence. It sounds pretty basic, but most automakers actually go through vast stretches of time when marketing and product development and design remain strangers. Many designers and engineers won't try to fathom, based on sketchy research, consumers' tastes five years down the line, which is when a car now just a sketch on paper will hit the showrooms. But swinging his weight on the BMW management board, Hahnemann made sure that marketing and brand management were equal to product development and engineering—a balance of disciplines that wouldn't hit its stride in the United States until the 1990s! Hahnemann believed products should be born of marketing ideas and that marketing would establish the current production deadlines and quantities. Everything BMW would do must be rooted in a marketing strategy. One principle Hahnemann established, which has served BMW well but still eludes many automakers, is constant upgrade throughout a series run. When BMW launches a new model, a four-door, for example, it brings out the two-door the next year, the convertible the year after, more powerful engines the following year, performance upgrades the year after that. That's done to keep the line fresh over the course of a seven-year run and to keep people interested. Basing its brand strategy in sporty driving and performance—and thus attracting customers who value performance—ensures that annual improvements and upgrades are very much noticed and appreciated by BMW's core customers. Those upgrades also keep the motor press interested over a seven-year run. Mass marketers like General Motors and Ford typically introduce a model, then leave it alone for several years except for cosmetic changes to headlamps and trim. People get bored with the old product, and the sales curve descends gradually after the second year. It is not uncommon to see sales of a BMW model, on the other hand, peak in its second year and then stay very close to that peak for an additional three to four years, occasionally even going up in the fifth, sixth, and seventh year (when prices are cut).

Called "Niche Paul" by the motor press and his colleagues, Hahnemann was the first of his time to tap into the idea of consumer perception. What the public thought was far more important than what any BMW staffer thought of the marque. It would have been a well-trod path for BMW managers to just talk to one another about their desperate situation after a decade of clumsy, overpriced cars and toy Isettas. Surprisingly though, Hahnemann's research showed that the public forgave BMW its recent past. He commissioned a market researcher and psychologist to conduct a focus group of sorts in which people were handed cards printed with names of automakers: BMW, Daimler-Benz, Glas, Volkswagen, and Auto Union, among others. Other cards had the words: "State-owned company," "Partially state-owned company," "Company with a major state shareholding."[17] Despite a lot of recent press about possible state takeover of BMW, people actually associated Daimler-Benz with being state-owned, probably because of its size and institutional character. Hahnemann was fascinated by how consumers picked up a brand *perception* that had no basis on any information conveyed by the media. Happily enough, most people associated BMW with the most favorably received models it had ever produced: the prewar 326, 327, and 328, not the recent Isetta bubble car. Strange, but true.

Hahnemann saw, too, that Mercedes-Benz was associated with an image of old Germany and that BMW could counter that stodgy image by striving to be a car of the new Germany. He aimed for BMW to fill a *psychological* gap in the market, not just a product gap. As Hahnemann tried to establish a real working culture at BMW, it helped that Mercedes-Benz openly regarded BMW as a quaint workshop but not as a *real* car company.

Hahnemann expressed the difference he perceived between Mercedes and BMW this way: "If a businessman has made something of his life in Germany and has to show his neighbor he is something, he can only drive a Mercedes. If, however, he has made something of his life, but feels not the slightest need to show off, then he can buy himself a BMW."[18] Hahnemann summed up the strategy as "unpretentious exclusivity." The director of advertising under Hahnemann, Fritz Lummert, would later come up with the ad slogan, "The New Class"—a brick-through-the-window dig at Mercedes-Benz. One of the things that helped define BMW in these years was its absolute focus on Mercedes-Benz, a rival that BMW executives pretended to think was beyond their scope in terms of product quality. Inwardly, however, the men of Munich believed they someday would build cars that consumers would come to think were better engineered than those built in Stuttgart. "Mercedes worried about itself and everyone else; we only concerned ourselves with Mercedes,"[19] Hahnemann admitted in an interview after he left BMW. Hahnemann came to be known around Germany as "Mr. BMW." That focus on Mercedes-Benz stayed baked into BMW well into the 1990s. "Achieving parity with Mercedes-Benz and besting it where it could in a specific category drove BMW's whole cultural engine until very recently," said industry consultant Jim Hall of AutoPacific in 2002.

A main problem with the whole strategy was that the BMW 1500, a design triumph, was riddled with the quality problems that were to be expected by shrinking its development from five years down to two. The brand needed to promise—and execute—quality to go with the car's exclusivity and sportiness, especially because the price, at DM8,500 ($2,125), was DM1,000 ($250) more than comparable Opels and Fords.

By 1965 and 1966, Germany's economy was in full swing, and would soon be second only to the U.S. economy for gross national

product. BMW prospered from the "New Class" cars and in 1963 paid
its shareholders its first dividend in 20 years. With BMW needing more
capacity to churn out more cars and extend the lineup, Hahnemann
moved the company's management to buy the Glas Werks, a maker of
agricultural machinery since 1883. Glas was an oddball company that
pursued making vehicles in even smaller niches than did BMW. It had
established itself over the years in lower Bavaria as a successful family
enterprise. With lagging demand for agricultural machinery after the
war, the company management decided to get into the personal transportation business after seeing Italy's Vespa scooter at a farm equipment trade show. Glas began manufacturing a scooter, the Goggo, in
1951. Though Germans were more interested in transportation with a
protective roof, the desire for a small car needed to be satisfied. A true
small-car boom developed, led by the Volkswagen Beetle. The most
famous of the Glas models was the Goggomobil. It didn't matter that
the Goggomobil of 1954 was basically a four-wheeled scooter with a
roll-up canvas sunroof, the first prototypes of which used a door
across the front of the car as in the BMW Isetta. Business improved in
1955, helped by a decent car with real doors and room for a family of
four that sold for less than the equivalent of $750.00. BMW annexed a
struggling Glas in 1966 to gain the additional manufacturing capacity
along with the company's 4,000 trained workers. By 1968, the only
Glas product the company was still making was the Goggomobil, with
all other Glas assembly lines converted to BMW vehicles.

In March 1966, BMW introduced the 1600-2 to nearly unanimous
acclaim in the motor press. The lighter body made the car as fast as the
more powerful 1800, while the sports car handling that made Bavaria
famous was back in the garage. The motor press immediately made
comparisons with the Alfa Romeo saloons of the day, just the kind of
praise the still struggling restart, if not upstart, was looking for to earn
credibility.

BMW had never made much of a dent in the U.S. market, enjoying
just a small cult following of German expatriates and driving enthusiasts eager to be the only ones on their block to own a BMW. For this
group, driving a BMW was something that made them seem "in
the know" among their friends. Anyone could own a Volkswagen,
Mercedes-Benz, or Porsche in 1966. Owning a BMW was starting to

be seen as chic among so-called early adopters, the people who relished being the first ones to discover a new product.

From 1960 to 1966, the popular sedans and coupes in the United States were Ford Fairlane, Falcon, and Galaxie, Oldsmobile 88s, Chrysler Imperials and 300s, Chevrolet Impalas, and Pontiac Bonnevilles. Stately cars and muscle cars that were heavy and fast were the rage. But postwar hostility to German cars was thawing, helped immeasurably by the cultural phenomenon Volkswagen was becoming with the cognoscenti and the increasingly rebellious youth movement. VW's Beetle, Karmann Ghia, and Microbus were not just the choice of students, but their teachers as well.

Meanwhile, BMW was doing what came naturally, improving, freshening, and leveraging engine blocks and existing chassis. Not long after the 1600-2 was launched, Alex von Falkenhausen had a two-liter engine installed in his 1600-2 for his own use. Quite by coincidence, planning director Helmut Werner did the very same thing. Neither man knew the other had done so until one day both found themselves in BMW's Munich workshops at the same time working on the same hardware.

After much debate between production and manufacturing board members who did not support the idea of mass-producing the car, BMW made the Falkenhausen-Werner "tuner" cars into a production car destined specifically for the U.S. market, where Max Hoffman said he and other dealers could sell a more powerful and still sportier version of the 1600-2. And the car, dubbed 2002, was able to pass new U.S. exhaust emissions standards.

Hahnemann's thinking about BMW's niche strategy at this time and his gamesmanship with the German media and upstate rival Mercedes-Benz shows through in an interview he did in *Der Spiegel* in 1969. He was queried about whether it was a coincidence that BMW had introduced a 2800, which had the same engine displacement as the Mercedes 280. "How are people to see your big cars, if not as an anti-Mercedes car, which has exactly the same engine size?" asked the interviewer. Hahnemann responded: "That's right, if you're only comparing product with product. . . . Our psychological niche, however, is particularly noticeable here, because both these cars, do, indeed, have precisely the same capacity. . . . [But] We never thought of Mercedes when we developed this car. . . . *We* have built a remarkably well balanced car. Daimler-Benz is probably still a hair's breadth ahead of us in production. It is simpler, you see, if cars are built heavier, as they are done in Stuttgart. But we can certainly take on any competitor when it comes to fine balancing."[22] All in one interview, Hahnemann perfectly played up BMW's mystique. On the one hand, he says the company never even thought of Mercedes when developing the car; on the other, he denigrates Mercedes' "heavy" engineering. It was pure Hahnemann, tweaking the nose of Daimler-Benz, which BMW customers loved, but doing so in such an understated way that it did not seem as though he was merely pitching BMW to *Der Spiegel* readers.

BMW had seen profitable growth in the late 1960s on the strength and acceptance of the "New Class." As in the United States, the years 1966 to 1970 in Germany were awash in student protests and cultural expressions of individuality, especially among those under 30 who were at odds with their parents' generation over politics, music, art, and commerce. BMW was the upstart, the opposition, to Daimler-Benz, which was the establishment company in Germany—the brand of BMW customers' parents. Sales at BMW, though, trailed off in 1970, especially sales of the new upper-priced six-cylinder models. Hahnemann's customer surveys showed that the older buyers who wanted the six-cylinder were suddenly put off by BMW's spare interior designs. For more money they expected more creature comfort. BMW quickly reacted with leather and wood trims, but not to the degree of Mercedes saloons. It would be wrong and possibly damaging to some of BMW's core brand attributes if they became too much like Mercedes.

The biggest breakthrough for BMW in the United States, it is agreed by most company followers and those inside the company, was David E. Davis Jr.'s review of the 2002 in *Car and Driver* in 1968. Davis in 1968 was one of the most listened-to voices in the motoring press. His words then, as now, carry a lot of weight.

Davis not only praised the performance of the 2002 and hailed it as a breakthrough vehicle, but in his unique style of giving his readers the idea that he is always writing with a Cuban cigar burning and a glass of 30-year-old brandy at hand, he scolded most of the auto industry for the gas-thirsty, sloppy-handling, oversized rattle wagons and muscle cars they were turning out. The review rippled through the motoring press, the community of driving enthusiasts in America, and Detroit.

Davis's use of delirious 1968 American idioms is priceless. "To my way of thinking, the 2002 is one of modern civilization's all-time best ways to get somewhere sitting down," said Davis, who went on to praise the car's handling, build quality, gear ratios, and overall feel as something only the most discerning car buyer would appreciate. "Something between nine and ten million squares will miss out on this neat little two-door sedan with all the cajones and brio and élan of cars twice its size and four times its price, but some ten thousand keen types will buy them in 1968, so the majority loses for once."[23]

As much as Davis believes the 2002 represented the best German know-how of the time, he also extolled the virtues of the 2002 for being "American." "Not American in the same sense as the contemporary domestic car, with all its vast complexity and nouveau riche self consciousness, but American in the sense of Thomas Edison and a-penny-saved-is-a-penny earned and Henry Ford I. The 2002 mirrors faithfully all those basic tenets of the Puritan ethic on which our Republic was supposedly based. It does everything it's supposed to do, and it does it with ingenuity, style and verve." Not flash.[24]

So began BMW's modern era and the true beginning of a new brand of motorcar that would be studied and benchmarked by competitors for the next three decades.

The Ultimate Family

THREE

The BMW brand including its market worth belongs to perhaps the strongest automobile companies in the world. For this reason, you can rest assured that the BMW spirit lives on in the fourth generation.

—STEFAN QUANDT

Recognized everywhere, BMW is the world's most admired car company, yet it is controlled by one of the least-known, most-secretive, wealthiest families on the planet. The second-wealthiest family in Germany (behind the Albrecht clan), the Quandt family—including matriarch Johanna, son Stefan, and daughter Susanne Quandt Klatten—has a combined wealth, depending on gyrations in the stock market, of around $17 billion.

Johanna Quandt is the widow of Herbert Quandt, who took over BMW in 1959 and died in 1982. Johanna and the two children she had with Herbert, Stefan and Susanne, hold 46.6 percent of BMW's shares. Their wealth from the car company grew from $7.5 billion in 1997 to about $12 billion in 2002. Herbert's four children from his previous marriages do not hold stock directly in BMW, but some of them have their wealth tied up in other Quandt businesses and holdings that Herbert Quandt portioned out for them before he died.

Stories abound about Johanna Quandt's almost Greta Garbo–like lifestyle—stealthily traveling around the world on commercial flights in economy class despite all her billions. Johanna was born in Berlin in 1926

to a middle-class family; her father, Wolfgang Bruhn, was curator of the
Prussian National Library of Art and a published expert on German
native dress. After finishing her secondary schooling, Johanna got a job
around 1957 as a secretary in the offices of Herbert Quandt, whose businesses then included the big battery maker Varta, textile maker Stohr,
a petrochemical firm, as well as shares in BMW and Daimler-Benz.
Already married twice before, Herbert divorced Lieselotte Blobelt
Quandt in 1959 although they had three children under age 10. As he
had grown disaffected with his wife of a decade, Johanna's appeal grew.
With Johanna, Herbert played the role of a lonely man with deteriorat-
ing eyesight (he eventually went blind). As he came to depend on
Johanna more and more for his business needs, a relationship flowered,
and the two married in 1960.

After Herbert Quandt's death in 1982, Johanna took a seat on
BMW's supervisory board. Seldom seen in public even after taking on
this responsibility, Johanna retired from the board in 1997 at age 71.
She is almost clinically shy and suspicious of the press and has no use
for stock market analysts and reporters who cover the markets (no
doubt a carryover from her husband's disdain of the media). While she
remains "a force," says one BMW executive, the family's BMW oversight is now handled by Stefan and Susanne, both of whom have seats
on BMW's supervisory board.

From the time Susanne and Stefan were small children, they were
kept under tight security. In the early and mid-1970s, Germany was hit
by a series of politically motivated kidnappings and killings of prominent bankers and industrialists by the Red Army Faction. Theo
Albrecht, scion of Germany's wealthiest family, which controls the
Aldi retail stores, was kidnapped, held for three weeks, and released
only after a ransom of more than $2 million had been paid. The Revo-
lutionary Cells also put the Quandts on guard by murdering Israeli
Olympic athletes in Munich in 1972, literally in the neighborhood of
BMW headquarters. That, and the painful knowledge of what had
happened to Charles and Anne Lindbergh's baby in 1932—a sensational kidnapping case that occurred less than 40 miles from where
Herbert was living in Philadelphia in 1932—sent him and Johanna into
paranoid spasms about the prospect of losing a child to terrorist kid-
nappers. In fact, in 1978 there was an attempt made at kidnapping
Susanne and Johanna, as well as a separate attempt on Susanne's

cousin. A gang of 14 armed men led by convicts on a day-release pass from the local prison had intended to snatch the two Quandts from their home in broad daylight and demand a $10 million ransom. The plot was foiled by German police at the last moment.

Stefan Quandt, born in 1966, is on the five-member executive committee of BMW's supervisory board that appoints the *Vorstand,* the management board. Besides his BMW holdings and board membership, Stefan has several other businesses. He owns 100 percent of Delton AG, which is made up of several companies: Ceag, a fast-growing manufacturer of cell phone battery chargers; Thiel, a German logistics company that he is trying to expand; Heel, a company that makes homeopathic remedies; and Sparte, a maker of household products such as plastic bags and coffee filters. Delton AG reported earnings of 850 million euros in 2002. He is much more driven by new-technology businesses than old-line industries. Stefan also owns a controlling share in Datacard, a lucrative Minnesota-based supplier of magnetic-strip security cards that the Quandts bought into in 1987. Datacard has the world's biggest market share of that booming business.

Associates say Stefan is a fairly uncomplicated son of wealth whose idea of a good time is a soccer game and a couple of beers. He has said that he regrets aspects of a sheltered childhood, not being able to freely mix with other children and having to be chauffeured everywhere, even for short distances, for security reasons. He spends a great deal of time at the Quandt offices in Bad Homburg working at his father's desk and is widely expected to one day become supervisory board chairman of BMW, a far more public and direct role than his father ever held.

A bachelor, Stefan has seldom been photographed squiring a woman around in public. Hardly a photo of him exists in the German press archives in which he is smiling. He likes to shop for himself, accompanied by a sole, discreetly positioned security guard, or alone. He served in the German army after high school and then earned a degree in economic engineering. After attending university, Stefan worked for Boston Consulting, which, not coincidentally, has frequent BMW assignments. He then worked at Datacard in the early 1990s. He is said to like the Datacard business and extended what was supposed to be a six-month stay into a year's sojourn in Minnetonka, Minnesota. He then went to work at the company's Hong Kong office, where he was in charge of its Asia-Pacific region. Returning to Bad Homburg in 1996, he took up where his father had left off, managing the multifaceted Quandt empire.

Stefan's older sister, Susanne, born in 1962, sits on the supervisory boards of BMW and pharmaceutical company Altana. At her rare public appearances, she retreats into an almost mechanical official role. She has a quiet style and is never seen wearing any jewelry other than earrings and her wedding ring. BMW managers who have dealt with her say she prepares carefully for conversations and meetings about the car business, often with written questions on a legal pad. One outside industry consultant who has been present at meetings with Susanne says, "She is very smart, quite engaged, and very focused . . . I liked talking with her very much."

After finishing college in 1983, Susanne held a series of jobs in advertising and at BMW to learn something of business, always working incognito under an assumed name. Susanne Kant and Susanne Edge were two of her aliases. She was able to work incognito because few people had ever seen photographs of her, cameras being routinely banned by security guards at the few public appearances the Quandts made. She worked at the ad agency Young & Rubicam, which handles Ford business internationally; at Dresdner Bank; and at BMW's Regensburg factory, in purchasing and logistics. There she met Jan Klatten. Susanne, in fact, did not reveal her identity to Jan until seven months into their relationship when they began discussing marriage, preferring him to think she was just a hardworking girl from Munich until she knew of his true intentions and reasons for marriage. After marrying Klatten, the two had three children in four years.

As much as the Quandts are tied to BMW, Susanne is more involved in Altana AG, which has become one of the fastest-growing drug companies in Europe, as chairman of its supervisory board. Altana came into existence in 1977 when Herbert Quandt was rearranging his empire for disposal to his heirs. Its core is a chemical company that was started in 1873 and acquired by Susanne's grandfather, Günther Quandt, in 1941. But the growth driver is drugs. Altana developed the anti-ulcer drug Panto, which reverses the damage of stomach ulcers with just four weeks of treatment. Demand for the drug surpassed all expectations, achieving 650 million euros in sales in 2000 and 1.3 billion euros in 2001. Earnings for the whole company in 2001 were

3 billion euros. Altana saw a doubling of total sales over five years, with a 20 percent profit margin. From 1987 to 2001, the value of Susanne Klatten's Altana holding increased by about $4 billion. Largely on the strength of Panto, Altana was added to the German Stock Index (DAX), and it was listed on the New York Stock Exchange in 2002.

Tradition and service are important to Susanne Klatten, especially as they relate to her parents' interests in fostering entrepreneurship. She spent 2.8 million euros of her personal fortune to establish a training center for young entrepreneurs at the Technical University in Munich. "Whoever wants to accomplish something should be able to find support," she told historian Rudiger Jungbluth for his book, *The Quandts,* published in 2002.[1] As part of the Herbert Quandt Institute, she also personally backs a program to educate students in the foundations of the Christian, Jewish, and Muslim religions. At the family's Sinclaire House in Bad Homburg, scientists, artists, and politicians gather to germinate their thoughts in various symposia sponsored by the Quandt Institute. Susanne today is the wealthiest of the Quandts, and she is considered to be the wealthiest woman in Europe. She and Stefan each came into their inherited money at age 30. Her net worth was estimated to be around $7.5 billion in 2002, while Stefan and their mother were worth about $4.5 billion apiece.

Politically, the Quandts support exclusively—and quite generously—the Christlich Demokratische Union (CDU), a conservative political party in Germany. In fact, Johanna, Susanne, and Stefan each contributed DM500,000 to the party in 1998. There has been much executive crisscrossing between Altana's and BMW's boards and the CDU party hierarchy, but a government investigation into party contributions from Altana, with public disclosures devoured by the press, chastened the family a bit.

The family's near anonymity outside of BMW and German banking and society circles would baffle most Americans who have some basic knowledge of the Fords and Rockefellers. Ask an average Bavarian or Prussian merchant about the Quandts and chances are they'll simply shrug. They give very few interviews and when they do, the results aren't exactly the stuff of great storytelling. Stefan told historian Jungbluth, "Giving interviews to gain advantage is one thing. . . . To give interviews to become famous is useless."[2]

The Quandts have controlled BMW since its post–World War II restructuring in 1959. What's more, Herbert's father, Günther Quandt, was a leading German industrialist who controlled some of Germany's biggest companies in the 1930s. But with all that, the Quandts for the most part fly happily below the celebrity culture radar. Their intense privacy has foiled so many journalists for such a long time that most have simply given up trying to interview them. BMW managers interviewed for this book, such as chairman Helmut Panke and design chief Chris Bangle, when asked about the Quandts, get very quiet. Any interviewer knows that to linger on the topic will mean a quick end to the meeting. As one BMW executive said to me once, "Who wants billionaires mad at you?" During the mid- and late 1990s, when BMW's ownership of the British Rover Group was causing billions in losses and speculation about thousands of British jobs being lost, British journalists tried to prevail on the Quandts' media spokesman for an interview with Stefan or Susanne, making the case that they "ought to" speak on the subject of the collapsing marriage between BMW and Rover. The answer came back simply: "Why should they?"

————

The known history of the Quandt family stretches back as far as the late eighteenth century. The Quandts emigrated from Holland to Prussia in the early nineteenth century, when Wilhelm I invited Protestants who were being persecuted in their homeland to settle in Prussia. The first Quandt about which anything in much detail is known is Emil Quandt, born in 1849. Not born to wealth, he worked hard from the age of 14. But he married well, to Hedwig Draeger, the daughter of a rich textile manufacturer, and took charge of the family firm in 1883. Not long after, Emil landed the exclusive contract to supply uniforms to the German Imperial Navy and Prussian army, cementing the business's solid footing. Emil's son, Günther Quandt, born in 1881, didn't strike out on his own until after marrying Antonie Ewald in 1906, at which time he was given a linen factory out of the family holdings to run. From that base he made savvy acquisitions and funded several start-ups. By the time World War I broke out, Günther was running a conglomerate that included battery-maker AFA, a company that made land mines and shell casings, a petrochemical firm, and the garment company that supplied most of the German military's uniforms—all in addition to several other companies in which he simply held stock.

Antonie's mission in life quickly became her two boys, Helmuth, born in 1908, and Herbert, born in 1910. Günther continued to build his fortune into something he imagined Helmuth would inherit. Herbert was not viewed by Günther as a viable heir because of his lame legs and wretched eyesight; diagnosed as nearly blind as a boy, total blindness seemed an eventual certainty.

When Antonie Quandt died in 1918, swept away by the influenza epidemic that overran Europe, Herbert was a nine-year-old and a near stranger to his father. But Günther and Herbert became closer by necessity. Lost without a woman to care for himself, his sons, and his household—which now included three newly adopted children of a dead business partner—in 1920 Günther married Magda Ritschel, who was 18 years his junior. Günther met Magda on a train and was immediately captivated by the young beauty. Strongly taken by this teenage girl, he visited her at Holzhausen College, where she was a student, more than once claiming to be her uncle as he whisked her away from the campus in his open landau for outings in the surrounding countryside.[3] Magda soon dropped out of college, and Günther continued the courtship, frequently inviting Magda and her mother to his lakeside villa. Günther already showed signs of the anti-Semitism that would later crush Germany, and after the two were engaged he insisted that Magda's birth certificate be amended so that she was declared the legitimate daughter of Oskar Ritschel, her birth father. Thus his fiancée shed the, to some, undesirable name of Friedländer, her Jewish stepfather's name, which she had taken several years earlier. Quandt also required that his bride attend a Protestant church with him. They were married on January 4, 1921, at Ritschel's parents' house in Godesberg. After the honeymoon, said her mother later in an interview, Magda rushed into her arms wailing, "How could you have let me marry him!"[4] A brusk sort of man who paid far more attention to sums and share prices than postnuptial courting, Günther wanted a live-in nanny, housekeeper, and appealing distraction more than a true soul mate. Harald, their first and only child, was born just 10 months after the wedding.

Historians have painted Magda as a charming, attractive opportunist, no doubt swayed by Günther's money and position. Love, if it

sparked for even a few months, seemed to quickly fade. A rigid Günther made his young wife justify household accounts on a weekly basis
as if she were running one of his businesses, with expenditures for
nearly everything, including food, being approved and *initialed* by Günther. They did little of the entertaining that would have pleased Magda
but bored Günther. As the early years of the marriage passed and Helmuth became a young man, Magda reportedly took an unhealthy interest in Günther's eldest son. David Irving reports in his book, *Goebbels:
Mastermind of the Third Reich,* that Magda's lengthy infatuation finally
led to an affair with her 18-year-old stepson Helmuth prior to his death
from peritonitis in 1927.[5] His death took place on a trip Günther forced
him to take to separate him from Magda, according to Irving. Günther
would say later that Helmuth's death was the end of the marriage, but
it was clearly over for Magda before that.

Magda Behrend Ritschel Friedländer Quandt Goebbels is at the
center of what the Quandts view as the darkest and most embarrassing chapter of their family's history. Günther Quandt's profiteering
from both world wars, including the employment of slave labor at his
factories in the 1930s, would be a deep enough stain for most German
industrial families. But Magda took the stain and literally turned it into
a lake of blood at the side of two of the most reviled characters of the
twentieth century. Obsessive about privacy and uneasy about the family's considerable past business connections to the Nazis, the Quandts
no doubt recoil from having had a family member known as "First
Lady of the Third Reich." Magda earned that black title with her second marriage, this one to Nazi propaganda minister Joseph Goebbels
after her divorce from Günther, and for her close friendship with Adolf
Hitler. In marked contrast to Hitler's seldom seen mistress Eva Braun,
Magda was the most public female face of the Third Reich.

Magda's story is too rich and intertwined with the Quandts of the
1920s and 1930s not to merit a bit more discussion in this examination
of the Quandt family. Her dark chapter in Quandt history was often
mentioned in newspaper stories in the 1990s about BMW's struggle to
remain independent and the possibility of the Quandts selling out.

———

Magda Behrend Ritschel was born in 1901, the illegitimate daughter of
Auguste Behrend, a domestic servant. After Magda's birth, Auguste

maintained that she had married Magda's biological father, Dr. Oskar Ritschel, an engineer and builder. If the marriage actually occurred, it didn't last long, and Auguste soon married a Jewish man named Friedländer who was in the leather business. Friedländer's first name is disputed by historians, with some believing it was Richard. Ritschel and Friedländer, who knew and liked each other by all accounts, vied to provide support and fatherhood for Magda, who eventually grew accustomed at a young age to men competing for her affection. Raised and schooled in a Brussels convent school, when World War I broke out she returned to Berlin and took Friedländer's name, despite the fact that he and Auguste had divorced. She loved him as her true father. She completed her secondary education in 1919 and then enrolled in an exclusive girl's college, Holzhausen, in the Lower Saxony town of Goslar.

Returning to school in the fall of 1920, she found herself sharing a train compartment with 38-year-old Günther Quandt, who was struck by the young woman's beauty and magnetism. But the life she was seduced into thinking she would have never materialized. Not yet 40, Quandt seemed in an odd hurry to reach middle age. He was smitten, as most men might be with a girl not yet 20, but he had scant interest in the cultural doings that tantalized Magda and no interest in entertaining. His emphasis was on Magda running his house, which included not only Herbert and Harald, but also those three orphaned children of his deceased business partner.[6]

After Helmuth's death in 1927, Günther took Magda on a six-month trip to the United States. There, it was reported in Irving's book, she met and shared intimacies with the nephew of President Herbert Hoover, who would subsequently travel to Germany, after Magda and Günther separated in 1929, to beg her hand in marriage, only to be rebuffed. But in the summer of 1929, while still married to 47-year-old Günther, she had an affair with a Russian-born Jewish lawyer, Chaim Arlosoroff. Günther, who was having her followed by detectives, verified the affair and chased her from the family residence; Magda herself had already been pleading with him for months to let her out of the marriage. Magda ensconced herself in a luxury apartment in Berlin with Harald and a 4,000 Reichsmark monthly allowance. An associate of Joseph Goebbels's noticed her in 1930 and encouraged Magda to join the Nazi party as a women's organizer.

Little interested in the toil and tedium of grassroots organizing, which had her mixing with working-class German fraus and frauleins rather than the men of substance in the party, Magda quickly ingratiated herself with the hierarchy of the party and soon met Goebbels himself.

By early 1931, it is clear from Goebbels's diaries that Magda was in the propaganda minister's close circle and was, in fact, his lover. In her book, *The Women of the Third Reich,* Anna Maria Sigmund notes that Hitler was impressed with Magda and saw her as a perfect wife for Goebbels, adding as she did a glossy sheen to the party's public face.[7] Hitler promoted their marriage, says Sigmund, by telling mutual confidant Dr. Otto Wagener that "this woman could be of vital importance in my life, even without my being married to her . . . too bad she is not married."[8] Hitler had no notion of wooing Magda himself, but he wanted her in his orbit. She would have to be married to someone senior in the party lest tongues wag about her and Hitler. Wagener relayed Hitler's thoughts on the matter to Magda, and soon enough she and Goebbels were wed. Oddly enough, their wedding took place in December 1931 at Severin, the Quandt family farm—without the knowledge of Günther Quandt! Both Hitler and Harald Quandt, who'd begun wearing a Hitler Youth uniform, attended. By marrying Goebbels, Magda relinquished both official custody of Harald and her alimony from Günther. Leni Riefenstahl, Hitler's propaganda filmmaker, was also present for the wedding, and in her memoirs Riefenstahl said Magda confided to her, "I agreed to marry Dr. Goebbels because I can now be closer to the Fuhrer." None of the Quandts except Ello Quandt, the wife of Günther's brother Werner, had anything to do with Magda after her marriage to Goebbels.[9]

In 1933, Goebbels learned of the prior affair between his wife and Arlosoroff, who had subsequently become a prominent Zionist leader in Palestine. In June of that year, Arlosoroff traveled to Germany to try to get Hitler to release certain Jewish assets from German banks in exchange for Zionist support against the worldwide Nazi boycott. Numerous entries in Goebbels's diaries record his suspicion that Magda was still emotionally connected to a Russian Jew, whom he referred to only as *"der fremde Mann"* (stranger or foreigner).[10] And, by no small coincidence, Arlosoroff turned up dead that month, murdered.

Almost continually pregnant from 1933 to 1940, Magda also constantly played hostess for dinners and other social gatherings for various

Nazi bigwigs in Hitler's private headquarters, where the Goebbels had an apartment. After her marriage, neither her beloved Jewish stepfather nor her natural father wanted anything to do with her. Friedländer, the former, would later be sent to the Buchenwald concentration camp near Weimar in 1938. His family contacted Goebbels to plead for help, but neither he nor Magda intervened. Friedländer died at Buchenwald the following year.

Magda fussed over Hitler like a wife and mother, regularly cooking his special vegetarian meals, which were often sent to his office in insulated travel thermoses. Her six children with Goebbels: Helga, Hilde, Helmuth, Holde, Hedda, and Heide all carried names that began with *H* as homage to Hitler. Magda had seven children over the course of 19 years, plus three documented miscarriages and reportedly several that were not documented. In 1938, fecund Magda was the first recipient of the "Honor Cross of the German Mother," an honor bestowed on German women for having a number of children (eight children earned a gold medal, six a silver, and four a bronze) and for meeting racial and political standards exalted by the Reich.

In the waning days of the Third Reich, Magda wrote at length in her diary of her belief that she and Goebbels would certainly die with Hitler rather than take their chances with the invading Allies. Standing by Hitler to the end, she wrote that to die with him for the cause was an honor she and Goebbels had not dreamed of so many years before.[11] "To end our lives with him is a favor of fate that we never dared to hope for." In late 1944, with the Allies marching toward Berlin, there had been some planning to evacuate the Goebbels children from Germany if possible. But Magda's diary entries of April 1945 make it clear that she and Goebbels had decided to keep the family intact, however briefly, before consigning them to a monstrous suicide fate. In late April 1945, Magda wrote a letter to Harald, whom she didn't know had been captured by the Russians and was being held as a prisoner of war in Cairo:

My dear Son.
We, Papa, your six siblings and I have been with the Fuhrer for six days now. Our purpose is to bring our National Socialist lives to the only possible, honorable conclusion. I do not know if you will receive this letter. . . . You must know that I have stayed

with Papa against his will that the Fuhrer wanted to help me escape last Sunday. You know your Mother—we are of the same blood, there was no doubt in my mind. Our wonderful idea has perished—and with it everything beautiful, admirable and good I have known in my life. The world that is coming after the Fuhrer and National Socialism will be a world not worth living in, and therefore I have brought the children here with me. They are too good for the world to come. The merciful Lord will understand me if I personally give them release. You will live on, and I have only one request of you: never forget that you are a German, never do anything dishonorable, and take care that through your life our death has not been in vain. . . . The detonations shake the bunker. The bigger ones [the children] protect the smaller ones, and their presence here is a blessing, if it only makes the Fuhrer smile every now and then. . . . My beloved Son, live for Germany!

Your Mother.[12]

Hitler's secretaries and Eva Braun's maid pleaded with Magda to let the children be spirited away to safety. These women, plus the kitchen and office staff, literally begged on their knees to take them. Hanna Reitsch, the pilot who carried the Goebbels's last letters out of Germany in a private plane, implored Magda to let her take the children aboard as well. But she maintained her resolve. Magda dressed all the children in white outfits and combed their hair. They were then given lemonade laced with poison or a sleep-inducing drug. Accounts vary about whether they then received an injection or whether cyanide was dripped into their innocent mouths as they slept a drug-induced sleep. In their own suicides, Goebbels shot himself and Magda took poison.

Such misery, this grim chapter in the Quandt family history, has understandably helped make the Quandts leery of attention. It's a rare German who can speak comfortably of the country's history between 1930 and 1945; mention of the war to a German, young or old, typically elicits a quick and awkward conversation. One can imagine the reticence of people whose relations played a prominent role in the horror.

After Helmuth's death in 1927, Günther began to ponder Herbert anew, especially as he had proved himself resourceful and fairly clever despite his diminished eyesight. Homeschooled, he had learned his subjects well by way of oral learning. Not surprisingly, Herbert developed a keen sense of hearing, sometimes going out into the forest near the family home before dawn with his tutor to track deer in the dark and learn bird species by their call and nesting places. He also learned to play the piano and organ well despite his problems with reading the sheet music.

Herbert's determination and resilience improved his father's view of his son's ability to perhaps succeed him in the family businesses. He began taking Herbert on a series of trips around Europe, Asia, and the United States. The two traveled to the United States in 1927, and Günther, ever the prescient businessman, saw signs of economic collapse in America's near future. As a manufacturer, he was worried by mounting inventories of unsold goods and by consumer goods companies expanding their product lines beyond all reason. He was also troubled by housewives and students, as well as the men of business, using credit to buy stocks on margin, thus speculatively driving prices up with no grounding in corporate performance or assets.

The American stock market's collapse two years later in 1929 was followed by a collapse in consumer prices. People who owed money because of margin calls rushed to liquidate hard assets to pay the bills. Such fire sales flooded the markets with goods, driving down prices. Even the value of gold and diamond jewelry plummeted because supply far outstripped demand. The U.S. stock market's crash soon washed over Europe, especially Germany, which had received the most American investment during the 1920s in postwar reconstruction. Now, it suffered the most as America liquidated its foreign investments. German companies had grown during the 1920s by using short-term borrowing to finance long-term expansion; they failed when American banks wouldn't roll over the loans. Unemployment in Germany soared from 2.8 million in 1928 to 6.7 million in 1932. Unemployed men received 51 Reichsmarks per month as unemployment compensation, with 31 Reichsmarks earmarked for rent and heat. That didn't leave much for food or clothes for a bachelor, let alone a family man.

The Quandts' AFA battery business was in decent shape prior to the Crash of 1929, but a steep drop in orders for both large industrial batteries and car batteries rapidly changed the picture. Günther then began buying shares in AFA in a way that alarmed German stock regulators. As the value of shares in AFA fell—in part due to Günther's publicly stated pessimism—he was buying them on the cheap, increasing his control of Germany's biggest battery maker. He was quickly accused of misleading shareholders about the company's prospects by hiding reserve funds as well as some new breakthrough products that would soon pay off. Small shareholders sold their AFA stock as Günther publicly trashed the company. But after this big sell-off, the news broke in the papers that AFA planned to pay huge dividends out of the reserves it had set aside for war reparations that would be forgiven and whose existence was known only to Günther and a few senior managers who were in on the scheme. As AFA's largest shareholder, Günther would reap the largest share of the new dividend, essentially pocketing much of the company's reserves for himself. Small holders induced to sell also discovered that AFA would soon manufacture advanced dry-cell batteries, a much anticipated and sought-after breakthrough that was revealed only after Günther increased his holdings. A Frankfurt newspaper described Quandt as an extremely "well versed manipulator of all opportunities and possibilities for gaining control of stocks."[13] Historian Jungbluth noted that Günther was, "a man who understood perfectly well how to occasionally sing the tune of appropriate pessimism, which well-informed men use in order to get poorly educated securities holders to part from their wealth."[14] The price of AFA shares shot up some 40 percent in a flash, while most other industrials tanked.

Quandt had been so proactive about shielding his wealth from the market crash—and he had started with so much to begin with—that he sailed practically unscathed through the Depression that ravaged Germany. As his businesses variously muddled through, Günther decided to go on a world tour. Herbert wasn't keen to go, having become secretly engaged to Ursel Munstermann, the daughter of an industrialist. But Günther insisted on the trip, wanting to get to know his son better—indeed to take his measure—and to continue molding his heir. The two visited such far-flung places (for 1931) as Cambodia, Japan, and Darjeeling, then on to the United States, Mexico, and Cuba. The two spent time in Hawaii, Hollywood and elsewhere in California,

Detroit, Miami, and Niagara Falls. They visited Ford's legendary High-land Park assembly plant in Michigan, Packard's works, General Electric facilities, and some airplane companies. And they were bowled over by the just completed Empire State Building in Manhattan, as there was nothing remotely like it in western Europe.

In late 1931, Herbert and Ursel became formally engaged, and the two spent a few months in London at a subsidiary of one of his father's companies where Herbert received more training. In 1932, he left for the United States, where he spent six months working as an intern at a Philadelphia battery concern. Forty miles away, the Lindbergh baby was kidnapped and killed. Herbert was deeply affected by the experience, seeing how the Lindbergh family was turned into a circus sideshow by the media; the tragedy colored his views on security, the press, and privacy for the rest of his life.

The trips abroad were a means of educating Herbert in the ways of global business. Especially in the United States, Herbert toured as many plants as he could to observe the mass-production processes that hadn't yet gained a foothold in Germany. While in Philadelphia, he tooled around in a Chevrolet coupe that he bought for $75 and sold for $110 on his return to Germany—a bit of legerdemain that impressed his father and stayed with Herbert as a favorite anecdote until he died. Observing the rise of communist sympathies among the U.S. Eastern establishment in 1932, Herbert grew extremely hostile toward communism, deeply suspicious of the cause and its promoters, even while remaining nearly oblivious to the fascist activities building in his homeland during his absences and the ever-mounting popularity of a no-longer-minor politician named Adolf Hitler.

Returning to Germany in late 1932 from his internship abroad, Herbert Quandt began an internship at AFA under the tutelage of the head bookkeeper. Herbert would soon learn how German companies routinely hid large sums in opaque "reserves" rather than distributing profits as dividends to common shareholders. Herbert married Ursel in 1933, but their incompatibilities were soon obvious. Rather superficial and immature, Ursel preferred the company of her own parents to that of Herbert.

In early-1930s Munich, Günther Quandt found himself in a tough spot as head of an industrial conglomerate. His companies were of great interest to the Nazis looking to rearm Germany. Besides his own

battery company, he was also on the board of AEG, the German version of General Electric. Günther has been variously described as
being—at first—a simple opponent of the Nazis, as a staunch foe of
Hitler's, or as one of the madman's key financial advisors. The truth is
that Günther Quandt was a man of his wealth and of his times, a businessman most concerned with maintaining his personal wealth and
status. In the late 1920s, Quandt behaved as did most gentile industrialists: He didn't allow himself to get too closely associated with any
one political party; rather, he showed enough respect and support to
all the major politicos of the time to cover his bases. He didn't join the
Nazi party until May 1933, after Hitler was appointed chancellor. His
1933 contribution of 25,000 Reichsmarks ($7,600) to the Nazis trailed
those of just about every other rich businessman that year. But he and
his companies made out very well as Hitler rebuilt Germany's war
machine. His rechargeable battery business went up exponentially
with sales to the growing military complex, as did sales at his weapons
and munitions outfits. Like other companies deemed vital to Germany's military interests, starting around 1939, his plants were
manned by slave labor. And when Henry Pels & Co., an engine works
owned by Jews, was confiscated by the Nazis, it was folded into the
Quandt holdings with Günther's full complicity.

Günther's first meeting with Hitler took place in 1931. According
to Nazi Party records, the meeting was also attended by deputy führer
Rudolf Hess, and economic adviser Otto Wagener. Said Günther
Quandt in his memoirs: "I cannot say that Hitler made a significant
impression on me. Not an attractive or repulsive man. He came across,
in fact, as completely average."[15] Hitler was looking for counsel from
leading industrialists about how to solve the economic calamity in
Germany. There were 6 million unemployed. Graduating students had
no hope for jobs. No wonder they were ripe for Hitler's Nazi Party
promises! Quandt advised Hitler to shorten the workday from eight
hours to six to cut back production of goods, because there was an
oversupply, and to cut salaries by 25 percent. He also advised Hitler to
eliminate welfare payments to the unemployed, to put the money into
public-works projects like roads, train stations, new schools, and
canals, and to put the unemployed to work. It is common knowledge,
advised Quandt, that the economy will flourish when construction
heats up.

Günther Quandt was an opportunist, though he later tried to portray himself as an unwilling Nazi conspirator. Like many businessmen of the day, he had misgivings about Hitler and his evil practices and war machine. But as long as the party wasn't after him, he was fairly content to go along. In fact, Günther stood to make a great deal of money with Hitler as chancellor, and he knew it. Besides the battery company, Quandt's munitions business would flourish. As a condition of the Treaty of Versailles signed at the end of World War I, Germany was forbidden to rearm, so all munitions-related products were being manufactured for export. But Quandt told Hitler and party leaders that he had the means to quickly expand production and build new plants to satisfy the Reich's appetite for arms. Günther had anti-Semitic feelings, though not as strong as those of the true party faithful. Jews came and went from the Quandt household before and after Hitler seized power, but he was all for German rearmament for the economic windfall it would mean for his companies and because he genuinely believed Germany had paid the price for World War I and had too long been humiliated on the world stage. Again, in his memoirs, Günther hatched a squirrelly argument to defend his position: He had felt a reconstituted German military would be the best check against Nazi abuses. Did he forget who the military was working for?

After Hitler came to power in the spring of 1933, Quandt immediately joined the Nazi Party. Six days later, he paid a call on Goebbels, whom he had met at Magda's thirtieth birthday party. Not surprisingly, the two men didn't get on. This second visit was obviously an attempt to gain favor with Goebbels for business reasons. Goebbels entered a short line in his diary about the meeting: "Herr Quandt came to visit today. He is full of . . . and this all because of our victory."[16] Günther was arrested in 1933 and detained for, he claimed, "unknown reasons" for four months. The truth was that he was in prison for about six weeks and then released on bail. The reasons are, in fact, sketchy, but seem to have been connected to a general uprising of the young Nazis after winning election. No fan of the industrial power structure, these zealous youths were out for some revenge for being left out of work so long. In the early days after the election, confusion was the order of the day and "taxes" that were, in fact, unorganized extortion were rampant. It was suddenly illegal for Quandt to enter the offices of his own company, and party leaders were organizing Quandt's workers. SS-uniformed "soldiers" occupied the plants and offices and chucked Günther in prison for "tax evasion." Goebbels, feeling sorry for Harald Quandt, whom he genuinely loved, helped get Günther out on bail.

Günther's opportunism can be seen in this light. No industrialist of the day wanted Hitler to run amok. Hitler made foreign governments nervous even before he began invading other countries. Most large German companies, Quandt's included, had extensive business holdings in other parts of Europe and even in North America. Nervous foreign governments didn't make doing business with German companies any easier. All German foreign investment was at risk as Hitler's expansion policy took hold. In exchange for lost assets and markets outside Germany, businesspeople like Quandt seized every opportunity to ride Hitler's back to economic prosperity through supplying the military and building a new German national infrastructure. In company brochures that survive from the 1930s, Günther is seen praising Hitler for rearming the German people. Besides manufacturing ordinary munitions such as bullets and artillery shells, Quandt worked closely with the SS in developing specialized munitions, and he built a separate factory for product development. To most historians, this puts Günther Quandt all the way in bed with the Nazis even if he didn't want to admit it later.

In 1937, Herbert Quandt was made head of one of AFA's subsidiaries, and the die seemed cast for him to take over from his father when Günther either chose or was forced to retire. But that same year, Günther met a young man named Horst Pavel, a lawyer he would soon look upon as a second son. Indeed, Günther effectively positioned Pavel as a rival to his own son—why he did so remains debatable. Herbert speculated in an unpublished memoir that his father was just testing his mettle, seeing whether Herbert might shrink from the challenge. And meeting that challenge would be good training for the tough competitors he would face soon enough. His father worried that Herbert might be too soft for the rough and tumble of business. Pavel clearly had the right skills, so he was a worthy alternative if Herbert faltered.

As the Third Reich's conquest of most of Europe loomed on the horizon, business was good for the Quandts and AFA, with the company manufacturing batteries for submarines, tanks, and military vehicles. Herbert, as head of human resources at AFA, was definitely involved in the transactions for and training of slave labor for the assembly facilities supplying the war effort.

In his postwar memoirs, written while he was imprisoned by the Allies for war crimes as an industrial collaborator, Günther stated that he saw "the negative side" of the Third Reich when he was arrested.[17] He said he realized that "a new phase of insecurity of personal rights had begun in Germany with the Nazi coup."[18] Not exactly a soul-searching mea culpa given the six years of death and destruction Günther had helped support. After all he had been through at that point—two imprisonments (one by Hitler and one by the Allies); having the onetime love of his life die by her own hand in Hitler's bunker, taking six of her children with her; having had Hitler's chief political adviser as his son's stepfather; witnessing who knows how many slaves punished, degraded, and slaughtered at his own facilities and those of his friends—this tepid remorse falls awfully flat.

It wasn't just cruel fate foisted upon him, for Günther was a crucial cog in the Nazi war effort. In AFA's Hagen, Germany, battery factory, more than 3,500 slave laborers toiled away, and the DWM munitions factory had more than 4,000 forced laborers. SS officers terrorized and tortured workers by whipping them with cables and, after a full day's work, forcing them to stand at attention all night inches beyond the reach of killer dogs. Though no evidence links Günther and Herbert to directly participating in such inhuman acts, they were clearly neck-deep in the horrors of the Third Reich even if these actions took place while they were off-site, tucked in warm beds and gaining weight on the best food.

A very savvy businessman, Günther Quandt was sometimes a con-niver who pushed the limits of legality and humanity, but he was largely bored with politics unless it impacted his station in life. Günther wrote in his memoirs, "In *Mein Kampf* was to be found everything that would happen, if Hitler were ever to come to power. It wasn't just about bread and work, but also about war and the oppression of other peoples. Unfortunately, most of us didn't read the book in time. If we had, perhaps we would have been spared the most horrible chapter in German history. I blame myself as well for not having taken Hitler more seriously."[19] This was a bit more telling than his earlier remorse, but at this point Günther was trying to rehabilitate his image with the Allied occupiers and in Germany society.

During the postwar denazification of Germany, Günther enlisted a lawyer's aid to fashion himself not as a collaborator with Goebbels but as a rival who fought with him over Harald's custody and upbringing. He claimed to be a Nazi from compulsion rather than personal inclination. He claimed, falsely, that Goebbels threatened to deny him custody of Harald if he didn't join the party. The lawyer was able to get Günther's Nazi classification diminished, which meant he did not have to stand trial at Nuremberg with more notorious Nazis. Instead, he served 18 months in prison and was released in 1948, six years before his death in 1954.

The Quandts' most important business, battery maker Akkumulatoren Fabrik Aktiengesellschaft (AFA), had been the sole manufacturer of batteries for German submarines between 1915 and 1918. Between the wars, the company continued to supply products to companies both domestic and foreign. After the second war, Herbert Quandt concentrated on rebuilding the battery company, which would take the name of an AFA subsidiary, Varta, in 1960. The family's properties in Pritzwalk and Berlin were confiscated by the Russians, so the Quandts relocated their base of operations to Frankfurt and later to Bad Homburg, north of Frankfurt, though Varta remained based in Hagen until the 1970s. Much of the business was located in Hanover immediately after the war, as the company lost control of seven foreign subsidiaries—the price paid by German companies that were part of Hitler's war machine. Herbert not only refocused Varta on industrial, automotive, and eventually consumer batteries, but he diversified the company into pharmaceuticals, food, cosmetics, and plastics. It was a true conglomerate of its time.

After Günther died in 1954, the family's holdings were divided between Harald and Herbert. Herbert took over shares in Daimler-Benz and, later, BMW. With a window on the industry through his position on Daimler's supervisory board, Quandt began buying up more shares of BMW in 1959. BMW had not hit its stride after the war as had Daimler and Volkswagen, and it was being positioned for takeover by Daimler despite protests by Bavarian shareholders who took pride in the BMW marque, such as it was, and who wanted to keep a car company intact that was uniquely Bavarian. Despite his position with Daimler, Herbert was not keen to see BMW squashed, in part because of his love of cars. Though his poor eyesight meant he didn't drive, his leisure time was spent with fast boats, horses, and fast cars. He loved his involvement with Daimler, but knew he'd never fully participate in the design and production, the automobile industry's glamorous, romantic side. BMW's shareholders and dealers, of course, didn't welcome Daimler coming in and "bigfooting" BMW. Shares in BMW were held mostly by middle-class Bavarian families who rarely sold them, passing them down within the family.

Through a complex play of obscure corporate bylaws resting on the fact that BMW had made errant financial filings, in December 1959 shareholders were able to reject a sale to Daimler. In January, the company's supervisory and management boards dissolved, leaving BMW essentially rudderless.

Quandt used the false name of Lindemann to set up a meeting with the Bavarian Finance Ministry, which was trying to come up with a plan to preserve BMW as an independent car company. Quandt had bought enough shares to give himself the opportunity to take over BMW, but he wouldn't pull the trigger until seeing the car that would determine BMW's success or failure over the next few years: the 700. BMW's head of finance, Ernst Kampfer, drove a 700 prototype to Quandt's office in early January 1960. Quandt walked around the car, running his hands over every contour, literally reading the car like Braille. He opened and closed all the doors, listening for quality in the mechanicals. He sat in the seats, front and back, discerning the quality of structure and leather. Kampfer drove the car to Stuttgart for Daimler engineer Fritz Nallinger to drive on the Mercedes test track. The Mercedes engineer told Quandt it was a fine piece of machinery. There was a clear safety issue with the gas tank being in the front of the car, and it was powered by an enhanced motorbike engine, but Nallinger said it was a good vehicle. "Yes, build it," he told Quandt.[20]

Then Quandt went about infusing the company with new capital and talent. He plucked some engineering and development men from the Borgward Works, a car company on its last legs that nonetheless harbored some top engineers and production managers. He got shareholders to agree to buy a new class of stock, which helped raise some fresh capital. Yet Quandt hardly ventured into this new enterprise with wild abandon. Even after his plan was accepted by BMW's shareholders, he tried to put together a deal for Daimler-Benz to own 51 percent of the company; Daimler refused, having been outmaneuvered after the December shareholder meeting when Quandt came to the rescue of the shareholders who wanted BMW to stay out of Daimler's control. He then tried to get American Motors, Ford, and Fiat to each buy in, but they all wanted majority control over the BMW brand for themselves. That would have left Quandt in a position little better than his supervisory board role at Daimler.

In the end, though, Quandt retained control because enough shareholders bought the new class of stock to give him the capital he needed without putting an unacceptable amount of his own assets at risk. And this near brush with capitulation to a behemoth like Ford or Daimler has made BMW guard its independence fiercely ever since.

———

In the 1970s, as Herbert's health varied seemingly on a yearly basis, he began planning the distribution of his estate—the largest private fortune in Germany. Quandt disapproved of how Günther had handed down his fortune to him and Harald. It came to them in one solid piece, and carving it up caused many problems. So he began dividing and separating his quite intertwined holdings. He saw the need to keep shares of the estate quite distinct to accommodate his very separate families. Johanna, Stefan, and Susanne's inheritances would have to be quite separate from those of his children from his two previous marriages. Equal, debt-free shares in Varta would be left to three of his children, including Sven, who joined the supervisory board at the battery maker right after finishing college. His daughter Silvia from his first marriage, an artist who had no interest in business, would inherit a fortune in stock and real estate.

Harald Quandt had died in 1967 when he crashed his turboprop plane in Nice, France. Some 10 years later, the Quandts, no strangers to tragedy or scandal, were gripped by the sensational death of Harald's widow, Inge, which attracted tabloid newspaper coverage. Inge Quandt had never truly recovered from her husband's death. A nervous and insecure woman, she took up with a family friend almost immediately after his death. She had five daughters with Harald; with no son to take over the family businesses, she sold her sizable shareholding in Daimler-Benz to the ruling family in Kuwait. She was not a socialite and rarely circulated off the grounds of the family estate. She joked that the only friends she had made over the years were the two doctors who delivered her babies. She abused prescription drugs and was a chain-smoker, too, inhaling more than 100 unfiltered cigarettes a day. In 1977, she married her financial advisor, Hans-Hilman von Halem. On Christmas Eve, 1978, Inge was discovered dead in her bed, apparently having died from heart failure. A few days later, Halem shot himself in the same bed in which he had found his dead wife.

It wasn't until 1974 that Quandt relinquished his last remaining shares in Daimler-Benz. He was completely blind by then, able to discern only people's profiles as they stood before his office window. He and Johanna had long practiced a daily ritual where she read aloud to him the newspaper and magazine articles he deemed worthwhile. This practice, over 22 years of marriage, made Johanna a savvy businesswoman, as she learned on a daily basis what her husband thought was important. Herbert conducted business, assimilating contracts and the like, via audiotape. Over the years he'd honed the skill of assessing people by the modulation of their voices. One day as he and BMW chairman Eberhard von Kuenheim were interviewing a candidate for the management board, for example, he asked how long it had been since this man took a vacation. The answer: four years! Quandt could *hear* the stress and strain in the man's voice, and he ordered him to take a two-month vacation before starting his new BMW job.[21] He recorded all of his phone conversations and many of his in-office meetings so he could play back the tapes both for content and to get the best handle on what the others were thinking. Even his own half-brother Harald was not spared this treatment. He had BMW modelers make models of proposed vehicle designs, which were brought to his office so he could run his hands over every contour. This was how he kept his hands in, or on, the main business of his favorite company.

Herbert Quandt died of heart failure just shy of his seventy-second birthday in 1980. A shrewd man of business, Herbert maintained two sides until his death, according to family biographer Rudiger Jungbluth:

He never stopped worrying about disappointing his father, and he continually advanced his own power and wealth by rendering other men deeply dependent on his goodwill.

———

Johanna Quandt seldom attended BMW functions aside from the annual shareholder meeting, though one exception was the opening of the Spartanburg, South Carolina, factory—BMW's first in the United States—which builds the Z Series roadsters and X5 SUV. Stefan and Susanne are seen around the company's "Four Cylinders" Munich headquarters far more often, typically getting briefed on business and product plans. Their involvement in the family's main moneymaker peaked in the late 1990s when BMW's ill-advised acquisition of Britain's Rover Group so drained its resources that rumors circulated regarding the sale of a big chunk of the company to Volkswagen or Ford. Stefan and Susanne began to move against chairman Bernd Pischetsrieder, prodding supervisory board chairman Eberhard von Kuenheim to come up with a transition plan that involved replacing Pischetsrieder, his handpicked protégé, with an eye toward also divesting the Rover Group, or parts of it, to end the drain on BMW earnings and prestige.

Stefan maintained throughout 1998 that the family wouldn't sell even a portion of its holdings to a rival automaker. Volkswagen chairman Ferdinand Piech had "suggested" to reporters that the Quandts were looking for a partner, and German media was full of reports that a sale was impending. When Piech suggested in public that Volkswagen would like to buy a chunk of BMW and might have the opportunity to do so, Stefan issued a public admonishment of Piech, as well as a letter directly to the chairman. It took Piech, another billionaire auto industry scion, to draw Stefan out in public; Stefan had once said that he would rather see falsehoods printed about him than to have to give an interview.

Having the worst of the Rover debacle hit BMW in 1998, the year after the Quandt heirs took positions on the supervisory board, provided a trial by fire. It was the worst time at BMW since before their father had taken over in 1959. Some say, in fact, the heirs waited too long to flex their muscles, leaving von Kuenheim too long on his own to rein in Pischetsrieder, whose plan to revitalize Rover was putting

BMW at risk. Susanne and Stefan, according to former and current BMW managers, finally pulled the strings and forced the resignation of Bernd Pischetsrieder in 1999, replacing him with Joachim Milberg rather than longtime product chief Wolfgang Reitzle. Both objected to Reitzle's very public persona and frequent interviews with the German media about BMW business.

Von Kuenheim is known to describe the proper way a true BMW manager conducts himself with a French term, *comment*. The literal translation is simply "how," but in his own idiomatic use of the word, according to one BMW executive, it means "you just know it." What this means at BMW is that BMW managers, especially the chairmen, are expected to always act discreetly. Never air the company's laundry in public. Never discuss private meetings, especially with the Quandts. Be poker-faced and speak in professional terms—and then only when you have something worthwhile to say. Don't ever put the company's business in the street. This is something that doesn't have to be written down or even spoken to BMW managers. The ones who will rise high within the organization "just know it." This was the style and pattern of Herbert Quandt, and it is still a part of the company culture more than 20 years after his death, because the merits of discretion and privacy are so ingrained in his children. No one crosses the Quandts.

In the coming years, Stefan is expected to step into the role of supervisory board chairman at BMW. Either way, the influence and impact of the young Quandts will continue to be felt. Outsiders may be hard-pressed to know exactly how and in what form their impact is truly felt—whether a new plant is built or not built, whether a new model is produced or not produced, or even in the naming of a new model. And that is exactly how they seem to want it.

The Ultimate Brand

FOUR

Authentic: *Trustworthy; authoritative; not imaginary, false, or imitation.*

Consistent: *Possessing firmness and coherence; resistant to movement or separation of constituent particles; showing steady conformity to character, profession, belief, or custom.*

Brand: *A mark made by burning with a hot iron to attest manufacture or quality or to designate ownership.*

—WEBSTER'S COLLEGIATE DICTIONARY, NINTH EDITION

The words most often used to describe BMW's brand and the way the company manages and molds it year after year are *authentic* and *consistent;* authentic because the company never seems to turn out a dud; consistent, because no one ever seems to have doubt about what BMW stands for. Sporty, performance-oriented cars of a high level of craftsmanship and ingenuity has defined BMW since before World War II. Though the company had 15 difficult postwar years in which it struggled to regain its focus, the company has stood unwaveringly on the same brand platform since 1962 when it introduced the 1500 saloon as the start of its "New Class" under new owner Herbert Quandt. Other companies strive to be known for *something.* Oldsmobile was known for decades as a maker of well-styled, powerful, performance sedans. Cadillac was known for prestigious and comfortable luxury sedans with big engines. Volkswagen was known for decades for its cheap, reliable, dependable cars, full of basic German engineering, a brand that conveyed its personality through its exterior designs. Ford was long a brand with a quality car for every person and every family at affordable prices. Mercedes has been all about engineering excellence, quality, and prestige. Rolls-Royce was the ultimate automobile, engineered and crafted like no other. All these companies and brands, though, have experienced a lot of drift over the decades because of products divorced from their brand promise and image; advertising slogans changed almost annually to try to refocus the brand around product that was not designed or developed with any brand idea in mind in the first place. For decades, GM and Ford, especially, developed vehicles that fit a business case or filled a market segment but that were not developed with a brand anchor. Only after the marketing and advertising staffs got the vehicle from the engineering and production department could they go to work making the latest vehicle fit the brand scheme in vogue that year from Chevy, Buick, Cadillac, or Lincoln. In the auto industry, brand communication often chases product down the street, hoping to catch up to it like a dog after a bus. The smarter strategy, but one that is harder to execute, is to establish brand identity and to have that identity anchor, color, and permeate all the products and processes so the brand and products are mutually dependent, growing in lockstep. This is what BMW has done better than any other car company over the decades and better than most companies outside the auto industry as well.

BMW owners, in contrast to customers of most other car brands, are easy to visualize. They are people who are particular about the brands they buy and wear; people who are young or young-minded; and people who are driven in their lives and careers. What does a Chevy owner, an Audi owner, or a Lincoln owner look like? In some cases, we have an idea, but unlike the image we have of a BMW owner, the de facto owners of those cars aren't nearly as attractive to conjure in one's mind. Is that a subjective opinion? Yes. Certainly for many people, the image of a BMW owner is negative. A person who views the purchase of a car on mostly rational terms (How much does it cost? What is the fuel economy? How many people will it carry? Will it pull my trailer?) may view someone with a *Bimmer* in the driveway as wasteful, affected, and unimaginative with his or her money. That's okay. BMW doesn't target the buyer who lusts for the bulletproof quality and reliability of a Toyota Corolla or Honda Civic. This is where BMW's focus comes in. BMW is interested in appealing to only those consumers who aspire to the same value BMW is built upon: sporty driving. Let others court the rest of the driving population who prioritize size, fixability, reliability, interior space, or a cheap price tag above all else.

BMW's focus, which has made it the most admired brand in the global auto industry with the best yearly profit margins (with the exception of the much smaller Porsche AG), is why Ford, Volkswagen, General Motors, and Renault all knocked on BMW's door in the 1980s hoping that they could buy their way into a brand they had long studied as a textbook case for how to do cars right. To the company's credit, the principal owners, the Quandt family, seem never to have seriously considered selling the company. That steadiness of ownership, says BMW chairman Helmut Panke, is "no small advantage and no small ingredient in the company's strength." There must be something to what Panke says, because even after taking a $3.2 billion charge against earnings in 1999 and losing five key members of its management board, the company nevertheless put up record sales and earnings in 2001 and 2002, while the United States and Western Europe were mired in economic recession.

Who thinks BMW has the best brand? Automotive historian and leading industry analyst Karl Ludvigsen simply says, "BMW is an object lesson on how to build a brand. . . . All my clients want to be like BMW."[1] *Fortune* magazine in the spring of 2003 ranked BMW twelfth among the Most Admired Global Companies, one small notch below Toyota, which barely edged out BMW among auto companies.[2] Noteworthy, BMW beat Toyota in the categories of "innovativeness" and "employee talent." That second honor is nothing short of astonishing, as the survey was done just two years after the loss of the five management board members in 1999 and 2000, four of whom became chief executives or chairmen of major companies after leaving BMW.

Panke, a physicist who has held several jobs at BMW, including human resources director and chief financial officer, seems to know exactly what BMW stands for and is not shy about articulating it. "The BMW brand stands for a promise of fascinating individual automobiles, and we shall continue to keep our promise in this respect. A part of this promise is never build a boring BMW." The last sentence is the key to the brand inside the company, says Panke. "That's the message that resonates the most. It is the simplest language, and it centers everyone on the mission."

BMW's customer profile is the envy of all its competitors. In the United States, the mean household income of BMW buyers is above $160,000, ranging from just above $140,000 for 3 Series buyers to more than $260,000 for the 7 Series. In 2000, 2001, and 2002, sales and operating income kept rising despite a stock market crash in March 2000, followed by two years of rising layoffs in upper-middle management at many companies, the crash of Internet companies, and the evaporation of bonuses at many companies. Still, BMW sales climbed, and an impractical premium small car, the Mini, was launched with enormous success, as more than 30,000 people in the United States plunked down more than $20,000 apiece in 2002 for a slice of Bavarian crème Brittania, and 110,000 more worldwide did the same. As more evidence of BMW's financial prowess, driven in no small part by its indelible brand image, *Automotive News* and PricewaterhouseCoopers in 2002 recognized BMW for best shareholder value among all car companies in 2001, just a year after it divested the Rover Group.

Former BMW executive Victor Doolan, who moved on to Ford and its Volvo division in 1999, says the key to the success of BMW is that its brand products have long been built more on substance than status. "The status followed the substance. Status has a way of coming and going, and other brands rise and fall with status as it is affected by fashion. Part of BMW's core strength is that it is one of the few premium brands that has historically transcended fashion changes." What's the evidence? One example is how, in late 2002, despite a spate of competitors, including the Jaguar X-Type, Infiniti G35, Lexus I30, and Acura T1, the 1998 3 Series not only outsold those brand-new models, its sales were up on the year despite the newer models crowding its turf.

In the late 1960s, when BMW was just getting its tires planted in the United States, BMW's advertising not surprisingly played up its performance attributes and its growing image among import-car enthusiasts for being a serious "driver's car." A 1968 print ad, for example, pictured the BMW 1600 and brand-new 2002 sedans. Under the 1600 was the word, "Fast." Under the 2002, the ad read "Faster than Fast." Simple and to the point without trying to convey more than one idea.

BMW's slogan on all its advertising at that point was "The Sportsman's Car," which frankly made it sound like the top choice among hunters and anglers. By 1972, ad content remained largely the same. One ad for the BMW 2002 Tii was headlined, "The BMW 2002 Tii. It'll really move you." The new slogan that year, written below the BMW logo was simply, "Munich. City of the Olympics." The Summer Olympics in 1972 were being played in Munich. Besides linking BMW to the city that was so much in the news that year, the company correctly played up the accolades thrust on it by the motoring press from which it had gained most of its credibility. That same year, one ad for the 2002 reminded readers, "For five years straight, the readers of *Car and Driver* have voted the BMW the world's best sports sedan." *Car and Driver*'s David E. Davis Jr., had, in fact, done more than any other motoring writer at the time to put BMW on the map in the United States when he wrote a glowing, almost rapturous review of the 2002 in 1968. Most, but not all ads, pictured BMW models in motion rather than stationary to emphasize the brand's performance. Though advertising wasn't yet centrally managed for BMW in the United States—regional BMW distributors were each doing their own ads—there was wit, humor, and a sense of confidence in advertising befitting a German performance car. Headlines like, "Goes Like Schnell!" "Fast-Poke," and "If you know about BMW, you either own one or want one." That last headline spoke directly to the fact that BMW in 1972 was still a kind of insider's car, a brand that wasn't yet in the U.S. mainstream, like a terrific rock band whose notoriety wasn't yet national. Ads played up performance and fun, but without a clear idea that could be distilled into one clever line of ad copy. Ads in 1971 for the critically praised six-cylinder Bavaria read, for example, "You get it in the new BMW Bavaria: 6 cylinders. 2.8 liters. 130 mph. Under $5000. Wundercar!" Pretty basic stuff with no centering thought in the ad that conveyed a sense of *brand*. One ad for the Bavaria pictured a fetching young woman leaning against the car under the headline, "Take Me To Your Husband." The ad suggested in cheeky fashion that a wife was better off supporting her husband's choice of a BMW Bavaria to enliven his life than to take the chance he might choose to spice things up with another woman. A better ad showed BMW's distinct front end with vertical twin kidneys under the headline, "Think Fast."

The import-car market was active in the United States in the early

1970s, though it was dominated by Volkswagen, which sold a half million vehicles there. VW was a cultural and business phenomenon, which even prompted Disney's film studios to make three movies starring a Beetle, *Herbie The Love Bug*. Largely through VW, American drivers were thoroughly indoctrinated to the benefits of German engineering. With rising oil prices, heightening concern about pollution caused by automobiles, and the start of an economic recession, performance cars were still desired by millions of drivers—but at a rising social price in some neighborhoods. The business climate was difficult for car companies, both domestic and imports. Americans were still gobbling up large, heavy sedans like Buick Elektra, Oldsmobile Delta 88, and Ford Country Squire station wagons, but there was also a strengthening small-car market with entries like Chevy Vega and Ford Pinto. BMW was envious of its German competitor, Volkswagen, which was so successful that it had begun plans to open its first U.S. assembly plant. BMW wasn't ready for that commitment, but the reason for Volkswagen's U.S. plant was a concern to BMW management: Currency fluctuations left German imports vulnerable. The U.S. greenback had weakened against the German deutsche mark by 40 percent in 1972 and 1973, forcing BMW's, as well as Volkswagen's, Porsche's, and Mercedes-Benz's prices higher. By 1974, the dollar had settled at 2.5 marks, but that compared with about $4 to the mark throughout the 1960s. Meantime, the U.S. political scene and pop culture were volatile, and changing tastes in pop culture and the national mood often dictated changing tastes in automobile design. In the postwar 1950s, for example, Americans, liberated from two decades of sacrifice they endured during the Depression and then a world war, pined for big, chrome-laden land barges full of shark fins and gimmicks such as headlights that turned with the car and push-button gearshifting. In 1973, the Vietnam War was still raging in the public consciousness, and the flames of the electorate's discontent were further fanned by the Watergate scandal that was dogging the Nixon administration. Music was in transition between the folk and rock scenes that dominated late 1960s. The softer teenybopper music of an adolescent, Mormon, angelic-voiced singer named Donny Osmond was grabbing the hearts and newspaper-route earnings of American pubescents. "Tie A Yellow Ribbon 'Round The Ol' Oak Tree" by TV pop-music act Tony Orlando and Dawn was the number one song in 1973, swapping places in some months with the Rolling Stones' "Angie" and Jim Croce's gritty "Bad, Bad Leroy Brown." Television, too, was caught between and betwixt the vanilla custard of hit shows like *The Brady Bunch* on Friday nights and the highly controversial and often antiwar-themed *All In The Family* and *M*A*S*H* on Saturday nights. This was the national consciousness and rapidly changing cultural landscape into which BMW was planting its stake.

BMW had decided, as Volkswagen had already done, to acquire the regional distribution companies that had built up BMW's U.S. sales in the 1960s and to centralize sales and marketing in northern New Jersey, just across the Hudson River from Manhattan. The area there near the George Washington Bridge had become a kind of "import alley," with transplanted executives from Germany, Italy, and France working for VW, BMW, Mercedes, Fiat, Peugeot, and Renault tripping over one another at the same restaurants and golf courses. The decision on an ad agency for BMW of North America, though, would be made at BMW's headquarters in Munich, where the company just happened to have an American, Bob Lutz, in charge of sales and marketing. Lutz had joined BMW from General Motors' Opel division, and part of his job was to guide BMW's expansion in North America. In the spring of 1974, BMW began a review of U.S. ad agencies. BMW put out a request for proposal to New York ad agencies, which stated that it was looking for a general strategy for growing its presence in the United States with a unified advertising message that could be "used in every aspect of its communication, including print and newspaper advertising, billboards, radio and television, as well as dealer communications and consumer brochures." The three ad agencies vying for the job were two Madison Avenue giants, the Ted Bates Agency and Benton & Bowles, and a newcomer, Ammirati & Puris. Bates was the iconic ad shop, having been in business since 1940. Benton & Bowles had an even deeper history, going back to 1929. These were agencies that worked to elect presidents and governors, as well as to pump sales for some of America's consumer product giants like Procter & Gamble, Philip Morris, and General Foods. Martin Puris and Ralph Ammirati, the new guys on the block, had been a copywriter and art director, respectively, at Carl Ally Inc. Ally, like Volkswagen's famous and celebrated agency Doyle Dane Bernbach—which had turned advertising on its head in the 1960s using humor and irony to sell products—was a rebel, challenging and disdaining the old traditional ad agencies like Bates & Bowles. Whereas DDB was known for humor, though, Ally was known for grabbing the consumer and the marketing problem at hand by the throat. The agency, for example, pushed against network television rules that banned mentioning competitors by name in advertising. A 1971 campaign for Fiat outright named Volkswagen as their competitor. And for Volvo, Ally executed a TV commercial shot from above, perhaps in a helicopter, showing a box-shaped Volvo with its name written across its roof pulling far ahead of five obviously familiar but unlabeled rivals in a 10-second race. Martin Puris and Ralph Ammirati had done top-drawer work on the Fiat U.S.A. account on ads for both the Fiat and Ferrari brands. Trying to challenge VW's hold on the small-car market, the two had successfully infused Fiat's U.S. brand image with some European cachet, with ads pointing out that Fiat, not VW, had the best-selling small car in Europe. BMW's Lutz had especially liked a TV spot done by Ammirati & Puris that showed a stunt driver careering around Italian roads and landmarks like Rome's Spanish Steps. The ad won awards in both the United States and Europe and left a lasting impression on would-be Fiat buyers. The two creative men also produced a high-impact ad in which they made the point that no less a driver than Enzo Ferrari, in fact, drove a Fiat.

BMW was, in 1974, the only European import that was still struggling for mere name recognition outside of hardcore driving enthusiasts and readers of *Car and Driver*. "A lot of people actually thought BMW stood for 'British Motor Works' when we did some consumer research," recalls Puris. The year before the review, it had managed less than 15,000 sales.

Ammirati & Puris quickly came up with the strategy they wanted to pitch. Says Puris: "The cars handled like no other. That was for sure. We knew about BMWs, of course, having worked on Fiat and Volvo at the Carl Ally agency. We knew they handled, in fact, better than the cars we had been pitching. While Fiat was a company led by designers, BMW was a company dominated by engineers. The chassis on a BMW was a thing of beauty compared with other makes of the day. It was like driving on rails compared with Fiat and Volvos, or Mercedes, for that matter. So we had the strategy of always emphasizing handling and driving pleasure. But it took us a few weeks to come up with a line, a slogan, to go with the idea. The ads done by the distributors did a decent job of conveying the hardware, but there was no over-arching idea to bind every ad to one idea we wanted to get across to the customer." The moment he wrote the famous line of ad copy doesn't stick with Puris. He just recalls working out a slew of frag-mented words and phrases at his desk until one jumped off the page at him: "The Ultimate Driving Machine." It's ironic that although that line has endured longer than any other in the auto industry, Puris had to win over his own partners before he pitched it to the Germans. "Ralph [Ammirati] and the others weren't sure. They thought it might be too brash, too forceful. I said, 'No, this is it.' It says everything we want to say in one line, one thought. I knew, among other things, that it would be great on billboards and bus shelters to just run a great pic-ture of the car and that one line of copy if we wanted to, without any other copy," says Puris.

The BMW 2002, while putting BMW on the map with the rela-tively few Americans who had embraced BMW in its early days, was viewed as a problem by the agencies and BMW. It was smaller than a Cadillac or Mercedes, but nearly as expensive as some Caddy and Benz models. Part of the agency's big pitch for the business involved taking the 2002 to country-club parking lots and talking to members about what they thought—parking lots that almost never had a BMW parked in their spaces. "You gotta be kidding," was the most common response received when the price was disclosed to the argyle-sweatered golf crowd. The agency took away from its research the notion that it would have to pitch BMW as a "new kind of luxury." That, in fact, was a line that was tacked up on a board in the agency before the big pitch day in Munich, but Puris's "Ultimate Driving Machine" won out. "Luxury to that point was defined mostly by size, plush interiors, and pretty wallowing ride from Lincolns, Cadillacs and Mercedes, so we were going to have to change the discussion about luxury and center it on performance. BMW's were not only smaller, but the interiors were rather spare. The value in the price tag was under the hood and in the guts of the car, not in the interiors," says Puris.

"Ammirati & Puris was more like us in the U.S.," recalls Bob Lutz. "The other agencies we were looking at were big institutional agen-cies that worked for the biggest soap and toothpaste companies in the world. Ammirati & Puris was a start-up, entrepreneurs, just like BMW liked to think of itself. They had the experience with Fiat and Volvo, and then the strategy was just dead right. They were a clear winner in the pitch. It wasn't close." BMWs were to become the thinking person's and the cool man's luxury car.

Among the first ads created by the agency was a print ad for the 2002. "The 2002 is practical, roomy and economical. But in spite of all that it isn't boring." Another ad, for the 3.0Si, spoke more directly to the idea of performance as found in a BMW being the "new luxury." The headline: "The BMW 3.0Si. For those who deny themselves nothing." That line is a departure from the "fun" and "sport" messages in the earlier ads by BMW's distributors, and there were no Germanisms like *Wundercar* in the ads. "There was a higher price to justify, so some ads needed to address that this wasn't an overpriced car when compared with other cars. "It was a car for people who appreciate the better, finer things, like the better stereo, the better tools, the cooler vacation" says Puris. Too, the car was photographed in a stationary pose against a black background for dramatic effect. BMW was readying the U.S. launch of the 5 Series in 1976. The country was still in recession. BMW chairman Eberhard von Kuenheim had been directly involved in the hiring of Ammirati & Puris. He did not pretend to be a marketing expert, but he had definite opinions about such things as photography and which poses made the vehicles look their best. One ad for the 530i showed an illustrated cutaway of the car that exposed some of the car's mechanical innards, as well as an off-center frontal photo of the car rather than a full side profile. Turning the BMW's less-than-lush interior into a positive, the headline read, "The BMW 530i. An engineer's conception of a luxury car, not an interior decorator's." Playing up the Bavarian engineers in ads would become a hallmark of many BMW ads. A year later, the agency adopted a print ad and billboard style of using bold all-capital letters in headlines as a device to exude power and confidence. One ad from 1977 for the 3 Series announced, "YOU DRIVE A BMW. IT DOES NOT DRIVE YOU." Sales jumped from 19,000 in 1975 to 26,000 in 1976. Introduced in July 1975 as the successor to the 2002, the new 3 Series helped drive sales to 31,000 by 1978. The 3 Series expanded the appeal of the 2002, as it had more interior space, a better ride, improved fuel economy, and better occupant safety.

All of Ammirati & Puris's ads in these early years on the account punctuated the BMW roundel logo with "Bavarian Motor Works, Munich, Germany," as part of the ongoing campaign to educate the broad buying public about BMW's origin and heritage. In fact, BMW's Bavarian origins have always been an integral part of its culture and brand identity.

———

In order to evaluate the relevance of the Bavarian connection to BMW's culture and history, it is first important to understand one or two key points about Bavaria. Bavaria may be politically part of Germany, but its soul remains independent and somewhat aloof. Until the early 1900s Bavaria still had its own king, and its affiliation with the German federation under Kaiser Wilhelm was relatively loose.

Historically, Bavaria's affiliations have often been closer to the Austro-Hungarian Empire than to the Prussians in Germany. It is, in fact, not uncommon for a displeased Bavarian to mutter "damn Prussian" under his breath if the source of his displeasure is non-Bavarian. This, of course, is ironic, since BMW's most celebrated executive in its postwar history is Prussian aristocrat Eberhard von Kuenheim. And it's biggest embarrassment was the 1999 ouster of its chairman, Bavarian Bernd Pischetsrieder, who had been handpicked by von Kuenheim.

The state's fiercely Roman Catholic religious positioning is perhaps the most significant factor to have affected its somewhat isolationist culture. The rest of Germany is strongly Calvinist and, for a long time, it was the perceived threat to their religious freedoms that kept the Bavarians out of the political federation. Bavaria has more public (religious) holidays than any other state in Germany. In fact, it is for this historical reason that Bavaria still maintains certain political differences from the rest of the country. Staunchly conservative in nature, the German right-wing party, the Christian Democratic Union (CDU), is not represented in the country's southern-most state, which affiliates itself instead with the independent Christian Socialist Union (CSU). While policies are largely similar, the CSU has a tendency to be even further right than the CDU and is either criticized or applauded (depending on your own persuasions) for its so-called *Kinder, Kirche, Küche* policies (children, church, kitchen), which hold great value in the traditional family unit, where the woman's role is largely domestic.

Ethnic Bavarians not only think differently from their Prussian neighbors, they also look different. Typical Aryan features of blond hair and blue eyes are hard to find in these parts. Most look more southern European, with olive skin, dark hair, and dark eyes. They are typically smaller and more stockily built than the willowy northerners. Munich is labeled as "Italy's northernmost city" in some guidebooks. The Bavarian dialect is also something of a shock to the system of those who learned *hochdeutsch* (high German) at school. Not only is much of the terminology different from high German, the thick guttural accent quickly removes any recognition even from those words that are the same.

Bavaria is a wealthy state. It has rich farmland, breathtaking scenery, a pleasant climate, and, since the end of the nineteenth century, a solid manufacturing and technology base. As well as boasting the headquarters of BMW in Munich and Audi in Ingolstadt, it also lays claim to German giants Siemens, Infineon, and MAN, to name just a few of the internationally known blue-chip companies. A quarter of the technology patents filed in Germany each year originate in Bavaria. The relative wealth enjoyed by the state in modern times has led to its having the highest living standards in Germany and the lowest crime rate. These elements combine to create an impression of aloofness. In the United Kingdom, in contrast, the Scots are often accused of having a national inferiority complex when it comes to their English neighbors. In Bavaria, quite the reverse is true.

Walking or biking around Munich, it is not difficult to see how the city provided a ready incubator for Germany's most unfortunate chapter—the rise in the 1930s of Hitler's Third Reich. Among the disaffected veterans of World War I and the antisocial types found in any city, the political ferment sweeping Germany found fertile ground in Munich. What's more, Munich's style and sophistication was a magnet for unemployed students who had finished their studies amid skyrocketing unemployment. Its sprawling English Garten Public Park, founded in 1789, became an ideal Nazi rallying spot, as did the city's numerous biergartens. Later, one of the most notorious of the Nazi concentration camps, Dachau, was located just a few miles beyond the city's border.

Postwar Munich is very much a city for walking and biking; full of wide public plazas, it seems a city literally laid out to inspire public gathering, and despite its strategic importance, it was not as heavily bombed during the war as were Berlin and Frankfurt, so many of its historic prewar buildings remain intact. Munich remains the most historically and architecturally significant city in Germany today.

The Quandt family, which owns 47 percent of BMW, is not Bavarian, but their conservative and isolationist approach to running the company meshes well with Bavarian sensibilities. As can be said to a large degree of Bavarian culture, the BMW brand has been diluted very little by external influences. One outdated yet stereotypical image many foreigners have of Germany is of men in lederhosen, listening to brass bands and quaffing beer in liter mugs, all of which is exclusively Bavarian. It is not unusual to walk the streets of Munich on a Sunday and see families out for a stroll in traditional lederhosen or *Tracht*. But someone so dressed in downtown Hamburg would be as out of place as a man wearing a kilt in New Orleans or chaps and spurs in Boston. By some lights, much of what is perceived as German culture is really distinctly Bavarian culture. Typically, Bavarians are considerably more stubborn and, to some extent, more conceited than other Germans. Yet, these days few key people at BMW are actually Bavarians, and they say that the so-called Bavarian factor is not particularly relevant. Maybe so. But that belies BMW's fierce, historical attachment to independence, especially vis-à-vis its rival to the north, Mercedes-Benz. BMW's overriding commitment to its independence is still fueled by its close call with bankruptcy in 1959, when proud Bavarian shareholders shuddered at the prospect of BMW being gobbled up by Daimler-Benz. Former chairman Bernd Pischetsrieder says BMW's culture has always been "far closer to being Mediterranean than Prussian." And he recalls that Eberhard von Kuenheim, when introducing Pischetsrieder as his successor, quipped, "I'm not sure we are strong enough to have a Bavarian chairman."

As sober-minded traditionalists, Bavarian workers tend not to jump around a great deal; those who start life with BMW tend to stay the course. Most Bavarians consider life there good, so why would they want to live anywhere else? Despite the external influence from the likes of such Prussians as von Kuenheim, a good deal of local blood has made its mark in recent BMW history. Besides Pischetsrieder, Wolfgang Reitzle, the dominant product development chief from 1984 to 1999, is Bavarian; and, though both chairman Helmut Panke and today's product boss Burkhard Goeschel were born outside Bavaria, they were reared in Munich.

One former non-Bavarian BMW engineer reckons that most non-Bavarian Germans coming to Munich do so with a conscious desire to adopt the Bavarian way of life. "The good weather, high standard of living, the beer gardens. . . . You also have to be prepared to accept the Bavarian culture, which isn't easy for everyone," he says. His comment implies that Bavaria has a tendency to attract like-minded souls, which, of course, is the heart of BMW's brand philosophy of not *chasing* customers, but rather *attracting* buyers who believe, as the BMW collective does, that driving should be fun for its own sake.

BMW's culture is more of a piece with big-city Munich, which is dynamic, cosmopolitan, and extremely international, than with the sleepy surrounding Bavarian countryside. If not exactly a thriving counterculture, there's remains an audacious and independent streak evidenced by the still-common nude sunbathing in the city's main park, the *English Garten*. In a way, Munich's undercurrent of independence is a bit like BMW's. The company, like Munich, is quite small compared with its rivals. Considering its position on the world stage when it comes to fashion, culture, industry, and business, Munich has a huge profile for a population of just over a million. The same could be said for small-scale BMW as it continues to set the world standard for engineering, vehicle performance, and profitability.

Bavaria is very much baked into BMW and is well represented in the BMW logo. The logo itself is meant to depict a spinning propeller against a blue sky, an image that long ago made more sense than it does today, given that the company started life designing and building world-class airplane engines. The BMW logo matches the colors of the Bavarian flag; it's also the only logo in the auto industry that depicts *motion*. Every other car company logo shows an initial (Lexus), symbol (Mercedes' star or Audi's interlocking rings), or a crest (Cadillac and Porsche). Beyond the symbolism, the logo is graphically striking, with its sharp blue, white, and black colors. "It's a detail that works very much to the brand's benefit that we have such a visually striking and active symbol of our brand staring the driver back in the face from the steering wheel and adorning all our products," says BMW chief designer Chris Bangle. In short, it is probably the best-looking piece of jewelry in the car business.

Such striking symbols of accomplishment that tie into the BMW brand, culture, and history are never far removed from employees or customers. One of the jewels of Munich's, and Germany's, postwar architecture is BMW's world headquarters, known as the "Four Cylinders"—a full expression of architecture as semiotics—designed when modern architecture was gaining force in the 1960s. Rather than just conveying an image or mood, in the way that a Greek style or Colonial Revival bank is designed to convey permanence and trust, the goal was to have BMW's headquarters evoke more than static corporate solidarity. Twenty-two stories high, each tower is connected at the center by a core; a cross section of the building would loosely resemble a four-leaf clover. As BMW employees walk from office to office, the outer pathways on each floor are always curving. The BMW tower proved a showpiece for Munich during the 1972 Olympics, visible as it was from several vantage points all around the games, especially from the nearby Olympia Park. Termed "conspicuous" by many Munich guidebooks, a 1972 BMW press release declared it ". . . situated within sight of the pavilion-type roof of the Munich Olympia Park. It will be a symbol of prosperity, autonomy and technical perfection with a hint of utopia." A revolutionary construction, it has never been exactly replicated. Construction engineer Helmut Bomhard developed a unique suspended, prestressed concrete structure dependent on a specific—and quite peculiar—construction method; oddly enough, all 22 floors were preassembled on the ground and installed one after the other in *downward* sequence. Starting at the top, each individual floor was hoisted up hydraulically from the central tower, the concrete backbone of the building. Then the next floor was hoisted up and suspended from the one above. The "Four Cylinder" building is consequently a suspension structure.

To see the building going up was to know that the project perfectly mirrored BMW's goal of being seen as a serious engineering company producing motorcars for the world's most sophisticated buyers. The construction was a thing of German mastery. This passage from Horst Monnich's *The BMW Story* is a fine description of the process:

The unusual design meant that the building was not standing, but hanging. Suspended on a supporting cross with four arms (each of these measured 16 meters) storey after storey would be raised by hydraulic presses over steel tensioners called "hawsers." All eighteen had already been fitted with an aluminum façade and had been fully glazed on the ground. They were raised 20 centimeters at a time. They would then be lifted in unison over a final 14 meters, to bring them to their final position, leaving the space below them empty. While work could be done fitting out the interior in the suspension house, it was also possible to erect the entrance building on the ground, as well as the 30 meter long, four-storey, low building which was linked to it.

The Four Cylinders stands in stark contrast to Daimler-Benz's headquarters in Stuttgart or the Ford or General Motors buildings in the United States. Ford erected a world headquarters in Dearborn, Michigan, in the 1960s that is known simply as "The Glass House" because it's basically a giant rectangle of glass and concrete. GM's decades-old headquarters was a row of Greek Revival "chimney" buildings that looked more like a fortress than any bastion of ahead-of-the-curve thinking. And Chrysler in 1972 still inhabited a warren of puny buildings in Highland Park, Michigan, so depressing as to make executive recruitment difficult. That, too, was part of Hahnemann's thinking when pushing such a progressive building—it would be an obvious symbol of a company where talented and clever people would *want* to work.

In 2006, BMW will open BMW World, a new customer reception and delivery center near the Four Cylinders building and Olympia Park. The BMW Museum, long neglected and outdated, will also be updated as part of the project. Along with collecting their newly minted cars at the BMW Center, the buying public will be able to view artistic and technological exhibits, go to events and conferences, and patronize restaurants and shops. The new building is meant to be in the style of a covered piazza, a marketplace with flexible, transparent areas and an expansive suspended roof. The hope is to make the BMW Center an even more distinct and spectacular landmark in Munich than the Four Cylinders.

———

Throughout the 1970s, under the leadership of Eberhard von Kuenheim, BMW advanced year after year in profit and volume by following a simple, and now Bavarian, recipe for success. It built coherent and simple designs, leading, he believed, to cars that were attractive from every angle and would age well. Conventional design schemes were adequate and low risk, like the classic suits he wore to work very day. But each model year would bring with it technical innovation. The vehicles weren't to be flashier from one year to the next or from one development cycle to the next, but each year and each cycle the cars should be smarter. Innovations were often pitched in advertising and press material in a way that was just a bit over the heads of many BMW followers, though motor journalists could always decipher it and nearly always lauded BMW for every advance. Trispherical combustion chambers were described in ads as *Dreikugelwirbelwannenbrennraum*. In such a combustion chamber, thanks to BMW engineer Alex von Falkenhausen's theories on the travel of the flame front and its relation to combustion efficiency, air and fuel were transformed into torque and horsepower that exited through a new five-speed transmission to be fed to the rear wheels. It was also here that the unique sound of the big six-cylinder engine originated, changing from a deep-throated burble in the midrange to a clean, high wail at the upper reaches of the rpm range. BMW was great at getting away with this sort of stuff. Technical jargon like that worked for BMW the way marketing Beetles as "ugly" worked for Volkswagen. Another ad flogged something called "anti-dive front suspension." This, however, was not a technical breakthrough so much as it was an invention of sales and marketing executives like Bob Lutz. Lutz not only knew what he wanted the car to do on the road, but how best to describe it. Other companies like Mercedes and Audi had, in fact, adopted similar technology and design geometry to keep the front end of the car from diving during hard braking, but it took BMW to advertise it so directly. The image of BMW by the mid-1970s had translated into the company's de facto mission statement. "The Ultimate Driving Machine" was an idea, recalls Wolfgang Reitzle, "that seemed to take over everything we did." Auto industry historian Martin Buckley says, "As the marque developed in later years, this learned behavior seemed to become instinctive. BMW always felt and looked right, always had a distinctiveness, and always seemed to find customers happy to pay high prices for its product. This was not an achievement of engineering, but of management and organization."[5]

Von Kuenheim was driven by his rivals north to Stuttgart. It burned him to play second fiddle to Mercedes-Benz. A large part of what drove the company's culture throughout the 1970s and into the 1980s was "earning a seat at the table with Mercedes," says auto industry consultant Jim Hall. Behind his aristocratic and genteel outward appearance and demeanor, von Kuenheim was a fan of speed and performance cars. Perhaps most important, recalls former board member Lutz, "he almost always knew what he didn't know and made sure he had the right people around him who did know." When Lutz arrived at BMW in 1971, he was already an admirer of what BMW was doing. At Opel, Lutz could not engineer into the brand he was responsible for the same level of cachet that BMW had built up through "The New Class." "BMW had that youthful image everyone wants and spends an awful lot of money trying to manufacture or cultivate," says Lutz, who was easily wooed to BMW because GM had promoted him so fast and in such rapid succession that his salary hadn't had a chance to catch up to his executive grade, leaving him earning less than $35,000 while his peers were earning three times as much or more, plus bonuses. Upon his arrival, Lutz was appalled to learn from von Kuenheim that BMW had commissioned a corporate identity project from a German consulting firm that had sold von Kuenheim on the idea of changing the BMW logo to eliminate the black bezel around the blue-and-white propeller as well as the BMW initials, leaving just the blue-and-white propeller. Von Kuenheim had been convinced that the idea was a good one for a company eager to play in a more advanced league, reasoning that it was a cleaner, more modern look. Lutz strenuously disagreed. Said Lutz, "There is no reason to tinker with this. You have got an image represented in this beautiful logo that other car companies would kill to have." Lutz carried on at some length with his objections, ultimately winning von Kuenheim over to his side.

Von Kuenheim is most often referred to as a Prussian aristocrat or a "Cool Prussian." He recognized immediately upon being offered the job as chairman of BMW by majority shareholder Herbert Quandt that his success depended on retaining the trust of Quandt and putting up sound financial numbers. The two went hand in hand. One without the other would spell failure. Toward that end, say associates, he spent a good deal of time simply managing his own power base with the Quandts and German bankers. He managed more through intimidation than by encouragement.

Von Kuenheim was left fatherless as a teenager when his father died following a fall from a horse. He graduated from a technical high school in Stuttgart and entered the German navy at age 17. While he was in the service, his mother was captured by the advancing Russian armies at the family estate in Juditten, a village south of what was then known as Königsberg in East Prussia but which is now Russian territory called Kaliningrad. She died in a prison camp.

After the war, von Kuenheim went to work at Bosch on the production line, making refrigerators and car parts, until he was able to attend university on a grant from Bosch and earned his engineering degree. By age 35, von Kuenheim had worked his way into the Quandt Group as a staff executive in charge of technical questions for the businesses controlled by Herbert Quandt's brother Harald. After Harald Quandt's death in 1967, von Kuenheim took over technical responsibilities for all of Harald's businesses. Then, to test his mettle, Herbert Quandt sent von Kuenheim to run one of Harald's businesses, Industrial Werks at Karlsruthe (IWK), a problem company with disorganized operations and disappointing profits. Quandt was convinced after a short time and better results at IWK that he had his next BMW chairman, and so it was announced at the 1969 Frankfurt Motor Show that the largely unknown von Kuenheim would succeed Gerhard Wilcke in the top job.

————

By 1980, BMW was a legitimate worldwide brand that stood for performance and sporty driving in every market in which it marketed cars. Sales reached $4 billion, up from just $1.7 billion worldwide when von Kuenheim took over the company in 1970. The brand stood unwavering from the strategy it set forth six years earlier after it began adoption of "The Ultimate Driving Machine" in the United States, complemented by the European version of the ad strategy, "Freude am Fahren," or "Sheer Driving Pleasure." Von Kuenheim, in a 1980 interview with *Fortune,* stated without hesitation that BMW was about ". . . fast, responsive cars for people who relish the sheer pleasure of driving." As I have followed car companies for nearly 20 years, it is a rare thing to find a company that can stick to a brand mission for 5 years, let alone 10. During a rich period of product development and lineup expansion in the 1970s and into the 1980s, "It was invaluable to have such a clear idea of what we were doing so that everyone was able to stay focused on one idea," says former product chief Wolfgang Reitzle. By 1980, BMW had not only weathered the assault on the auto industry from environmental and safety regulations and high gasoline prices, it had thrived. The lineup stretched from the 3 Series and all its variants (the 316, 318, 320, 320i, 323i), the 5 Series, the 6 Series, and the 7 Series. The product portfolio also included the hand-built M1 277-horsepower performance car that had kicked off the now storied and financially successful M Series. The M1 enabled the autobahn driver to accelerate to 100 miles per hour in just 13 seconds and to cruise at 160 miles per hour.

BMW sold 350,000 cars worldwide in 1979, 35,000 of them in the United States, where it had 400 dealers, but it had still not cracked most of the Midwest and Midsouth regions of the country. BMW's cars didn't rile environmentalists like Detroit's and Stuttgart's products did. The fuel economy of BMW's fleet in 1980 was 26 miles per gallon. That is *still* above the auto industry's fleet average for fuel economy in 2003. BMW saw early that straight-six-cylinder engines, in which the cylinders are lined up in a row rather than in a V shape, were better for its rear-drive designs and for fuel economy. BMW's six-cylinder engines, in fact, offered their power with fuel economy similar to the four-cylinder engines being produced by others to deal with the energy crisis of the mid- and late 1970s. This was an important key to BMW's brand management, too. In the mid-1970s, when oil shortages drove gasoline prices skyward and emissions regulations toughened, BMW didn't work on the issues of fuel economy and cleaner tailpipe emissions only to accommodate creeping regulation—it set out to conquer the challenges without compromising BMW's performance reputation because it was critical to its obsession with leading in technology. It would have been a disaster to have the motor press, let alone customers, judge new models as "fast and sporty but gas-thirsty." Among other technical advances to make this possible, BMW pioneered the use of microcomputers that constantly adjust ignition timing and fuel injection to make the most efficient use of fuel.

Part of BMW's culture and its brand recognition in business circles, especially among investment bank analysts who track the company's share price and write reports for investors, is its financial strength and discipline. This was Herbert Quandt's strength that was executed by von Kuenheim at BMW. A 1980 snapshot of the company, 10 years into von Kuenheim's leadership, shows that BMW had one of the strongest balance sheets in the industry despite its small size; the interest earned on its cash actually surpassed interest paid out on long-term borrowings. This was and still is an unusual discipline to be found in modern industrial companies. Throughout the 1970s, the company financed most of its development out of its healthy cash flow instead of increasing debt. By 2000, although GM, Ford, DaimlerChrysler, and Volkswagen sold many more vehicles, BMW earned more than twice as much as any of these giants on the cars its sold. The 9.9 percent operating margin reached that year was second in the auto industry to the much smaller Porsche's. Until the financial debacle resulting from the acquisition of the Rover Group in 1994, BMW had posted 40 straight years of profits, a record matched only by Toyota in an industry notorious for its sharp cyclical swings.

———

By the early 1980s, the 3 Series was in the midst of its first makeover since it replaced the 2002 in 1975. The changes to both the 3 Series and 5 Series were subtle, such as raising the trunk lid to a more horizontal line in keeping with modern styling trends and allowing for greater luggage space. Five-speed gearboxes were introduced. A four-door version of the 3 Series was offered to bring a more practical family package to BMW's sport sedan image. BMW had mastered the art of getting the customer to trade up. It had a long list of options on every car, many of which were standard items on competitor cars—for example, power steering and the five-speed gearboxes. Transaction prices have long been around $3,000 or more above the manufacturer's sticker price. Dealers played to the vanity of BMW buyers, selling pricey wheel treatments, sunroofs, and interior upgrades to fatten the already plump profit margins on each car.

The 1980s proved a rich decade for BMW. The mid-1980s were especially prosperous for BMW's target customers as the boom in the stock market swelled the ranks of those whose income enabled them

to claim upper-middle and upper-class status. U.S. ad agency Ammirati
& Puris was carefully trying to balance the images of "luxury" and
"performance." Some ads still spoke to BMW's history and Bavarian
roots. At the same time, Wall Street was becoming not just the traditional seat of power it had always been, but also more of a cultural
phenomenon. More than ever, college graduates were aspiring to get
jobs as bond traders, investment bankers, and deal makers. Curiously,
many ads did not herald a specific model in the headline. One ad, for
example, read "A Luxury Sedan That Satisfies Both The People Who
Know Money and The People Who Know Cars." A reader had to take
in the small print to see the ad was for a 3 Series, to learn of the car's
ties to the celebrated 2002 and, of course, to get the spiel about German engineering. In fact, print ads heavy with copy had become a hallmark of Ammirati's work and often included technical information
over the heads of most readers. Says BMW's marketing director Jim
McDowell, who worked at Porsche in the 1980s, "The backstory of
BMW and its products was important to buyers and part of the mystique. German engineering was known then as something desirable,
though certainly most buyers didn't know exactly why. For many, it
was like ordering French wine because it was French and not from California." As BMW's mystique grew and sales climbed, rivals, including
Mercedes-Benz, began chasing the 3 Series success. Mercedes introduced a new 190 in 1984, often called the "Baby Benz." BMW shot
back indirectly, though unmistakably, in advertising, as it had done as
far back as the early 1960s when it began advertising BMWs as the
"New Class," a rabbit punch to it rival. One ad in 1984 shouted, "Introducing the only sports sedan morally entitled to borrow these innovations from BMW."

———

In the early twenty-first century, marketers refer to young consumers
born after 1979 as Generation Y. The significance of using *Y* to define
the group is debatable, but it may just as well as stand for those children born when the United States was gripped by a cultural phenomenon in which baby boomers, especially those born after 1955, were
dubbed by marketers as "yuppies," slang shorthand for young urban
professionals.

The late 1960s and early 1970s saw the cultural movement of the "hippies," politically and culturally rebellious participants in the counterculture of the 1960s. The late 1970s ushered in the "preppies," materialistic and upscale, obsessed with status, who believed the privileges they took for granted were due them thanks to an accident of birth. The word *preppie* derived from "prep school," the private preparatory high schools for the children of wealthy parents who aspire to have their offspring attend Ivy League schools. Yuppies, though, melded what they deemed the best of both worlds—the materialism of the preppies, minus the snobbery and self-absorbed perfectionism, with the mind-set of the hippie, minus the antiestablishment edginess. The term *yuppie*, say some researchers, was first used in print by *Chicago Tribune* columnist Bob Greene in a March 1983 piece on Jerry Rubin, a hippie-turned-yuppie, and was bandied about extensively in the 1984 presidential campaign in which Colorado senator Gary Hart, a contender for the Democratic nomination, seemed manufactured to appeal to the fiscally conservative but socially liberal yuppie voter.[6]

Newsweek dubbed 1984 the "Year of the Yuppie," young urban professionals whose lifestyle and outlook made them synecdoches of Reagan's America. Yuppies were criticized in the media and by their nonyuppie peers as wasteful consumers pursuing the American Dream without much regard for those left behind. Market researcher Daniel Yankelovich said of yuppies: They "desire to do things 'my own way,' want to exercise maximum control, and manipulate other people for one's own ends. Characteristically, Yuppies are needy and demanding people who crave attention and who insist on *their* prerogatives."[8] The yuppie heyday was short-lived; critics gleefully described the stock market crash of October 1987 as the consequence of yuppie folly—and the beginning of the end of yuppiedom. The BMW, or *Bimmer,* had become *the* official car of the yuppie phenomenon, and the term *yuppie* quickly became liability. There can be little doubt that the yuppie phenomenon had a lasting cultural impact.

Considerable debate raged about the number of genuine yuppies. The *Newsweek* cover story estimated that there were 1.2 million, while *American Demographics* determined that about 5 percent of baby boomers (4.2 million) qualified.[9] Nearly 75 percent of yuppie households were headed by couples, and a yuppie subset called DINKS—

double-income, no-kids couples—was identified as well. Married or not, DINKS worked long hours at their jobs, postponed having children for the sake of their careers, and had lots of discretionary income that they used in consuming conspicuously. Not just BMWs, but Mercedes-Benz, Cadillac, and Jaguar all benefited.

Obsession with career was the religion of yuppie culture. As *The Yuppie Handbook* (Pocket Books, 1984) pointed out, work had to be personally meaningful, emotionally satisfying, and a vehicle for self-expression. It sounded like an excerpt from BMW's marketing plan. Since staying busy was de rigueur for yuppies, advertisers targeting them found the print media more effective than television—yuppies were likely to record their favorite television shows and skip the commercials when playing back the videotape. *Metropolitan Home, Architectural Digest, Esquire,* and *New Yorker* magazines were authentic yuppie publications and a major part of BMW's regular media plan. Meanwhile, upscale mail-order catalogs proliferated. Richard Thalheimer's San Francisco–based *The Sharper Image* earned a whopping $78 million in 1983 as the "ultimate toy store for yuppies." From espresso-cappucino makers and the Corby trouser press to a $5,000 tanning bed, the most popular yuppie items had to be useful as well as fun to own. Again, BMW's brand image fit the yuppie like Bavarian reindeer skin gloves. A 1986 Louis Harris Associates survey showed the following: 73 percent of Americans believed that yuppies were *primarily* intent on making more money; 81 percent of yuppies agreed that they were; 72 percent of the public believed that yuppies were *more concerned with their own needs than with the needs of others;* the same percentage of yuppies agreed; 70 percent of those surveyed thought yuppies bought flashy cars and clothes in order to set themselves apart from others; 81 percent of yuppies said this was so.[10]

———

BMW's sales began falling off after the stock market crash, from 96,000 in 1986 to 73,000 in 1988 and 65,000 in 1989 and 1990. Ammirati & Puris, with guidance from BMW of North America's own management, fed the yuppie image with TV ads for the 7 Series, for example, that showed people even after the stock market crash with their cars at polo matches and opera houses. But the agency also produced the usual diet of speed and performance ads. A 1989 ad for the 3 Series showed, for example, a group of young, attractive people at a soccer match, with the headline, "The BMW 3 Series. It's Why Some Enthusiasts Are More Enthusiastic Than Others." A year later, a print ad for the 3 Series looked more aggressive, with a car driving out of the ad toward the reader (a similarly shot TV spot was also created), with the headline, "The BMW 318 Is Back. With a Vengeance!"

Watching sales stagnate, worried that its image was mired in the negativity of yuppiedom, BMW in October 1991 shocked the advertising world by placing its account, which had been at Ammirati & Puris since 1975, up for review with the intention of switching agencies. Signs of conflict were seen at BMW and at Ammirati's lower Fifth Avenue offices in early summer that year. Victor Doolan, a longtime BMW executive, some months earlier had rotated in from BMW's Canadian operation to the United States to take over sales and marketing, and, as Martin Puris recalls, "It was different from the start of Doolan's arrival. He didn't seem to like us, and we didn't like him. We knew things were going to change, though it took several months for us to realize a review of the business was absolutely inevitable." Advertising industry consultant John Slaven, a longtime director of advertising at Volkswagen of America, was called into BMW by Doolan the previous June to discuss options, such as which other agencies were available that would be up to the job if Ammirati had to be replaced. Slaven's response was to tell Doolan that his first option was to "have a nice lunch, lie down for a while, and forget the whole idea." It's not that Slaven didn't need the consulting fee, but his first advice was to keep Ammirati on the job. The agency was considered one of the few "Tiffany" agencies in New York, and he implored Doolan to work out whatever differences had interrupted the relationship. Doolan says he was following orders from Munich to replace Ammirati and that the order came from von Kuenheim. There is one story that kicks around BMW that von Kuenheim, already frustrated with BMW's sliding sales in the United States, was pushed over the edge one day when he was informed that a team from Ammirati & Puris arrived at the Four Cylinders building in a chauffeured non-BMW car; some say it was a white Cadillac, others say a Mercedes-Benz. Puris denies it happened. In any case, the relationship that was the envy of Madison Avenue and one of the most celebrated accounts in the ad business was doomed.

"The situation was that we had done about 50,000 sales in 1991, which simply wasn't enough, and there was talk about whether BMW would stay in the U.S., though it's hard to believe we would have gone that way," says Doolan. The yuppie stain was on BMW from the 1980s. By 1991 and 1992, five years after the 1987 stock market collapse, with a poor economy raging that would soon be the undoing of George Bush's presidency, *yuppie* was a dirty word, not even cute any more. The feeling in Munich was that Ammirati hadn't done enough to counter the yuppie effect; now the company engaged fully to turn the situation around.

In retrospect, BMW and Ammirati's luxury positioning of the brand in the mid- and late 1980s went too far too fast, perhaps followed too closely the fickle wave of fashion. The best ad agencies and marketing companies don't merely follow society's fashions, they anticipate the changes coming and help lead them through the right words and images. Puris maintains that the agency never wavered from the strategy of performance and luxury and that it never catered to the yuppie factor. That's probably true, but it perhaps didn't do enough to counteract the yuppie stink on the brand. Another truth, though, is that BMW, and von Kuenheim especially, was never very good at admitting mistakes. Earlier in the 1980s, BMW had an obvious quality problem with transmissions, and complaints were flowing into Munich from all corners of the world; von Kuenheim was loath to admit it, even in a meeting with his regional managers. When one raised the problem in one such meeting, von Kuenheim dismissed him with a withering stare and rebuked him later for airing the problem in too public a setting.

Clearly, the product line itself had shortcomings that had led to the falloff in sales, as evidenced by a sweeping makeover and improvement of offerings undertaken at the same time the advertising account was going into review.

- *Introduction of a number of new models in its core series.* Most notably, the 325i Sedan was introduced in 1992; it represented a complete, bumper-to-bumper redesign. The following year, BMW introduced a 740i sedan with the first eight-cylinder BMW engine to cross the pond.
- *Aggressive pricing.* The new 325i was priced under $30,000, while the new 740i was priced under $55,000. These prices retained the

premium BMW believed was warranted for its brand over its Japanese competitors, but kept the models within 10 to 15 percent of a comparably equipped Lexus.

- *Reorganization of its dealer network.* By the early 1990s, BMW had almost 400 dealers in the United States (only 106 of which sold BMW exclusively), compared to fewer than 150 dealers for Lexus and Infiniti, respectively. Dealer frustration with BMW was high, and the quality of customer service at BMW dealerships was mixed. As a result, BMW restructured its account management approach and reconceptualized its dealer operating system to ensure greater consistency in the customer experience across dealerships.
- *Cup holders, one-touch windows, and other amenities.* Items absent from BMWs in the late 1980s were added to knock down some of the barriers to purchase identified in market research.

By the late 1980s and early 1990s, the luxury-car landscape had changed considerably in North America. A new pragmatism had begun to replace the conspicuous-consumption patterns of the early 1980s, and BMW found itself saddled with an outdated image. More significant, the company faced new competition with the introduction of luxury brands from Japan. Honda had moved in with Acura in 1986 and was joined in 1989 by Toyota's Lexus and Nissan's Infiniti. The Japanese companies were not only delivering astonishing quality in these cars (the $75 BMW oil change and monthly garage visits to Helmut or Wolfgang were no longer charming), but their cars were less expensive. Clearly, the Japanese were taking losses on their early vehicles (known as *dumping*) in order to build up sales volume and credibility. "Lexus changed the world for us. . . . We had a lot of come-to-Jesus meetings in those days about what we were going to do and how we were going to do it," recalls longtime BMW executive Tom McGurn.

In 1991, Helmut Panke had succeeded Karl Gerlinger as president of BMW North America. He immediately began working on a plan to make BMWs sold in the United States more competitive in price and features, as well as to build BMWs in the United States for the first time by middecade. Talk of pulling up stakes in the United States was officially over. Panke, his hands full, left it to Doolan to sort out the advertising issues and saw no reason to try to buck Munich's desire to hire a new agency. Doolan went to Ammirati's offices on a damp, dank day in September to finally put it to Martin Puris and Ralph Ammirati—a review would happen. The incumbent agency that had invented "The Ultimate Driving Machine," and had built its whole business around the BMW account, was invited to compete with other agencies to hold onto the business. Puris sat down with Doolan, while Ammirati had stopped off in the men's room before entering the conference room. Doolan started his speech before Ammirati arrived. Puris took no time to consider the offer and said, "You're fired!" Puris knew his agency's standing on Madison Avenue. He had confidence and he wanted the last word. Doolan left him an opening to compete; Puris slammed the door in his face. BMW hadn't fired the agency, the agency had, technically, fired BMW. Just then Ralph Ammirati walked in, hands probably still damp from the restroom visit, and said, "Did I miss anything?"

Following a review of a handful of ad agencies, Doolan and a team from BMW chose the Mullen Agency of Wenham, Massachusetts to succeed Ammirati & Puris. Mullen was at that time an agency off the Madison Avenue track, situated in a mansion in a woodsy hamlet north of Boston. Known primarily as a top-drawer print ad agency for genteel clients like Rockport Shoes, founder Jim Mullen nevertheless craved a car account. Mullen, like a lot of wealthy men, was a collector of fast cars and modern art, a combination seemingly made for BMW. Doolan and the BMW dealers were mesmerized by Mullen and his enthusiasm and taste for cars and art, and they awarded the outsider agency the roughly $100 million account, which was worth about $12 million in revenues and increased the firm's business by about one-third overnight. While print advertising, of course, was an important element of BMW's business, TV advertising was more important. And this is where Mullen couldn't get out of first gear. The agency quickly proved it didn't have the staffing or in-house talent to produce a big TV ad campaign and strategy. Too, there quickly developed a feeling at BMW that Mullen must have used freelance help to develop the winning strategy and the presentation, because the people he hired to staff the account didn't seem to know their way around a car account and the complexities that go along with the size of the business, the hundreds of dealers, and so on. The first campaign from Mullen showed a profound lack of understanding of the task at hand, which was elevating the brand beyond yuppiedom and positioning it against the encroaching Japanese brands. One TV ad, for example, showed the 7 Series zigzagging around the countryside as a voice-over extolled the virtues of Bavarian engineering. As edited, the film transitioned from a wide camera shot of the landscape, at which point the voice-over said, "Everything else . . ." and the ad then shifted to a beauty shot of the 7 Series rolling gracefully down the road, ". . . *is senseless luxury.*" The coordination, or lack thereof, of film editing with the voice-over left the viewer with the impression that the BMW 7 Series was, in fact, "senseless luxury." "The Ultimate Driving Machine" remained the advertising theme and slogan on all advertising. But in this campaign, the ads didn't seem to solidly connect with the idea, besides being technically off-kilter.

Nevertheless, from 1991 to 1992 and into 1993, sales were going in the right direction, up from 53,300 in 1991 to 78,000 in 1993, but that was to be expected from the additional product and product changes and a brightening economy. But measurements of brand equity and performance were not going in the right direction. Besides, Jim McDowell, who had joined BMW from Porsche in late 1992 after the selection of Mullen, was having a difficult time working with the new ad agency. Said McDowell, "BMW is blessed with a great brand; that will go a long way toward carrying sales when the product itself is correct and the economy helps a little, but you still have to do things right, and the advertising wasn't up to the standards we were trying to set. And the people on the business weren't the right people. It was a big, bad chemistry problem." There is a tenet in advertising that it can take five to seven years for a bad marketing strategy to seriously affect a solid brand. McDowell wasn't about to wait.

McDowell had come to BMW from Porsche AG, where his agency had been Fallon McElligott, formed in the mid-1980s in Minneapolis, Minnesota, by Pat Fallon and Tom McElligott. Fallon had been an account manager at Minneapolis ad agency Martin-Williams, and Tom McElligott was a talented creative. The two had started a small freelance business—advertising guns for hire—before opening their own full-service agency in 1981. Soon after, it picked up big accounts like the *Wall Street Journal*, McDonald's, and Porsche. The late 1980s were not kind to Porsche, as the company with the iconic sports car brand suffered from a limited product line and financial mismanagement. But

Fallon's advertising had consistently won awards, and it had a reputation in the ad industry as a smart and strategic agency absent the opulent trappings and wasteful expense accounts of Madison Avenue, not to mention Mullen's mansion offices. McDowell held a stealthy review of a couple of ad agencies. He had a feeling from the start that Fallon was the right choice, and so the agency was awarded the business in 1994. Fallon had two tasks to tackle right away. Get ready for the placement of the company's first U.S.-built car, the Z3 roadster, in 1996. The car would actually launch as a costar in the James Bond film, *Goldeneye*, in late 1995 and create a coherent ad strategy that had eluded Mullen.

In 1996, BMW had a series of memorable ads created by Fallon that were not "BMWesque," and they garnered mixed reaction among dealers, customers, and the media. One TV ad involved a computer-generated penguin struggling to make his way up an icy hill, sliding down after managing a few forward steps. The penguin disappears, only to come back in a BMW 3 Series equipped with traction control to climb the hill. Another TV spot that year, titled "Canals of New York," depicted a 7 Series sedan driving through New York City streets turned into canals via the art of special effects, weaving around yachts sharing the canals. "Why float through life when you can drive," said the ad's voice-over, clearly a dig at American and Japanese luxury cars, as well as Mercedes-Benz. Cadillac and Lincoln had well-known "floaty" rides. The new Mercedes S Class, too, was heavily criticized for its massive size. Lexus, while successful in terms of sales, was harshly critiqued in the motor press for having too isolated a ride, placing cabin silence above all else, especially handling and performance. But the "Canals" and "Penguin" ads, while memorable, were also, BMW would find out, softening its hard-won status as *the* sport sedan. The ads were too cute. Fallon's creative director on BMW says the agency, like many other agencies handling car brands, was creating 30-second ads that told little stories to convey the selling point. "But with everyone telling little stories, ours had difficulty standing out. In 1996, BMW saw survey results showing that, of 180,000 customers who shopped BMW but bought the competition, the top reason people didn't buy a Bimmer was that the car they ultimately purchased was "more fun to drive." Ouch! Lexus, Mercedes, Audi more fun to drive than BMW?

McDowell called it "a slap in the face," and a wake-up call to get down, dirtier, and grittier in its advertising. In August of 1996, BMW began a much different ad strategy, one with a clear bloodline to the hard-core performance and gritty ads of the mid-1970s. Shot in black and white and underlined by a pulsating heavy-metal rock music sound track, the ads are what Bildstein calls "point-of-view" advertising in which the camera is on the hood of the car showing, for example, the nose of the car on the road, or on an outrigger, trained on the tires of the car as it maneuvers over the road. The star of each ad was the car and the experience of driving it, with some clever ad copy salted in. One TV ad for the Z3, for example, showed the car being driven all out on a twisty road, with the words, "Shall We Dance? Right foot forward." Another TV spot showed the tires and front end of the car taking corners hard and fast, but completely in control. The accompanying ad copy on the screen, reprised in print ads, read, "Happiness isn't around the corner. Happiness is the corner." Key to the success of these ads in reestablishing BMW's sporty driving credentials was the heavy-metal music sound track and the sound mixing of the ads that conveyed the almost musical roar of the BMW engines even through small speakers on a mediocre television. For BMW customers and prospects with upmarket TVs channeled into their stereo speakers (of which there are many), the ads were arresting. After 18 months of the campaign, sales were climbing, and BMW's own research showed "fun to drive" climbing back and reclaiming its rightful place in consumers' minds.

———

In 2001, BMW faced competition from a reinvigorated field of competitors in the luxury/performance category: Mercedes-Benz, Jaguar, Lexus, Infiniti, Volvo, Porsche, Audi, Saab, and Ferrari. Jaguar and Saab, for example, had been weak rivals for years. Under new ownership, though—Ford bought Jaguar in 1989 and GM bought Saab in the mid-1990s—they were receiving investment from their U.S. parents to take on the established Germans. Volvo, also bought by Ford, was out to chase BMW in the 3 Series, 5 Series, X5, and even M Class segments. The vehicles in these categories shared a number of common characteristics. They all touted elegant design, high performance, and up-to-date technological features for driving and safety. Despite the crowd of entries, BMW's U.S. managers, like their Munich masters, believed that their target customer was fundamentally different from that of competitors.

BMW, like many other marketers, stopped emphasizing demographics (targeting customers based on age and income) in favor of psychographics (targeting based on mind-set and lifestyle). Says BMW's McDowell, "We don't think anyone serves the particular psychographic we do. Take Mercedes, for example. People buy Mercedes because they care about status, and the Mercedes says, 'I've arrived.' Volvo is another example: People buy a Volvo because they think of it as being very sensible and practical and they are very impressed by the concept of safety. BMW is targeting a different psychographic than they are. No one's really playing in our field. Porsche comes close, but they're much more niche than us."

In mid-2001, two-thirds of BMW customers were male; the average BMW customer was about 46 years old; median income was $150,000; the majority were well educated, married, and had no children. Beyond the vital statistics of BMW owners, though, BMW carefully tracks the tastes, personalities, and lifestyles of its core customer base. As McDowell says, "BMW customers are such active people that we often joke that the best way to find a BMW prospect would be with X-ray vision. If we could see through to the trunk of their car and determine that there were athletic bags stored back there, we'd know that we'd have a prospective BMW customer in the car." BMW, says McDowell, appeals to people who tend to be leaders, who work hard, play hard, and achieve a lot very early in life. They tend to be very active and engaged in sports as part of their daily regime. According to McDowell, "They tend to be as demanding of the people around them as they are of themselves. Because they work hard, their free time is extremely valuable, and they are very particular about what they surround themselves with. These people typically have an eye to detail. They care about how things are assembled. They are willing to pay more to get an absolutely perfect product, as opposed to just a very good product."

Peter Hampton, 43, is such a buyer. In fact, he seems like a poster boy for BMW. The owner of an electronics business, the Ann Arbor, Michigan, MBA is a discerning shopper of everything that goes into his house. His home entertainment system is Bose. His refrigerator is Sub-Zero. His stove range is Viking. He does not live in an $800,000 house, but rather in a $350,000 bungalow-style house. "I could afford to buy a bigger house, but I love this one, and I love the street where I live," says Hampton. Is he a brand-conscious snob? "Brand-conscious, yes. Snob? Maybe some people think so. But I have high-end appliances because I respect the products I buy, that I surround myself with. I cook a lot. I entertain pretty frequently. I love my BMW 530i. I love driving it. When I drive a car every day, as I do, I want to feel that it is more than just a conveyance. It's the same as my Bose stereo. If I didn't care about excellent sound, I'd get a Panasonic boom box. But when I listen to Keith Jarrett on piano or Billie Holiday, I want to hear everything. I want to be *in* the music. When I drive, I want to feel like I am an extension of the machine and the machine is an extension of me. That's what I get from my BMW."

Jim McDowell was on a roll in early 2000. Sales for BMW in the United States were at a record high and he had no new models to launch for six months. Twice named "Marketer of the Year" by *Brandweek* for deftly managing BMW's marketing communications, decades of healthy sales gains behind him, no doubt helped by a booming dot-com economy full of new millionaires with a taste for Bavarian sheet metal, McDowell could have done much worse than prepare for another year of "Ultimate Driving Machine" ads. He saw this time, though, as an opportunity. With no new products to launch, he could do something to promote the BMW brand without having to bog down with practical concerns of advertising engine derivatives, horsepower, or torque. But he had two problems. Clutter on TV, in magazines, and even on the Internet was becoming a serious problem for advertisers, especially companies like BMW with limited advertising resources. For all the products BMW offers in the market every year, it has a surprisingly small advertising budget compared with rivals such as Lexus and Mercedes-Benz. Advertising has become so prevalent and so bad (creatively speaking) that consumers, especially BMW's discerning customers who are pressed for time, have been increasingly turning away from mass media. Even McDowell admits, "We had done three straight campaigns about responsive performance. . . . It was getting repetitive rather than consistent in a positive way." Worse, other automakers were mimicking what BMW was doing in its 30-second ads, making even the best BMW ads struggle for notice. On the Internet, most companies by 2000 hadn't figured out much beyond annoying banner ads, hideously annoying pop-ups, or gimmicks to get Net surfers to go to an obviously corporate web site. Says McDowell, "BMW introduces many more new products every year than we could ever hope to support, given our marketing budget. We're a funny little company. We have a huge brand image, we have relatively small market share, and to earn that relatively small share, we have a huge number of models. And that means that we have relatively modest marketing budgets, but a lot of new products to introduce." Eighty-five percent of BMW buyers do extensive research on the Web before heading into a showroom, besides the normal day-to-day consumption of the Internet. In fact, BMW customers under age 50 by 2000 were spending more time on the Net than watching TV. Given the clutter problem and the worry that even BMW was starting to clutter the Net, instead of merely cranking up for another season of TV and print ads and perhaps the odd Internet promotion, McDowell wrote a letter to Fallon, saying, "We're taking the gloves off. Let's get beyond thinking about ads."

After a series of brainstorming sessions, a couple of nontraditional advertising ideas began to emerge. One idea was to produce a series of short films that might run in theaters before the main feature. Another was to incorporate the Internet into an advertising campaign. Soon into the process, the two ideas had merged into the idea of producing a series of short films for the Internet. McDowell recalled, "What excited us about the idea was that we knew we were dealing with an entirely new genre, an entirely new way of communicating our brand to the world. We also knew that if we produced a bunch of short films for the Internet, they wouldn't be seen by as many people as, say, a series of ads we aired on television. But we believed that what we lost in terms of audience size could be made up for in terms of *involvement*. We convinced ourselves that we could create something so involving that people would remember the experience 10 years down the road."

Fallon's creative team put together a videotape of car chases from well-known films: the 1998 Robert Deniro film *Ronin;* the Steve McQueen classic, *Bullitt; The French Connection.* The memorable scenes, which generally lasted less than 10 minutes, showed how a car could be a costar of heart-pumping action in a short story. The agency had studied the growing phenomenon of Web films and felt the medium had great appeal for BMW's brand because the people who had the means (high-speed Internet connection) and interest to view Web movies were both young and in the heart of BMW's customer audience. There were two ways to go: BMW could reach out to unknown film directors or students, or it could go big with Hollywood star directors. The stars won out. "We wanted A-list everything: A-list directors, A-list actors, A-list production values," says McDowell.

Some at Fallon thought it would be tough to get big-name directors to agree to make films that were commercials. On the contrary, director David Fincher, who had directed *Fight Club, Seven,* and *The Game,* jumped at the chance. Fincher's company then helped Fallon convince other big-name directors to participate: John Frankenheimer (*Ronin, Birdman of Alcatraz, The Manchurian Candidate*); Ang Lee (*Crouching Tiger, Hidden Dragon*); Wong Kar-Wai (Cannes Film Festival Best Director Award in 1997 for *Happy Together*); Guy Ritchie (*Snatch, Two Smoking Barrels*), who had the added notoriety of being married to pop diva Madonna; and Alejandro González Iñárritu (*Amores Perros*). Not only did the idea of working with a corporate entity like BMW not bother the directors, they were, in fact, eager to be able to work on a project that would have such immediate results. The films, which would take no more than two weeks to shoot, would be about 8 to 11 minutes long, to be downloaded from the Net and promoted by BMW. Compared with the creative and financial headaches and hassles of distributing a feature-length film, BMW's project was a walk in the park. The international flavor of the lineup of directors fit with the global nature of the Internet. People from all over the world would be encouraged and interested to download the films, so it wouldn't do to draw all the directors strictly from Hollywood. The star power wouldn't stop with the directors, though. Once the directors were lined up, the project attracted the interest of well-known actors, including Forrest Whitaker, Mickey Rourke, Gary Oldman, soul singer James Brown, and Madonna.

BMW had previously struck good fortune with Hollywood. When the company launched the Z3 roadster in 1996, it hoped merely for a high-profile product placement—a cameo in the James Bond film, *GoldenEye,* which began showing in theaters six months before the car hit dealerships. The Z3 replaced James Bond's signature Aston Martin from previous films. Though it got only 90 seconds of screen time, it was a very *good* minute and a half. Bond is presented the Z3 by the legendary research and development chief from the British MI-5 Intelligence agency, "Q," who says, "Now, pay attention, Bond. First your new car. A BMW . . ." The car's movie role was also supported by a series of traditional ads featuring scenes from the movie and a Special Limited Edition Bond Roadster available in the Neiman Marcus Christmas catalogue. Movie scenes were viewable on the BMW web site, which also offered the ability to custom-order a Z3. Hits to the Internet site tripled, from 35,000 a day to 125,000. The whole program fed into other benefits that transcended traditional print and TV advertising. During the 1996 Academy Award telecast, for example, Apple Computer bought an expensive 30-second ad, but the BMW custom configurator was on the screen for 25 of those seconds. Over 9,000 Z3 roadsters were prebooked by dealers by December 1995, twice the normal level for a new model. Still, McDowell says he doesn't like to sing the same note too often. He agreed to a subsequent Bond movie, *Tomorrow Never Dies,* in which the 7 Series and a BMW R1200, its first cruiser motorcycle, were featured, and the success of that program was not nearly as high in terms of splash and notoriety. Too, the Z3 campaign had led to several copycat movie placements by other car manufacturers.

Once the decision was made to create the short films, Fallon McElligott and a film production company team produced a series of 15 scripts ranging between 6 and 12 minutes. The protagonist in each film was a professional driver who helped people out of difficult situations. Played by actor Clive Owen, McDowell describes the character as "the guy James Bond should be, but isn't any longer . . . much closer to the young Sean Connery version than today's Pierce Brosnan Bond, but even grittier than Connery. Owen's character is a man who will get the job done, but not transition to a beautiful girl at the end or have the car turn into a speedboat."

Making a film with an independent director is not the same as making an advertisement. Companies spending money on 30- and 60-second ads often strip so much interesting content out (after having spent perhaps $500,000 or more to shoot it) that it winds up looking an awful lot like . . . advertising. McDowell says BMW has been finicky enough to scrap ad footage because the car got too close to the centerline of the road. Now, here was BMW, turning the whole process over to temperamental film directors. BMW could tell an anonymous commercial director or producer it wanted more footage with the light gleaming off the hubcap and the car closer to the white centerline, but McDowell wasn't going to be able to tell that to Ang Lee. He was smart enough to realize that to try it would defeat the whole reason for hiring directors like Lee in the first place. In fact, the enthusiasm for the project and for BMW expressed by the directors, who clearly felt they weren't merely shilling, worked well in the over-all scheme of positive public relations. "I drive a 1995 minivan," confessed Ang Lee. "The first time I drove this car [the 540i] I just went crazy. Usually I am a timid driver, but once I drove this car, it brought out the worst in me." At the Hollywood screening of John Woo's 2002 BMW film *Ticker*, Woo went over his thank-you list and concluded with, "And I thank the Z4, my new hero. I'm dancing with the Z4. I've found my fair lady."

To flesh out the character of the driver for all the directors, the creative team at Fallon, who wrote the scripts despite having competition from Hollywood writers (directors and production company staff as well as BMW reviewed Fallon's work and that of the professional Hollywood writers and opted for Fallon's), a dossier was written for Clive Owen's character, Luc Velant: "Born in 1963 in Alençon, France, his wife and two children were killed in a terrorist car bombing in Algiers. Schooled at Harvard, he served in the French Foreign Legion Special Forces as a critical-mission driver/transporter. He was discharged in 1989. Since then, he has lived in Bangkok, participating in high-stakes, bare-knuckle extreme fighting competitions. He hires himself out to perform critical-mission driving jobs. He is highly sought after by persons in discretion-imperative, crisis, and high-risk situations. CIA/Interpol is unable to ascertain how clients contract Velant or what his fees are, though they are estimated to be in excess of $75,000. While it has proven extremely difficult to track Velant as he moves among nations, it is hoped that he will lead CIA/Interpol to more significant suspects and/or fugitives. Velant is not guilty of any crime. While it is important to continue surveillance whenever possible, do not approach or attempt to apprehend."

The end result was a series of five films collectively titled *The Hire*. Altogether, the films cost about $15 million to produce, or about 10 times what it might have cost to shoot five 30-second ads. The films were released one at a time, and because they were done by directors with vastly different styles, each had a distinct voice and flavor. In one film, titled *Star*, by Guy Ritchie, according to the official description: "The driver faces a most perplexing challenge: a hugely talented and beautiful rock star who always gets what she wants. The most humorous of the five films, Guy Ritchie directs Madonna in this hilarious spoof of a bitchy rock star and her ride to the Venue, a club. The Driver relishes each quick move and tight turn the BMW speeds into, as Madonna (and her cup of coffee) are flung from side to side, top to bottom and front to back of the interior of his titanium silver M5." In another film, titled *Powder Keg*, by Alejandro González Iñárritu: "Soldiers patrol fields surrounding a rural village in search of a photojournalist who has snapped a picture certain to unite the world against their leader. The Driver's BMW X5 negotiates the rutted live-stock-filled tracks of an unnamed Latin American country. The tension mounts as the soldiers' pickup truck closes in on the X5 at the border, finally forcing The Driver to take to the fields to escape. You hold your breath to find Jacob still alive, shooting from his emptied camera through the window at the guard, precipitating The Driver's palpable fear. Jacob's blood, almost black in the sharply contrasted production, pools all over the X5's interior. The final scene where The Driver returns Jacob's dog tags to his mother—she is blind—closes the film with sharp poignancy." The breadth of story lines and moods created in the series was a key to their overwhelming positive reception in the media, which is always ready to bash a bad advertising idea or feature film directors who sink to directing ads.

The films could be accessed only at www.bmwfilms.com, not at BMW's official product and sales web site. McDowell and the Fallon team believe the distance from the sales site was important to keep it from being viewed as advertising. They even dithered over whether to call the site BMW Films, but felt in the end that it was necessary to anchor the project with the BMW brand in the consumer's mind. Too, BMW doesn't have a bad or crass image with the people who would be going to the trouble of downloading or viewing the films. Thirty-second trailers were prepared for television audiences. To unsuspecting television viewers, the trailers looked just like previews for movies released in theaters. Each trailer, though, directed the viewer to the BMW Films' web site.

In just a few months, BMW films attracted 9 million viewers to the web site. BMW customers and noncustomers (many of whom were without the income or lifestyle to purchase a BMW) raved over the films in the web-site comment area. Moreover, major media noticed the creative breakthrough and reviewed the films just as they would feature films. *Time* magazine's film and culture writer Richard Corliss wrote, "The ultimate in new-media, high-end branding has arrived. . . . It surely deserves the attention of discerning movie watcher."[11] About one of the films, Corliss wrote, "A fine, full movie in miniature, a perfect showcase for the director's obsessions: voiceover, slo-mo, the glancing connection of two lonely souls in the night."[12] *New York Times* film critic Elvis Mitchell wrote, "Startlingly effective. . . . The BMW Films tingle with zest in a way that car ads don't do anymore. . . . *The Hire* is what movies might be like if someone decided to give James Bond a soul."[13] *USA Today*'s Mike McCarthy wrote, "BMW has struck gold. . . . Three out of four stars." Even the antiestablishment, left-leaning *Village Voice,* a New York City weekly, praised *The Hire* series as, "A landmark in a hybridized media landscape," calling one of the films "ravishing."[14]

These publications and these writers hadn't ever written about BMW advertising in such terms; they hadn't paid attention at all. That was the point all along. Creative directors yearn to have some of their most inane advertising written about in the *New York Times* or *USA Today* advertising columns; it is a coup to have film and cultural writers take enough notice to write about the films, let alone in such glowing terms.

If simple Internet traffic is a measure of success, BMW Films made its mark. Nielsen/NetRatings reported that traffic to www.bmwfilms .com for one week in May 2001 spiked to 214,000 unique visitors, compared to only 138,000 surfers the previous week. Males—the target audience—comprised more than 68 percent of the audience, with 33 percent of the surfers falling between the ages of 35 and 49. Bullseye! On average, surfers spent more than six minutes on the site, and 39 percent of site visitors watched a movie on the site, not including those using the customized player. BMW Films was cited by Media Metrix, a company that tracks Net traffic "top newcomers," for attracting 787,000 unique visitors in six weeks.[15] For BMW, it was more traffic in six weeks than it had expected in six months, and the people fit BMW's targeted audience. More than 40 percent of visitors made $75,000 or more a year, and more than half of those visiting had broadband connections—another indicator of a high level of disposable income. How does this stack up against running a 30-second ad on NBC's *Friends,* where BMW can reach 10 million people for about $300,000 to $500,000? "Great," says McDowell. There is a larger principle at work. Run an ad on a popular TV show, and it could be blotted out by increasingly popular devices such as TiVo, which tapes programs on the equivalent of a computer hard drive and allows viewers to easily wipe out the ads when they play back the program. Indeed, as many as 80 percent of TiVo owners—which include a prominent number of BMW owners—use the devices to blot out ads on recorded programs. Even if BMW aired a 30-second ad it thought brilliant, people are becoming trained to ignore the ads or use the opportunity to go to the bathroom or raid the refrigerator. An effective ad has no impact if no one watches it. "It's the push-pull dynamic. Most of the time we are pushing messages, information, and deals on consumers and we hope for the best. Here, we created an incidence where they came looking for us," says Fallon group director and cofounding partner Fred Senn.

McDowell and Fallon began considering how to follow the success of *The Hire.* More short films? Wider distribution of the films on DVD? Run them in theaters as warm-ups to feature films, perhaps before feature films by the same director? Put them on videos and DVDs as warm-ups or bonuses to those directors' films? As soon as attention focused on how BMW had busted through the clutter like a 540i through a plate-glass window, other car companies began laying plans to make films, as Jaguar had tried to do. Indeed, by 2003, Buick and Nissan had both turned to Internet films.

BMW decided to produce another batch, believing that it still had the franchise on the medium. It had started the Net film sensation among car companies and did the best job. Fans, too, were clamoring for more stories. Three more films were commissioned for 2002 to help launch the all-new Z4 roadster. The directors this time were Joe Carnahan (*Walk Among the Tombstones, NARC*); Tony Scott (*Spy Game, Top Gun*); and John Woo. When these films hit the Internet, some reviewers commented that not only had BMW rival Mercedes-Benz aped the BMW films with a faux film-trailer-cum-ad that it aired in movie theaters, but a full-length feature film, *The Transporter*, directed by Corey Yuen and starring Jason Statham, seemed to copy the look and feel of *The Hire*.

The new batch, besides answering the demand from fans and customers for more Luc Velant, would also be key to solving a marketing problem for the Z4, around which all three of the new films would center. The predecessor of the Z4, the Z3, had become the 1990s definition of a "chick car." According to Hennie Chung, BMW North America's executive in charge of developing the Z4 with Munich and launching it in the United States, "Toward the end of the Z3's cycle, we had the stigma of being a 'girlie car,' which in Europe is sometimes called a 'hairdresser's' car." Men, she said, will not buy what they view as a "pink" car, but women will always buy a car with a masculine image. The Z3 didn't have the "pink" problem when it launched in 1996 as BMW's first U.S.-built car. The boost from its cameo role in *Goldeneye* helped. At that time, though, the only competitor to the Z3 was the much-lower-priced and less powerful Mazda Miata and the much pricier Mercedes SL. But in 1997, Porsche introduced its Boxster roadster and Mercedes brought out the SLK. As *Automotive News* put it, those roadsters "kicked sand in the Z3's face," even though Z3 outsold the newer competitors.[16] Despite the pink halo on the Z3, the car's customers were, in fact, 70 percent male, slightly higher than the 67 percent male average for the roadster segment and higher than the 65 percent male average for BMW overall. The problem remained, though. "You have to look beyond the registrations . . . the fact was that the Z3 was taken less seriously by serious roadster fans after the Boxster came out, and that kind of 'buzz' wasn't healthy for our brand or the Z line when we started planning the launch of the Z4," said Chung.

The reviews of the 2002 *The Hire* films were every bit as strong as those for the first group of films in 2001. *Adweek*'s Barbara Lippert said, "There's usually a curse with sequels, but these three are clever, challenging and great looking—easily as good as last year's batch. The third one, starring James Brown, is even better. . . ." More gratifying to BMW, Lippert wrote, "All the films are about mortality and money, and what a human life is really worth. . . . The series manages to get BMW away from its '80s yuppie image and into a thoughtful world of human possibility (where it helps to drive a really great car). In the past two years, the films have humanized Madonna and given new life to advertising. Can reinventing the wheel be far behind?"[17] Besides Net distribution, BMW distributed the films on DVD, aired them on the Independent Film Channel and Bravo cable channel, and even took a channel on DirectTV in spring 2003 to run the films. The awards, again, were plentiful. Fallon garnered "Best of Show" for the second consecutive year for BMW Films at the 2003 One Show Interactive awards.

One of the dynamics that appealed to Fallon creative director Bruce Bildstein was the idea of turning commercial ad production on its head. In producing an ad campaign, 10 to 15 percent of the budget is spent on production, and the rest is spent on distribution. BMW films reversed that by spending 80 percent of the budget on production, making the content so compelling that it would actually eliminate the need for high media spending. BMW and Fallon devised a method for comparing traditional TV and print campaigns with Web campaigns in terms of consumer participation. McDowell says past media buys were analyzed to determine how much time BMW's core customers were exposed to the automaker's message via broadcast commercials. Then BMW compared that figure of what it called "BMW minutes" to the amount of time its prospects spent on its Web site. McDowell was surprised to find that a major fraction of the total BMW minutes consumers were devoting to BMW were Internet minutes. That finding convinced BMW to invest in the films and in the quality of the Net content. Companies pay tens of millions to TV networks and cable stations just to buy time, and, clearly, BMW customers and potential customers were not nearly as invested in TV watching as they were in Net surfing. On a creative level, says Fallon creative director David Lubars, the films didn't look like ads because there were no "beauty shots" of the cars that would make the films seem and look like ads. The cars actually get very banged up in the films, just as they did in *Ronin* and *French Connection* and *Bullitt*. That surprised some of the directors who expected that they would have to baby the cars a bit. One of the disappointments with the last James Bond movie, said Lubars, was that the whole production, including star Pierce Brosnan, was too pretty, almost cartoonlike. Says Lubars, "We were relieved when Aston Martin bought back into the Bond movies. By the time they did, the specialness was over. We had done it.

It was time to move on. And the best review of the films was the *New York Times* reviewer who basically said that our films are what James Bond movies should be like. That was incredible."

"Traditional advertising will not go away, but we have to expand our palette of ways to reach increasingly hard-to-reach people," says Lubars. "The way to reach these people is to have them reach you, and that requires an entirely new set of creative tools." By late summer 2003, almost 50 million people had been to www.bmwfilms.com to view or download the eight films produced to date. But that number is only the tip of the iceberg. It doesn't reveal the pass-along factor, the number of people who went out of their way to view the films on a friend's computer or who had the player and films passed to them without going to the site. Tens of thousands DVDs were distributed. And then there is the tough-to-measure audience who viewed the films on cable and satellite TV. All of those millions of consumer contacts, which have resulted in BMW collecting millions of e-mail addresses and other information about the people who went to the site, came to BMW, instead of BMW pushing an ad message onto them. In that regard, BMW pulled off the *opposite* of marketing in the single-most-effective brand-building exercise the company has ever executed.

Herbert Quandt: The Quandts are a family with a difficult past. Though extremely private, they have been effective owners.

Stefan Quandt: Together with his mother, Johanna, carrying on the style and tradition of Herbert.

Chris Bangle and Dr. Burkhard Göschel: Enlightened risk takers on the firing line in a new era of rapid growth.

Dr. Helmut Panke has proven to be the right CEO at the right time and with the right team-building style.

Dr. Wolfgang Reitzle: His unparalleled taste and aesthetic instincts led to the best-designed cars in the world.

Bernd Pischetsrieder: Though smooth and smart, he was undone by his flawed attempt to grow the company through the acquisition of The Rover Group. After his ouster, he won the job of chairman of Volkswagen AG.

Eberhard von Kuenheim: Having led the company for two decades as chairman and a third as supervisory board chairman, he carried the title "Mr. BMW." His tenure is unmatched in the modern auto industry.

The company's roots are in aviation. No wonder their cars make drivers feel like they are flying.

The Four Cylinders Headquarters Building: BMW is steeped in an engineering and innovation culture, and defined by the vehicles it makes.

The 1928 Dixi 3/15: Not a homegrown BMW, but it got the car business started.

The BMW 328: It established the prewar mystique for speed and style.

The BMW 2002: It began the sports sedan phenomenon that would define BMW's postwar boom.

The Original 6 Series: Paul Bracq's coupe for the ages.

The 1998 3 Series: From its classic look to its extraordinary balance, handling, and rear-wheel drive architecture, the 3 Series is widely considered to be the world's most perfect car.

"The Hire:" Director John Woo chats with actor Clive Owen in a scene from BMW Films. The film series, widely watched on the Internet, set a new benchmark in advertising creativity and strengthened BMW's already formidable brand image.

The Rolls-Royce Phantom: The best "Roller" in decades, with BMW know-how to boot. But at $350,000, does the world want a new Bavarian Rolls?

The Mini Cooper: Salvaged from the Rover deal, it's lighting up the small-car market worldwide. What's not to love?

BMW Motorbikes: Cycles for men in suits. "Real" BMW executives have ridden or ride motorcycles, exemplifying the sporty, two-wheel, unsung side of the company.

The X5 SUV: The first BMW utility, it's the best in its class for road manners — even if it's not much of an off-roader.

The 7 Series: Techno-marvel or flawed flagship? Only time will tell.

The Z4: A land shark with a new design scheme that BMW fans either love or hate.

The Ultimate Stylists

FIVE

Those whom heaven helps we call the sons of heaven.
They do not learn this by learning. They do not work it by working.
They do not reason it by using reason.
To let understanding stop at what cannot be understood is a high
*   attainment.*
Those who cannot do it will be destroyed on the lathe of heaven.

—CHUANG TSE

No designer in the auto industry, perhaps no designer in any commercial enterprise in the new century, has been talked about, debated, and scorned as much as BMW's chief of design Chris Bangle, who cited the preceding quote from Chuang Tse during an interview with me in 2003.

Bangle has been the head of vehicle design at BMW since 1992. He was hired by former product development chief Wolfgang Reitzle, himself acknowledged to be one of the industry's most talented product executives during the second half of the twentieth century. By the time Reitzle resigned in 1999, Bangle had headed design for seven of BMW's most successful yet most tumultuous years—successful due to the brand's sales growth and attendant critical praise, tumultuous since between 1994 and 2000 the company was bedeviled by the ill-fitting and costly acquisition of the British Rover Group. It must be said that being head of design under Reitzle is like being Alfred Hitchcock's cinematographer. Hitchcock so intensely molded every frame of his films that his personality, more than that of any of his actors or technicians, dominated his films. In a similar fashion, Reitzle's personality simply fills any room and vehicle program he enters.

More than a few auto executives at other companies, industry analysts, and journalists refer to Reitzle's school of product design as "Savile Row," a reference to the London neighborhood known for the world's finest tailoring. This flattering comparison stems from the notion that Reitzle's vehicles look fresh and attractive 5, 10, and even 15 years after their introduction. The auto industry is littered with vehicles that look bad from the start or dated and tired after just a few years—in short, cars that don't measure up to BMWs. On Reitzle's watch as product boss, BMW brought out two generations of 3 Series, 5 Series, and 7 Series, one 8 Series, one X5, a Z1 and Z3. The best example of Reitzle's sure hand is probably the 1998 3 Series, widely considered to be the best current all-around motorcar in the world. "The 3 is set apart from just about any car I can think of. . . . It came out in 1998 and will look fresh and classic in 2020," acknowledges Ford's top designer J Mays.

"Reitzle is one of the very few people in the industry who can clear a room with his opinion, because when it comes to a design, establishing the way something should be and how it should look, he is very nearly always right," adds General Motors product chief Bob Lutz. He ought to know. Lutz is about the only other executive in the industry who can clear a room of chatter in the same way. Lutz was BMW's board member in charge of sales and marketing during the early 1970s. "People who know exactly how something should look before it is finished are few and far between," says Lutz, who briefly courted Reitzle to come to GM after he left Ford in 2002. Reitzle ultimately became chairman of Linde AG in Germany, a diversified company that sells natural gas technology and forklifts, among other things. "Product Czar," "Product Lord," and "Product Guru" are terms that crop up in a string of newspaper and magazine articles about BMW and Reitzle, seeming appropriate accolades given the sway he held at BMW.

It couldn't have been easy for Bangle, who likes to work with a large design palette, to toil under Reitzle. At the same time, Bangle benefited from the presence of such a singular force. Many car companies, such as GM before Lutz arrived, develop vehicles by committee. A good idea or design is often tortured until it confesses to being a mere mediocre common denominator pleasing a group of perhaps 10 or 12 engineers, accountants, and perhaps a marketer. Given the post-Reitzle product offered by Bangle and an almost entirely new management board, it's clear that Bangle did not always agree with Reitzle's relentless insistence on ultra-clean, smooth-sheet-metal surfaces, traditional twin-kidney grilles, and minimal front-end overhang. As soon as he was able, Bangle broke free of the handcuffs Reitzle had slapped on him and immediately began writing a new BMW design strategy with Reitzle's successor, Wolfgang Ziebart, and then Ziebart's successor, Burkhard Goeschel, and BMW's management board bought into it. The first car substantially designed after Reitzle's departure, the Z4, would never have cleared the "Product Guru's" filter. That's not to say the Z4 is poorly designed. Design, after all, is as subjective as art, music, or religion. Who is to say what is good? Bangle is going his own way, and so far BMW's board of management, the *Vorstand*, is showing confidence in his partnership with Goeschel.

Yet somehow, four years after Reitzle's departure, Bangle still labors in the long shadow cast by his former boss. And he, not Goeschel, is the lightning rod for praise and protest over the new designs. People inside and outside BMW say Goeschel is a well-rounded, affable, and talented engineer who has what's known around BMW as a "sensitive bottom," which means he is good at feeling all the right feedback from cars in development. When Goeschel drives a prototype on a test course or track, he is one of those canny and invaluable engineers who knows whether the tires should be a centimeter wider or the shock absorbers adjusted another millimeter or two. In stark contrast to Reitzle, he is apparently content to let others, like Bangle, occupy center stage; Goeschel handles the spotlight fine when it is thrust at him, but he does not appear to seek it.

As BMW progresses through its most aggressive product and brand expansion ever without the man who defined its greatest era of success, it's worth examining both Reitzle and Bangle, including where they came from, what they have done, and how their thinking and talents have driven BMW.

————

As head of BMW design, Chris Bangle hires and manages a small army of more than 300 designers who generate ideas, sketches, and models, not only for a vehicle's outside appearance, but the inside as well, including the thousands of bits and pieces that make up its total design statement. Sure, the general shape and proportions, the curves and bends, come from the designer. But so does each inch of the dashboard; every bezel, bumper, and button arise from a designer's pen or computer. This is no different at BMW, of course, than at any car company—or *any* consumer product company, whether it makes sneakers, skateboards, or staplers. Yet while the stapler designer may enjoy 15 minutes of fame if some obscure trade publication thinks he or she has sung a new note in the grand continuum of stapler design, Bangle is under near-constant scrutiny outside the walls of BMW; inside BMW, the pressure is even more intense. Not only does he have a following of millions of global BMW customers minutely judging his group's work, but that work is also targeted by the broader design community for often public criticism because BMW has long set a standard of simple design elegance and athleticism in machinery that all designers have studied, admired, copied, and benchmarked. Despite the staunch public support of the BMW management board, the *Vorstand* behind Bangle and Goeschel, it can't be easy for the sales and marketing executives who read the sometimes withering reviews of the designs in the media. To be fair, Bangle is not designing in a vacuum. The *Vorstand* members cast votes for designs before they are advanced for full development; if one design falls flat in the market there is blame enough to go around. No product category is as globally celebrated as motorcars. And every designer in the business would like to design a vehicle to adorn the spectacular hardware that lives and breathes beneath a BMW's skin. In short, they'd all like to *be* Bangle— to have his opportunity, his brand, and his palette.

Is his job any more stressful than that of J Mays at Ford or Trevor Creed, chief of design at Chrysler? Modesty demands he demur. Still, as one would expect from an internationally scrutinized and even hounded designer, he doesn't give much ground to people, even in his own peer group of designers outside BMW, who say his design strategy is wrong for the BMW brand.

"We aren't copying anyone else's design language, not even our own, and I think that makes some people uncomfortable," says Bangle.

———

Passing time with Bangle is like hanging out with an amiable college professor at a campus café, albeit one who lapses into German or Italian to make a point. He willingly discusses the reasoning behind the designs that emerge from his shop, wanting us to understand what he's doing. An American, he's spent most of his professional life in Europe, working at first at GM's Opel division, then at Fiat, and on to BMW. He is the first BMW design chief to be formally schooled in design, having studied at the Art Center College of Design in Pasadena, California. He will happily give up chatting about car design to discuss art, museums, literature, film, or even Greek mythology. For all the pressure, unlike so many other creative kingpins, Bangle does not seem consumed by the work to the exclusion of his family or outside interests. During interviews with him in 2002 and 2003, including sessions at the chaotic Detroit, Frankfurt, and Paris auto shows, Bangle appeared alternately bemused, bored, exhausted, ticked off, and ebullient.

At the 2002 Paris Motor Show, the Z4 roadster's debut received mixed reviews, both on the show floor and in the media in subsequent months. Bangle was as unflinching about the criticism as he was when the 7 Series was shown a year earlier at the Frankfurt show to a somewhat savage reception. "I think we are doing something that the rest of the design world hasn't caught up with yet. . . . We aren't doing the predictable, and we aren't copying the past," said Bangle, looking a little like he knows something most of us don't.

Working in a country that got along for decades employing car designers who were shop-rat engineers with a flair for drawing, Bangle comes across more like a tweedy history professor who picks up his kids at Gymboree in a station wagon. He's not what an outsider expects of BMW's chief designer. Given BMW's seriousness about performance, one might more likely expect some Bavarian-accented gearhead in a white lab coat. He can present ideas and arguments like a seminary instructor, albeit one who is frequently found rearranging furniture on the church's altar. In fact, the most pondered, dissected, criticized, and lionized auto designer of the new century, scratching his pencil at the center of BMW's hallowed "FIZ" research and development center in Munich, is a transplanted Wisconsin boy schooled in California and trained at Italian carmaker Fiat.

Bangle was born in Ohio, but spent his formative years in Wausau, Wisconsin. Chris says his father, Edward Bangle, was, like most aeronautics engineers and craftspeople, a great enthusiast about high-performance machinery such as airplane engines and cars. During World War II, Edward worked for North American Aviation as the assembly chief for the P-51 Mustang. That gives rise, perhaps, to a bit of historical irony in that the very engines Edward Bangle helped make went up against Luftwaffe planes outfitted with BMW engines. Originally from California, Edward and his wife Lura traveled extensively, moving some 20 times before settling in Wausau. Says Bangle, "One of my earliest memories associated with the automotive world is the phonograph records he [Bangle's father] gave me with recordings of the most famous Grand Prix, 'The Sounds of Nurburgring.' I often went to races with him and then reproduced them on my toy track where model Ferrari Testarossas, GTOs and Lotuses went head to head."[1]

Bangle's first brush with the BMW mystique came when his father took him to a car show specifically to see the Isetta, the postwar curiosity BMW was forced to build from the bones of one of its world-renowned motorcycles as it struggled to resurrect its factory destroyed by the war's bombs. The Isetta answered Europe's need for small cars that only sipped gas. As a boy, Bangle became a fan of BMW's famous motorcycles. "Motorcycles ridden by men in suits," Bangle says.[2]

Located dead center in Wisconsin, Wausau embodies, socially and culturally, middle-of-the-road America. A provincial American small town that remained largely insulated from the social tumult of the 1960s when Bangle was an adolescent, Wausau is home to one of the largest U.S. insurance companies, Wausau, and shares Wisconsin's pronounced German culture, the state having attracted large numbers of German and Scandinavian immigrants in the nineteenth and early twentieth centuries. Bangle remembers his Wisconsin schooling fondly. There he took advantage of the technical disciplines that were part of the middle school and high school curricula in the 1960s: drafting, printing, wood shop, and metal shop. It was in Wausau's public schools that Bangle first began drafting designs of cars, boats, planes, houses, and spaceships.

He entered the University of Wisconsin in 1975 and took the philosophy, literature, psychology, and history courses that fit his aspirations of becoming a Methodist minister. But theological pursuits soon fell prey to thoughts of design, and a year later he submitted an application to the Pasadena Art Center that included comic strips along with sketches of sewing machines, telephones, and cars. Bangle abandoned car design for a while and filled his portfolio with drawings of space vehicles and hardware and began taking an interest in the special effects that were revolutionizing moviemaking. In mid-1981, Bangle scored an interview with Disney, but on the eve of the meeting, he was offered a job at General Motors. He moved to Germany to work at GM's Opel division.

One of his early successes was the interior design of the Opel Junior, which featured a modular dashboard whose instrumentation could be added or deleted based on the driver's preferences. The idea won a European design award. Bangle was unusual among his colleagues at Opel in that he was as interested, if not more so, in the *interior* design as he was in the bent metal of the exterior.

In 1985, he was offered a job at Fiat to work on styling car bodies, which he hadn't done at Opel. Fiat design boss Pier Giorgio Tronville expressly wanted a designer who had specialized in interiors and who could arguably design exteriors from the driver's vantage point better than a designer who was trying to create only an artistic exterior shape. "I was being asked to design a car from the inside out, without sacrificing the interface with the customer, which was a unique starting point, especially at Fiat," says Bangle.

Bangle received invaluable technical training at Fiat, yet Fiat was a frustrating place to work. Neglecting its in-house designers, it most often chose final designs that had been produced at outside studios. The staff designers' role was to generate ideas and provide counterpoints to the work of the outside designers. Before he left Fiat, though, Bangle had rammed through two significant designs of his own: the 1993 Fiat coupe and the 1994 Alfa Romeo 145. One Italian motoring magazine lavished praise on the coupe: "You could take apart every piece of the car, dropping every single part in a museum as a piece of art."

BMW lost its design chief, Claus Luthe, in 1990 under tragic circumstances when Luthe stabbed his drug-addicted son to death during an altercation at the Luthe home. The son was reportedly threatening his mother with the knife when Claus intervened. For the next two years, Hans Braun, head of interior design, led the staff. But he was a placeholder only, as Reitzle looked for a replacement for Luthe who might, under his close mentoring, usher in a new era of design at BMW.

Fortunes were changing fast at BMW. Though its cars were still highly respected, the company hadn't carved out a strategy for the 1990s to meet the challenge from the Japanese premium brands launched in North America, which seemed destined at the time for Europe as well, though in 2003 Lexus, Acura, and Infiniti still were barely marketed on the continent. BMW's worldwide sales in 1990 were 514,000 and climbed to 582,000 by 1992. In the all-important North American market, though, business was plummeting. The stock market crash of 1987 and subsequent recession staggered BMW in its most important market; sales had fallen from 96,000 in the United States in 1986 to 53,000 in 1991. More alarming even than the recession-induced slump, though, was that BMW was on the verge of becoming passé. BMW North America chief Karl Gerlinger, for example, was greeted by a front-page newspaper headline during the 1990 Detroit Motor Show that proclaimed a list of trends that were "in" and "out." Horrified, he read, "What's Out?—BMW. What's In? Lexus."

Toyota launched its Lexus brand and Nissan introduced Infiniti in 1988, with Acura having launched two years earlier. BMW and Mercedes started to pay grudging attention only in 1990 or 1991. "The Germans saw the Japanese as appliance makers, and didn't think people would take them seriously in the luxury segment. . . . Of course, they [the Germans] misread the market entirely at first," says J.D. Power and Associates chairman Dave Power. Adds BMW's then–marketing director, Carl Flesher, "There was denial, no doubt. We didn't want to believe that the Japanese could build cars engineered as wonderfully as BMWs, and I still don't think they can create the same driving dynamics. But there are plenty of people who value what they do more than they value what we do." Meanwhile, BMW managers noted the dark harbinger that Volkswagen, at one time North America's leading import brand, was seriously considering exiting the market in 1992, emulating the defeated Peugeot, Fiat, British Leyland, and Renault.

When Bangle arrived in 1992, BMW's design mantra was protecting its identity at all costs, and there was little appetite for risk. It was an approach that left all BMWs looking much the same from the mid-1960s to 1992—like sausages cut to different lengths. Great sausages, but sausages nonetheless. The 5 Series looked like a cut-down 7 Series, and the 3 Series looked like a cut-down 5 Series. This idea had served BMW pretty well, but Reitzle knew a new era was dawning. He had already been hatching a scheme with chairman Eberhard von Kuenheim to expand BMW through the acquisition of brands like Rolls-Royce and Bentley, hopefully Land Rover and Mini, and possibly even Porsche. Those brands would need design leadership, but besides growing through acquisition, BMW would have to expand its own product line since it probably couldn't survive with only sedans and coupes. Along with the need for a credible roadster, a curious but growing phenomenon was taking hold in the United States: An increasing number of people were buying pickup trucks and sport utility vehicles as personal transportation. How would this trend affect BMW's business?

Hiring Luthe's replacement was left entirely to Reitzle, who himself believed he would succeed von Kuenheim as chairman in 1993. Design was Reitzle's province, and the designers themselves didn't have much status in the company. Boyke Boyer, head of exterior design under Bangle, says that at the time of Bangle's arrival, the design team was near the bottom of the corporate food chain. Working for two years without a design director, the designers lacked a leader to champion their cause and nurture a point of view. Designers had no voice in any top-level meetings. "The attitude was, 'Oh, those designers, pshh, pshh. They're nothing but a bunch of picture makers!' " says Boyer.[3]

The company had gone outside Germany once before for a designer with great success. French-born Paul Bracq was head of design from 1970 to 1974, and he led design on two of BMW's most revered models, the original 6 Series and the 1972 Turbo concept that was shown in conjunction with the Olympic Games in Munich that year. Reitzle had heard of Bangle and met him at the Geneva auto shows in 1991 and 1992. Says Reitzle, "I was looking for someone who had a real global vision of design, especially because of how fast things were changing in North America. But also someone who was steeped in European culture and sensibilities. The person I was looking for also had to be a motivator of people. Chris is funny, too, and that I thought was a good asset in terms of attracting good young people." But, Reitzle adds—and this is key to understanding the dynamic tension between the two men during the 1990s—Bangle "was never in charge of design. . . . I kept it." Reitzle hovered over design with even greater zeal and control after 1993, when Bernd Pischetsrieder, not Reitzle, was tapped to be chairman.

Indeed, as designs rolled out after Bangle's arrival, including upgrades to the 1991 3 Series, the 1996 Z3, the 1997 5 Series, the 1998 3 Series, the 1999 X5 all-activity vehicle, and so on, Reitzle declares, "I was influencing every last radius of sheet metal." But, he added, "Chris was the motivator I wanted for the design staff and the one executing. He brought great, interesting, and talented people. He created a super atmosphere. He was the best person I could have found, and he built and ran a thrilling and motivating design team."

Whether it was an internal design study, a concept car for an auto show, or an actual production vehicle, Bangle and his designers would come up with their concept of what a vehicle should look like. Then, according to Reitzle, he would invariably say, "Go ahead. You get that team to produce yours, and I'll get three design teams for competing concepts." Reitzle wanted new people and new ideas flowing into BMW, but he also is a disciplinarian obsessed about the connection between brand and design. He recalls, "The concepts Chris's teams came up with were often strange to me. . . . They had what I call Pasadena lines." The reference is to the art school Bangle and many other BMW designers attended. Reitzle: "This is more for Honda or one of the Korean companies, I thought most of the time. . . . This is not for BMW. And then he would click his heels together and say, 'Jawohl, boss!' And we would laugh."

That Bangle was an American was greeted with a wary mixed reaction. Though he was by the time of his hiring head of the Fiat Design Center in Turin, one magazine called him "The Invisible Man." The attitude was, "BMW's head of design born in Ohio and raised in Wisconsin?" Though thoroughly German, BMW had already proven itself progressive and global in its search for ideas and talent, with French, Japanese, Italian, and Dutch designers. The United States was becoming BMW's biggest growth opportunity, so having a head of design plugged into its culture as a native certainly couldn't hurt.

BMW has design studios around the world to salt the company with different design perspectives. Designs for the 7 Series, Z4 roadster and 2004 1 Series, for example, which will be sold on five continents, originated at Designworks, the California design firm that did contract work for BMW up until 1995, when BMW gobbled it up. Started in Malibu, California, in 1972 by Pasadena Art Center professor Charles Pelly, Designworks still does contract work for other non-auto-industry companies, just as it had before the BMW buyout.

Buying Designworks in 1995 was Bangle's idea. He calls it a "critical listening post" for BMW. Though BMW is the subsidiary's chief client, Bangle has been careful not to tinker too much with the firm's culture. As a designer he understands the value of the firm being outside the close orbit of Munich. In fact, he has used Designworks to shake up the BMW design culture in Munich. BMW provides 60 percent of Designworks' business; the rest comes from a diverse group of clients, including Adidas, Atomic Snowboards, Nokia, Microsoft, Hewlett-Packard, and John Deere. Yes, this BMW unit designed a John Deere lawn tractor as well as an earth mover! It has designed chairs for renowned manufacturer izzydesign that are worthy of both office and art gallery. "This is an invaluable resource for BMW, being able to have its designers working for other companies in other categories," says Bangle. He adds, "The learning, the inspiration and cross-pollination that occurs—it keeps designers fresh."

––––––––

When the 2002 7 Series was unveiled at the 2001 Frankfurt Motor Show, a buzz filled the hall that lasted well into the next day. A DaimlerChrysler *Vorstand* member standing next to me examined the car's tail end and said, "It's horrible, and I'm not just saying that. The 3 Series and 5 Series are two of the best cars in the world, and I admit that. But this is horrible."

The 7 Series was largely developed by Wolfgang Reitzle. Yet, he maintains that the final designs for the trunk lid and the front fascia—the two most criticized elements of the car's exterior design—were not approved by him before he left in 1999 for Ford. Pischetsrieder, too, insists changes were made after he left. BMW officials steadfastly maintain, though, that the two men signed off on the designs, though there were aspects of the 7 Series, such as the trunk design, that both Pischetsrieder and Reitzle fought against. Reitzle initiated the development of the iDrive system, which is meant to control just about all of the car's functions other than driving, including the radio, air-conditioning, and navigation system, by way of a joystick-style electronic controller knob mounted in the center console. The iDrive has been savaged by many would-be customers, actual customers, and journalists from both the motoring and consumer electronics press. Says auto journalist Paul Eisenstein, editor-publisher of thecarconnection.com and self-professed gadget freak, "There's something about the iDrive that can send even a computer geek into apoplexy. Once you get the hang of it, the system usually does do what it's supposed to. But many functions are counterintuitive, and trying to get help, either from the manual or the car's voice control system, isn't as easy as it should be." For people who don't want to fiddle with the console controller while driving, the hundreds of functions can also be controlled by voice commands, but this, too, proved unreliable and confounding as voice-activation technology in 2000 and 2001, when the final touches were being applied, had not quite advanced to the same point as BMW's vision.

Even design school professors have weighed in on both ends of the 7 Series and the iDrive. Imre Molnar, dean of the College of Creative Studies in Detroit, deemed both the iDrive and the 7 Series' tail as "inexcusable." Tom Tjaarda, the independent Italian designer, was uncharacteristically outspoken given that designers do not often slam their peers in public. Tjaarda complained, "Unfortunately, the rear end was the first I saw of the car, and I could not believe my eyes. . . . It is lumpy, with confusing lines. And it looks as if the boot is open when it's closed."[4] Having one of its creations so ravaged in the media is unfortunate new turf for BMW. The car's proportions and its "tumble-home" (boatbuilding jargon meaning "curvature of the hull," it is used by car designers to describe a car's proportions and curb stance) appear straight out of Wolfgang's Reitzle's style manual with classic BMW proportions. Its ride and handling are first class. As the auto industry's über-consultant on productivity, Ron Harbour, says, "It rides like the frame is carved out of stone. . . . It's exquisite." The vast majority of the motor press agrees with this glowing assessment of the ride.

It's the car's clothing that upsets the critics: turn-signal lamps that sit like white Dame Edna (British cross-dresser celebrity) eyeglasses over the headlights; a tail (where a curved fender intersects abruptly with the high trunk lid) that, as one German journalist quipped, "looks as if a dining room table had been dropped on the car." Others offer the spitball that the trunk lid looks as if it had been bought off the shelf, designed for another car, and stuck on the rear of the vaunted 7 Series as an afterthought.

In one of the greatest examples of public relations overkill ever devised by a company, BMW in the fall of 2001 gathered some 800 automotive journalists from around the world in Munich for daylong presentations about the new 7 Series. But there was to be no driving. They came all the way to Munich to be *schooled* on the car. The vehicle's complexity, it seemed, required a special trip just for the preview. Besides its new engine and transmission, the 7 Series has more than 123 electric motors, 38 in the seats alone. Since the seats contain up to 18 fans for heating and cooling, a BMW acoustics expert worked overtime to dampen their noise. Then there's the iDrive, which controls some 700 functions for the telephone, entertainment, climate, and so on. To make room for it, the gearshift moved from the console to the steering column. To shift the automatic transmission, the driver gently pulls on an electronic stalk that feels just a little flimsy by Teutonic standards. It certainly isn't positioned for frequent fondling while driving at high speed on the autobahn like a console-mounted standard transmission or even an automatic shifter. It was all unsettlingly new for BMW—or any other automaker.

Fortune magazine, whose readership is the heart of BMW's customer base, screeched in a headline: "Do You Think This Car Is Ugly? If So, You Aren't Alone."[5] The article began, "The latest version of BMW's flagship 7 Series does not go on sale in the U.S. until Jan. 19, but already it is being raked over at auto shows, 'dissed' in trade publications, and badmouthed on the Web." "DESIGN TALK GETS UGLY FOR BMW 7," announced a front-page headline in *Automotive News,* a trade weekly.[6] *Automotive News* reporter Mark Rechtin opened his review with, "Let's get one thing clear: I am not calling for Chris Bangle to be fired."[7] No designer in the car business had ever been discussed in such personal and overtly hostile terms in the business and trade press.

Such caustic reportage about a core product was new for BMW. But if the criticism of the 7 Series makes either chairman Helmut Panke or Bangle cringe in private, they don't let on. About the 7 Series, Panke says, "The comments about the new design are more critical than I expected." He admits, "We had 20 different design concepts [and] I had put my vote on a different one that was more evolutionary."[8] Nine months after that comment, the 7 Series was selling well in both Germany and North America, despite isolated accounts of BMW customers asking dealers to take the car back a week after buying it because of the dang-blasted iDrive.

Over pretzels and Alsatian wine in his corporate dining room, Panke said in July 2002, "We are leading. Leading with the iDrive system, leading with the ride and handling, with the packaging, the interior. And when you lead you don't take everyone with you. There are those who don't follow. But it doesn't mean just because you don't get everyone going with you that you stop leading. I will tell you, though; we will sell more 7 Series in this generation than the old generation." Panke says the 7 Series was designed to be more "authoritative" than the previous 7 Series, which was to make it more attractive in the United States and Japan. "Look at the athletes of the 1990s like Michael Jordan, and how muscled they are, not like the sports heros of the 1960s and 70s, who were more lanky." The more audacious design has been more popular in the United States and Japan than in Europe. "In Europe," notes Panke, "people wear fur coats with the fur on the inside, not the outside like in the United States Satisfying both markets with new designs is getting more difficult." On a separate occasion, though, Panke made an admission about the forthcoming 1 Series that could just as easily be applied to the 7 Series: "The biggest thing to guard against is disappointment. . . . Many companies do not appreciate this. You can get 98 percent of a vehicle right, but the wrong 2 percent can spoil everything else." It's true.

Still, Bangle has, some might say, exhaustively defended and explained the 7 Series since BMW debuted the new flagship sedan on September 11, 2001. The 7 Series, he says, is much taller now to allow more headroom, and the rear passengers sit farther back and have more foot room and legroom. In aerodynamic terms, there is a direct connection between the peak point on the roof and the spoiler on the trunk. When one goes up, the other has to go up, he says. The trunk lid, while a bit clunky, allows for much easier access to the trunk for as many as four full-size golf bags, which is the new standard for trunk size and access—especially in Japan, where 7 Series owners frequently find themselves traveling in groups of four together with their golf clubs.

The introduction of the controversial iDrive had to begin with the highest-priced BMW, the 7 Series. Every company, when introducing new technology, whether a stability control system or an iDrive, puts it in the priciest vehicle first, where the profit margins are fattest. The problem is that more expensive vehicles tend to draw a company's richest and, yes, oldest customers. The 7 Series' average buyer was about 55, and at that age people historically have difficulty adapting to new, gadgety technology. As sales volume increases, costs come down, and the technology can be put into lower-priced vehicles. Furthermore, as an entirely new approach to cabin controls, iDrive naturally had some bugs to be worked out. The risk in introducing breakthrough technology is that the very people who are most interested in it, the gearheads, are also the harshest critics if it doesn't work perfectly from the start, especially after spending between $70,000 and $110,000 on the car. While BMW worked to fix and update the software in the iDrive system in the first year, early 7 Series buyers struggled and criticized the system on Internet message boards and to the company's customer-complaint phone line. "The next generation of iDrive in the 5 Series will be better than in the 7 Series, and I suspect the one after that will be better than in the 5, and the improvements will be dialed back into the 7 Series," admits product development chief Burkhard Goeschel.

Adrian van Hooydonk, president of Designworks and the man who first sketched the new 7 and developed its styling, says that BMW's flagship car was in danger of being stifled by the weight of its own history. Says Hooydonk: "Over the years, we've been very successful in defining the BMW look, which we've done by being very precise in our designs. But when you make only incremental changes, you find yourself in a corridor that gets narrower and narrower. Finally, you reach a dead end, and by then, the customer has abandoned you for a car that's fresh and new. We had to break through that corridor. The goal for the new 7 was to push the boundaries as far as we could."[9]

The 7 Series evolved through its development from the time the first concepts were created. Bangle typically has five or six teams initially competing for the right to design a new model, internal competition being vital to the culture he is creating at BMW. "The key here is diversity," says Bangle. If everyone on the design staff thought the same way, BMW wouldn't have a design culture; it'd just have mass opinion. That's why internal competition is a fundamental premise of the organization. It gives the company a dynamic exchange of viewpoints. The outcome, says Bangle, is far more powerful than what a single person could produce. Once a design is designated the front-runner at the start of a new model, another team is always assigned the task of creating a counterpoint design. Such was the case in the competition to design the new 7 Series. The early favorite had been a conservative design closer to the old 7 Series, perhaps the one Panke liked. But van Hooydonk's counterdesign eventually emerged the winner. Despite the fact that BMW is expected to have a redesigned tail on the 7 Series for the 2005 model, Bangle is comfortable with the car. He maintains, despite the 7 Series controversy, that the car is a linchpin in BMW's whole new design. "The model is a quantum leap into the future. . . . We had to design a car to fit the bill, one that still mirrors power, sportiness, and grace, but which also embraces new technology. It required a whole new design language to implement," says Bangle.

The other important vehicle in this new wave is the car that followed the 7 Series a year later at the 2002 Paris Motor Show, the Z4 roadster. It employs Bangle's so-called flame-surfacing idea, the notion being that BMWs should have lines and surfaces that occur in nature, like the swirls of a flame, as well as in geometry. The contoured surfaces of the Z4 caused nearly as much controversy as the 7 Series. "Imagine a bookshelf where books are initially stacked at the extremes of the shelf to establish parameters before the next volumes are placed closer to the middle," says Bangle. He says he wants to move from the extremes to the center in establishing a new identity for each model range. This also counts for interior design, where ergonomics play a larger role due to the advent of new electronic technology. Unlike the 7, the Z4 doesn't employ the iDrive system. The personality and real-life driving of a roadster don't lend themselves to such runaway automation. The small size of the cockpit and the prevalence of manual, stick-shift transmissions in the roadster segment would have made the console-mounted iDrive a problem.

Besides, there just aren't as many functions to control—no rear-seat climate control, for example, to worry about.

Amid all the hubbub, BMW is coping for the first time with a real division of opinion among the automotive press. The majority of high-profile critics don't unabashedly applaud the new BMWs as they once did. *Automobile*'s senior editor Mark Gilles wrote of the Z4, "Up close and in person, particularly with smaller rims, the Z4 is just plain goofy-looking. All those creases and lines distract you from what are essentially classic roadster proportions, which is worrisome, because one of the primary reasons for buying a roadster is to have a beautiful car in the driveway or the garage, a car you don't have to explain to your friends."[10] My colleague at *USA Today*, James Healey, on the other hand, wrote, "The school bus chuffed and squealed to stop to discharge a third-grader at the corner. All the kids aboard crowded the front windows, exclaiming over the BMW Z4 parked at the intersection. Thus, the Z4 easily passed a key test. A sports car should radiate so much fun that kids instantly connect. Would you want to drive what you thought was a hot-mobile only to find out the young ones were chuckling at the buffoon driving the dork buggy? No worry in BMW's redo of its small two-seater. The 2003 BMW Z4 is about as close to the perfect sports car as anybody has come, especially at a five-figure price."[11] Mark Vaughn of *Autoweek*, a magazine especially attentive to design, said, "[T]he new roadster sure looks good. Or, at least not frightening. After that last 7 Series, we were worried. Granted, there will be those who see only pictures of it and say the wavy lines on the Z4's flanks look schizophrenic, the grille and hood lines are clichés and the way the high-rounded deck-lid sits in back is just plain whack. But that's if you've only seen pictures. . . . We spent two days in the cars and liked the way the pinched, flowing edges lined up and undulated along the sides, as well as the sharply angular integrated roll bars and the steep rake of the windshield. It looks best in the flesh, we think."[12]

Will BMW lose some customers who don't go for the new designs? Of course, just like some Catholics stopped going to church when the Second Vatican Council did away with Latin-only masses. But for every rigid BMW purist who has a closet of blue suits and white silk pocket squares, there are probably two buyers, and younger ones at that, who *have to have* the new BMW 745 or Z4 for the same reasons that the BMW defectors and trashers passed it over.

———

When discussing BMW's design focus, Bangle likes to tell the tale of meeting with a BMW finance director who was carping at him for selecting materials he found too costly, especially since the customer has little or no contact with them. Just then, a design staffer brought to Bangle the prototype of a future sedan's middle console. The staffer lifted the lid and asked Bangle to reach his hand inside and feel around. "The supplier is having a terrible time getting the texture right in here. The surface is not good, Herr Bangle." The finance man watched for Bangle's reaction, given the conversation they'd just been having. Bangle is fond of getting his point across with metaphors, and he showed the finance man a picture of an ancient Gothic cathedral in Munich adorned with carved cherubs. "Those cherubs cost a lot to put on the church . . . but can you imagine the cathedral without its cherubs?" The accountant shook his head. "Funny thing about Gothic churches. You get cherubs regardless of whether you look at them or not. Making cherubs is how the craftsmen of the time honored their religion. So is your problem with the cherubs or with the church?" Then Bangle handed him the console and told him to poke his fingers inside the dark pocket to feel the surfaces that people will be rubbing their hands on as they grope for CDs, a cell phone, or gloves. As he did so, recalls Bangle, his eyes gleamed with comprehension.[13]

Says Bangle, "We don't make automobiles, which are utilitarian machines you use to get from point *A* to point *B*. We make 'cars,' moving *works of art* that express the driver's love of quality." It is precisely this sort of statement that gets Bangle's peers, including some he went to design school with, muttering around the auto show floors about his folly, his preoccupation with conceptual design and the subjugation of vehicle design axioms.

Where Bangle and BMW's design philosophy does pay off in both real and conceptual terms is the (often expensive) attention paid to detail, such as BMW's use of real wood veneers instead of the more easily molded but tacky plastic faux woods. Referring to the plastic simulated wood, Bangle says, "Those customers will wonder how else we're snookering them." Americans, far more than Europeans, love real wood in a car's cabin, and Bangle is no exception. "People are pay-ing a lot of money, in some cases a small fortune, to drive a car as *we* define it."

When Bangle arrived at BMW in 1992, he found a company that was making scads of money, but that had a befuddled design depart-ment. Bangle understands the psyche of the designer very well. "Emo-tional, sensitive, often egocentric artists don't respond to cold, rational arguments. They must be shielded from the comments of people who don't understand them or the artistic process." One of the changes he instituted, therefore, was to insulate designers from engineers and shield them from an engineer's comments and judgments too early in the process of choosing and finalizing a design. One member of his staff, Bangle says, who had worked up a design he was especially proud of, heard a manufacturing engineer denounce it as requiring too much new tooling. That designer was out for several days "sick"—probably updating his resume, Bangle reckoned. Manufacturing engineers are infamous for trying to kill off bold design innovations—sand in the gears that can cost a company too many good ideas. Sure, simpler lines and curves are easier to manufacture without glitches. The tooling tends to be cheaper, too, which makes the manufacturing group shine with the accountants. But every aspect of a design should be fought over in the proper forum so that the difficulty and cost of making a part is weighed against the return to the brand in customer appeal. The top dogs who are paid to make those decisions should be allowed to make them. If engineers with their own agendas are allowed to dis-suade a designer too early in the process, the decision makers don't have the best input on which to base their choices. The company loses the dynamic of debate between those who might settle for a boring car (the very antithesis of the BMW ideal!) and those who want the inside of a console to feel like a velvet glove.

At General Motors, for example, several models during the 1990s were released to the public with an abundance of plastic cladding on the vehicles' sides, front, and rear. Under tremendous pressure to cut costs and improve quality, manufacturing engineers figured out that it was cheaper and less problematic to have supplier companies contour plas-tic snap-on pieces than it was for GM to stamp contoured steel and fiberglass body pieces. These plastic cummerbunds threw a brick through an aesthetic window, but budgets were met and costs decidedly cut. Models such as the Pontiac Grand Prix, Pontiac Grand Am, Chevrolet Avalanche, and all of GM's minivans, however, were derided by the critics, including product boss Bob Lutz, who arrived at GM in late 2001 to fix the broken process. Lutz was hired precisely because of his well-regarded aesthetic judgment when it comes to how vehicles look—and for his unapologetic willingness to tell the manufacturing engineers where to get off. Lutz declared them ugly and detrimental to any effort to build up these cars' brand images, and he summarily decreed the cladding removed, except as an option to the dullards who actually liked a suit of plastic armor or a vinyl roof on a sedan or coupe, like some bald men insist on wearing a bad toupee. However, the vehicles, originally designed with the cladding in mind, now appeared in some ways denuded and not quite "whole." The cost of not having a strong dynamic internal debate over design can be far greater than the nickels and dimes saved by manufacturing "experts."

After his arrival at BMW, Bangle moved quickly to institute a strict monitoring process in the design studios, walling off sensitive models, prototypes, and scale models and actually placing "Stop: No Entry" signs on the doors. Engineering and cost-analysis types aren't allowed inside the studios unaccompanied; when they do go in, the designers and modelers are almost always out. When the designers do need feedback from the engineers, design team leaders are always present to keep the discussions productive rather than destructive.

Bangle often had his designs trampled flat at Fiat. At BMW, he has moved to protect his staff from even his own oversight. BMW was already thinking about moving toward more SUVs in its lineup long before the X5 was introduced in 1999. SUVs represent a whole new concept for BMW and thus require an entirely new design language that was still evolving even after the X5 was fully baked. Being the first BMW SUV, the X5 was fairly conventional in its form and lines. There was a greater sense of license with regard to the next vehicle, though, called the X3, which embraced a more daring design. In 1996 Bangle was authorized to spend more than $1 million to send a team out of Munich to a location unknown even to him for a project named "Deep Blue." Led jointly by a designer and an engineer, the team included members from both departments. Besides coming up with an SUV design, the goal was to create a new fusion of engineering and design: Engineers were to advocate for design, and designers were to champion engineering. The team settled down to work in Malibu, California, in a home that had once belonged to Hollywood icon Elizabeth Taylor. After six months, the team produced six product statements for what would eventually become the X3 SUV, first shown as a concept at the 2003 Detroit Auto Show. Bangle notes, "Both the designers and the engineers learned that the key to a passionate BMW is a synthesis of engineering passion and design passion. They saw that engineers do a better job when they work with designers, and designers do a better job when they work with engineers. You can't teach that. They had to learn it for themselves."

Bangle speaks inside BMW of "BMWness." It is a difficult concept to put into words for people inside or outside the company. In short, it means that people ought to know a vehicle is a BMW when they see it from 20 yards away, even if it is a brand-new design and the logo is not visible. It also should feel like a BMW, even if the occupant is blind-folded. Defining BMWness is especially difficult now that new designs, some of which seem radical to the company's loyal fans, spill forth at a rate unprecedented at BMW. It's felt, seen, and heard, says Bangle, in "buttery seats and the purr of the engine." To drive this idea home and get nondesigners in the company rooting for design, Bangle spends time running seminars inside the company for nondesign staff. It also involves spending money for gimmicks that Bangle says help bake design's importance deep in the guts of the company. While BMW worked up design schemes for a new 3 Series for 1998, nonde-sign staff, especially the purchasing department, were having difficulty seeing the changes from the old model. To breach this visual impair-ment, Bangle had a special working prototype built. By pushing a but-ton, the occupant could transform the height of the instrument panel from the classic BMW 2002 model to the level of the old 3 Series and then to the new 3 Series. Another button changed the door height of the 2002 to the proposed 3 Series design. And so on. To a designer, sub-tle line changes are vital, but to an untrained onlooker they're hard to see, and the accountant finds such subtleties hard to justify. Buyers may not apprehend any single improvement, but a collection of subtle line changes makes up the totality of a new design. The efforts to edu-cate the nondesign staff pay off, says Bangle, because once they truly understand the design process there is less resistance down the line. A growing respect between the two sides means the tension between the different factions of the company is elevated to a "dynamic tension rather than a political or destructive one."

Without his tutorials, some of Bangle's requests might seem downright nutty to the people looking at the bills. In January 1998, he decided that full-size clay models of the next 3 Series needed to be seen by the designers in sunlight for an adequate assessment. Normally, this was achieved by moving the bulky clay sculptures by trolley out to a public area near the FIZ (technical center), perhaps on a sunny Saturday or Sunday after road access was blocked off and guarded to keep prying eyes at bay. But sunny days in Munich are hard to come by in January. No problem. Bangle filled out a job ticket to have the models transported to BMW's test track in France, commandeered the corporate jet to fly the designers to the track, and set them up at a nearby hotel. Evaluating every line under the right light is crucial to making the right decisions. BMW's top seller, the 3 Series, will be photographed in all kinds of light, including natural sunlight, by professional photographers. These pictures will land in every piece of merchandising used to sell the car—every catalog, every advertisement. Customers may see it in sunlight on a dealer lot; magazine and newspaper photographers will shoot it in sunlight for their publications. When understood in these terms by the finance staff, when the enormous costs of getting the lines *wrong* are considered, a hundred grand or more spent on the exercise doesn't seem like much.

To help bridge the gap between design and the engineering and finance staffs, Bangle found an associate design strategist who also happened to be working on his doctorate in economics. These days, when finance folks come to Bangle with efficiency models that damn the design process as being over budget, he has his strategist pore over the assessment. This is done not merely to outfox Munich's green-eyeshade accountants, but to ensure that the two sides speak a common language. On a few occasions, Bangle has been able to massage the finance department's numbers to show compensating efficiencies down the line.

———

When Bangle arrived at BMW, its design capability was largely restricted to cars, and the staff numbered 150; today it's over 300.

BMW didn't seriously have a motorcycle design department or an ergonomics studio. There were no Designworks, Mini, or Rolls-Royce studios. Bangle says BMW is "operating at a much higher level today and still leading the industry in design. Not everyone has to agree with what we are doing and not everyone will love what they see. But that is what *leading* is all about," says Bangle. Referring to the botched 1994 acquisition of the Rover Group, Bangle says, "You know, this company made a grave mistake when it tried to be too big too fast and appeal to far too many people all at once." Bangle's not out to make fans out of every car buyer. "You can make money that way, although that's not the way *we* make money. . . . But that's not leading. And we have always prospered by leading," says Bangle.

If the only bad publicity is *no* publicity and the time to start worrying is when people *stop* criticizing you, Bangle has nothing to fear. Web sites have sprung up expressly devoted to having him stripped of his job, not to mention his health, hearth, and home. These are the handiwork of intensely devoted BMW brand advocates, worshippers of BMW's clean, athletic lines who don't think much of where Bangle is taking BMW design since Wolfgang Reitzle's exit. The worst of the Internet bulletin board postings and Web rants suggest that Bangle should be washing cars instead of designing them. A "Stop Chris Bangle" Internet petition was started in 2001, and by early 2003 it had nearly 4,500 signatures. Joe Pisano said simply in his posting, "I own a 1998 BMW M3 coupe [and] the current designs that BMW is churning out (7 Series and Z4) are a disgrace to the company." "Fire Bangle before he kills the 3 Series too," said a posting by Michael Rubin.

Sanguine about most things, Bangle is philosophical about the Internet attacks. "The best thing about the Internet is that it's unfiltered and completely democratic . . . [and] the worst thing about the Internet is that it's unfiltered and completely democratic." In the end, everyone is going to have their own personal web site to spew opinions. But BMW doesn't use consumer clinics to tell it how to design its cars; it doesn't allow consumers to vote on designs; and the company can't let web sites and web site petitions dictate future design strategy. Says Bangle, "People value BMW because they value what this organization values. We don't ask our customers what they would like us to value. We don't follow our customers so much as we act in a way that inspires them to follow us. Most companies get that backwards."

———

When chairman Bernd Pischetsrieder and Wolfgang Reitzle left in 1999 under the cloud of billions in losses due to the Rover disaster, Bangle's team started making immediate changes to the models still in the cooker that hadn't been frozen by the *Vorstand*. Bangle had a far looser rein in taking BMW's designs into the twenty-first century without Reitzle in the saddle. Says designer Boyer about that time period, "Reitzle is a very traditional man. By that I don't mean conservative—he is a forward thinker. However, you just have to look at the fountain pen he uses or the watch that he wears to see that his design thinking is traditional."[14]

With a whole design language defining BMW for two decades, a language that was successful and generally admired, it takes chutzpah to go in a drastic new direction. Companies with their backs against the wall often take risks, because the only option is to change or crash. But BMW and Bangle are making bold moves at the peak of their success. Jim Hall, a leading consultant to the auto industry in design and market planning, marvels, "This is the ballsiest thing anyone has ever done at a successful car company—knowing that they are going to lose some of these people who have bought four, five, and six BMWs."

While BMW's designs have been viewed as classics, like Chanel's "little black dress," the company, with a few exceptions such as the original 6 Series and Z1, simply wasn't known for design panache. Even the company's biggest postwar breakthrough, the 2002, was universally praised more for its agile driving character and driver feedback than for any curb appeal. Also, BMWs had long been admired for what they weren't. They weren't trendy like Versace dresses or Acura sedans, outdated six months after the debut. More so than Reitzle, Bangle wasn't comfortable with BMW continuing to prove a negative when it came to design.

Like it or not, design, by necessity, in the late 1990s was becoming more important to the Bavarians than ever before. Challenges loomed on the horizon. For instance, BMW was starting to think about sport utility vehicles shortly after Bangle's arrival in 1992, which would require a design language that was surely different from the sedans and coupes that made Bavaria famous. A true high-volume roadster was required that would have to look different than the BMW coupes yet still connected to the brand. And what about coupes? BMW coupes, while as cool as Munich's Isar River in February, still looked like cutoff sedans rather than true coupes. If Bangle were going to have to assemble a staff to come up with new design language to make these new SUVs, roadsters, and coupes—in addition to the sedans—with all of them looking like a brand family and all of them connected somehow to the blue, white, and black propeller, then it made no sense to freeze sedan design in time. Everything was going to change.

Pondering the sea change from Reitzle's era to Bangle's requires, somehow, a discussion about *skin*. For Reitzle, the skin of the vehicle needs to be pulled taut, shrink-wrapped, and stretched around the car's proportions. Smooth surfaces everywhere you look. Reitzle says he often stared at design models for dozens of hours and from every angle over a period of months, often after his regular workday. He scheduled it into his day planner. He would go to the design studio, put on some music, pour a glass of wine or a cup of coffee and stare. He liked to do this outdoors, too, in natural light when possible. The point was to see how it was to "live" with this car's design. How did he feel about a rear-quarter flank on the car in the second or third month of this exercise? By this method, he'd determined that smooth skin stretched over an athletic, almost catlike body was the most appealing body to look at over time.

To Bangle, on the other hand, the skin of a car is something to be sculpted, not just raked smooth. The Z4 is the most obvious example to date of Bangle's flame-surfacing idea, but it also exists in the 2003 5 Series, and it will appear in the 1 Series in 2004. Says Bangle, "There is an underplay of movement and surfaces in the Z4 that is not known in the culture of automobiles. It's known in other things, like sculpture. What you never see in automobiles is a transition of surfaces where one theoretical surface dives into another theoretical surface. We don't see it because automobiles have largely followed traditional architectural rules, and architecture is about simple geometric shapes and symmetry, and these shapes don't allow for complex interceptions. It's not how clothes are traditionally made, either. This is the surface vocabulary we have been using. Suddenly the Z4 has a message. It's not just a car, not just a roadster. Look how the light works on the car and plays with the surfaces on the car. This is characteristic of a new emotion and philosophy."

As a reflection, or perhaps a validation, of what he is after in car design, Bangle directs me to an exhibit at the Cooper-Hewitt National Design Museum in New York City, titled, "Skin." The exhibit includes examples from Swatch's "Skin" collection, which feature watches that have translucent bands and faces to show the inner mechanism as well as the wearer's own skin. There's a handbag that allows nylon threads to emerge across the surface of the fabric. Says the show's catalog, like hair "longer than human body hairs and more sparse than animal fur, the strands of thread invoke the skin of an anomalous being." Indeed, the effect created is that the handbag is hairy. A fabric pattern called *crease* optically creates the illusion of wrinkles on the material, an affront to those who want to see only ironed material. Finally, there were women wearing blouses with an image of a naked body on the fabric, making the fully clothed woman appear naked. The curators declared, "Skin, the complex membrane that holds the body together, also embraces the full spectrum of design today—from product to architecture, fashion, and media." Says Bangle, talking about the Z4 surfaces, "Is a beautiful woman less beautiful because she is wearing a beautiful set of clothes?"

What Bangle seems to be saying is that the automobile's skin is a seriously underutilized part of the palette in vehicle design. The emphasis in vehicle design has long been on establishing lines and proportions and in stretching the skin around a structure. Why not *play* with the skin!

BMW has long had a closer connection to the fine arts than any other car company. In 1975, French race-car driver and professional auctioneer Hervé Poulain transformed an icon of automobile racing, the Le Mans race car, by driving a BMW 3.0 CSL painted by artist Alexander Calder. Poulain's rolling-canvas idea—BMW race cars painted and signed by internationally famous artists—was enthusiastically embraced by BMW. Poulain's Le Mans race car, bearing a vibrant red, blue, and yellow Calder design, became the first BMW Art Car. Many more followed. In 1977, artist Roy Lichtenstein painted a BMW 320i with a comic strip dot pattern accenting a bold yellow and white graphic. In 1979, Andy Warhol was the first artist to paint the BMW M1; his performance car became an abstract in red, blue, green, and yellow. The Art Cars are not statically showcased in the BMW museum in Munich, but exhibited in the world's best museums: the Guggenheim, the Louvre, and the Bilbao in Spain. Artists from nine countries on five continents have created Art Cars over the years. By itself, such a program isn't that significant in the context of BMWs overall marketing budget. But looked at in the continuum of BMW's image crafting, it's a brilliant addition to the communication and management of its global brand. Art is a universal language. A Warhol or a Lichtenstein carries about the same weight in the United States as it does in Japan, India, Russia, and Saudi Arabia—all places where BMW sells cars and motorcycles. It's not a program that needs an accountant's imprimatur. "The benefits of the Art Car program are self-evident when you go to the Louvre or the Guggenheim and see our car on display and associated with the greatest artists of the last century," says BMW chairman Helmut Panke, a former chief financial officer who likes to see programs pay for themselves. Bangle continues that association with the arts. At the Pinakothek der Moderne in Munich, his staff installed an exhibit titled "The Art of Car Design," which exemplifies his philosophy of surface design. A 14-meter-long marble relief contains a surface theme similar to that found on the sides of the Z4, and an accompanying film shown on several monitors depicts BMW designers working to bring their arty thoughts and ideas to rolling sheet-metal reality.

Bangle clearly struggles with grounding BMW's designs in marketing's demands. Brand, yes—Bangle is passionate about what he believes constitutes the BMW brand, how his staff thinks about the brand, and what a gift it is to have such a well-defined brand. But basing a design on marketing—creating a product to match consumer taste—is problematic. "There is no car company that can touch BMW's clarity of brand. Porsche comes closest and may be right there with us. . . . But I don't think we as designers should be too influenced by what consumers tell us about what they want except for dealing with the last 10 percent of a vehicle." By Bangle's definition, that 10 percent means, "How big is the trunk egress? How does the cup holder work? What do the wheel covers look like? How easy is the convertible top to control? The idea of not doing a design like the Z4, not following a design idea we collectively think is beautiful and correct for the brand because we listened to some focus groups or customer clinics is not any way to be successful in creating the right designs."

Bangle subscribes to a theory advanced by author and paleontologist Stephen Jay Gould. Gould promulgated a controversial theory known as *punctuated equilibrium,* which argues that evolution proceeds slowly, but not always steadily; it is sometimes marked by sudden, rapid change. Bangle believes that cars evolve the same way. BMW, he says, is entering a period of abrupt, accelerated change. Says Bangle, "When you spend an enormous amount of money developing a new model, you don't just throw all that money out the window seven years later and do something completely different. Instead, you refine the car, you improve it, and you get your money out of it. Ultimately, you develop two generations of cars that are very close in their evolutionary nature. But then, 14 years later, the conditions have changed so radically—competitive pressures, technological advances, safety and environmental regulations, consumer preferences—that it's time to make the big jump."

AutoPacific, a leading marketing and design firm, consults with BMW, and partner Jim Hall believes Bangle is right to shake things up. "If BMW stays a stationary target, the number of things that make the brand and product portfolio become fewer and fewer. . . . Four and five years from now, BMW is going to look incredibly progressive. The 7 Series and maybe even the Z4 will look a lot more mainstream, but by then they will be on to the next design already." Longtime BMW communications and marketing executive Carl Flesher puts it this way: "Our competitors have had a long time to zig closer to us; now it's time for us to zag."

In the meantime, Bangle has to stomach some barbed attention. *New York Times* reporter Danny Hakim wrote a 2002 page-one article titled "BMW Design Chief Sees Art on Wheels; Some Just See Ugly."[15] Bangle "often speaks in language that floats beyond pedestrian conversation and can leave one a little puzzled," Hakim wrote. He also called Bangle's approach to car design hypercerebral because in the course of their interview Bangle conjured up references to Archimedes, Vermeer, Pythagoras, Euclid, and the British art historian Kenneth Clark. Maybe that whole crew was a bit much for one interview, even if it did take place at the Detroit Institute of Art. But who should a highly educated, world-renowned design leader summon up as philosophical and artistic reference points, TV gab mogul Oprah Winfrey and Home Shopping Network artist Thomas Kinkade? Framed under the headline's "Ugly" comment, it makes Bangle seem esoteric and obscure, when in fact he directs a talented and worldly design staff responsible for selling more than a million cars a year.

———

Wolfgang Reitzle, forced to resign from BMW in 1999 in a management overhaul, is generally acknowledged to be one of the top three or four product men in the global auto industry. From 1985 to 1999, Reitzle was BMW's management board member in charge of product development for BMW AG. He was one of eight on the management board, but he stood out as a star among equals as early as 1984, occasionally overshadowing his own chairmen, Eberhard von Kuenheim and later Bernd Pischetsrieder, in the German press as well as in the international business and the motor press. It is worth noting, too, that during the same time period that Reitzle was head of product development at BMW, Mercedes-Benz employed four men to do a similar job. His longevity speaks to his talents and to the consistency of product design coming out of BMW during his tenure.

Reitzle is blessed with great knowledge and instinct about how a vehicle should operate under the hood, and he has a tremendous sense of that which cannot be taught—good taste. He is also a superb strategic thinker. A slim man, about six feet tall, Reitzle is always nattily turned out in the best suits and silks. Sporting a meticulously trimmed mustache, he loosely resembles the late actor David Niven. He is a rare mind in the industry in that he thinks and studies both design and marketing at the same time. While at BMW, he didn't just think about how to design a car to be a true BMW, but where each product would nudge BMW's brand in the global fabric of premium brands of all kinds—fashion, hotels, retail, jewelry. In his book, *Luxury Creates Prosperity: The Future of the Global Economy*, Reitzle conspicuously never talks about BMW, but he does offer analysis on such brands as Ritz-Carlton, Gucci, Davidoff, Restoration Hardware, and Starbucks.

During his time at BMW, especially as head of product development, Reitzle generated a certain divisiveness inside BMW that men like him do. There were those who followed him and deferred to his judgment willingly and faithfully—and those who grudgingly deferred to him because they respected his judgment but resented his annoying habit of being right. There were, and are, plenty of people who just don't like him. As in any large organization, some feel he grabbed too much credit for vehicles as successful as the BMW 3 Series, 5 Series, X5, and the Mini. But BMW experienced its greatest surge in sales, profitability, and critical success for its product while *he* was in charge of product, so it's hard to deny him his due. Is the creation of great product the result of a lot of dedicated people in an organization, some of whom make the boss look better than he is? Sure. But as the conductor of a first-class orchestra playing his arrangements, Reitzle gets the credit. Did the economic boom of the 1990s help drive BMW sales as an abundance of new wealth flocked to the brand? Absolutely. But other car companies, like Acura, Infiniti, Cadillac, and Jaguar turned out a lot of dogs during that time, and Reitzle consistently turned out winners that customers snapped up. BMW sales continued to rise after the stock market crash of 2000 and the subsequent three years of economic malaise in Germany and the United States, mostly on the backs of models executed by Reitzle.

———

Reitzle grew up in the town of Ulm, Germany, on the Danube River, just on the border of Bavaria and the state of Baden-Württemberg, almost midway between BMW's Munich home and Mercedes-Benz's Stuttgart base of operations. The town is known for having the highest church spire in the world, on the Munster, and also for being the birthplace of Albert Einstein. Though evidence of a quaint fishing-village life still exists, a single devastating Allied air raid in 1944 wiped out much of the town's historic center. Wolfgang Reitzle was born into a solidly upper-middle-class family in a city rapidly rebuilding after the war. Reitzle's father owned a small firm that sold paint and painting systems to small and medium-sized companies in Germany. When Reitzle was four or five years old, recalled his mother, he could close his eyes on a street corner and tell his parents what kind of car had passed. When Reitzle was a teenager, his father deferred to his judgment about what kind of car the family would buy.

When Reitzle started at BMW in 1976, he began on the shop floor, working with specially trained technicians and tradespeople to make testing equipment used to develop the latest manufacturing processes. After a year of that, Reitzle became department chief for testing manufacturing processes and equipment. Among his tasks was testing the first robots employed at BMW plants.

At the time Reitzle joined the company, BMW was still known as a boutique carmaker that elicited a lot of positive emotion from performance-driving-oriented buyers, but a lot of angst when it came to repairs, which the cars needed far too often. "It was a workshop sort of atmosphere," says Reitzle. Mercedes had it all: quality, reputation, engineering resources, sales. BMW excelled in designs seen as more modern than Mercedes and in driving "fun." Already, BMW had adopted a marketing theme in North America, "The Ultimate Driving Machine" (loosely translated, "The Pleasure of Driving" elsewhere), and this very much colored how people viewed BMW both inside and outside the company. Reitzle says BMW had the better engines and chassis, but Mercedes still far outclassed Munich in body manufacturing and design aesthetics, especially inside the cars.

Reitzle moved through BMW ranks like oil through an engine. In rapid succession, he went from his job as department chief for process and machine testing to being deployed on an ad hoc basis, often in "emergency" situations, he recalls, to fix problems at the new plant in Dingolfing that was turning out the 7 Series. A new car from a new plant has many bugs, and many were flagged by BMW dealers as problems before they could be sold. From this experience, Reitzle came up with the idea to establish a pilot plant for new models so that manufacturing bugs could be detected and fixed in a small, controlled environment before they became a problem when dealers were sitting on months' worth of orders. The proposal was adopted by von Kuenheim, who put Reitzle in charge of building the pilot plant and then running it. Reitzle then ruffled his first feathers at BMW, taking up space in the Munich assembly plant for his pilot facility and angering the plant manager, who objected to his lack of jurisdiction over Reitzle while he was working under *his* roof. From that experience, Reitzle developed new processes for painting, stamping sheet metal, and so on. It was valuable experience for the young Reitzle, because he was literally remaking the way BMW went about its business of manufacturing cars, and he would come to know better than most in the company just what was possible in terms of turning designs on paper into real motorcars that BMW could build in its plants and sell in showrooms.

When a manufacturing engineer complained that a body panel or chassis component was too tough to make, Reitzle gave little ground.

Reitzle played a key role in launching the second 5 Series saloon, which was the most successful in BMW's postwar history for quality and execution. That breakthrough grabbed the *Vorstand's* attention, and he was promoted to chief of engine manufacturing and foundry for the company. In 1983, von Kuenheim fired his research and development chief and assumed the task himself in addition to his job as chairman, but he knew he needed a clever executive to work closely with him and to take over the post full-time. He turned to the 34-year-old Reitzle, who was willing to work the required six-day workweeks. Then von Kuenheim became squeamish about naming such a young executive to the vital job of research and development, and he went outside BMW and named a more experienced man from German truck-maker MAN. Reitzle, clearly disappointed with von Kuenheim's decision, told his chairman he wouldn't work for the new boss. Instead, Reitzle convinced von Kuenheim to send him to Harvard Business School for an advanced business program. On Reitzle's return, von Kuenheim appointed him boss of all technical planning at BMW. That meant he headed planning for a new plant in Regensburg, Germany, which included all the company's manufacturing processes and purchasing for manufacturing. After a year, von Kuenheim realized his R&D chief from MAN was not working out. He then made Reitzle chief over vehicle development as well, while he split off the research job to another executive. It was a lot on the plate of the 35-year-old.

The workshop atmosphere, with a lot of people "working with their sleeves rolled up," as Reitzle describes it, was part of the company culture. But it was not resulting in processes and manufacturing standards that were up to the reputation of its vehicles. For the sake of BMW's reputation, quality had to improve. Cars were arriving at dealerships with serious glitches. There did not yet exist a company mandate to deliver a problem-free car to the dealer. The 2002, as good as it was, for example, suffered a high rate of window failure. Drivers who drove around a corner quickly, pushing the car to its limit, stood a better than 5 percent chance of having a window disappear into the door structure—this because the window was held in place on the rail with adhesive instead of screws. Drilling holes into glass and then screwing the glass in place created a problem of excessive breakage at the plant. The company had not yet established advanced hot- and cold-weather testing, nor did it perform durability testing, where parts and adhesives are subjected to prolonged vibration and harsh temperature change. The situation serves as a glimpse into the company's thinking in the early 1970s. The goal was to eliminate breakage at the plant, not necessarily to deliver a window that wouldn't fail for the customer. BMW enthusiasts accepted the problems because of the pleasure derived from taking a corner like few other cars allowed. Certain other cars, like British MGs, had the same poor quality and the same loyal following. But BMW certainly didn't want to be the German MG.

Besides the quality issues, Reitzle believed that as good as the cars were to drive, BMW hadn't been progressive in fostering enough creative thinking. The 2002 broke conventions and established the sports saloon segment, but the organization didn't seem to be focused on innovating—only on improving what it had done after a burst of fresh ideas in the 1960s. The company was engineering-driven, as it should be, but it was set up only to advance the existing lineup of cars—the 3 Series, the 5 Series, and the new 7 Series. And the 7 Series, while a new model, was only a subtle evolution of the basic sport sedan strategy. BMW was not a fertile place for new ideas for new models and lineup expansion, except for engine derivatives. It was only with much lobbying and persuasion, for example, that Bob Lutz and Paul Bracq had convinced von Kuenheim to let them build the GT show car to showcase at the 1972 Olympics in Munich instead of the new 5 Series (von Kuenheim's choice). The GT, of course, caused a much bigger sensation than the new 5 Series. All of the company's electric car experiments were merely derivatives of existing models. No one bothered to design one from the ground up. When the company reached outside its normal operations to develop the M1 performance car in the 1970s, following an idea hatched by its Motorsport division to develop a limited-run performance car, the project fell apart after BMW first went to Lamborghini, which flubbed the project, and then to Baur, the German coach builder, to build it. The experience soured BMW on breaking out of the envelope it had created for itself. Such a task as the M1 should have been undertaken inside the company from the start, but there was no system to support the project. Reitzle set out to change that.

Reitzle set up a new division at BMW, which operated as a "skunk works" (an engineering and development unit that works outside the normal structure of a company to try to expedite projects), staffed by talented and creative engineers and designers working outside the BMW product development center. The idea was somewhat modeled after Reitzle's earlier idea to have a pilot factory for each new model so bugs could be worked out before they infected the actual production facility. Reitzle set up BMW Technik GmbH near BMW headquarters so he and others could easily go back and forth in a few minutes. The group, run by ex-Porsche engineer Ulrich Bez, began with about 60 people but soon grew to about 100, and that is roughly the size it has remained.

The first project undertaken by Technik under Reitzle was the Z1 roadster. BMW had cabriolets based on coupes that were in large part chopped off sedans. But its product lineup cried out for a two-seater sports car, designed from the ground up to be nothing but an open-air roadster. Technik could prove its worth right away by coming up with a model around which the whole company could rally. Who doesn't like a sexy sports car? The Z designation derives from the German word *Zukunft,* meaning "future." The Z1 was unlike anything BMW had in its lineup or had even suggested since the short life of the 507 (introduced in the 1950s). It used the engine and transmission from the 1982 to 1987 BMW 325, mounted in a specially designed chassis made from galvanized steel. The body, made from various composite resin panels, was fixed onto the base frame. The front suspension was made up of reworked 325 components, but with a wider track. The rear suspension was the new and specially designed Z axle. The Z axle developed by Technik was an entirely new design for BMW; a space-saving multilink rear-suspension layout of weight-saving construction. Apart from its compact dimensions, its outstanding features were optimum directional stability and excellent control of lateral forces.[16] In short, it was, and has been since, a key engineering invention toward achieving the controlled, agile, and stable ride that has made BMW famous, and it has been used on BMW cars ever since. The most distinctive features of the Z1 body were the electrically powered doors, which in the open position drop down into the side sills, thus creating the ultimate open car when the soft top is lowered. Remarkable aerodynamics of the Z1 were created through a clever flat composite tray that covered the entire underbody, forcing air under the car to the rear wing. The effect of the design created a vacuum between the car and road, sticking it to the pavement as though the tires were coated with glue.

The Z1 was an unusual car when it went on sale in 1988 after causing a sensation at the 1987 Frankfurt Motor Show. But it was badly timed. When Technik developed it, there was nothing else like it. It was a far sportier car than the Mercedes SL. Nevertheless, at $68,000, it was priced high, and it looked sky-high after Mazda launched its affordable and wonderful Miata roadster in 1989 at less than $20,000. A total of 8,012 Z1s were sold between 1987 and 1991, when production stopped. The best year was 1990 when more than 4,000 sold. In its last year, sales fell to 1,451. The Z1, though, was hardly a failure. Besides establishing BMW credentials anew in the roadster segment, Reitzle's Technik had succeeded in developing new engineering approaches (the car's aerodynamics and the Z axle, which would be used in the next 3 Series), and it paved the way for BMW to develop a more affordable roadster, the Z3, which became the first model built at BMW's first U.S. assembly plant. *Autocar and Motor* magazine in Britain wrote, "What the Z1 does is to bring luxury convertible refinement to the squat, nimble, compact roadster—and set new standards for both."[17] Wrote German magazine *Auto, Motor und Sport,* "The Z1 delivers the shock of a fallen power line the first time you drive it hard on a twisty road."[18] This kind of praise wasn't new for BMW, but the decibels of the praise were higher, and the Z1 gave BMW's sporty and fun-driving image its biggest boost in more than a decade, since the 1972 Turbo hit the circuit.

One of the first big high-volume vehicles Reitzle tackled as the new product chief was E36, the third generation of the 3 Series, BMW's bread and butter. The car wouldn't see showrooms until 1990, as a 1991 model. The design was under way, but there was still plenty for Reitzle to affect. Heretofore, BMW had launched its 3 Series models with the two-door model, then the four-door, then the convertible, and so on. It was the company's method of keeping the product fresh through the seven-year life cycle. But this new 3 Series would be launched as a four-door, because the company had seen that sales of the four-door version of the E30, second-generation 3 Series, sold briskly and was in greater demand than the two-door. Launching the four-door first allowed the company to follow with a "coupe," not just a two-door. The semantic difference was worth more money on the sticker price for the coupe. A touring wagon was added as well. They further freshened up the line with a combination of four-cylinder, six-cylinder, and diesel engine configurations. All the variations broadened appeal and added sales and rich profits over the seven years of the car. Says *Car and Driver* editor Csaba Csere, "People have accused our magazine of writing too much about BMW, but it is really that they always have something new coming off the same line of vehicle. . . . They really are the best at keeping a product line fresh and worth writing about over its life. Most other companies just launch a vehicle, and forget about it until they freshen it up with a new grille or headlamps."

In the E36 3 Series, Reitzle's attention to styling is evident. The chief designer of the car was Claus Luthe, who certainly deserves credit as well. But Reitzle's input was considerable and critical to every car beginning in the early to mid-1980s. He was the maestro. Besides guiding the key elements such as proportion and minimizing front-end overhang, Reitzle is especially known for his attention to details that make up perhaps 10 percent of the vehicle's impression, but are *the* things that help it hold up over time as a fresh, modern design. The E30 3 Series had sold well, but it was looking dated already in 1986. Reitzle recognized that the next car had to transcend the usual five- to seven-year styling window for which most car companies planned. Reitzle believes a winning design looks good for at least 15 years. The E30 was too small. It had an overly vertical, upright stance that was too conservative for BMW's sporty image. The E36 had to become more aerodynamic for both styling and fuel-economy reasons. It would, of course, have to be faster than the old car, too. Handling had to improve, and it needed a stiffer chassis. Overall, the new car was four inches longer and two inches wider, but the wheelbase was five inches longer for a smoother ride. The most obvious change, though, was the new catlike curb stance of the car, literally inspired by the way a cat haunches up its rear and draws its head back before taking off for a pounce on an unsuspecting mouse. The roofline was more contoured than the straight roofline of the previous models. The front end had a minimal overhang from the front wheels. Says Reitzle, "I started this discussion of overhang at BMW. Audi and Mercedes cars, I always thought, looked like dachshund dogs being dragged across the carpet by their chins. The minimum overhang gives a more athletic and streamlined look; that and pushing the wheels out to the most extreme four corners as possible. I used to drive our packaging engineers crazy with this obsession of mine with the front end." A steeply raked windshield added to the aerodynamic stance of the car. The twin-kidney grille was smaller than in previous BMWs, horizontally laid out (wider than it was tall) instead of the E30's vertical grille (taller than it was wide), making for a more elegant and modern face. The air dam below the grille and the trunk lid's trailing edge looked fully integrated into the whole design. Nothing looked tacked on or added as an afterthought on the E36. Notes auto industry historian James Taylor, "[The 3 E36] still looked good a decade after it was conceived."[19] The list of vehicles that share that distinction is mighty short! Fifteen-inch wheels became standard, two inches bigger than the E30's. Reitzle said he also obsessed about the look of the wheels. "They should fill up the well as much as possible. . . . The black empty space must always be kept at a minimum." The quality of everything in the car went up: the leather, the matching of leather grains, the carpet, the plastics, the use of wood. It was as though a professional decorator had come to a house that had been styled at a hardware store. The E36 3 Series coupe wasn't just chopped down as in the past, but the roofline changed. This, too, was where Reitzle's influence inside BMW was paying off. He had the authority and the will to stare down people who would have otherwise done things the old way for the sake of saving a few dollars. The new roofline lowered the car by more than an inch, and the front and rear windows were more steeply raked than in the saloon version. These clearly noticeable changes gave the car a true sense of being a different car, not just a two-door version of the four-door. Rear legroom was compromised, but a strategic decision was made to emphasize trunk space over rear legroom because the vast majority of backseat passengers, Reitzle reckoned, are children, who don't need as much legroom as adults. "My thinking was, and still is to a degree, that a BMW should be like an Italian suit," says Reitzle. "It has to fit, and it only goes up to a certain size. . . . If the customer needs more room and more space, they can go to another company like Mercedes or Audi or Opel. We made the cars bigger one generation to the next, but never put a priority about making things bigger for the sake of utility—only about performance, handling, style, and making more profit. This was key to our consistency, and we always felt that there is profit in consistency."

———

Before Bangle, Reitzle worked with chief designer Claus Luthe, who came to BMW in 1976. Recruited at the Geneva Motor Show in 1975 by BMW design director Wilhelm Hofmeister, Luthe could hardly believe the offer to move to Munich, so he didn't even follow up with Hofmeister for several months after the show. Luthe in those days was working for Audi under Dr. Ferdinand Piech, grandson of Ferdinand Porsche and future chairman of Volkswagen. Luthe finally left Piech and Audi in October 1975 after seven months of wooing by BMW. He inherited a design department of fewer than 30 people. In just a little more than a year, though, the department swelled to more than 100, with about 25 designers and the rest modelers and craftsmen. Made up of a combination of new college graduates and young up-and-comers from other automakers, Luthe's team would be the core of BMW design for the next 14 years of his tenure.

The 1981 (E28) 5 Series was the first design that Luthe's team is credited with developing, though he says that because of BMW's six- to seven-year development cycles much of the design was already locked down before he arrived, leaving him only details to affect. To say that the E28 was similar to the preceding (E12) 5 Series is extreme understatement. The motor press at the time *harumphed* the E28 because of overly conservative styling and the absence of a desirable 3.5-liter engine at the launch. Luthe has said in later interviews that he was instructed to "go conservative" by BMW chairman Eberhard von Kuenheim. There were many improvements under the hood and in the chassis; BMW took the position that the motor press would respect the company for putting so much of the investment into the guts of the car rather than the skin. What changes there were to the car's proportions and outer skin were largely done to improve aerodynamics, and thus fuel economy. Better fuel economy was made a priority for all new models after the oil shortages and run-up in prices in the mid-1970s and the stiffer government fuel economy standards in both Europe and the United States. The car retained the reverse-angle front fascia and vertical twin-kidney grilles, which, though not aerodynamic, had become part of BMW's design "furniture" since the

1960s. It would be the last of those reverse-angle fascias as fuel-economy needs trumped design aesthetics and traditions. The front end of the car was sculpted for a quicker drop off from the windshield and a less level hood to aid airflow over the car. The rear trunk line was raised and flattened to generate extra downforce. The (E30) 3 Series that followed in 1982 under Luthe and Reitzle also suffered early brickbats for being too conservative and too much like its predecessor. As with the E28, BMW's conservative *Vorstand,* which votes on final designs before they go forward, had voted for evolutionary change rather than anything that would startle. Said Luthe at the time of introduction, "We don't have to create models that are radically different from the ones they replace. To maintain our tradition, we do not need to design 'way out' designs. The important thing to keep in mind is to make sure there is continuity from the old model to the new model. It is absolutely essential that we build a lasting image of what a BMW is and not be swayed by ever changing fashion trends."[20] It was straight out of von Kuenheim's strategy playbook and auto show speeches.

Though the E28 5 Series was, in the long run, a commercial and ultimately critical success, Luthe wanted his first from-the-ground-up designs to push the limits of what BMW's culture would allow. But there was an overriding principle decreed by von Kuenheim: "Mistakes in design should never occur." The first ground-up design was the E32 7 Series, presented to the press in 1986, eight years after Luthe's arrival! Von Kuenheim, ever the Prussian aristocrat, requested a "truly noble car" from Luthe and Reitzle that would challenge the Mercedes-Benz S Class. Full of classic proportions and elegant lines, it was well received by the motor press and went on to become the best-selling luxury car in Germany. The car won the 1987 Car Design Award presented in Turin. The 7 Series styling was fashionproof; it had to be. Luthe first sketched the design in 1979. Given BMW's long incubation time, it wouldn't do to embrace the styles in vogue that year, only to see them become hopelessly passé by 1986. The E36 3 Series, which followed the 7 Series, also won the Car Design Award, but was not as readily embraced by the *Vorstand,* which thought it too radically different from the outgoing 3 Series. Luthe and product chief Wolfgang Reitzle, though, convinced enough board members of the need to take a design leap once in a while rather than baby steps.

———

Two principles have long dominated BMW's culture: *consistency* and *Mercedes-Benz*. Says Reitzle, "If there is one single element that makes BMW a success, it's consistency. In whatever we did over many years, we aimed to be consistent. . . . We always said we would never bring out a car that we ourselves wouldn't be pleased to drive. That may sound very simple or trivial. But it isn't. BMW was always the underdog and tried to measure up to Mercedes-Benz; the company that invented the car is just two hours away in Stuttgart."

The unwritten law at BMW, says Reitzle, is that everyone who came to work at the company had to love driving and know that driving pleasure is what the company is about. It wasn't just about solving engineering problems. Everyone in engineering, development, purchasing, the controllers office, and manufacturing has to be focused on driving performance. Everyone is expected to be curious about any car's performance attributes. The company's top managers have always been driving and performance enthusiasts. Most members of the *Vorstand,* for example, have been motorcyclists at one time in their lives.

Reitzle says that many meetings in his early days and into the 1980s focused on inventing processes that eliminated the company's, and therefore the brand's, weaknesses. He says focusing on Mercedes-Benz as its standard at times seemed like a bad idea because it meant always being number two no matter how much the company improved. "Always walking in someone else's footsteps," says Reitzle. But he came to appreciate von Kuenheim's strategy. "By always focusing on the best, but a company that had a different brand image and position than BMW, it focused the organization and kept us from getting comfortable even when we booked very good profits," says Reitzle. It seems to have paid off—BMW surpassed Mercedes in U.S. sales in 2002 and 2003, and is within striking distance of surpassing Mercedes in worldwide sales by middecade, especially if the Mercedes A Class, which few people consider a true Mercedes, is taken out of the comparison.

———

Key to understanding Reitzle's impact on BMW—on the company's product development and brand evolution—is to understand that he has long spent a great deal of time thinking about what *luxury* and *premium* mean; not just in the context of the motorcar business, but in the entire global landscape of consumer brands, consumer behavior, psychology, and anthropology. Give Reitzle an opening to talk about luxury and branding, and the questioner had best be in a comfortable chair. Reitzle's book about global economics and luxury brands reflects the breadth of his thinking on the subject beyond gears, chassis development, torque curves, and "tumble home." Reitzle cites David Brooks's *Bobos in Paradise,* for example, in a way that illustrates his thinking about vehicle design and development, as well as brand, though Brooks never mentions BMW cars in the book. Reitzle notes "Bourgeois Bohemians, or *Bobos* [Brooks' term]" are the new elite. Their elite status doesn't come from family background, property, or possessions, but rather by their consumption behavior. There is virtuous consumption and wasteful consumption, and determining which is which is not tied to the price tag. Bobos reject profit for the sake of profit and possession of wealth.[21] Especially during the 1990s, Bobos flush with the winnings from stock options and the Internet boom may have spent up to $5 million a year on "experiences," from elaborate vacations to frequent spa treatments to renting a remote Pacific island. Bobos redefined necessity for themselves. For example, $25,000 or more for a new bathroom could be seen as a necessity, and $15,000 simply not worthwhile. Lining a bathroom with imported slate tile came to be seen as smart, not ostentatious. Hundreds of dollars for hiking shoes was smart, while the same amount for patent leather shoes would be stupid. A $10,000 Sub-Zero refrigerator or Viking stove was smart. Skimping on a kitchen redesign was stupid. Country club memberships in the 1990s were down and looked down upon by Bobos.[22] Like brands such as Makita and Sub-Zero and Viking, BMW by the early and mid-1990s became seen as the "professional's car," the car that driving enthusiasts respected and wanted to drive more than others. The M Series performance cars, engineered for autobahn speeds of more than 130 miles per hour, were gobbled up in the United States for 65-mph speed limits, helping to cement the image that BMW nurtured for its vehicles. Too, the cramped backseat of the 3 Series or 5 Series was a case in which elevating design aesthetics over passenger utility drives home the elevated status of BMW vehicles and their drivers that is at the core of the company's product development schemes. Reitzle could have ordered more legroom for the backseat and satisfied an utterly practical consideration, but such a change would have spoiled the proportions and meticulously calibrated aerodynamics of the car. Likewise, when Reitzle set out to develop the Range Rover, there was a growing interest for a third row of seats in SUVs. General Motors, Ford, Chrysler, and Toyota were all engineering room for a third row of seats in their SUVs. Reitzle spent an astonishing $1.8 billion to develop its Range Rover, enough to stop the heart of any chief financial officer. The SUV rides like it was glued to rails, a contrast to the far floatier rides of the Chevy, Ford, and Chrysler, and has jewel-like quality in the interior. But it had no third-row seat and none was possible. Reitzle allowed for only two rows of seats for the BMW X5, too. GM's North American chief Gary Cowger recalls being shown the Range Rover by Reitzle after its motor show debut. Curious about the third-row potential in the car, he queried Reitzle about it. "No . . . it is not needed. . . . When the parents go to Gstaad [Switzerland] skiing they leave the children at home,"[23] said Reitzle. Shortsighted? Elitist? Even a little pompous? Maybe. But for Reitzle, the vehicle is all about style and desirability packed into every square inch of sheet metal. General Motors' Trailblazer EXT, with seating for seven, is never going to merit consideration for a design exhibition in a museum. The 2002 Range Rover just may. For Reitzle, that is the point; it's what separates a well-managed premium brand from a mass brand.

Reitzle subscribes to the ideas of economist Thorstein Veblen, who in 1899 coined the phrase "conspicuous consumption." Veblen believed that the lower classes were not out to overthrow the upper class, but rather were striving to reach it. The presence of the upper class, indeed, served the larger community by setting the example and giving the working class *purpose*. Wrote Veblen, "Since the consumption of these more excellent goods is an evidence of wealth, it becomes honorific; and conversely, the failure to consume in due quantity and quality becomes a mark of inferiority and demerit."[24] Reitzle's mantra, too.

Creating and maintaining aspiration among people whose economic or household situation doesn't yet allow them to buy a BMW has been at the core of BMW's growth and success. Maintaining BMW's consistently high critical praise has always been crucial, because it keeps a storehouse of pent-up demand among people with not enough income or too many young children to buy a BMW sedan or coupe. Reitzle says both the engineering and marketing of BMW's focus on such factors as safe driving at high speeds and better brake performance has long been intended to feed the *rationale* for buying a BMW, while its performance attributes and styling feed the *desire* to own one. Says Reitzle, "We always talked about, for example, running brake tests from 100 miles per hour to 0 in 2.5 seconds to test our brakes. We wanted to be successful in America where the speed limit is 55 miles per hour or 65 now in some places. Can we really play up the strengths we have in Germany on the autobahn, and will it make sense to U.S. drivers? Of course. We decided that we wouldn't be different. We would be consistent. Our customers in the U.S. will know when they go 70 miles per hour that they have a car that was designed for 160 mph for the autobahn, and this they will find valuable. Many people buy BMWs or Porsches or Land Rovers because of what they could do, or what their friends think they do. This is the aspiration we created."

———

Both Reitzle and Bangle are blessed with the gift of being able to articulate their thinking and intentions better than most businesspeople. They are both among the most compelling conversationalists on the subject of car design I have ever encountered. Is one smarter or better than the other? Given the subjective nature of art and design, answering this question would be like debating Democratic versus Republican politics or Middle East policy. I choose another path. Given the success of BMW's designs during Reitzle's time, it is correct to say that designs executed under his direction are among the best of the twentieth century. Bangle's designs under Burkhard Goeschel are different, and they may prove, in time, to be among the best loved of this century, though this century is awfully young. For a signpost, I turn to *Automobile Magazine,* which writes on a BMW product almost monthly and saw fit to name Bangle its "Man of the Year" for 2002. When Bangle began working with Reitzle, the objective was to change the look but not the character of BMW, according to magazine editor Robert Cumberford, writing in the magazine's January 2003 issue: "Bangle is a man with the courage of his convictions and solid character, and he is worthy of our admiration for that alone."[25]

The Ultimate Blunder

SIX

What do you call an MG with dual exhaust pipes?
Answer: *A wheelbarrow.*

—ANONYMOUS

BMW's first inclination to buy up the last bits of the once proud British auto industry came, oddly enough, during a trip to Japan in 1991 taken by BMW chairman Eberhard von Kuenheim and product development chief Wolfgang Reitzle. The two men went calling on their counterparts at Toyota, Honda, and Nissan. All three companies had in recent years launched premium brands—Lexus, Acura, and Infiniti—to compete against BMW in Japan and North America, so the two Germans decided on a cordial fishing expedition among their newest and most mysterious competitors. BMW had long pondered the eventual threat posed by the Japanese. How far and wide should BMW take its brand? How far up or down in price? Should BMW do a minivan or panel van like Mercedes? No. Should they do a super sports car costing in excess of $100,000? Maybe. A small city car? No.

Expansion was the one subject that had confounded von Kuenheim for almost two decades. Believing in BMW's focus on cars and motor-cycles, he wouldn't follow the Daimler-Benz example of buying tech-nology companies far afield of the auto business. His only forays into diversification were a financially unsuccessful return to the aero-engine business in a joint venture with Rolls-Royce and an in-house venture capital operation that invested in technology firms. Neither amounted to much. Both schemes lost money, according to inside managers. Von Kuenheim's expansion conundrum remained.

The Japanese had lately staked their claim in BMW's premium-car territory with their exceptional quality, manufacturing prowess, and productivity. They already had the mass market covered, and now they were studying and benchmarking BMW for how to create a premium *image* for their new luxury brands. It worried the two men.

Von Kuenheim had long dithered over how to expand BMW's business to protect both the integrity of the brand and the company's financial independence. Daimler-Benz had invested in companies like Fokker Aircraft. GM and Ford had bought up savings banks, digital technology firms, and defense contractors. Chrysler had purchased the Gulfstream aircraft concern.

Since taking over as chairman in 1971, von Kuenheim felt that BMW's place was in cars, particularly in niche markets. Stay sporty, stay special, and be the brand that young people aspire to—whether for a sports car, coupe, or sedan. But some BMW executives had been worrying for many years that focusing on the premium niches to the exclusion of the mass market left the company vulnerable to cyclical recessions. Reitzle had been working on a "2 Series" front-drive concept car to be priced below the company's 3 Series, thus potentially generating more sales at lower prices. That car never met BMW standards. Besides, it violated the basic tenet of the BMW brand—always rear-drive vehicles. Expansion befuddled von Kuenheim.

BMW's problem, as outlined in research conducted in 1992 by the company, was that only 20 percent of consumers shopping in the premium segments even considered a BMW. The other 80 percent simply were not impressed by BMW's sporty performance attributes. Nor did they relate to BMW's image as a badge for high-flying corporate and finance executives. BMW was indeed the "Ultimate Driving Machine," the world over, yet a disturbing percentage of buyers didn't care. It confounded management. Some at BMW, especially von Kuenheim and then–manufacturing chief Bernd Pischetsrieder, had come to believe the answer lay in tapping the mass market for greater volume by buying someone else's brand. This was viewed as an easier and cheaper task than spawning new BMW models to grab more of the 20 percent who were shopping BMW but not buying. Reitzle, however, advocated acquiring additional niche brands to complement BMW's own niche brands, staying clear of the mass brands he considered contrary to BMW's strategy and culture.

As von Kuenheim and Reitzle rode the bullet train around Japan they discussed how BMW should grow. While other automakers, including GM and Ford, had been interested in buying BMW to possess its iconic status in the premium segment, Reitzle told von Kuenheim he thought BMW would do well to acquire a portfolio of sterling brands itself rather than stretch the BMW brand to cover all bases. Brands that Reitzle wanted *defined* their segments. "I felt that we needed iconic brands and that we would know very well how to manage them because we would manage them just as we managed our own BMW brand . . . always with tight focus and definition," says Reitzle. Over tea and sandwiches on the train, Reitzle spelled out his vision to his boss on a yellow legal pad.

- *Buy Porsche.* The vaunted German marque was suffering dismal product development decisions and overall poor management. The unsuccessful and critically lambasted 928, for instance, and a costly four-door sports sedan exercise had drained 500 million deutsche marks (DM) from its cash reserves. But the marque was still revered worldwide and virtually defined the performance sports coupe segment.
- *Buy Rolls-Royce and Bentley, owned by Vickers plc of Britain.* Formerly the brand of kings, Rolls-Royce had fallen on hard times under Vickers, a British conglomerate that didn't invest in the brand. But it was still the ultimate iconic brand in the super-premium segment, literally defining regal luxury, albeit undeservedly. With Rolls-Royce fading a bit, Mercedes-Benz's 600 Pullman luxury saloon had become the choice of the vastly wealthy. BMW had no offering there and would not try to boost the BMW brand into that rarified price neighborhood. "BMW had no credibility with that class of buyer, having long established itself in the 3 Series segment," Reitzle reasoned. He added, "The center of gravity for our brand was too low for that." By contrast, Vickers had plowed investment into Bentley, thinking that Bentley appealed to a sportier superpremium audience and

had more upside sales potential than Rolls. BMW, too, saw great growth potential in an expanded Bentley line, as a more natural progression from the BMW product image.

- *Buy Land Rover.* Though BMW was especially interested in the Range Rover flagship, it saw the long-term potential of reinvigorating Land Rover as a whole. Neglected by British Leyland and then British Aerospace, it was still the iconic sport utility brand, possessing the greatest off-road capability and rivaled only by Chrysler's Jeep for combined utility and prestige. In fact, Land Rover was the upmarket premium "Jeep" to the world, instantly recognizable as *the* SUV from Great Britain to Mongolia, Australia, Africa and South America.

- *Buy Mini.* Also long neglected by British Leyland and British Aerospace—the tiny, tinny, but lovable car hadn't had a complete overhaul since its 1959 introduction—Reitzle nonetheless saw Mini as *the* minicar. Minicars were becoming an important segment in Europe and Asia because of ever-increasing fuel prices and, as always, the narrow, centuries-old city streets and village roads and the dearth of parking places in Europe. Reitzle didn't want to take BMW itself into the déclassé segment, but he felt it was a market BMW should pursue through the right acquisition. Mini was the natural choice.

It was quite a shopping list the 42-year-old Reitzle presented to von Kuenheim, BMW's elder statesman. (Reitzle also wanted Aston Martin, but it had already been snapped up by Ford.) Von Kuenheim was open to acquisition. At the same time, McKinsey & Co. had recently presented BMW management, along with all of the consultancy's other clients, with a heavily researched prognostication of consolidation among the car companies. General Motors, Ford, and Toyota were the only sure bets to stay independent. Companies like BMW, Volvo, Honda, and Renault were seen as on the bubble, since their modest size hobbled them in regard to product development, production costs, purchasing, and economies of scale in general. BMW remained fanatical about its independence, particularly about avoiding the giant maw of Daimler-Benz, which had nearly swallowed up BMW in 1959.

The first company on BMW's shopping list, Porsche, had been run by Arno Bohn for three years. Not a car man, but rather a skilled industrial manager, Bohn was chosen by the Piech and Porsche families, who controlled Porsche's supervisory board, because of his reputation as a financial disciplinarian and strategist. But the company was being whipsawed by flagging economies in Europe and North America after the U.S. stock market crash of 1987. When the stock market fell, so did sales of sports cars, which no one *needed*. While Porsche AG was slimly profitable in 1992, Bohn had made the mistake of funding a sport sedan as a way of expanding Porsche's customer base. The project consumed almost 500 million deutsche marks, a huge sum for Porsche, especially since the car would never grace a showroom. BMW asked the Piech and Porsche families how much it would take to acquire Porsche AG. The price was 1 billion deutsche marks ($600 million in 1991 U.S. dollars), far exceeding BMW's notion of paying only about $350 million for a battered but still valuable Porsche. "Ridiculous," said von Kuenheim of the asking price. "Madness!" It would have been a bargain.

The Porsche deal fell off the table with a thud, and the focus then turned to Rolls-Royce. It was Reitzle's idea, so it was he who flew to London to talk to Sir David Plasto, chairman of Rolls-Royce, about acquiring the storied brand. Vickers and BMW were already in business together producing aero engines. Vickers had acquired the legendary, but now antique, factory at Crewe, England, that built Rolls-Royce and Bentley automobiles. Vickers never showed much interest in the business, taking it on almost as a kind of favor to the nation after its previous owner went belly-up. Quality and innovation, the onetime hallmarks of the brands, had fallen woefully absent from the cars. By the time BMW began its pursuit, both Rolls and Bentley had been using the same engine and chassis for 30 years. And the Rolls-Royce brand had been neglected in favor of the growing Bentley brand. Combined sales for Rolls and Bentley had dwindled to anemic levels in 1988 and 1989, and Plasto was delighted to find a taker in BMW. Reitzle returned to Munich with a deal in his pocket to acquire Rolls for DM350, or about $200 million.

Soon after, von Kuenheim was lunching with BMW's management board members, including Reitzle, and just as the customary Bavarian pretzels were served, he said, "Reitzle thinks we should buy Rolls-Royce—what do you think?" Reitzle was understandably bothered: He had already negotiated a deal in principal with Plasto, and now von Kuenheim was undermining him in front of his fellow *Vorstand* members. Reitzle had thought that this was his deal and that von Kuenheim would get approval from the supervisory board, and then it would simply be presented to the management board. This unfolded as Reitzle held some weak cards. The 3 Series, "Reitzle's baby," had just been introduced, and quality problems were hurting the launch. Pischetsrieder was the board member in charge of manufacturing, and the company had built a new "flexible" body shop that was not up to BMW's usual standards. The body panels fit together poorly, production lagged behind schedule, and too much corrective handwork was required to make the cars salable. The chief financial officer, Volker Doppelfeld, was, as one BMW executive recalls, "throwing oil all over this fire." Reitzle was the most popular candidate to succeed von Kuenheim, but Pischetsrieder had also emerged as a strong candidate. For his part, Doppelfeld wanted the job himself and thought he might be able to make both men look bad to von Kuenheim as well as to supervisory board chairman Hans Graf von der Goltz and chief shareholder Johanna Quandt. Reports of cost overruns and quality issues had reached von der Goltz, and von Kuenheim summoned both Reitzle and Pischetsrieder to von der Goltz's office for an explanation. Pischetsrieder was in charge of manufacturing, so it was his bailiwick. But there was enough blame to heap some on Reitzle as well. Doppelfeld didn't mind torpedoing Reitzle, so he'd been quick to paint Rolls as a poor investment. Von Kuenheim seized the opportunity to assert his authority, informing von der Goltz at the meeting, "You know, Dr. Reitzle has for months been trying to get us to buy Rolls-Royce. You may hear something about this in the press. In case you do, it's true, we have had discussions. But I do not think this is a good idea. I was in London this month at a government meeting and outside the House of Lords, and I saw only two Rolls-Royces. These are cars now bought only by movie stars, red-light-district bar owners, and aged royals."

BMW canceled Reitzle's deal with Plasto. After an embarrassing meeting at Vickers, Reitzle went to Rover's owner, British Aerospace, to discuss buying Land Rover and Mini without taking on the entire

Rover brand. "The numbers on Rover were terrible. . . . We only wanted Land Rover and Mini, and I was not interested in any deal that included Rover," says Reitzle. But British Aerospace rebuffed that offer. The fortunes, if you could call them that, of Rover, Land Rover, and Mini were intertwined in the last of the mainstream British car companies—Rolls-Royce notwithstanding. (Ford had already snapped up Jaguar for $2.5 billion.) The Brits didn't want the last vestiges of their once proud auto industry simply picked clean by the Germans.

After the deals for Porsche, Rolls-Royce, and Rover fell through, Porsche board member and soon-to-be Volkswagen chairman Ferdinand Piech tried to hire Reitzle as chairman of Porsche AG. Perhaps the two biggest personalities in the German auto industry, along with von Kuenheim himself, Piech and Reitzle liked and respected one another. The deal included a Porsche ownership stake for Reitzle, an unheard-of offer in the German car business; it would have made Reitzle happy *and* wealthy. But von Kuenheim rightly valued Reitzle as the best product development man around; what's more, the boss hated disloyalty. Reitzle wanted the Porsche job badly, but von Kuenheim wouldn't rip up his contract. While he consoled Reitzle with a spoken intent, if not a promise, for Reitzle to succeed him as chairman, the breach of loyalty actually sank Reitzle's future at BMW. The top job went instead to Pischetsrieder in 1993.

———

Within weeks after Bernd Pischetsrieder became BMW's chairman, the bearded Bavarian rekindled the Rover plan, even if it required taking on the Rover brand, and informed von Kuenheim. A new chairman has the right to pursue such deals even though von Kuenheim had dismissed the notion himself a few years earlier. Pischetsrieder was anxious to stamp his imprint on the company and to launch his tenure. Now he would work with Rover chairman George Simpson, who had succeeded David Plasto. Pischetsrieder opened negotiations by repeating Reitzle's gambit of two years prior: Land Rover and Mini only. But Simpson echoed Plasto's refusal, knowing that the marginally profitable Land Rover was the tasty buttercream icing hiding Rover's rotting, rancid cake. It was his ace. Anyone who wanted Land Rover or Mini would have to absorb Rover as a whole. Simpson, a 25-year Rover veteran, knew the company had to be sold to a better-resourced and more engaged (in the auto business) company than British Aerospace.

What was Rover? The company had been sustained only by its partnership with Honda, which owned part of the company and supplied Rover with vehicle platforms and development expertise. The Rover name had been applied to all the cars marketed by the company after 1986 when the old Austin name was dropped. But quality never reached Honda levels, and marketing failed to establish Rover as a true premium brand, which had been the strategy. Cars were either too small, priced wrong, or too dull. There was almost no credibility surrounding the brand in Great Britain or continental Europe except among old-line Brits who bought the brand out of stubborn national or brand loyalty. The plants were antiques and the workers clung to old, oftentimes sloppy, work practices. Land Rover made the company look marginally profitable, but the Rover brand was bleeding money.

Concerned about the fate of Rover's 33,000 workers, Simpson had three options:

1. Rover and Honda had built cars together for a decade, with the Japanese automaker owning 20 percent of Rover and providing much of Rover's product development know-how. Convincing Honda to purchase the rest of the company was the most attractive, if unlikely, option.
2. Convince either Daimler-Benz or BMW to buy Rover. Ford, Volkswagen, and GM had all offered to buy Rover in the mid-1980s, but they, too, were now struggling for profitability and were no longer interested.
3. Try a management buyout. That was most unlikely since the British banks knew how sick Rover was and would be loath to fund a takeover.

Pischetsrieder offered 550 million pounds, well short of Rover's book value of 1.3 billion pounds sterling. BMW also needed Honda, 20 percent owner, to agree to any deal. Pischetsrieder wrote to Honda CEO Nobuhiko Kawamoto blithely asking him to step aside while BMW gobbled up the company. But Honda was happy with its Rover stake, and Kawamoto didn't even bother to answer, offended by Pischetsrieder's and Simpson's approach to the whole affair.

Meanwhile, Simpson wanted Honda to stay at the table to run up the price on BMW. If Honda was irritated by the whole business, it was understandable. Honda had saved Rover from going belly-up years earlier; it and the other Japanese companies had juiced Britain's moribund auto industry, creating and preserving tens of thousands of jobs. A grateful British government had formed close ties with the Japanese. Rover paid Honda for vehicle platforms and engines from Honda and paid royalties to Honda on each car Rover codeveloped with Honda using Japanese components. BMW executives never even properly asked Honda if it might take Rover off its hands after BMW pocketed Mini and Land Rover. Regardless, Honda would have refused, knowing only too well the depth of disease at Rover. Dancing with Rover was far preferable to marrying it.

In January 1994, BMW upped its offer to buy Rover to 700 million pounds, but Simpson told Pischetsrieder that it wasn't enough, though he was, in fact, desperate to unload the company, and no other offer came close. On a cold, miserable day in January 1994, BMW pulled out the stops. It offered 800 million pounds for Rover, plus 20 million pounds to Honda as an incentive to continue supplying engines, plus assumption of Rover's 200 million pounds in debt and 700 million pounds in off-balance-sheet commitments. The deal added up to 1.7 billion British pounds.

The deal would have to be blessed by Britain's Department of Trade and Industry (DTI) and the British Board of Trade. Pischetsrieder and corporate strategy chief Hagen Luderitz met with the British Minister for Science at the DTI, Lord Sainsbury, to explain BMW's plans. The British ambassador in Tokyo advised Sainsbury that Honda and Nissan executives were privately warning that their further investment in the United Kingdom would be in jeopardy if BMW bought Rover. To assuage egos and worries, Pischetsrieder had to make grand assurances to the government of job security for Rover workers and further investment in Britain. Meanwhile, von Kuenheim had advised Luderitz and Pischetsrieder to downgrade the decrepit Longbridge assembly plant near Birmingham, England, to a components plant making engines and other parts for Rover and BMW vehicles. This would reduce the workforce by thousands and concentrate vehicle assembly at the Cowley plant, which was smaller and more efficient than the one at Longbridge. That idea, wise as it was, though, would have sunk the deal. The DTI was concerned only with preserving jobs in the politically important British Midlands, so Pischetsrieder ignored von Kuenheim's counsel. After the protection of jobs and further investment in both plants was guaranteed, the deal was inked at a posh hotel in the Bavarian mountain village of Aschau over dinner, drinks, and cigars. Pischetsrieder, Simpson, British Aerospace chief executive Dick Evans, and finance director Richard Lapthorne were present, as were their wives. The following Monday when the deal was announced, Pischetsrieder promised, "We are not in this for a short-term dividend. If we wanted that, we would have put the money in the bank."

He would soon wish he had.

Pischetsrieder and Luderitz had negotiated privately with Rover, sidestepping discussion with the rest of the *Vorstand*—not a terribly unusual move for a corporate chief and his chief strategist in a deal of this magnitude. Pischetsrieder announced to his management that BMW was buying the Rover Group and intended not only to leverage the Mini and Land Rover brands, but to rejuvenate the Rover car business as well. He also expressed some interest, over the longer term, of pumping new life into old British marques owned by Rover—MG, Riley, Wolseley, and Triumph. Despite the initial table thumping—the German equivalent of a round of applause—several of the executives privately winced. Several *Vorstand* members, including Reitzle, almost immediately began expressing reservations about the deal. Mini and Land Rover, yes, but Rover? Run Rover? Why? What did this rotting brand have to do with BMW's business, its premium brand?

The support of CFO Doppelfeld was key to completing the deal. Having seen the company's chairmanship go to Pischetsrieder, he now saw an opening to one day succeed von Kuenheim as supervisory board chairman. Well liked by both von Kuenheim and the Quandts, Doppelfeld helped Pischetsrieder make his case to the supervisory board for this pig-in-a-poke Rover deal. He argued that Rover's upside for greater sales in markets outside the United Kingdom—boosted by BMW's engineering and product development prowess, discipline, and quality processes—might offset the current losses within five or six years at the most. Reitzle tried in vain to make the case for immediately dumping Rover to whomever would take it. "Give it away or even pay up to 700 million pounds or so to some investor group with a misguided itch to make dowdy, midpriced British cars to take it off their hands," he said. Even at 2.4 billion pounds (the purchase price plus this theoretical payoff), it was a decent, if slightly inflated, price for Land Rover, Mini, and two plants that would have to be extensively refurbished and downsized.

But Pischetsrieder knew he couldn't do this, having just made a shipload of promises to the British government about BMW's commitment to Rover workers. From this point, a power struggle ensued between Pischetsrieder and Reitzle. Besides being correct about the Rover situation, Reitzle was, of course, embittered (who could blame him?) about not becoming chairman, especially after von Kuenheim prevented him from leaving to head Porsche in 1991.

Reitzle minces no words: "My thinking on this was clear about why we should not try to run Rover. If we want to get into the jeans business, then we should buy Levis, not some third-rate brand. And we should not try to use the BMW brand to get into the jeans business. What could we do with this brand that meant nothing outside the U.K., and had only diminishing value inside its home market?. . . . Land Rover and Mini were both iconic brands with obvious value. Rover had nothing. It was madness from the beginning."

Not long after Pischetsrieder closed the deal to buy Rover, he rang up Sir Nick Scheele, who was running Jaguar for Ford. The two had crossed paths for years, and Scheele, one of the most amiable men in the international auto business, was a trove of knowledge and perspective on the British auto industry, having worked for Ford of Europe for years, as well as in the United States, before taking over at Jaguar. Pischetsrieder wanted to sound out Scheele on his newest acquisition and ideas. Since Scheele was running Jaguar with a well-resourced American parent, his perspective about working with a foreign parent was attractive as well. Jaguar had been in Ford's hands since 1988, but was still struggling to fix the old classic Jag brand. The two men talked for three hours.

Without bias about what a revitalized Rover might mean to Ford's business in Great Britain, Scheele told Pischetsrieder that he thought Land Rover and Range Rover were excellent and valuable brands but that he would have to start right away in making over the Land Rover plant in Solihull in Warwickshire and start a process of reforming the workforce, which Scheele described as "entrenched." That's a polite way of saying that the workers were not very open to progressive work practices designed to improve quality and productivity. Mini, too, was "a helluva brand" with which BMW could do "great things." Scheele told Pischetsrieder, though, that he could wind up spending a lot of money trying to rehabilitate Rover and make it worth trying to export. Said Scheele, "Rover was a brand for small-village solicitors and chemists, and that's all it would ever be. There is no future in trying to export a brand with no desirable brand value in its home market." Scheele compared Rover with Ford's Mercury brand, which Ford had no reason to export since it had little brand equity in North America at that time. Lincoln, too, was a brand with a finite appeal that would flounder if it were exported to Europe. In the United States, General Motors had spent billions trying to modernize the geriatric image of Oldsmobile before it announced in 2000 that it would fold the brand. Rover had "gone off," a Britishism used to describe cheese that is past eating. About Pischetsrieder's other plans for Triumph, MG, Wolseley, and Riley, Scheele was equally skeptical: Wolseley had become a brand of socks; Triumph had become a brand of brassiere and other lingerie; and Riley was best known in Britain as a spy character on a BBC television program, *Riley: Ace of Spies.* "As brand names, they didn't exist anymore in the car business except in classic cars shows," said Scheele. In the United States, small companies have tinkered with bringing back brand names such as Studebaker, Packard, Nash, Dusenberg, and Auburn, but these ventures never last long and are usually promulgated by shady entrepreneurs. "I told him that, honestly, outside of Land Rover and Mini and maybe MG, I wouldn't give him a tuppence for the lot," said Scheele.

———

The Rover Car Company began when the Rover Cycle Company, founded in 1896, progressed into making motorcycles in 1903 and cars in 1904. First came an eight-horsepower, single-cylinder car designed by E.W. Lewis, who had previously worked as senior designer at Daimler. Two- and four-cylinder cars soon followed. One of Rover's most popular cars was an air-cooled twin-cylinder model, which achieved high sales in the 1920s. In 1933, Rover underwent a managerial housecleaning, and new models soon followed. Rover steadily gained a reputation during the 1930s as a manufacturer of high-quality, well-appointed cars for professional men and their families. It was comparable to what Buick and Audi became in their home markets.

During World War II, car production was halted, and Rover built aircraft parts and tank engines and helped develop jet engines. At war's end, auto production was moved from Coventry to the Rover factory in Solihull, where a range of new models was produced and the Land Rover utility vehicle was eventually launched. The company's mainstay during the 1950s and early 1960s was the P4 series of saloons aimed at what we now call the executive end of the market. In 1958, Rover introduced the large and luxurious P5 3-liter saloon, its first unibody car. It was also the first Rover that eventually employed the 3.5-liter, Buick-derived engine, which is now considered one of the best V8 engines ever produced. Available in saloon and coupe versions, the P5 went on to become a favorite with British prime ministers, including Harold Wilson, James Callaghan, and Margaret Thatcher. Queen Elizabeth II was also known to drive the P5 as her private transport. Rover's next new model was the sporty P6 2000 saloon. Launched in 1963, this car was technically quite advanced for the day, featuring four-wheel disc brakes, independent front and rear suspension, and a newly designed overhead camshaft, four-cylinder engine.

During the 1960s, Rover was acquired by the Leyland Group, who in 1968 merged with British Motor Company (BMC) to form British Leyland, and Rover was merged with Triumph and Jaguar. The now famous Range Rover was launched in 1970, and in 1976 Rover produced its next major success in the form of the SD1 3.5-liter saloon, which, like the Rover 2000 of 1963, won the title of "Car of the Year" in Britain. In 1968, the Leyland Motor Corporation and British Motor Holdings merged to form one large car and commercial-vehicle organization, British Leyland Motor Corporation. In 1975, the company became British Leyland, shortening that in 1978 to BL.

In 1986, as the Rover 800 was introduced, Sir Graham Day was appointed chairman of British Leyland. He quickly named the company Rover Group, dropped the Austin name from products, and began a program of moving the company and its products upmarket, away from mass-produced cars. Then, in 1988, the Rover Group was sold to British Aerospace.

Pischetsrieder remained wedded to his plans to fix Rover, figuring that it was the only affordable and available acquisition candidate. Underlying this thought was the consultants' contention that any car company selling fewer than 1.8 to 2 million units a year would not survive the coming shakeout in the global auto industry. BMW in 1994 sold just 574,000 vehicles worldwide. Recoiling from the prospect that BMW might become a fob on the watch chain of GM, Ford, or worse, Volkswagen or Daimler, the Quandt family remained fixated on that minimum sales number. To start a new brand, as the far larger Toyota had done with Lexus, would cost a minimum of $5 billion, because it would cost more to start a nonpremium, high-volume brand than a premium, small-volume brand like Lexus was when it launched. Also, the rules of brand gravity would not apply to BMW. That is, while Toyota could reasonably apply its reputation for quality to a new brand of premium cars, there was little benefit in starting a new high-volume brand that people would inevitably view as "the cheaper BMW." There'd be too much temptation to ferret out where BMW was cutting corners.

As the Rover takeover rolled toward completion in 1994, Pischetsrieder was fed and feted by peers and politicians at manor houses throughout England, each host seeking assurances that he wouldn't close the creaky Longbridge complex and lay off significant numbers of Rover's workforce of 33,000. Unbeknownst to Pischetsrieder, though, Rover's workforce had swollen by the thousands in the months prior to the deal's consummating move. In 1994, according to a 1996 study by McKinsey & Co., Rover added more than 4,000 employees to the payroll. BMW managers argued that Rover used the months of negotiation to staff up what was arguably already the most overstaffed, bloated, and inefficient carmaker in the world, aware that once workers are hired, axing them isn't easy. Charitably, the 4,000 new hires represented enthusiasm for an overly optimistic growth plan. At worst, it was a low-down move to take advantage of a foreign interloper they saw as having bottomless pockets.

In 1995, the depth of the Rover problems and the potential profit losses were becoming evident. Sales of BMWs were up by 20,000 units worldwide and Rover sales were up by 16,000 vehicles. But net income went down. Pischetsrieder, already starting to feel the heat of his decision, felt compelled to write the following in BMW's annual report:

"Short-term opportunism should not take priority over long-term opportunities. It should be disregarded if it is incompatible with the established identity of the company and its marques. That is why decisions which are right and necessary in the medium to long term must be taken, even if they look risky or wrong in the short term."

Throughout 1995, Reitzle reasserted himself with von Kuenheim, arguing that Pischetsrieder was driving the world's most admired car brand into the gutter with his foolishness about turning around Rover. Von Kuenheim eventually became concerned as well that he had given Pischetsrieder too much rope—rope that the swaggering Bavarian chairman seemed not only ready to hang himself with, but to use to wound von Kuenheim's carefully honed legacy as well. As supervisory board chairman representing the Quandts' interests, von Kuenheim obsessed about his legacy as chairman, associates say. But once Rover was a done deal, von Kuenheim had little choice but to hope Pischetsrieder could somehow muddle through a viable Rover turnaround plan that would cost no more than $2 billion or so in restructuring costs on top of the purchase price.

Pischetsrieder has a reputation as marketing expert, yet he hatched a curious and unrealistic marketing scheme for Rover. Continuing a flawed and poorly executed strategy that began at Rover in the late 1980s, Pischetsrieder felt he could make Rover a premium choice in any segment. Whether a compact sedan, a midsized sedan, or the Mini, the Rover product would always be the premium choice. Rover had an image in the United Kingdom and a few other markets similar to that of General Motors' Buick brand. It was "slightly premium," the sort of car that might be driven by a bank manager or attorney who was too conservative or not wealthy enough to buy a Cadillac or BMW. Pischetsrieder's scheme was just the sort of plan that a marketing maven can render well on paper, but that lacks any basis in the rough-and-tumble world of selling cars in the mass market. Enjoying some lingering customer loyalty in Great Britain, Rover maintained a tenuous brand position there; but it had no real cachet of any kind in continental Europe. In the United States, Rover had tried to sell sedans under the "Sterling" brand with little success, and there was nothing in any of the research done to date by firms like J.D. Power and Associates to suggest the Rover brand would fare better. To suggest that Rover could become the premium choice in every high-volume segment was to discount what drove the volume of such sales: quality, reliability, and service. To think Rover could challenge the Japanese on these fronts and establish brand cachet in short order was pure fancy. Were they going to conjure up cachet on Rover through startling and breath-taking advertising? Not bloody likely. Asked what a Rover should be, Pischetsrieder gave a short, cavalier answer: "Cheap Jaguars"—just as Buicks were long positioned as cheap Cadillacs. Seeing Volvo and Audi as Rover's natural rivals, Pischetsrieder told *Car* magazine, "Rovers should be cars of a special character, cars that won't please the major-ity but will please a large minority." He added, "As well as the tailor-made Italian suit for which BMW might stand, there would also be the comfortable and nevertheless elegantly tailored suit from the London workshop for which Rover cars might stand." It's all very poetic, but didn't take into account the breadth and depth of problems at Rover, for which Pischetsrieder was clearly unprepared, nor the riddle of what the British government would do about its perennial currency valua-tion issues and Britain's well-established resistance to joining a com-mon European currency.

The chairman had convinced himself as he bought the Rover Group in 1994 that he could grow sales of the brands by threefold from the 467,000 it turned over that year if he could transform its image with a new generation of Bavarian-tinged cars. BMW's backing alone, the optimistic thinking went, should be enough to convince buyers that Rovers had more cachet than Hondas or Fords.

Pischetsrieder declared in 1995 that Rover's turnaround would cost $5 billion over six years, which included capital investment and restruc-turing. The staggering figure was seen by many as a target BMW would handily beat, thus making Pischetsrieder a hero. Chief execu-tives are not in the habit of setting goals they don't think they can sur-pass. He never truly thought it would cost that much or take the full six years to turn a profit. But then Pischetsrieder's blunders began unravel-ing his plan. Rather than rolling up his sleeves and digging into the qual-ity and productivity mess that was Rover, Pischetsrieder let Rover's management fester in the problems they'd created. Pischetsrieder understood that BMW was on trial with the government and the media in Britain, BMW's second-most-profitable market after the United States. With plenty of anti-German sentiment lingering in Britain from two world wars and the British tabloid media given to sensational and jingoistic coverage, he didn't want to move too fast. After all, BMW engines were in those planes that blitzed London a half century before, and British memories were long. The Japanese escaped similar jingoistic vitriol because, though fighting was fierce in the Far East, the Japanese had never attacked England. So Pischetsrieder walked softly, not wanting to deliver too Teutonic a shock to the British-Japanese (from Honda's decade-long involvement in codeveloping cars) culture at Rover. The irony, of course, was that Pischetsrieder, while clearly enjoying the trappings of power and prestige afforded him by his position, was not the aloof German in the arrogant tradition of Volkswagen's Ferdinand Piech or DaimlerChrysler's Jürgen Schrempp. An anglophile, Pischetsrieder is the grandnephew of Mini designer and British auto legend Alexander Issigonis. With the company suddenly lacking Honda's sure hand on the tiller after BMW bought out the Japanese automaker's 20 percent stake, he adopted a hands-off policy.

As astute a corporate planner as any company around, BMW shockingly didn't even ponder the lessons of Ford's 1989 purchase of Jaguar—either before the Rover purchase or afterward. After Ford paid more than $2 billion for Jaguar, it didn't crack the whip on management and workers until almost 1994; five years of steady losses at Jaguar, including the two under Ford, almost forced a closure and write-off of Jaguar in 1991. Both Jaguar and Rover's MG brand were the butt of jokes the world over for poor quality, so neither purchaser could plead ignorance.

Says current BMW chairman Helmut Panke: "We made an extraordinary number of overestimations when we bought Rover. We overestimated the value of the brand and the competence of the workforce. Those are the two biggest factors. As a company, we decided we would buy something and make the numbers look convincing, rather than looking at the numbers to convince us as to whether we should buy it." Panke, of course, was at that time running BMW North America and not in a position to be blamed for lack of due diligence.

Pischetsrieder defended the purchase of Rover in terms of acquiring four entire brands for the price of a single vehicle program; that is, for the $1.5 billion it takes to develop a sport utility vehicle, BMW bought Rover, Land Rover, MG, and Mini. Pischetsrieder even mused about resurrecting the Austin name, which Rover had dumped in

1986, and he had a pet idea of reviving the dormant "Riley" brand name for a special limited-edition model. Riley had been a much loved brand of saloons and sports cars until 1969. Too, Pischetsrieder owned an old classic Riley.

In North America, where SUVs were becoming all the rage, Pischetsrieder planned to quickly leverage the Land Rover franchise. A classy established brand like Land Rover could clean up if BMW pumped up volumes and also built a new entry-priced model—the equivalent of a 3 Series Land Rover. Pischetsrieder was encouraged by the fact that even with some of the worst quality scores in the industry, the Land Rover franchise was making money. Shortly after the 1994 deal, he was delighted to see a prototype of the Freelander, an entry-priced SUV already in development. However, Rover management had failed to engineer it to meet U.S. safety standards; an internal BMW document referred to that decision as "incredible." These were the same professionals who let the Mini Cooper remain unchanged since 1959 despite a European and Japanese minicar boom. The Freelander hit European showrooms in 1996, but none appeared in America until 2001, when it got tepid reviews in a then-swamped SUV market.

Rover was using twice as many vehicle platforms in 1996 to sell about the same volume of vehicles as BMW did, but at much lower profit per unit. Productivity at Rover's plants was 30 percent below BMW's, itself not exactly an industry standard. When the $5 billion cost over six years began looking far too conservative, in a move of almost cruel irony, Pischetsrieder appointed Reitzle chairman of the Rover Group. Reitzle had been issuing plans to both Pischetsrieder and von Kuenheim for over a year on what to do with Rover, so he drew the assignment. Von Kuenheim felt Reitzle was the only choice to untangle the Rover mess. With great trepidation, Reitzle saw the assignment as a long-shot chance to become chairman if he could pull BMW's chestnuts out of the fire, though he ran the risk of saving Pischetsrieder's job if he were successful.

Rover executives knew by this time that Reitzle hated the original deal, held no regard for them, and saw no future for Rover. They also knew that Reitzle had advocated closing or disposing of Rover as soon as the deal was consummated in 1994. And these Rover executives, aware of Reitzle's views, spoke freely to the British press, auguring for a Reitzle reign of terror. The *Birmingham Post and Mail* ran a cartoon of Reitzle wearing a spiked, World War I Prussian helmet, riding a German tank into the Longbridge plant. It was typical of the British press, but also reflected the strong and lingering distrust of the Germans.

Reitzle agreed to the Rover assignment provided he had the freedom to employ whatever rabbit he might pull from his hat. By necessity, his strategy would mean either a disposal of the Rover car business or a drastic restructuring and deep job cuts. Reitzle assembled a small team that included several McKinsey & Co. consultants. They worked long hours, often 14 to 18 hours a day, for six months studying Rover's core operations: productivity, quality, absenteeism, cash flow, and management. Just how deep was the quagmire?

Reitzle presented the team's findings to the *Vorstand* in mid-1996: Rover would lose 2 billion deutsche marks within two years. That was equal to BMW's combined earnings over the previous three years. Oddly enough, the presentation drew a range of reactions, from snickers to derision to alarm. Some members of the *Vorstand* believed Reitzle had ordered up the dire predictions before the study even began—for how could it really be that bad? Others saw it as a ploy to trash Pischetsrieder to von Kuenheim and especially to the Quandts. Others supported the analysis as validating the misgivings they'd harbored from the start. In any case, the report's findings were all true.

The McKinsey report made these charges:

- Rover had shown a net profit in 1994 only by manipulating the balance sheet.
- Absenteeism at Rover plants ran 6 percent, compared with an industry benchmark of 1 percent.
- Downtime (time that the plant was not producing vehicles) at Longbridge was more than 15 percent, compared with an industry benchmark of 5 percent.
- Rework time (the time workers spend fixing assembly-line errors by hand) was four times the industry standard.
- While Land Rover as a division earned $171 million in the year examined by McKinsey, Rover overall lost $22 million. The parts business declared a $52 million profit—a sham since the parts, which were bought by Rover, not by dealers or parts stores, mainly went to satisfy warranty claims. Spare-parts manufacturing, often

a handsome profit center for automakers, was outsourced by Rover, so it earned nothing from the replacement parts purchased by mechanics and owners at parts stores. Given Rover's quality problems, a spare-parts business would have been lucrative.

- All Rover vehicles were far below the industry quality average, as measured by J.D. Power and Associates.
- Longbridge was a whopping 62 percent less productive than industry leaders' factories.
- Nearly one-third of Rover's production remained in inventory as unsold vehicles—twice the desirable amount. A car company carries unsold inventory as assets on its books, but Rover's inventory was overvalued by hundreds of millions of British pounds because of falling prices at the discount-driven dealerships.
- Rover had given, sold, or leased at a loss to company employees and their families more than 31,000 vehicles, compared with just 5,000 provided to BMW executives under less generous terms over the same period. And Rover was hardly a global player in BMW's league. Amazingly, 18 percent of Rover "sales" were to their own employees and family members at a loss! Top executives were allowed to acquire up to five cars each under this arrangement.
- Owner loyalty (repurchase) for Land Rover and Mini was average in the United Kingdom, but below average in every other market in the world; owner loyalty was almost nonexistent in Germany, Spain, and France.
- BMW earned a return on sales of 8 percent, compared with an industry average of around 4 percent. Rover's return on sales was negative. The company had been operating on negative cash flow, consuming 200 million British pounds per year in debt. Yet Rover's own internal documents anticipated a robust 14.6 percent gain in revenues from 1993 to 1995—coupled with a 17 percent cost increase. Yes, Rover actually planned for cost increases to run faster than revenue growth, an imbalance not usually built into a company's plans up front!
- In all the years since the Mini was launched in 1959, the car had *never* been profitable. Despite amortizing the cost of tooling and development over more than 30 years, Mini lost money every year. In the auto industry, this is a remarkable feat of ineptitude.

Most vehicles have earned back their investment by the third year of production.

That this due diligence was not done before the deal was signed, but two years afterward, that all these findings were compiled only after BMW began to realize how murky was the Longbridge swamp, is difficult to explain. Pischetsrieder maintains all the problems were fixable, but that the economics of fixing Rover fell apart as the British pound rose against the deutsche mark. Reitzle says, "Management did not know how deep the problems were because they didn't look until two years after they decided to buy the thing. They didn't want to listen."

The profit and productivity targets set by Rover management for 1997 and 1998 departed similarly from reality. They were merely targets set by the English managers to buy more time for Pischetsrieder and themselves. Though the McKinsey report branded the notion as laughable, the 1997 target was to earn 150 million pounds. *Losing* 150 million pounds was the actual best-case scenario, with a loss of $450 million pounds more likely. Stymied by the rising British pound, losses did reach that level. The pound climbed from DM2.35 in 1996 to DM2.90 at the end of 1997. BMW's hedging plans had revolved around a worst-case currency scenario of the deutsche mark at 2.62 to 2.68 to the British pound.

Pischetsrieder's position weakened with both von Kuenheim and the Quandts. Staffers at BMW Four Cylinders headquarters and the FIZ technical center chattered constantly about "the Rover mess." "Even the greeters at the FIZ knew of the problems," says longtime communications chief Richard Gaul. Von Kuenheim and the Quandts reviewed Reitzle's McKinsey report, and the product chief personally briefed Stefan Quandt and Susanne Quandt Klatten. Slice the numbers as you would, the conclusion was unavoidable: Pischetsrieder had accepted from Rover management financial expectations far divorced from reality. Having been snookered by Rover, how could he be expected to run BMW? While the Quandts had approved the Rover acquisition specifically to help guarantee BMW's financial independence, the deadweight looked like it would propel BMW straight into the fire. Disheartened by the Quandts' and von Kuenheim's cool reception to his lightning bolt of a report, Reitzle offered to step down as chairman of Rover.

Reitzle was succeeded by Walter Hasselkus, a Munich native who was even more of an Anglophile than Pischetsrieder. Hasselkus was known around BMW as "Sir Walter." He had approved a new Mini to be launched by 2001, two years after the desired 1999 launch, plus an all-new Range Rover to be introduced in Europe in 2001, to be followed by a U.S. launch in 2002. (BMW decided to rechristen Mini as MINI—all-capital letters—in conjunction with the brand's new beginning under Teutonic parentage.) An internal BMW document shows an almost freakish and delusional optimism at BMW about Rover's prospects. By 2002, BMW targeted a whopping 470,000 Rover sales, 200,000 Minis, 30,000 MGs, and 200,000 Land Rovers, despite a projected loss of 103 million pounds in 1996, slightly less red ink than the year before. But BMW's accounting was more conservative than Rover's standard British accounting, and applying BMW's currency translation and depreciation formulas, an additional loss of 200 million pounds could be factored in. Heavy discounting succeeded in ringing up 522,000 Rover Group sales in 1997—the highest in eight years, while sales overseas surpassed sales in Britain for the first time. But each Rover-branded car bled red ink, while each Land Rover vehicle earned a decent profit of about 9,000 pounds.

BMW's lack of alacrity didn't help. It took two years after BMW acquired Rover to start consolidating purchasing in Munich to save money. BMW pared back free and discounted cars to Rover managers and even dismissed close to 7,000 workers, though their hands were pretty well tied by the contract signed by former Rover chief John Towers in the early 1990s guaranteeing lifetime jobs for union members as long as the company kept the lights on.

In 1997, Pischetsrieder finally understood a distressing fact well known to Rover managers, to Honda, to the rest of the British car industry, and to virtually every Land Rover owner since Twiggy was a pop star: While Rover's quality was lacking, Land Rover's was beyond awful. On top of the poor design and lousy assembly quality, Land Rover workers and middle managers were more resistant to BMW's encroachment or criticism than were their Rover counterparts, because drivers, blinded by Land Rover's considerable cachet, largely overlooked the problems. The Land Rover workers at the Solihull plant were well known for resisting change or improvement: They had to vote twice before agreeing to stop smoking on the assembly line, to get rid of howling radios, to remove pens from pockets while on the line (they tend to find their way into the crevices of the vehicles and get sealed in during assembly), and to forgo wearing metal belt buckles (they scratch paint on the assembly line.)

Seeing the error of letting Rover and Land Rover muddle on in a sea of red ink, BMW executives began intoning "we are one company" at auto shows and to the media. Behind that facade of unity, though, Munich engineers and managers descended en masse on Birmingham, bossing the Brits like domestic servants, exhibiting open derision at the Rover processes, segregating themselves at mealtime, and even moving some design and engineering functions to Germany—away from what they viewed as the contaminated Rover atmosphere. BMW showered 600 million pounds onto Rover in 1997 alone, 20 percent more than in 1996, and managers throughout BMW increasingly resented having their own projects hampered or delayed in order to prop up "The English Patient" (a reference to the film). Three years after the deal was done, BMW finally sent one of its own quality control experts, Hans-Peter Lange, to ride herd at Rover. Meanwhile, as if Pischetsrieder didn't have enough British cheese and sausage that had "gone off" on his plate, he embarked on negotiations to buy the decrepit Rolls-Royce as well.

In 1997, BMW officials could see where they might get Rover within $100 million or so of profitability. But the 1997 rise of the pound above DM3.00 made everyone in Munich sweat, especially CFO Doppelfeld. Pischetsrieder's version of history—that his plans were crippled by the staggering rise of the British pound—is undercut by the fact that Honda knew for years what a lousy bet it would be to own Rover and expose the whole corporation, saddled with Longbridge, to the gyrations of Britain's pound sterling. The higher pound could have been endured longer if BMW had done a better job of slashing costs over the prior three years, but the hands-off policy that lasted too long made the rising pound a disaster. BMW hedged against the pound's rise until mid-1998, thus ensuring sales from England to mainland Europe would be valued at DM2.40. But the British government gave no indication that it would ever intervene to stabilize the pound through monetary policy. And, unlike much of continental Europe, the British steadfastly rejected joining the European Union and its uniform currency. There was no light at the end of the currency tunnel. The Quandts, up to this point concerned and wary about Rover, by 1998 began to dig deeper into the problem with von Kuenheim, whom they wanted to take a more active role in sorting it all out. In a rare public display, Stefan Quandt reassured workers that the company was not seeking to sell to a partner company, because rumors had circulated in the press, fed in part by comments to reporters by Volkswagen chairman Ferdinand Piech, that the Quandts were looking to sell a stake in BMW. "The fact that Stefan did that was an indication of how bad things looked from the outside and how enormously angry he was becoming over the Rover issue," said one senior BMW manager.

BMW pinned its goal of breaking even at Rover on the first Rover sedan it developed from scratch: the eventual Rover 75, launched in 1999. Meant to take on Volvo and Audi in the premium/subluxury market, the company planned to eventually export it to the United States. German and British stock analysts wrote that the 75 would "make or break" BMW's English foray. An upmarket British sedan built by Germans in a dire financial atmosphere was a far from sure bet with the public.

Basic to BMW but foreign to Rover was BMW's quality system, a veritable institution at BMW that applied rigorous quality checks throughout the development process of a new vehicle. The theory is that there are perhaps a dozen checkpoints throughout the development of a new car at which things can go terribly wrong. Many other automakers have long made the mistake of continuing a vehicle's development in the face of impending disaster hoping the wrongs will be righted in the end. At BMW, the development process doesn't progress past any of several checkpoints until all phases of the project check out and are equally sound. Once the vehicles are shipped, any remaining glitches detected by the dealers are rapidly communicated back to the shop floor to be fixed. Despite several years of exposure to Honda, the idea of continuous improvement had simply never taken hold at Rover. Now, BMW proposed to shake it into Rover, hoping that a rapid increase in quality would be met with applause in the British market and drivers would snap up 75 saloons absent big discounts like Rover had never seen. The plan, sadly, banked on the competition doing absolutely nothing. But with Honda, Toyota, and Nissan in the U.K.

market for many years, quality was hardly much of a selling point—it was expected, like a steering wheel and tires.

By March 1998, the pound rose to a startling DM3.10, enough to fry the nerves of BMW's money counters, since BMW's currency hedge expired in June. Though the pound retreated later that year to DM2.70, it still exceeded BMW's worst-case scenario. Hasselkus could see the firestorm ahead; he tried to reach British monetary authorities through the media since they wouldn't listen to his private entreaties. In a press release, Hasselkus complained, ". . . At a time when Rover Group's exports are increasing, the negative effect of currency on our business is considerable. The service and financial sectors of the U.K. economy give a false impression of what is happening in a real world of manufacturing and international competitiveness. The current value of the pound means our revenue from vehicles sold abroad is reduced, while cheap imports are sucked into our home market." The statement yields two notable points: It was a politely phrased broadside fired at the British government for not moving to adopt the euro; then there was the perhaps ironic remark about "our" home market. With a healthy appetite for traditional English cooking, ports, and clarets, as well as an interest in the British football league, Hasselkus professed solidarity with the Rover family and the company's British employees. The Brits, on the other hand, still saw BMW as German interlopers.

In summer of 1998, Rover sales went south in a hurry. Cheaper Volkswagens, Peugeots, Hondas, and Nissans went flying out of dealerships while Rover sales got hammered in the United Kingdom and on the continent because BMW couldn't discount enough to offset the currency disadvantage. The British government, ever resentful of criticism of their financial policies, especially by Germans, comically charged that BMW hadn't increased productivity enough. BMW's failings explained the problem at Rover and the deepening losses. Never mind that Rover's Longbridge plant was a century old and twice as big as needed for the sales volume; never mind it hadn't received any significant investment in 20 years; forget that it employed 30 percent more workers than necessary—with lifetime job contracts. In truth, BMW had cut the productivity gap between Rover and BMW from 50 percent when it took over down to 30 percent, no mean feat. Even that was hardly enough, since BMW's better profit margins allowed it to book some of the best profits in the industry while being less competitive in productivity with volume makers like Honda.

Exports, always key to BMW's plan for Rover, proved that plan's undoing. With the pound's ascent, the cost of a Rover 400 in Germany rose from DM29,000 to DM39,000—far costlier than competing models. Rover's 1998 losses looked like they would escalate to more than 700 million pounds. Wondering whether they had backed the wrong horse and whether Reitzle might have been the better choice for chairman, in September 1998 the Quandts and von Kuenheim warned Pischetsrieder that such losses would be unacceptable in 1999. Moving quickly, Pischetsrieder suspended all new investment in Rover, meaning the only projects going forward were the ones too far along to be stopped: Range Rover, Mini, and Rover 75.

The 75 debuted at the all-important (in England) Birmingham Motor Show in October 1998. Auto shows are not known for provocative speeches by auto industry lions like Pischetsrieder, who would prefer to occasionally drop bombshells in private interviews with top-tier journalists. But fearing his grand strategy was falling to pieces and frustrated with his lack of traction on labor and monetary policy with Trade and Industry Secretary Peter Mandelson, Pischetsrieder and other officials told a gaggle of reporters at the 75's introduction, "With these products, the future of Longbridge will be secure. Without them, there will be no plant. We have made good progress with Rover, but it is not enough . . . and the parameters under which we planned the next couple of years for Rover have changed." In a scrum with reporters after this statement regarding jobs, Pischetsrieder told reporters in no uncertain terms that if the British pound stayed above DM2.70, the future of Longbridge "could be seriously affected."

The British government got the message and hunkered down to generate a BMW aid package. Along with Longbridge and Rover's 39,000 employees, a host of smaller companies in the British Midlands supplied Rover. If Rover sank, so would those companies and their additional tens of thousands of jobs. BMW wanted at least 200 million pounds from the government, a cut of 3,000 jobs, support for a 10 percent cut in prices from suppliers, and support for flexible work rules that had already been rejected by the unions. The unions came through with a cost-cutting plan unique in the British auto industry. The workweek would be reduced from five days, or shifts, and 37 hours to four shifts and 35 hours. And workers accepted lower pay raises for 1999 and 2000. It was a good offer from the union, but not enough. By late 1998, more than 100 engineers from Munich were running roughshod over their Rover counterparts, trying to drive down costs, improve quality, and speed up new model development, which included the new Mini.

The strong pound kept relentless pressure on Pischetsrieder; by late 1998, von Kuenheim and the Quandts were telling board members they had grave doubts that he could ever overcome the currency problem no matter what his marketing schemes and productivity gains. Given the crisis at Rover, they felt his protracted negotiations in 1998 to buy Rolls-Royce were an unnecessary distraction. Currency problems aside, Pischetsrieder's marketing plan for Rover was not widely supported. Wall Street firm Goldman Sachs in December 1998 published a report that starkly declared, in frank terms, "BMW is discovering, as many others have, that taking a volume brand up market is not the easiest task to accomplish." What's more, the investment moratorium now delayed for years the high-volume replacements for the Rover 200 and 400 models that were supposed to benefit from the model 75's glow. Rover would likely be left in 2001 with two old Rovers engineered by Honda, an overpriced Rover 75 from BMW, the new Mini by BMW, and a glitchy out-of-date Land Rover Discovery. There'd also be a new, high-priced BMW-engineered Range Rover, and a new smallish and mediocre Freelander engineered by Rover but built under BMW's direction. It was quite a hodgepodge.

By early 1999, BMW was a mess. Hundreds of engineers, troubleshooters, and bottleneck breakers shuttled between Munich and Birmingham. The attention Rover and the British labor unions demanded from BMW as the British pound rose ever higher was proving so worrisome to the Quandts that they started to suspect the Rover purchase might cause them to lose control of BMW rather than ensuring their independence. Meanwhile, the unseemly battle for control of BMW between Pischetsrieder and Reitzle that played out almost weekly in the German press and the *Financial Times* was offensive to the hyper-private Quandts and von Kuenheim. BMW's image was being kicked through the streets like an empty beer bottle. As Christmas ran into New Year's, it became clear to everyone at BMW that Pischetsrieder wouldn't last until Easter as chairman of BMW.

A supervisory board meeting was called for February 5, 1999, a Friday, at BMW's Munich headquarters. The prior Friday, several of the influential supervisory board members, including von Kuenheim, Stefan Quandt, Susanne Quandt Klatten, and the members representing the German banks, met in a Munich hotel to prepare for the showdown. They agreed that Pischetsrieder had to step down, but who was the logical successor? Some board members clearly came away from the meeting with the idea that Reitzle would be named chairman. At least two even called Reitzle with congratulations. Von Kuenheim's true role in this is still sketchy. One senior BMW executive says that von Kuenheim was well aware before the February 5 board meeting took place that Reitzle could not and would not be the choice of the Quandts. Intensely private and demanding that their top managers place a premium on discretion, Stefan Quandt and Susanne Klatten were reportedly livid to see a report in the German media about a meeting between Reitzle, von Kuenheim, and von Kuenheim's wife at the chairman's home the previous December. The assumption was that Reitzle had divulged the details of the meeting. "This will not be tolerated," Susanne Quandt Klatten told von Kuenheim. "He [Reitzle] may have thought he was to be named, but Reitzle was not one of the options for chairman that day," says one well-placed BMW official.

At the Friday morning meeting the supervisory board sat on the opposite side of the conference table from the executive board. The executive board left after five minutes, which was customary on matters of personnel so that the supervisory board could speak freely. Managers on the executive board such as Reitzle, Doppelfeld, and production chief Joachim Milberg anticipated the meeting would last perhaps 45 minutes and then they would be called back. Reitzle expected to make a speech—a speech one onlooker said he'd actually left at his chair in the conference room. The media, many at BMW expected, would be granted interviews arranged for that afternoon or the next day. But an hour ticked by, then two, then three. Food was sent in for lunch. *Lunch?* What was going on? Four hours, five, six elapsed. Something was terribly wrong.

The Quandts, it is known now, were already set against Reitzle. But their opposition wouldn't be heard. It was labor in the person of Manfred Schoch, chairman of the Central Works Council, who was not buying into Reitzle as chairman. One story circulated was that Tony Woodley, national secretary for the Transport & General Workers' Union in Britain, which represents Rover workers, reached out to his German counterparts to put the kibosh on Reitzle's candidacy. Woodley knew that Reitzle would move swiftly to sink Rover, sell it off piecemeal, and boot tens of thousands of British workers into the street. Without labor's support, von Kuenheim and the Quandts couldn't realistically elevate Reitzle to the top spot. Pischetsrieder's role in helping to orchestrate labor opposition to Reitzle is hard to pin down, but it's clear he wanted to keep his chief rival from succeeding him. Was the Central Works Council's opposition really an insurmountable obstacle to Reitzle or just the excuse the Quandts needed to appoint a less controversial figure? BMW was in turmoil, and Reitzle was the rock star of the German auto industry. Was a rock star the right man to quell the unrest? The Quandts didn't think so.

Some days before the meeting, Pischetsrieder had somewhat brazenly told Reitzle he would not get the top job despite von Kuenheim's apparent support (Woodley had already told Pischetsrieder about his discussions with the German Central Works Council). Reitzle didn't learn what was in the wind until the day before the meeting. A supervisory board member was missing from the meeting. This gave von Kuenheim an excuse for not being able to make Reitzle's case, as the missing board member carried with him a needed vote for Reitzle, von Kuenheim said at the time. BMW insiders believe the Quandts had soured on Reitzle long before the board meeting and that his fate was sealed after his meeting at von Kuenheim's home was reported in the media. In addition, at the Detroit Motor Show, said one BMW executive, "He may have made one or two criticisms too many *in public* about the Rover debacle." In truth, according to well-placed sources at BMW, it was Stefan Quandt and Susanne Klatten who prevailed on Works Council chairman Schoch to oppose Reitzle's candidacy and who arranged for the missing supervisory board member. Though Woodley had reached out to Schoch as well, the labor leader's attitude toward Reitzle's candidacy was even more affected by the Quandts. While the

Quandts did not want Reitzle, they didn't want to be seen as overtly sinking his candidacy for the chairmanship, so they got Schoch and von Kuenheim to do their work for them. Reitzle still had a huge following within BMW, and rightly so. More than any other one person, he was responsible for the company's most successful era of new models. He had literally established the style of vehicles for which BMW had become known and admired the world over. Moreover, Reitzle had warned anyone who would listen for five years that Rover was a sink-hole that could swallow BMW's jealously guarded independence. The Quandts wanted distance from the exercise of forcing Reitzle's resigna-tion, preferring instead to play the role of blessing a conclusion that was reached by the rest of the board. Without the Central Works Council, the rest of the board, including those who supported Reitzle, had to backpedal. In truth, when the rest of the board realized the Quandts were not on board with Reitzle's candidacy, their support quickly evaporated. "No one on the supervisory board has much stom-ach for opposing the Quandts," says one BMW executive. The Quandts, with their 47 percent interest, simply wanted *their* man, which was not Reitzle. Why would Schoch cave in to the Quandts? There was a perfectly fine alternative to Reitzle: Joachim Milberg.

Von Kuenheim emerged from the board meeting late that after-noon, said one onlooker, a "desperate look on his face." This was unusual for the normally poker-faced Prussian. "What can I do . . . I cannot get the support for you," he told Reitzle in a bit of theater to appease his former protégé. With the German newspapers writing for a week that Reitzle would take over as chairman, the dejected product guru who bled BMW blue now had no choice but to offer his resigna-tion. To remain as product development chief would have been a tremendous loss of face. Besides, it is doubtful that Joachim Milberg, the new chairman, would have wanted an embittered Reitzle in charge of product development on his watch.

What BMW needed now was a conciliator to unite the *Vorstand*, receive labor's embrace, and be trusted to carry the Bavarian flag for the Quandts. A relative newcomer to the company, Milberg had been at BMW only since 1993, but he had impeccable credentials. Milberg had been a professor of engineering at Munich's technical university and a manufacturing and productions expert who had connected with most of the automakers and parts suppliers in Europe and North

America before joining BMW. Pischetsrieder had recruited Milberg to be his own head of production. A known quantity to the Quandt family even before joining BMW, Milberg benefited, says one BMW executive, from being the Quandts' "kind of man . . . quiet, unassuming, very smart, and almost as shy of the limelight as they are." Milberg was named chairman, to the surprise of most of Munich and those inside BMW's Four Cylinder building.

Instead of accelerating a Rover spin-off, as Reitzle advocated, Milberg pursued Pischetsrieder's overlapping, multibrand strategy, while more ruthlessly trying to wring the waste out of Rover's system and lower costs by more integration with BMW. BMW had chartered two Avro jets and one Airbus to fly planeloads of managers and engineers with sharp pencils back and forth almost daily to dissect cost overruns, bottlenecks, and excess labor. The kid gloves donned by Pischetsrieder were cast aside. Milberg had no attachments, sentimental or otherwise, to the Brits and had made no promises he was afraid to break. He just knew that the bleeding had to be stopped. Under Milberg's prodding, German managers began supplanting Rover managers. Milberg moved swiftly. He also put pressure on the British government to kick in the 200 million pounds it had been dithering over for months to support BMW's revitalization of the Longbridge plant, where BMW eventually planned to build two new Rover cars. When the British offered only 118 million pounds—and stipulated it would be phased in over a period of *years*—the usually subdued Milberg hit the ceiling. At the BMW shareholders meeting in spring 1999, he threatened, "The longer the negotiations drag on, the greater will become the likelihood of a production site outside of Great Britain." And *poof* would go the 50,000 assembly and supplier jobs connected to Longbridge. Milberg lacked Pischetsrieder's public swagger, but in this instance he was proving far tougher than Pischetsrieder.

———

By the fall of 1999, less than a year into Milberg's tenure, support for Rover among some key BMW board members (namely, new finance chief Helmut Panke and strategy chief Hagen Luderitz, who had helped engineer the deal) was dwindling. When two Brits, Eric Walters and Jon Moulton of the London-based venture capital firm Alchemy, called on the two men in Munich to propose that BMW sell

Rover, they got a receptive hearing. Rover was on track to lose about 600 million pounds in 1999—about the same as in 1998. And future prospects looked equally bleak, at least until 2000, with no prospects of any profit until 2002 at the earliest, but even that was doubtful.

Says Panke, "What we saw was the increasing number of qualified engineers flying to Birmingham on Monday and returning on Friday, engineers who were doing nothing but fixing, fixing, fixing. It was as if my wife was continually asking me to fix a cuckoo clock week after week, and I kept spending my time fixing this clock rather than doing something rewarding for both of us. After all these weeks, if I'm not successful, I have to say . . . 'Forget it. Let's start over. Buy a new clock. Whatever. But we are getting rid of this one.' "

The two Alchemy venture capitalists told Panke and Luderitz that they had been "barmy" from the start, that Rover was dead when BMW bought it in 1994 and that it was madness to keep throwing good money after bad. Alchemy proposed to take the company off BMW's hands and boil it down to making the model 75 and MG-branded cars, the only ones in the mix they saw as having a viable future. Alchemy was the first to suggest to Panke that BMW sell Land Rover separately for about 1.5 million pounds to offset both BMW's losses and the money it would have to pay Alchemy to pay off workers. It was a controversial idea, but one that Panke began entertaining immediately.

While Milberg was still publicly wed to remaking Rover, Panke felt it was hopeless. "Rover had become a virus in the organization. . . . There was an incredibly negative atmosphere in our management meetings and it dominated all our meetings with the motor press even when we were introducing a new BMW model," said Panke. "This was, I thought, putting our culture at risk." Panke was reluctant to part with Land Rover, but BMW was introducing the X5 sport utility, whose nifty on-road manners proved that BMW could put its marque on SUVs without diluting its sports car heritage and brand equity. And he definitely wanted to keep the Mini as part of the mix since BMW was well under way toward launching the new "Mini" in 2001. In addition, BMW wanted the Mini as a hedge against rising fuel-economy requirements in the United States and elsewhere in the world. The Mini's 24 mpg city / 33 mpg highway fuel-economy rating would boost BMW's corporate average in the United States.

By early 2000, BMW put the word out to Volkswagen, Toyota,

Honda, Fiat, General Motors, and Ford that it was ready to sell Rover. But BMW quickly learned what it would have to pay to unload Rover. In exchange for the headache of Rover and its two creaky British factories, it would have to allow the acquiring patsy the privilege of buying a stake in BMW—perhaps as much as 25 percent. Ford, GM, and especially Volkswagen were all interested in taking on Rover, but they also wanted to stir pots in BMW's kitchen. The Quandts, however, would not entertain the sale of even one share to an outside car company—that would have been the beginning of the end of BMW's independence. The Quandts did, though, want the Rover matter decided upon before the mid-May shareholders meeting. With no other suitors bending a knee, Panke focused on the Alchemy proposal.

Alchemy drew up a complicated road map to separate Rover from BMW. It called for Alchemy to pay BMW 20 million pounds and for BMW to pay Alchemy 500 million pounds to dim the lights at Rover, reducing it solely to a niche maker of MG sports cars and Rover 75s. Even at that, Alchemy would eventually try and sell off that last sweet little MG niche, probably to Ford or Volkswagen. On March 16, 2000, the two sides announced an agreement to sell Rover and the Longbridge plant to Alchemy. The other shoe to drop was the sale of Land Rover to Ford for 1.8 billion British pounds. The decision to sell Land Rover—which made perfect sense to Panke—caused a rift on the management board that prompted the resignations of manufacturing chief Carl Peter Forster, engineering boss Wolfgang Ziebart, and sales chief Henrich Heitmann. In just 14 months, nearly the entire management board had turned over, which was certainly remarkable for BMW, as it would be for most companies.

Says Panke, "I won't say this was not a very difficult time for the company. But I also think that this time crystallizes why this company is as strong as it is. After 1999 and 2000 and all these changes of personnel, we not only replaced everyone on the management board from inside the company, but we restored earnings despite economic recession in Europe, the U.S., and Japan and achieved our strongest sales in history." The strength of BMW's management is astonishing when you look at where those who left BMW in 1999 and 2000 landed: Pischetsrieder is chairman of Volkswagen, Reitzle is chairman of Linde AG; Forster is CEO of Opel; Ziebart is chairman of Continental AG. To lose such talent and barely miss a beat is remarkable.

The deal with Alchemy, however, came unhinged. Over the six weeks following the announcement, the British firm would not meet some of BMW's demands. BMW pondered adopting the Alchemy plan themselves: Wind down Rover, sell Land Rover, and sell or mothball MG. But that flew in the face of BMW's main goal of ridding itself of Rover. Then came an offer from an investment group called Phoenix, which was headed by former Rover chief John Towers. Towers was emotionally committed to saving Rover, and after piecing together a basic plan of attack, he received the British government's support. Towers proposed that Phoenix take over the company, including Mini. The Towers' group would require at least 200 million pounds in borrowed working capital. However, keenly aware of Rover's dire straits, the British banks turned Phoenix down. Meanwhile, protests and marches against the Alchemy plan to shutter Rover were taking place in Birmingham and indeed throughout the Midlands. Public opinion was rising against BMW, with a call for boycotting its showrooms. British government officials were trying to blame BMW mismanagement for Rover's demise, while BMW and most independent analysts more correctly slammed the government for allowing the British pound to skyrocket out of control. Despite its public posture, the British government was starting to realize that Longbridge was going to close. The only real issues to be hammered out were how much money the workers would receive and who would shoulder most of the blame and cost. To protect its image in one of its most significant markets, BMW opted for the Phoenix plan. To push the deal through, BMW used its clout with an American bank, First Union Bank of North Carolina, which BMW was showering with business via its Spartanburg, South Carolina, assembly plant, to help finance Phoenix. And so a deal was done: Phoenix would pay BMW a token 10 pounds for Rover, the Longbridge plant, responsibility for 7,000 workers, the Rover 25, 45, and 75 models, MG, and the old original Mini. BMW would pay Towers' group 500 million pounds to take it all off its hands. BMW would keep the new Mini and the Oxford plant, though it would have to go through the extraordinary chore of shifting Mini's production and tooling from Longbridge to Oxford.

In total, BMW lost about 3 billion pounds over six years on top of the purchase price. In 2000, it cost 3.2 billion euros to sell Rover, though it recouped 2.9 billion euros by selling Land Rover to Ford.

When everything is added and subtracted and currency valuations are summed together, it looks like BMW paid out around $7 billion to end up with Mini.

———

How could the "most admired car company in the world" make such a colossal blunder?

By acquiring Rover, BMW nearly doubled in size—an enormous challenge for a company as tightly managed as BMW, especially when that meant half the company was now operating in another country, with workers and managers who speak a foreign language. Factor in Britain's well-known economic isolationism from the rest of Western Europe, and it was a bad bet any way you slice it. At bottom, the best odds were lengthened by poor reasoning: BMW had decided it wanted to expand, and no other company was for sale, so it bought Rover. And unlike Ford's acquisition of Jaguar, which remained a prestigious, if tattered, brand when Ford pounced, Rover had no cachet or even brand equity outside Britain.

British journalists Chris Brany and Andrew Lorenz in their fine book, *End of the Road,* correctly note, "Pischetsrieder was caught up in what business psychologists call 'The Concorde Fallacy,' so-called because the Anglo-French airplane was financed even after it became obvious that by an economic evaluation it should have been scrapped. Those responsible for the project had invested so much in it that they were unable to withdraw." Pischetsrieder acknowledges the theory when he says, "To withdraw from Longbridge would have meant acknowledging a reversal of strategy. . . . The reason companies fail is because they do not have the courage to continue with the right strategy in the face of problems."

As BMW jettisoned Rover and sold Land Rover to Ford in 2000, its share price rose 53 percent. Despite an economic downturn in both Germany and the United States, in 2002 it posted its best first quarter in history, with profits up more than 400 percent over previous years, and proved BMW could sell SUVs on its own. Saluted by the motor press as a "genuine" BMW, the X5 was born a winner, as the 3 Series continued to dominate the entry-level premium segment. An X3 SUV was developed for launch in 2004.

Wolfgang Reitzle calls the whole Rover affair "the Rover exercise."

Since *exercise* means bodily exertion to develop or maintain physical fitness, it's an apt phrase. After all, BMW learned a lot about itself during the six years it owned Rover. At a total price tag in excess of $8 billion, it was forced to reevaluate the elasticity of its own brand and reeducate itself about BMW's core values. Exercise also means to "cause anxiety, alarm, or indignation." Needless to say, the experience certainly did all that, too.

The Ultimate Brand Expansion

SEVEN

Provided you already have a Mini,
a Rolls-Royce makes an ideal second car.
—Motor MAGAZINE

Out of the expensive rubble of BMW's purchase of the British Rover Group has emerged a small, sparkling gem that should deliver handsome operating profits for decades to come: Mini. It looks like the jewel of the deal since BMW had much grander initial plans for the Land Rover and Rover brands; this despite the fact that by the time BMW came along in 1994 even the British had come to look upon the Rover as some aging, beloved rock star in orthopedic shoes being trotted out onstage. Yet the BMW-designed Mini Cooper actually captured the North American Car of the Year award in 2002. It's arguably the toughest accolade an automaker can win, determined as it is by the votes of some 50 automotive reporters—so companies can't seek to buy it with reams of advertising at one magazine or another in the hopes of winning *that* publication's car of the year award.

While BMW struggled with its acquisition of the Rover Group in 1997, the company also ventured into an all-out bidding war with Volkswagen for ownership of Rolls-Royce and Bentley. The outcome of that contest was that BMW won the rights to the Rolls-Royce brand and to develop future products adorned by the storied "flying lady" hood ornament. Volkswagen ended up with Bentley and an aging factory in Crewe, England, that was in desperate need of an expensive overhaul. By 2003, BMW introduced the first of its homegrown Rolls-Royces, the Phantom.

The Rolls-Royce and Mini additions lie at the heart of BMW chairman Helmut Panke's vision for BMW AG's growth. "Always premium. Always premium" runs Panke's mantra. He continues: "We have two brands now that are uniquely suited to BMW's way of doing business. We have a brand in Rolls-Royce that uniquely defines luxury the world over to which we can bring our resources, expertise and processes to put it back on the pedestal intact where it belongs. In Mini, we have a brand that is and will continue to be the undisputed premium choice in the small car market—that is a totally unique positioning that no other brand in the world will be able to claim. So, in these two brands, we have characteristics and imagery that no other company can claim or copy. That, to me, is the essence of brand value and brand management."

————

Mini sales in 2003 were estimated to be 140,000 at the time of this writing, 15 percent ahead of BMW's expectations. In North America, sales were running 20 percent ahead of plans set forth in 2002. Mini North America chief Jack Pitney had two challenges during 2003: a few niggling product quality glitches and getting the factory to build more cars—a lot more cars. While other companies took to bribing customers with fat rebate checks of up to $4,000 to buy some small cars in 2003, Mini was oversubscribed, even with dealers often charging $1,000 or more over the sticker. To understand Mini's value to BMW, consider that it will earn more in 2004 selling 30,000 or so Minis in the United States than will General Motors selling 200,000 Chevy Cavaliers.

What makes the Mini Cooper the perfect complement to BMW? Five minutes of driving the Mini Cooper or the faster Mini Cooper S reveals all too plainly why BMW didn't let its vaunted blue-and-white propeller badge anywhere near the car. BMW chairman Helmut Panke says the decision was made primarily because the little car has front-wheel drive, "and no BMW would ever be front-wheel drive . . . the discussion about putting the BMW brand on the car didn't go anywhere because of that." Plausible perhaps, but—front drive or rear drive—the fact is that the car doesn't feel anything like a BMW. And it's not just that it has front-wheel drive with an engine Chrysler helped develop. One feels every rattling bump in the road in the Mini Cooper. Close your eyes, and the Mini Cooper feels every inch a $14,000 car in a $19,000 suit. Not that there's anything wrong with that; it's an indication of BMW's marketing prowess and eye for brand talent.

Pound for pound, the Mini is hardly a better drive than a Ford Focus or a Volkswagen Golf; some road-test evaluators even prefer one of the latter. But the Mini consistently wins hearts and wallets through its sheer *brand character* expressed by its design and packaging inside and out—and its obvious descent from the original Mini. Its unrefined road character, which is inherent in a car just 10 feet long, is quite overcome by its sheer style—style worth thousands of dollars per unit. Where other cars in a similar or somewhat cheaper price bracket, such as the Focus or the Cavalier, scream "basic transportation," the Mini Cooper simply delivers a *groovy* driving experience.

David Welch is one of *Business Week*'s Detroit correspondents, covering General Motors and some of the import companies, among other beats, for the magazine. Welch is a Detroit native. Like most auto journalists, he drives different cars every week as loaners from the car companies, so he enjoys a wide array of cars, trucks, and SUVs and can drive whatever he wants. Welch is physically and socially active and counts competitive fencing among his pastimes. In the fall of 2002, Welch, 32 at the time, plunked down his own money to buy a Mini Cooper S.

Says Welch: "The first time I saw the Mini Cooper, I thought it was the best—and yes, I admit it—the 'coolest' car that anyone has designed in decades. I was only looking at photos put out for the press by BMW, but I thought: finally, a car with some character. Sure it has retro styling, but it's not like the Ford Thunderbird, which is just a modern copy of a model from years past. And the looks didn't seem all that retro to me. But the car looked so good that I was hooked from the start. That was in summer of 2001. I went to the Frankfurt Auto Show that fall. I've always liked European auto shows because the car-makers actually go through the bother of trying to make cool passenger cars in the 'Olde World.' In the States, my options are a pickup, which I don't need, an SUV, which I don't like, and a relentlessly dull line of sedans like the Camry or Taurus. So when I got to Frankfurt, my first stop was BMW's auto show stand, which was a small dome they had erected outside the show hall. Inside they had three or four Minis along with the brand new and much anticipated new 7 Series sedan. The Mini, which had been shown in Paris a year earlier, got more attention. I had considered a Nissan Z, a Subaru WRX and a Mazda RX-8. But the Z was just too impractical, the Subaru too ugly and the RX-8 wouldn't arrive at dealers until 2003. That was too long to wait. Besides, the Mini was the most fun to drive and definitely the best looking car."

———

When BMW was negotiating to buy the Rover Group in 1993, the British assumed BMW had a twofold motivation: to obtain the prestigious Land Rover sport utility brand to complement its own golden BMW passenger-car brand and to boost sales volume with Rover cars. The Mini brand, which the Brits had neglected for years, was assumed to be slated for the scrap heap.

"It's funny given the history now that they couldn't see what a hidden gem Mini was," says BMW's Panke. "I think they were almost too close to it. It's like when someone has an old coat or table they are ready to throw out or give away, and then a stranger comes into your house and admires that table's construction or style or the way that coat is cut and hangs elegantly. The people at Rover didn't know the sleeping brand equity that was in the Mini, and neither, it seems, did Honda, which was building cars with Rover and could have funded a Mini program."

There are a lot of British who don't care much for steak-and-kidney pie or bangers and mash, especially those under the age of 50 who view old, classic British cuisine as boring and unhealthy. But Americans, Germans, and South Americans visiting the United Kingdom often scarf it up because no one at home makes it so well. British cars have enjoyed the same appeal outside Britain for decades; even the appeal of antique British motoring in the case of the Mini was recognized by the Germans. Some BMW executives had the same warm feelings toward the Rover brand, but that was clearly misguided.

Unlike the style and fun embodied in the very chassis of the Mini, the Rover brand had no such cachet, no such mystique.

The twentieth century offered three cars that, more than any others (though Thunderbird or Mustang partisans might make a good argument), transcended the automobile category to become landmark studies of design and consumer appeal and even cultural phenomena: the Ford Model T, the Volkswagen Beetle, and the Mini (the original Mini is spelled with upper- and lowercase letters, while BMW's reinvention of the car is branded as MINI). Historians and car buffs can debate the list of icons to the death. Pontiac GTO? Porsche 911? Ford Mustang or Chevy Bel Air? BMW 2002? But even on a longer list, there's wide agreement on the Model T, the Bug, and the Mini holding the top spots.

The Model T began a new era of personal transportation based on mass-produced, reliable vehicles. The Beetle, which achieved the same iconic status, made an even bigger jump from basic transportation into popular culture and art, and, of course, was built in its original form for more than 60 years before ending its run at a Mexican plant in 2003. Like the Beetle, the Mini also had a remarkably long production run, being produced for 41 years with hardware upgrades but no total makeover. The Mini was the first big-selling car to be produced with the combination of a transverse engine (mounted sideways in the engine compartment) and front-wheel drive. It proved such a dynamic way to pack an engine into a small space that virtually every other maker of front-wheel-drive vehicles later adopted the same layout. Mini also revolutionized the idea of how to use space on a vehicle platform. Though only 10 feet long, 80 percent of the car's space is devoted to passengers and luggage. To sit in a Mini is to marvel at how spacious it is, even for a six-foot-two, 250-pound man. It had laughably small, 10-inch, and later 12-inch, wheels, compared with the 16- to 20-inch wheels common on passenger cars today. It had independent rear suspension with rubber cushioning the body from the frame. When the Mini was launched in 1959, designer Alec Issigonis placed its wheels at the extreme outside corners of the car, a design characteristic that helped create a desirably stiff ride; it would become a staple in BMW's cars in the late 1960s and continues through today. The horizontally sliding plastic windows, rather than vertically retracting windows, allowed for extra-thin doors. Everything was geared to making the car as light and inexpensive as possible. Not only was Issigonis able to make use of an existing 848-cc, four-cylinder engine made by Mini parent company BMC, but the car's constant velocity (CV) joints were actually poached from a 1930s-era Cord automobile and supplied by parts maker Hardy Spicer.

Broad acceptance of the Mini didn't materialize though, until late 1961, when engineer, designer, and race car builder John Cooper got involved. Cooper built a modified Mini that generated a cool 100 horsepower, well above the basic car's power, and he attached seven-inch disc brakes. BMC chairman George Harriman approved the building of 1,000 "Mini Coopers" after a single, short drive on the track. The Coopers also sported two-tone paint schemes, with the roof painted a different color than the body. Thicker carpeting, chrome plate on the gearshift knob, and a key starter to replace the floor-mounted start button were among the interior niceties that distinguished the car from the basic Mini. That initial order of 1,000 blossomed to more than 20,000 Coopers by 1962. A peppier Mini Cooper S debuted in 1964 with a 0 to 60-mph rating of 13 seconds—4 seconds faster than the basic Mini.

Most of all, Mini became an icon, which makes the Brits' creeping indifference to the vehicle by the early 1990s perhaps harder to understand. Or perhaps not. As marketing consultant Dennis Keene notes, "The Beetle, too, was not something that Germans wanted to revive or had especially fond feelings for." In fact, says Keene, "The Beetle was far more appreciated outside of Germany, and even continental Europe after 1960, which explains in large part why the 1999 New Beetle has sold very few copies in continental Europe." The personality of the Mini is far more important than any transportation function it performs, Keene adds.

Says former BMW product chief Wolfgang Reitzle, "When we negotiated the acquisition of Rover, Mini was very key to the plan." He adds, "Mercedes-Benz was doing things with an A Class and Smart car, which were both funny looking, small cars with no connection to the Mercedes brand. Mini was *the* minicar brand. It defines a whole segment of the market. All we had to do was develop a very good successor to the old Mini, which I knew we could, and we did. The marketing would almost take care of itself, and this is a rare thing to find in any business. That's what made it, and still makes it, so valuable. Some cars and some products you don't really have to market. You just have to get the product right and then get out of the way."

Like the Beetle, the original Mini became a fashion accessory for people who could afford to buy a lot more car. Says Mini USA general manager Jack Pitney, "That's the difference between a product and a brand. . . . The Mini family was, and can be again, similar to the brand family that was Volkswagen Beetle, Karmann Ghia, and the Microbus, which were all built off the same chassis, of course, and were very different vehicles serving very different purposes—yet all working together in one brand symphony that spoke to a large number of people." And just as the Beetle transcended incomes and social stations so that rock stars, professors, bankers, and lawyers bought Bugs, Microbuses, and Karmann Ghias, the likes of British pop icon Twiggy, Beatle Paul McCartney, actor Peter Sellers, and Princess Margaret all owned the inexpensive Mini and were often photographed in them. Actor Patrick McGoohan's character in the celebrated mid-1960s TV series, *Secret Agent,* drove a Mini as he went from derring-do to derring-do. Owners treated Minis like a piece of canvas, painting and customizing them in ways a child might treat a favorite doll. As author Anders Ditlev Clausager aptly puts it, the Mini was "a car for the dustman as well as the duchess."[1] There just aren't that many brands in the world that achieve that kind of democratic appeal, especially not cars that are historically— because of their price and the infrequency of purchase—seen as an extension of the buyer.

BMW understands all this "car as suit" notion quite well. No one, for example, *needs* a BMW M5, capable of reaching 60 mph in 5.6 seconds and cruising easily at 140 mph or more on the autobahn. Yet, in the United States, where it's difficult to drive for long above 80 mph in most places without feeling the burn of a state trooper's radar gun, BMW sells all the M5s it can build and ship. People don't just drive BMWs—they wear them. The same goes for Minis.

———

When the Mini was launched in 1959, the British magazine *Motor* quipped, "Provided you already have a Mini, a Rolls-Royce makes an ideal second car." That kind of response immediately made it a car that would transcend class. The neighborhood butcher drove it—as did Princess Margaret.[2]

Oddly enough, the Mini has an almost bizarre connection to BMW and the executive most responsible for buying it. The Mini's designer, Alec Issigonis—born in Turkey, son of a Bavarian mother and a Greek father, who became a naturalized British citizen and was later knighted—was related to Bernd Pischetsrieder, the BMW chairman who engineered the purchase of the Rover Group. Pischetsrieder's grandmother and Issigonis's mother were sisters.

Issigonis's Mini was born at a time when the British public was keen for a cheap car that could be driven cheaply. In truth, the Brits were looking for an answer to the Volkswagen Beetle, a car the lions of the British car industry had passed over when they had the opportunity to take the Beetle and the factory that would build it in Wolfsburg, Germany, after the war. The Mini, the Brits' "people's car," had to get good gas mileage, be cheap to produce, and be reliable (by British standards) and fairly easy to maintain.

BMC, the merged operations of Morris and Austin, hired Issigonis in 1957 for his second tour of duty with the company. BMC chairman Leonard Lord tasked Issigonis with creating a small car that would drive so-called bubble cars off the road. Bubble cars, such as BMW's Isetta, were tiny cars barely able to seat two—but often asked to carry four—that were powered by motorcycle engines. They were a response to the oil supply crisis of the mid-1950s and rising gas prices. And so to beat back the "bubbles," Issigonis, who by then was a British citizen, came up with the Mini. Using a bubble car's 10-inch wheels, he set out to devise a space that could hold four people with "a bit of luggage." Working with engineer Dr. Alex Moulton, Issigonis laid out the transverse-style engine, a configuration that allows for a shorter front end, among other benefits. Space under the hood being at a premium, Issigonis also thought to locate the gearbox in the sump of the engine. This space-saving remedy, though scoffed at by many engineers of the day, allowed BMC to save big money by using an existing four-cylinder engine. Two subframes were used for the front and rear of the car, a design solution that dampened road shock and prevented violent torque reactions on such a small platform. Unsightly exterior welding seams, automotive anathema by 1960, nonetheless meant using unskilled, and cheaper, labor and simpler metalworking jigs—crude, maybe, but in a way that fashion designers said was "stylish." Five minutes after Leonard Lord began driving the prototype, he green-lighted the little wonder-car for production.

The driving world did not take the Mini seriously at first. Austin and especially Morris were known for conservative automobile design, and this was a revolution in British car making. Such a revolutionary and radical idea simply wasn't expected from BMC, which produced 20,000 Morris Minis in 1959—good enough. But just three years later, annual production at the Longbridge factory in the British Midlands was over 200,000. At just over 500 pounds when it was introduced, it was not the least expensive small car in the United Kingdom, but it was much better and more fun than any of the small-car alternatives. Mini owners generated a cult following around the car and brand, just as Beetle owners had. "You never forget your first Mini" became a common refrain. It also burst on the scene as a new decade presaged the coming revolution in music and design, of which the Mini was part. It became, in effect, Great Britain's national car, yet it never outgrew a kind of cult status. "That's rare for a brand and product to become so popular so fast and not flame out or become too commonplace. . . . That's what takes a brand from brand status to icon," says consultant Dennis Keene. Historian Anders Ditlev Clausager groups the Mini along with Ray-Ban sunglasses, Dr. Martens shoes, and Zippo lighters for functionality, ubiquity, and iconic status in the design world during the second half of the twentieth century.[3]

Like the Volkswagen, Mini inspired clever, fun advertising that other marques simply couldn't get away with. "You Don't Need a Big One To Be Happy" was one headline and billboard inspired by some 1960s sex manuals. The Mini itself—its unique character and personality—went a long way to inspire advertising copywriters to "get jiggy with" their ideas. Despite its diminutive size, the Mini was transformed by either the factory or aftermarket coach builders into an array of designs, station wagons, pickup trucks, and panel vans. Police departments even used them to slalom through city traffic.

When the original Mini ceased production in 2000, 5.3 million had been manufactured at Longbridge. The last ones put out 63 horsepower, compared with 55 in 1961. The curb weight was 1,580 pounds, up from 1,315 forty years before. Top speed was 90 mph, up from 85 mph for the 1961 model. Fuel consumption was 43 miles per gallon, quite a bit better than the 27 to 35 mpg it was rated at in 1961. All in all, much improved and refined in 40 years—but not much changed. Only a tremendous brand could get away with that!

———

British cars had a tough time of it in North America in the 1980s and 1990s. Jaguar had fallen to little more than boutique status until its revival around 2000. Land Rover was the same, generating sales of fewer than 20,000 in 1997 in the middle of a sport utility vehicle craze in America. MG was long gone from the United States. Rover had tried—and failed miserably—to sell one of its sedans codeveloped with Honda in the United States under the Sterling name in the late 1980s. And even the Mini, despite its huge overseas following, was little more than a mid-1960s passing fancy in the United States before packing up and heading back to England. It was a fad that coincided with the rise of the Volkswagen Beetle and "flower power."

A fad was decidedly not what BMW was looking for when pondering an icon's reincarnation. With the Rover acquisition crumbling around them in the late 1990s, and Mini the only piece left by 2000, BMW needed a solid initial business case for 100,000 Minis annually, with a clear path to 200,000 per year within a few years of launching. And the roman-candle performance of the Volkswagen New Beetle (shoot the moon, then crash)—which sold 83,000 in 1999 in the United States, its first year of full production, and was down to 61,000 by 2001—made a few Bavarians nervous. "The Beetle is a dead bird in Europe," said BMW chairman Helmut Panke at BMW's 2002 Detroit Auto Show dinner. "Mini is going to keep flying for many years."

The Mini has always been a global phenomenon, starting as it did with a German-Turk Britisher like Issigonis. It's fitting then that the new Mini should be the product of a marriage between the German BMW and the British Rover, and that the lead designer on the new car, Frank Stephenson, is an American born in Morocco, raised in Europe, and schooled in California.

When BMW bought Rover in 1994, the old Mini was still being produced in small numbers at the Longbridge plant, and some Brit designers had been working on ideas for a successor, following in the footsteps of prior fruitless plans. The word around Longbridge was that the company would continue to build the same car as long as it was legal to do so, but that if the government toughened up safety regulations to U.S. standards, then the business case for the Mini would evaporate since it wasn't worth the reengineering costs. Still, there was always somebody in some corner of the Rover design studios in the town of Gaydon working on a new Mini idea. "We'd always thought that the Mini was very interesting, but we'd never really had our eyes opened to what a powerful brand it actually was," said Mini engineering director Chris Lee. He added, "We'd tended to think of Mini only as a product name, not a brand name."

After taking over, BMW told Rover management that the company was prepared to invest hundreds of millions of British pounds in a new Mini. Rover managers actually discouraged the idea, preferring to see the money go into new sedans, touring wagons, and Land Rover SUVs. BMW had been toiling for years designing a front-drive small car, but it could never get the driving dynamics correct for the rear-drive BMW brand. And BMW believed that much of the development work it had done, rather than going for naught, could be applied to a new Mini. BMW also saw Mini as the correct brand to introduce zero-emission electric cars to satisfy the state of California's mid-1990s mandate. An important aspect of BMW's business plan was to sell a new Mini globally, especially in North America and Japan—two markets Rover managers had written off. Casting a wide net, BMW had set up competition for the new Mini among Rover, BMW's own Munich design staff, the company's Designworks operation in California, and one outside firm. Rover designers built two concepts incorporating some Mini characteristics—that is, small, with wheels pushed out to the extreme corners of the platform—and presented them in October 1995, but they looked more like a creeping class of European city cars, lacking the classic, tailored lines of the Mini original. And, contrary to the Mini tradition, the Rover designs also had rear-wheel drive. BMW executives, especially Wolfgang Reitzle, hated the designs.

The Munich-generated design, code-named E50, had many of the styling cues evident in today's Mini Cooper. It took the original Mini's design lines and made them bigger and roomier to match the drivers who'd grown bigger and roomier themselves since 1959. This also allowed for extra safety gear and stiffer structure. The "waist" line and roofline of the concept were strong and nearly parallel. Those lines, plus the clamshell roof panel sitting atop frameless windows and the muscled front end and hood give the Mini its distinctive look and tie it to the original. On the eve of presenting the clay model of the Stephenson design, the team discovered a problem after shaving two more millimeters of clay off. The designers, who by this point had been pounding a few beers, realized they'd forgotten to include a tailpipe. No problem. They quickly burnished the label off a can of Budweiser on a grinding machine and got it down to bare aluminum—voilà!—your tailpipe!

The Rover designers were angered that Munich had been designing behind their backs—and had gone so far as to use an American beer can for the tailpipe—so they generated a full-blown critique of the E50 as "too serious to have a sense of humor . . . doesn't shock with innovation . . . only better than average."[6] And the Rover folks accused the BMW camp of designing first and worrying about the critical packaging issues afterward. The criticisms jarred BMW's executives not only because of the way they were presented, but because Reitzle, whose sense of design and styling outclassed anyone at Rover by light-years, knew that the Rover designs were completely wrong for Mini. As Reitzle observed, "Don't forget, these were the people who really saw no future for the Mini before we arrived, so they were designing for a brand they had turned their back on. Their designs were very disconnected from the brand attributes that made Mini valuable. They looked more like city cars coming out of Mercedes or Fiat than anything correct for a new Mini."

The resulting Mini that is on the road today is a lesson in connecting brand to product. Gert Hildebrand, who took over the Mini design team in 2000, says too many companies make the mistake of not carrying the very notion of *brand* through to successive products. Rather than sticking tightly to certain brand attributes and allowing them to govern design, companies try to change the brand makeup by generating an array of disconnected products that suit the designers' fancy. "When you want to build up a brand, then you change a model. But you can't go far away from a certain feeling, a certain impression which people already have of the car. It wouldn't make any sense to make a Mini that looked completely different from what people had in mind about the old Mini." And that's what the Rover designers had proposed.

So an interesting point of debate ensued. The Brits wanted to capture a Mini design that would be true to Alec Issigonis's original ideals about space and economy. Given a clean sheet of paper, what would Alec design today? That was the Rover team's approach. The Germans, however, felt they should create a Mini that might have naturally succeeded the original in a single product cycle of seven years. The Germans and the American Stephenson believed that "filling in the missing Mini" was more on-target. The Brits' design, thought Reitzle and BMW design chief Chris Bangle, would have been too jarring.

Despite the friction between the Brits and the Germans about fundamental design in 1996, BMW's Pischetsrieder told Rover's design chief, Chris Lee, that his team was responsible for delivering a Mini, but the Mini that *Munich* wanted. The Munich team would retreat because, under mounting pressure to cork the red ink at Rover, Pischetsrieder couldn't afford further confusion and delay from a comingled British-German new Mini.

Munich had the idea of creating two body styles, one of which was to have a higher roofline than the Mini on the road today. But costs and aesthetics vetoed this notion. The higher-roofline version just wasn't appealing. The Brits never liked the idea of this second body style, but the Germans would have the last word, and this is where Reitzle's uncompromising obsession for design came into play. At many car companies, such a decision is perhaps made on the strength of how it all looks on a computer screen. Reitzle, though, approved the building of two prototypes—bodies that would actually be grafted onto a Fiat Punto, a car with Mini-esque proportions. The Mini team bought a couple of Puntos and then tore them down to the chassis and grafted on two proposed Mini shells. Reitzle felt that the bodies needed to be seen on the road and examined from every angle while in motion. How the cars appear to other drivers behind them or alongside them, how they look in the rearview mirror—these are the impressions potential buyers have of a car, not just visions of it parked at the curb or in an ad. On the road, it turns out the Brits had been right, and Reitzle conceded that the higher-roofline version the Germans had wanted simply didn't look like a Mini. So one body style it would be.

The Mini's front end is a design signature that clearly harkens to the original, with two large, angled headlamps that seem to glare with enthusiasm, like those of a pug dog. If the seating position and the relationship of the driver to the car and the car to the road seem especially good to drivers, it's because BMW lifted those proportions and precise metrics from its own successful 3 Series, a car that many enthusiasts deem the most perfectly designed automobile on the road today. BMW calls this the "h-point," or the precise position of the driver's hips relative to the pedals. This was among the many improvements on the original Mini, whose h-point was roughly akin to that of a delivery van, with a steering wheel angle more appropriate to a school bus than to a subcompact runabout. And the wheel arches on the new Mini grew to accommodate 17-inch wheels, a big step up from Mini's 12-inch, spine-separating wheels. Reitzle even envisioned 19-inch wheels on special performance versions of the car. The Mini also required a four-star crash rating to meet U.S. and European safety standards—quite a feat if you look at the Mini in profile. Despite the typical problems associated with creating a minimal front-end overhang—the amount of car and bumper that is in front of the wheels—the Mini's overhang is shorter than that of the BMW 3 Series, a rear-drive car that makes the overhang chore easier in theory. One of the design elements that makes a Mini genuine, though, is that its wheels are positioned at the extreme four corners of the car.

For all the sweat and tears over the design, only one obstacle remained in 1996: There was no engine, the choice of which affects many other design features including front-end packaging of parts under the hood, which in turn can affect the look of the front end. Typically, customers settle on an engine at the start. An existing Rover engine was deemed too wide and would have bollixed the carefully reckoned proportions of the car's front. And no BMW engine would fit in that tight space, nor could one be adapted. Reitzle discussed the problem with his friend Bob Lutz, then vice chairman of Chrysler, at the 1996 Geneva Motor Show. Reitzle wanted to know what engine Chrysler planned for its next Neon subcompact and PT Cruiser. Reitzle made a few trips to Detroit, and the result was BMW buying into a 16-valve, four-cylinder engine Chrysler had on the drawing boards and planned to build in Brazil. BMW agreed to take 200,000 engines a year. Given its expertise in developing engines, it may seem odd that BMW was willing to outsource such an important vehicle's power plant—

and have it made in Brazil by an American company! But BMW's engineers actually had a lot to do with the finished product's performance, and Chrysler was only too happy to share development costs and gain access to BMW's engine expertise. At bottom, both companies wanted to develop a world-class, low-cost 1.6-liter engine. In any case, this was the first time BMW used an engine that was not developed 100 percent in-house.

———

The answer for the Mini launch in North America, as in Europe, was to limit volume and create "a cultish atmosphere around the car and the brand before we had the first one to sell," says Mini USA chief Jack Pitney who ran BMW's North American public relations office before taking the Mini job in 2001. Pitney knew that guerilla and viral marketing—still useful, if overhyped, concepts from the 1990s—could achieve a real buzz—or be done very poorly. In any event, there was nowhere to go but up, as prelaunch research indicated that fewer than 2 percent of Americans were at all familiar with Mini as a brand. Pitney felt the job was to take what sparkled in the old Mini's brand mystique and make it fresh for those discovering it for the first time. Additionally, the effort had to resonate credibly with the Mini clubs, the brand's spear-carriers for the past three decades. If they declared the new Mini a joke, the wrong "virus" would infect the marketing, and BMW simply didn't have the resources available to fix a botched launch.

A real British car enthusiast, Pitney had owned a 1969 MGB, a 1970 MGB GT, and a Triumph TR7 when he was younger. And being younger had helped, for all the times he ended up pushing those cars rather than driving them. It takes a masochistic Anglophile to appreciate those romantic but horribly unreliable Brit sports cars. From the department of "I'm getting paid for this?," Pitney started lobbying for what was, for him, the dream job of Mini general manager in 1999—not a typical move for a PR chief. He went to Birmingham, England, to scout the situation and express his enthusiasm for export to the United States. Rover put him through a weeklong Mini immersion that included driving the original, first-off-the-line 1959 Mini. "The business case was easy for me," says Pitney. "Out of 17 million new cars sold in the U.S., all I wanted was twenty thousand. With a brand as unique and special as this, and my faith in what BMW could pull off as far as the quality of the product, the driving fun and styling, I knew I could sell 20,000 standing on my head." Not one to get bogged down in marketing semantics, Pitney says, "We approached this as a new brand in the U.S., not a reincarnation of an old product. It has been important for the team to think that way and to maintain the distinction. Because while we may look to Mini's past for inspiration, we don't want to look there for the answers. . . . This is a new brand and we have to treat it that way."

Research into who might be interested in a Mini showed what marketers call a *psychographic,* rather than a demographic, profile. In other words, Mini buyers would typically have similar lifestyles and personality traits, but their ages and incomes are all over the map. *Business Week*'s aforementioned Dave Welch is in the middle of the Mini mindset. He fences competitively and plays league baseball, not softball. So is Amy MacDonald. The 55-year-old grandmother and her husband, Angus, own a Mini Cooper S whose customized roof sports the McDonald tartan rather than the British flag. They travel the country playing competitive bridge, very often in their Mini, and also visit such unconventional destinations as Vietnam, Siberia, Tasmania, and New Guinea.

Reaching such people with marketing they wouldn't dismiss as tripe meant forgoing the usual 30-second TV ads on network television. Perhaps the clearest insight to emerge from prelaunch research, in fact, was that Mini people don't like to be marketed to at all. When they do watch television, they're more often watching public broadcasting stations with no traditional commercials. They are apt to own TiVo, the device that makes it easy to tape TV programs and filter out the advertising.

To start with, the U.S. advertising agency Crispin-Porter & Bogusky came up with the theme that would color all Mini communication: "Let's Motor." Said Pitney, "Motoring is a British term, as is 'motor car.' We wanted to stay away from the word 'driving' because of BMW's longstanding and entrenched 'Ultimate Driving Machine.' Motoring has the advantage, too, of being a word that no other car company was using in the U.S. And it is *bloody* hard to find a phrase that isn't some derivative of something someone else is using in your own category." Besides being a Britishism, *motoring* is meant to convey "enlightened driving." "Let's Motor" aimed at reflecting the typical Mini buyer's desire to drive; to drive to unique, interesting and adventuresome places; to drive off the map guidelines and to do so with a lovely picnic basket full of unique edibles. In June of 2003, the MacDonalds went on a weekend trip from their home near Cleveland to Michigan's Upper Peninsula. In their basket went sheep's milk cheese from France, three kinds of liver paté, and wine they had purchased from a small California winery. In their CD case for the trip were recordings of Nina Simone and an obscure Irish blues singer named Jeannette Byrne. No mainstream pop music for them and no "god-awful commercial radio," says Amy.

The goal has been to establish and maintain buzz around Mini. Before the car was widely available, the company put a Mini on the roof of a Ford Excursion SUV and drove it around such cities as New York, Chicago, and Los Angeles. The Excursion had been the largest "light" vehicle on the road, one scorned by the Sierra Club and other environmental organizations as the "Ford Valdez," a reference to the Exxon tanker that befouled Alaska's shores. A sign on the touring SUV/Mini combo asked, "What are you doing for fun this weekend?" The goal was a little humorous irony, theoretically, since people usually buy big SUVs for hauling trailers, boats, camping gear, and the like. But a popular Mini theory is that Excursions and SUVs like them are often driven by insecure adults who have a fetish for a high seating position amid automotive bulk. One can imagine such people, even those who live alone, driving Excursions and Hummer SUVs to warehouse-style grocery stores for 12-packs of paper towels and Campbell's soup in gallon-size cans. Size (hint, hint) seems to matter most to them. But these vehicles are dreadful to drive day-to-day, are menacing to park, and are the scourge of the highways. And a Mini is truly the anti-SUV. Business cards were handed out to those whose curiosity was piqued by the spectacle of a car driving around on top of the SUV. The cards carried a picture of a Mini on one side and "Coming to America—www.miniusa.com" on the other. Minis were also taken to sporting events and shopping malls. But instead of the convention of merely parking the car in a corridor or in front of a stadium, the Mini, for example, was "seated" at ballparks such as the Oakland Athletics' stadium, taking up a block of 12 seats that had been removed to make room for the strange British visitor. "A Mini is bound to become a member of the family, not just a car. That's why people often name them," says Pitney. At the Santa Ana, California, shopping mall, a Mini Cooper was turned into a coin-operated Mini-ride. A sign on the coin slot read: "Insert $16,850 in quarters only." Of course, an "out of order" sign was put up as well to add to the gag and keep yokels who didn't get the joke from trying to insert that many quarters.

On March 21, 2002, the day before the Mini officially went on sale, Pitney got a call from a dealer telling him of "a problem." Dozens of people were lined up outside his showroom, ready to camp out until the next day, so they could be the first to order a new Mini. Pitney told the dealer to just politely ask them to come back first thing in the morning. The dealer called back a few minutes later. "They won't leave. I'm going to have to call the police," he reported. Every fiber of the former PR man recoiled in Pitney as he bellowed into the phone, "Are you crazy, man, call the media!" At a Mini dealership in Las Vegas, a gang of customers ran out into traffic in the street to meet the transport truck bringing the first Minis, scaring the heck out of the driver.

Feature films have long been an important marketing staple for the original Mini, the BMW, and now the new Mini. From the late 1990s up to 2002, BMWs were featured prominently in James Bond movies. The original Mini was frequently used in films in the 1960s, especially in Britain and Italy. Mini has a starring role in *The Italian Job*. In a case of good planning and good luck, the original Mini played a starring role in a remake of the 1988 film *The Bourne Identity,* in 2002. Lead actor Matt Damon dragoons a pretty, Mini-driving Parisienne to help him elude his pursuers and is involved in several good chase scenes. Less than a year later, the new Mini was a full-fledged costar of a remake of *The Italian Job* starring Edward Norton and Mark Wahlberg. "Product placement will continue to be important, but the extent of Mini's role in *The Italian Job* made even me a little nervous, because some critics said the cars seemed to be featured almost too prominently," says Pitney.

Besides the conventional chores of finding a dealer and financing, Mini customers also come to the web site looking for Mini "Motoring Gear"—everything from clothing, video games, watches, and luggage to a Mini cuckoo clock. Like BMW, Mini has made use of short Internet films that can be viewed on a web site. In one early short film, a Mini owner is driving through the desert, listening to the radio, and enjoying the motoring. A police car appears and pulls him over. The cop actually turns out to be an English bobby who is stopping the young man for driving on the wrong side of the road. "But this is America," exhorts the driver. The bobby looks around, surveying the parched surroundings, and with typical British, buttoned-up reserve responds, "Right then. Carry on."

Once they order a car, Mini buyers can track its progress from the Oxford, England, plant to their dealer. Since the wait for a Mini, especially during its first year, could be six months (even the second year's wait could be four months), the company generates a digital dialogue with the customer during the delay, so it becomes more a matter of anticipation than inconvenience. Mini makes sure the radio's presets are dialed to the owner's preference, and a compilation CD chosen by the owner is in the CD player, ready to go. At Halloween, the www.miniusa.com web site offered a fully downloadable 120-page, paper Mini costume for people who wanted to go out *dressed* as a Mini.

There are some traditional TV and print ads, of course, and billboards have also played a key role in the launch. One ad ran in Texas: "Once You Have Small, You Never Go Back." This billboard caused a sensation, particularly on Texas drive-time radio. Though only hardcore fans of the original Mini would know, the ad paid homage to a 1960s ad for the original.

Mini buyers are customizing their cars far more than BMW has ever seen with its own brand. Considering the typical Mini buyer, Pitney notes, it's to be expected. "We want to see every Mini be almost a one-off special edition for every customer," he says. In this respect, Mini has been studying Harley-Davidson and its cash-cow business of selling accessories, clothing, and assorted Harley gear. Typical Harley customers may spend more than $5,000 on Harley products within three years of buying their motorcycle. To push the accessories potential beyond the typical automotive norm, Mini has hired a former merchandising expert from Armani apparel design to outfit the dealers' showrooms with the right atmosphere to try on clothing. This is new territory for the dealers, many of whom hadn't even thought of including a mirror in the showroom for customers trying on Mini apparel.

The Mini won the North American Car of the Year award for 2002, beating out such new, highly praised entries as the Mazda 6, the all-new

Honda Accord, the Nissan Z, and the Infiniti G35. Automakers are fond of saying they can't make any real money selling small cars because Americans don't want small when they're offered a $4,000 rebate to buy an SUV. But the Mini, the smallest car sold in America, won over auto journalists who drive every new car offered to the public. Other metrics were through the roof. It was number one on J.D. Power and Associates' 2002 APEAL ranking. Strategic Vision, which ranks automotive brands for "delight" in its Total Quality Index, ranked Mini in its first year. Eighty-six percent of Mini buyers have never owned a BMW car or motorcycle. Consumers' unaided awareness, or knowledge of the brand without prompting, was 12 percent in September 2001; in December of 2002 it had risen to 53 percent.

————

Upon driving the Mini in California during the press introduction, my *USA Today* colleague Jim Healey noted the car's fun factor and the attention it grabs in a sea of no-name, bloodless small cars: "A trio of teen girls eyeballed the line of Minis at an espresso stop here and broke into giggles. Motorists honked, waved and smiled. Always smiled. Too-cool street-corner kids did double-takes and threw their arms high. And smiled. The Golden Gate Bridge toll-taker, numbed by thousands of vehicles a day, remarked on the Mini. And smiled."

Here are some of *Car and Driver*'s notes on the Mini:[7]

- "Gone is the light, runabout character of the original, replaced by the substantive, capable feel that we've come to identify with German craftsmanship."
- "BMW says the structure of the Mini is between 1.5 and 3.0 times stiffer than that of its competitors and 50 percent stiffer than its own line of 3-series cars. The Mini's small dimensions help in that regard, but so do the 3800 welds on the structure (the much larger 3-series has only 800 more). BMW bolted to this rigid structure a much more sophisticated suspension than is found in most cars."
- The sport-tuned suspension allows virtually no body roll, even when pushed hard on the tight, twisting roads. It feels as if the Mini's center of gravity were a foot below the pavement. The

front-end grip, even with the standard 15-inch wheels and modest 175/65 Pirelli performance tires, is nothing short of *amazing*."

- Instead of thinking of the new Mini as an update of the old, one should think of it as the first BMW with styling guided by fun, nostalgia, and silliness.

These are the kinds of accolades for driving performance that the original Mini certainly hadn't seen in some 40 years, and such praise would have been highly unlikely had the Rover concept been allowed to proceed.

Mini's future is bright at BMW. Not only has BMW already committed to a convertible version of the car, but executives promote the view that the Mini is every bit the Trojan horse the original was. BMW designers from Munich to California have been working on Mini wagons, SUVs, pickups, and panel vans, though only the convertible has been officially green-lighted so far.

Says BMW North American chief Tom Purves, "We can do a lot with Mini that would never be right to try with our 3 Series or 5 Series. . . . There are so many ways to stretch this brand that would never be appropriate or correct for the BMW brand, yet are very complementary to our core BMW product line. We think of Mini as our front-drive cousin—separate identity and separate family, but definitely related."

———

The Mini is the smallest car on the road in the United States. At the other end of the market is BMW's other British marque, which is the largest passenger car and one of the most expensive: Rolls-Royce.

It's fun to talk, write, and argue about Rolls-Royce as a brand, as a car, and as a tradition. And therein lies the brand value to BMW, which paid a paltry $66 million for the right to develop and market Rolls-Royce. It spent another $100 million or so to build a unique factory at Goodwood, the country estate of the Earl of March, near Chichester, south of London. It probably spent $500 million or so developing the 2003 Rolls-Royce Phantom.

After driving the first BMW-developed Rolls-Royce, the 2003 Phantom, Andrew English wrote in *Telegraph Motoring:* "It is more than 19-feet long, weighs two-and-a-half tons, costs as much as a family house and will sell to a few stinking rich swanks with garages full of equally monstrous cars. So, just what is the relevance of the Rolls-Royce Phantom?"

English left out that to those on the political left, only *wankers* with far too much money and too little imagination about how to spend it will buy the $350,000 Roller. Among the buyers: contemptible, harem-keeping Arab oil sheiks; overpaid and undereducated professional athletes; greedy, dog-hating, child-neglecting investment bankers without consciences about the workers they put on the dole with every merger they execute; shallow-minded, oversalaried British advertising executives who grind underlings under their boot heels, torment their secretaries with personal errands, and keep mistresses in Chelsea apartments; and aging, potbellied rock stars. These, plus titled aristocracy, monarchs, and brothel keepers make up the imagery of Rolls buyers. Yet we care about this car because Rolls-Royce is in our language and in our psyches. "I just bought the Rolls-Royce of espresso makers," more than one Martha Stewart devotee has probably said while gabbing on the phone about plans for a June weekend soiree. It is a storied marque that has ferried some of the most important people of the twentieth century to and from Parliament, opera houses, and gorgeous country homes.

BMW came to own the Rolls-Royce brand by winning one of the great games of European industrial poker between BMW's Bernd Pischetsrieder and Volkswagen chairman Ferdinand Piech. BMW secured the rights to the Rolls-Royce name starting in 2003 when it introduced the Rolls-Royce Phantom at the Detroit Motor Show. Rolls-Royce CEO Tony Gott and BMW AG chairman Helmut Panke held forth at a press conference at the Detroit show, gushing over the traditions of British motoring and defending their investment in a century-old marque fallen on hard times. All the while, women in black evening gowns languorously tugged a tailored silk coverlet off the behemoth limousine as if they were rolling a silk stocking off a shapely leg. The car was gun-metal gray. (Take comfort, prospective buyers; for your $350,000-plus, you can get the car in any color you want.) An umbrella slid in and out of a vented hole inside the rear door so that water wicked away from the damp bumbershoot with the car's motion. The "RR" logos on the wheel covers stay upright and readable even as the car is in motion. The leather in the show car comes from 16 hides and is similar to that used in leather apparel, making for more supple and luxurious surfaces. No fewer than six different veneers are available for the woodwork: Figured Mahogany from West Africa; Burr Walnut, Birdseye Maple, and Black Tulip from North America; and Oak Burr and Elm Cluster from Europe. The woods are crafted into the car by British yacht builders in the south of England who are specially recruited for the task. The chassis, engine, transmission, and gearbox, though, are strictly Bavarian.

————

The man responsible for winning Rolls-Royce for BMW is not a typical German. A Bavarian, Bernd Pischetsrieder is independent minded, brash, urbane, confident. He loves to win—and he loves to win in style. Though his purchase of the British Rover Group was bringing his job at BMW down around his ears, on July 28, 1998, he was hitting on all cylinders as it became apparent that he had snookered the most lionized and feared titan of the German auto industry—Dr. Ferdinand Piech, chairman of Volkswagen, grandson of Ferdinand Porsche, billionaire.

As the deal went down, a photographer was summoned to a posh private golf club in Hoen Neuendorf in Bavaria to snap some shots for posterity. Pischetsrieder, BMW supervisory board chairman Eberhard von Kuenheim, strategy and legal advisor Hagen Luderitz, and communications chief Richard Gaul were countered by Ferdinand Piech, Volkswagen supervisory board chairman Klaus Liesen, Lower Saxony premier Helmut Schoeder, VW management board member Jens Neumann, and VW PR man Kurt Rippholz. The two sides assembled at the club to sign papers that would divide Rolls-Royce and Bentley Motors for the first time since 1931. BMW walked away with the rights to the Rolls-Royce brand name for 40 million pounds, while Volkswagen got Bentley, the antiquated factory in Crewe, England, and Cosworth Engineering for 640 million pounds. For months, Piech and Pischetsrieder had danced with Vickers plc, the owner of the auto company and aviation company Rolls-Royce Motors, which retained ownership of the Rolls-Royce brand name, over which *German* company would take over the last vestiges of the once proud British auto industry—the brands of English kings and queens. Both suitors wanted the whole auto company, but they would have to settle for dividing it in something short of Solomonic satisfaction.

Volkswagen had outbid BMW four months earlier, in April, for the spoils. But there was a hitch. After overpaying for the company, most observers agreed, Piech found that he had no right to sell Rolls-Royce-branded cars. Huh? Years earlier, the rights to the brand name had been transferred from Vickers to Rolls-Royce plc, the company that made jet engines under the Rolls-Royce brand—a company in which BMW claimed a 10 percent stake. For four months, Piech and Pischetsrieder met each Monday in a Munich hotel, to try to thrash it out. BMW's threat to cancel its contract to supply the Rolls-Royce Silver Seraph and Bentley Arnage with engines, air conditioners, and other key components had VW over a barrel since no BMW parts meant no Rolls products, and no Arnages, to sell for the four or five years it would take VW to develop new models.

Stuck, VW agreed it would sell the Rollers only until 2002 while BMW developed a new one that it would sell from a new company. Piech had been beaten, and he knew it, though to this day this proud man won't admit it. He still insists he was really interested only in Bentley. But if that's true, why did he later offer to swap the Bugatti brand for Rolls-Royce? It was an offer that Pischetsrieder entertained, but turned down after determining that true ownership of the Bugatti name was embroiled in complicated Italian trademark law. Did he already know that he was headed out of BMW to Volkswagen within a few months?

Pischetsrieder had expected to succeed in his desire to own Rolls-Royce and Bentley for years, based in part on his friendship with Rolls-Royce plc chairman Sir Ralph Robins. Rolls-Royce had been forced into bankruptcy in 1971 after a contract to develop turbofan engines for Lockheed went bust when the project fell behind schedule. The car side of the business was spun off, with shares issued in Rolls-Royce Motors on the London Stock Exchange. The Rolls-Royce aerospace company, though, retained the Rolls-Royce brand name and flying-lady image. Permission was granted to Vickers to use the name years hence on motorcars. Pischetsrieder and Robins forged a business and personal relationship in the early 1990s when BMW and Rolls formed a joint venture to develop engines for small jet planes. This was a scheme favored by von Kuenheim to return BMW to its glorious airplane engine roots, the business that launched the company before the Great War. Then, Pischetsrieder inked a deal to provide critical components for Rolls and, in 1994, Bentley automobiles, beating Mercedes-Benz for the contract. A grand egotist and perhaps a bit oblivious to the realities, Piech never even bothered to lobby Robins himself, delegating negotiations for Rolls-Royce to his sales and marketing chief. Having created a culture of fear at Volkswagen—with Piech's own board members often loath to challenge him—nobody saw fit to tell the old man that he ought to go to London if he hadn't thought of it himself.

After the papers were signed at the Munich golf club, the executives drove off in their respective BMW 7 Series and Audi sedans to a nearby airfield to board VW's Falcon jet for a flight to a former Royal Air Force field just outside London. The British media was waiting for the group at London's Institution of Civil Engineers. Some reporters groused over the Germans taking over Britain's storied brands, practically the country's national brands. But they had nothing to be bitter about, at least not toward the Germans. The company was more of a car museum than a viable concern, sabotaged by countless decisions over the years by successive British governments. BMW was already trying to salvage Rover, Land Rover, and Mini as the government mostly threw marbles at its feet while the same members of Parliament and Whitehall officials bent over backward to assist Ford's acquisition and rehabilitation of Jaguar and help Japanese companies set up shop in the United Kingdom. Anti-German sentiment ran high, often fueled by the tabloid newspapers that resented BMW's takeover of the Rover Group in 1994.

The press conference to announce the deal was dominated by Pischetsrieder. With a ready command of English, he was strutting like a rooster. With poor English and a distaste for press conferences—never mind one dominated by English reporters—Piech was obviously uneasy. It didn't help that all the German reporters linked by satellite were in BMW's Munich headquarters. It was a BMW show all the way, despite VW coughing up 10 times as much cash—a point nailed by a reporter's nasty question: "Dr. Piech, don't you think you've made a fool of yourself?" Laughter from the press gallery followed, and Pischetsrieder couldn't help but crack a grin. BMW's British PR man, Chris Willows, had the unenviable task of repeating the question for the chastened, steely-eyed, and slightly hard-of-hearing Piech. Piech also puzzled most of his audience by repeatedly referring to the Spirit of Ecstasy flying lady as "Emely," a German nickname for the hood ornament not commonly known in Great Britain.[8]

After 90 minutes or so, Pischetsrieder exited to a waiting 7 Series. No one had thought to have a Roller on hand to take him back to the airport. He lit his trademark Cuban cigar. "It was a great day. In the end, I'm sure we got the better of the deal," said Pischetsrieder.[9] He would change his tune four years later after being ousted at BMW and hired by Piech to succeed him as chairman at Volkswagen, where he had charge of Bentley. "Bentley is the more dynamic of the two brands and a better car for drivers. Rolls-Royces are for people who like the backseat," Pischetsrieder said at the 2002 Paris Motor Show, where he introduced the Bentley Continental GT.

————

Frederick Henry Royce, son of a miller, was 41 in 1906 when he lunched at the Midland Hotel with the much younger Charles Stewart Rolls, who was 26. Royce, an electrical engineer and owner of a manufacturing concern, and Rolls, an engineer and motoring enthusiast with access to capital, were brought together by Royce's friend, Henry Edmunds, who knew young Rolls from his association with the Automobile Club of Great Britain. On the train from London to Manchester, Rolls spoke presciently of his ambition to "have a motor car connected with his name so that in the future it might be a household word, just as Steinway for pianos or Chubb in connection with safes."

Royce had successfully built up the F.H. Royce Co. (and later Royce Ltd.), a manufacturer of electrical components as well as a high-quality electric crane. By 1903, with the electrical business tapering off, Royce set about using some of his excess capacity to develop a motorcar. Commissioning the bits and pieces from nearby foundries and forges and hiring a carriage maker to produce a four-seat body, the first Royce car was a 10-horsepower, two-cylinder 1800-cc machine.

A born aristocrat, Charles Rolls was the son of John Allan Rolls and the grandson of the seventh Earl of Northesk. He later became Baron Llangattock. Fascinated by the promise and potential of electricity, Rolls left Cambridge in 1898 at age 18 and pursued his love of motorcars for four years, racing and rallying, before opening his own firm,

C.S. Rolls and Co., in 1902. Rolls wanted to develop British cars that would compete with the leading French and German makers of the day, Peugot and Mercedes. But he was not keen on delving too deeply into manufacturing the cars.

The lunch at the Midlands went extremely well, the two men bridging the divide of their different ages and social backgrounds with their love of cars. In his memoirs, Edmunds said the two took to one another almost immediately. Following lunch, Rolls was allowed to give the Royce car a thorough inspection. Upon returning home, Rolls pulled his associate, Claude Johnson, from his bed to announce that he had met "the greatest motor engineer in the world." By December 1904, the two had struck a deal for Rolls to market and sell the cars developed by Royce under the name Rolls-Royce. If the order sounds unfair, try saying "Royce-Rolls." Both men agreed it lacked the right verve. A batch of nineteen 10-horsepower cars and one 15-horsepower car were built, all of them with the signature radiator design that would forever grace Rolls-Royce automobiles. The two didn't sign the papers forging the partnership until almost Christmas that year, but they had been working on designs in the meantime; three Rolls-Royce cars and one 30-horsepower engine were displayed at the Paris Auto Show that same December in 1904. The actual incorporation of the two companies as Rolls-Royce Ltd. didn't take place until 1906. That year's London Motor Show marked an important turning point when they showed a car now known as the Silver Ghost, a 40/50-horsepower six-cylinder. The car looked like it could fly, with a gleaming chassis and enough shining brass to outfit a marching band.

The 1906 car was dubbed the Silver Ghost only after Rolls-Royce stopped making it. The car was longer than Royce's previous cars since coach builder Montague Graham-White convinced the partners to build a longer car to compete against Mercedes, Panhard, and Napier for the limousine business of the rich and powerful. Not only was the 40/50 Silver Ghost longer and more opulent, but Royce had solved the problem of his previous V6 engines vibrating too much, which had caused crankshafts to break. The modified engine was extraordinarily smooth and quiet for the day, and it catapulted the Rolls-Royce brand into international prominence. All the other Rolls-Royce cars that had been for sale and commissioned stopped production so the firm could concentrate on high-end motorcars for the wealthy.

By 1909, Royce's health was poor, and he cut back his administrative duties, making way for Claude Johnson as CEO. And Rolls, although healthy, had grown weary of the day-to-day grind of running a company and now preferred to play the role of guiding hand. Rolls had become even more enamored with the fledgling aviation industry than he had been with motorcars. That love of flight ended what looked like a brilliant life prematurely when Rolls was killed in a flying accident in 1911. Royce soon moved to the south of France to live and convalesce for the next 20 years, returning to England for part of the year for design work.

The Spirit of Ecstasy mascot—the flying lady—that has adorned Rolls-Royce bonnets for almost a century was born of Claude Johnson's distaste for the varied hood ornaments that customers commissioned from silversmiths. Johnson commissioned a standard mascot from artist Charles Sykes that was originally called "The Spirit of Speed." Sykes had previously painted the illustrations that adorned Rolls-Royce catalogues. Sykes did the Spirit in 1911, but it wasn't installed on Rolls-Royce cars until after World War I. For his part, the purist Royce never had one because he felt such an opulent trophy spoiled the design line of the bonnet.

In 1914, at the behest of the British government, Royce began developing an aero engine at its Derby, England, factory. Up to that point, English planes had been powered by French engines. Given the assumption that the looming war would be fought almost entirely on French soil, a safe source of engines was needed. Aero engine business soon came to dominate the company, with the profits from aero engines subsidizing the often money-losing automobiles. The cars were also drafted for military use; a Silver Ghost armored car soon appeared with a gun turret and a Vickers .303 machine gun mounted on top.

After the war, Johnson began a two-model strategy that would endure for the rest of the century, with the company producing a large limousine as well as a smaller, personal-use car. The Ghost was looking a little dated by the early 1920s, having been conceived on paper back around 1905. A new engine was put into a 40/50 chassis, resulting in the New Phantom, later to be known by collectors as Phantom I. The car didn't break much new ground in chassis design. That would come, however, in 1929 with the introduction of the Phantom

II, the car, amazingly enough, that served as a starting point for BMW AG designers and engineers when in the twenty-first century they set out to produce the first Rolls-Royce under German ownership.

By 1928 Claude Johnson had been dead for two years, but Henry Royce was still a presence, and he directed the team designing the Phantom II. The new head of Rolls-Royce was Arthur Sidgreaves, who had come to Rolls in 1920 after working at limousine builder Napier.

The Phantom II, the last design that Royce himself supervised, was nine inches shorter than the Phantom I, which had a tall roofline that sheltered the owner and passengers in comfort while the chauffeur was left to cope with the elements in the open air. The early Rolls-Royces weren't meant to be driven in rain, though with English weather it seems beyond silly—or selfish—not to have a roof covering the driver. The Phantom II covered the passengers as well as the driver, whether that be the owner or a chauffeur. A proportional change in the Phantom II had passengers seated inside the axles (previous models had passengers' bottoms directly over the rear axle), which made for a softer ride.

The Phantom II also contained some of the luxury craftsmanship that has made the marque famous. Royce dictated that the paint was to be sealed in an artificial pearl lacquer made by finely grinding herring scales into the paint solvent. Interior materials included fine French leathers and sycamore wood tinted faintly with azure to echo the blue exterior.

Rolls then purchased the all-but-bankrupt Bentley Motors in 1931 in part to forestall a competitor revitalizing the firm and also to provide a secondary marque developing sports cars.

Plans for a Phantom III were under way as well. This car would benefit from some input from Royce, but he died in 1933 before it came to fruition. The Phantom III was a technically advanced but finicky car. It was the first Rolls to have an independent front suspension, and its crankcase and cylinder heads were made of Hiduminium, an exotic aluminum alloy that Rolls used in airplane engines. Owing in part to the decade-long Depression, only 770 IIIs were sold, compared with 1,767 Phantom IIs. The III marked the end of the Henry Royce era as well as the end of unlimited development costs. After 1939, Rolls-Royce cars were developed in tandem with Bentleys, neither marque ever entirely its own.

———

During World War II, Rolls-Royce ceased car production to throw all its resources at building aero engines for British Spitfire and Hurricane fighters, which surely saved English cities from being leveled, as well as tank engines that far outclassed the U.S. Sherman tanks. After the war, Rolls-Royce and Bentley cars became closely allied. In the mid-1950s, the Rolls Silver Cloud and Bentley S Series were differentiated only by the radiator and badging. Some buyers then spent additional funds having custom coaches built around or in place of the standard bodies.

The truth was, however, that after the war, Rolls-Royce's fortunes were in jet engines, not cars. After the war, the old coach builders were out of business. The whole British car industry went through rapid consolidation. Austin, MG, Riley, Nuffield, Morris, and Wolseley were merged into British Motor Corp. (BMC) in 1952. BMC later took over Jaguar and British Daimler in the mid-1960s. Standard-Triumph hooked up with Rover and Land Rover. And all of them merged into a kind of British General Motors in the form of British Leyland in 1968.

The first postwar car built was the Bentley Mark VI in 1946. It was correct, given the British economy and social atmosphere after the war, that the first new model would be a Bentley—sportier and arguably a bit more egalitarian than the snootier Roller brand. The Rolls Silver Dawn, built off the Bentley chassis, followed two years later. The first postwar Rolls on its own chassis, the Phantom IV, was built for Queen Elizabeth and the Duke of Edinburgh, and it was decreed that the car would be built only for heads of state. That decision was meant to elevate the superpremium, exclusive marque. But it also marked the beginning of a certain cut of the population—self-made wealthy men—losing some interest in the brand. Bentley quickly became the "money brand" for Rolls-Royce, as the company sold almost 8,000 Mark VIs between 1949 and 1955, while it sold less than 1,000 Silver Dawns during the same time. The 1955 Silver Cloud and Bentley S started a new era for the company and were timed to economic boom in Britain, Germany, and the U.S., tapered only by the oil shortages and high petrol prices that came with the Suez Canal crisis of 1956 and 1957. Sales of the Cloud and S Series were almost evenly split by the time they were replaced in 1965 by the Silver Shadow and T Series. The Shadow was a thoroughly modern, postwar shape, following the three-box style that would permeate most car design for the next 35 years. The Shadow also began Rolls's use of unibody construction, which had come to dominate most automobiles. No more separate chassis and body. The Shadow became the best seller in Rolls's postwar history, selling 32,000 copies over 15 years.

Bankruptcy hit Rolls-Royce in 1971 because of the colossal failure on the aero engine side of the company, and the modestly profitable car business was spun off as a new company on the London Stock Exchange. By 1978, trouble was in view despite brisk Silver Shadow sales. Investment in replacement cars was scant. The company replaced the Shadow and Bentley T Series with the Silver Spirit and Bentley Mulsanne, which carried over most of the engineering and components of the old cars. That same year, defense conglomerate Vickers took over the car-making operations of Rolls-Royce. The two companies were shadows of their former selves, and Rolls-Royce had become a bit of a rotting cake like the one on Miss Havisham's table in Charles Dickens's *Great Expectations*—frozen in time and decaying in a sad, crumbling mansion. Author Richard Feast, in his fine book *Kidnap of The Flying Lady,* cites Patrick Sargeant in the *Daily Mail* as saying: [The merger] looks nothing so much as two dukes falling upstairs out of Annabel's [a West-End nightclub], propping each other up."

Beginning in the mid-1960s, Bentleys and "Rollers" were identical but for the grilles, hood adornments, and a few bits and pieces inside. But by the late 1980s, Rolls-Royce made a decision to emphasize the Bentley brand, which it felt had more draw with customers. By 1990, 52 percent of the company's sales were Bentleys. The Continental R was shown at the Geneva Motor Show, making it the first Bentley to have a dedicated design since 1959. By 1995, Bentley accounted for 61 percent of worldwide sales. The decision to build up Bentley, effectively turning the company upside down from a Rolls-dominated company to one dominated by Bentley vehicles, resulted in the creation of smaller Rolls-Royces than people expected. During the last decade, says Rolls chairman Tony Gott, compromises were made to Rolls's suspension, quality, and craftsmanship. "They hadn't been honest Rolls-Royces, with everything the brand is meant to stand for, in more than thirty years," he said in 2003. Writing about the Silver Seraph, *Telegraph Motoring's* Jason Barlow said, "Even the company's legendary craftsmanship appeared to have gone AWOL. Large chunks of center console aren't supposed to come away in your hand in any car, but a Rolls-Royce? Heaven forefend. As I drove down the motorway waving a piece of errant hand-crafted walnut, it seemed that this particular Rolls-Royce had become just another bad British car."

By 1994 when Rolls-Royce Motors agreed to take much-needed technology from BMW for its Silver Spirit and Corniche models, including engines and other key parts, the cars' basic technology, underpinnings, and engineering dated to 1965. They were improved on and tinkered with year to year, much like the Volkswagen Beetle had been since the 1940s. But Mercedes, BMW, and now Toyota's Lexus brand had surpassed Rolls on every level of technology. Was Rolls-Royce "the best car in the world" as its marketing slogan suggested? Hardly. What was left, and what BMW would build upon, notes historian Richard Feast, was what was left of Rolls-Royce's aura.

———

Driving through the back roads and canyons near Santa Barbara, California, in early 2003 in the BMW-built Rolls-Royce Phantom with worldwide sales and marketing director Howard Mosher yields some surprising perspective about arguably the most historically cherished automobile brand in the world now being managed by the company with arguably the most admired brand in the business. Mosher says the key to the success of the Phantom and the whole business case for BMW resurrecting the brand will be whether the car compares favorably with the Ford *Taurus!* No, he wasn't in his cups when he said this.

Taking Mosher's logic to extremes, his notion is that the Phantom may be viewed by Edmunds.com and *Consumer Reports* as a "best buy" because if he and his mates do their job correctly with a hybrid of Bavarian and British aplomb, the Phantom will be cheaper to drive than the Taurus. It's all about residual values. If the Phantom holds its roughly $350,000 value after three years, as is the company's hope, with free maintenance and bumper-to-bumper warranty thrown in, Phantom owners drive for free. A Taurus during the same time period will drop in value by more than 50 percent, from about $20,000 to less than $10,000.

Mosher knows residual values speak louder than marketing messages to prospective Rolls owners. In the 1990s Rolls-Royce Silver Seraphs, Silver Spurs, and Corniches, like Tauruses, commonly lost 50 percent of their purchase price in just 36 months. "We have the product now. This is the best, most sophisticated and hopefully the most reliable Rolls-Royce since the 1930s," says Mosher. "If we hold the line on supply, and not exceed demand, we should be able to return Rolls-Royce to the status of investment, not just image," says Mosher.

Mosher ran Rolls-Royce's U.S. operation in the late 1980s and early 1990s before going to Land Rover. When at Rolls-Royce, he coped with the de-emphasis of Rolls-Royce in favor of Bentley and the general neglect of the car's engineering. One memorable marketing ploy during his tenure in the United States was a rare magazine ad campaign for Rolls-Royce that used a cheek scratch-and-sniff device usually employed for a perfume ad. The Rolls ad gave the reader the smell of Rolls-Royce leather.

Says Mosher about the strategy to rebuild Rolls-Royce's brand credentials: "We aren't stupid. No one *needs* a Rolls-Royce. One of the problems we have had when the company was not producing the product we'd come to expect from Rolls-Royce [was] we built too many of them and discounted them in part to make up for the fast depreciation. That scenario does away with the only reason to build a car or brand like this in the first place—exclusivity. That's what people are paying for. They are paying in part for a brand few people can get their hands on. That said, it still has to be every inch an excellent automobile. It has to represent something about uncompromising engineering, comfort and excellence."

Rolls-Royce's plan is to sell 1,000 Phantoms a year for a decade before introducing a replacement. If demand slips, either because of a soft economy or because customers wealthy enough to buy one just don't fancy the car, says Mosher, the company "must have the nerve to limit supply rather than cut the price." That wasn't the case in 1989, for example, when Rolls sold over 1,000 vehicles in North America alone, as the factory cut prices to dealers and the dealers discounted even more on their own—all while the United States was gearing up for its first war with Iraq.

BMW is counting on the people assembled to run Rolls-Royce to see to it that the product is correct and sufficiently British. Casting for the key roles was inspired. The chief engineer on the Rolls, Tim Leverton, a Brit, was the engineer seeing the 2002 Range Rover to market, and so he worked with BMW on the vehicle while it was developed under BMW ownership in the late 1990s. He is also the son of a former

Rolls-Royce engineer who grew up around the marque and had Rolls-Royces in his driveway as a boy. His experience working with the Bavarians on the Range Rover perfectly prepared him for the Phantom project.

Rolls-Royce CEO Tony Gott, an engineer at Rolls-Royce going back to the early 1980s, had run Rolls-Royce and Bentley under Vickers plc and then Volkswagen before VW turned over Rolls to BMW in 2003. Gott spells out the task simply. "We've got to get the world's most cherished brand taken seriously again." Gott resigned from running Bentley for Volkswagen in a shake-up and was quickly snapped up by BMW. It was vital to Helmut Panke to have people involved in Rolls-Royce who knew the brand and knew British motoring.

Besides Gott, of course, many of the Germans at BMW are steeped in British engineering. Karl-Heinz Kalbfell, who led Project Rolls-Royce for BMW, is a lifelong enthusiast of British cars and bikes, as was his former boss, Bernd Pischetsrieder, who bought the brand. As soon as Kalbfell could ride a motorbike as a young man, he bought a Triumph Bonneville. Its mechanical deficiencies and poor reliability didn't dissuade him. "It sounded great, and sound is a very important consideration," says Kalbfell. Today, Kalbfell keeps an old Rickman-framed Triumph in his Munich garage. His first motorcar was a Triumph Spitfire. Later that was displaced by a Triumph TR5. "A lot of us [Germans] have a love for British cars and motorcycles, probably because we recognize that the British have always been very good at creating desire in their machines if not always reliability as good as the German machines," says Kalbfell.

To come up with a Rolls-Royce under BMW that would garner credibility, designers in 1999 leased an old bank building on Basewater Road, north of Hyde Park. There the designers, often seen out on the sidewalk sipping espresso with pads and pencils in hand, observed many a Rolls-Royce and the people who owned them getting in and out of banks, restaurants, government offices, and clubs. Among the misconceptions, says Leverton, is that most Rolls owners don't drive their own cars. The vast majority do, and they enjoy driving. "But the people you see photographed in Rolls-Royces, heads of state and celebrities, are usually chauffeured, so that's where the image comes from."

Rolls spent about 100 million euros building the Rolls-Royce plant at Goodwood, the estate of the Duke of Richmond, in Chichester,

England. Eighty percent of Rolls buyers will go to Goodwood to customize their Phantoms and then drive their cars before having them shipped to their own estates. When Volkswagen bought Bentley and Cosworth and the Crewe factory from Vickers, it also bought all of its workers and tradespeople. A gentleman's agreement between Volkswagen and BMW stipulated no poaching of talent. There is no automobile trade in southern England. But there is a world-class premium yacht-building trade. Rolls plucked dozens of craftspeople from the boat trade to build the coaches around the Bavarian hardware. It's no wonder that the hardware closures and feel of the wooden bins bear an uncanny similarity in touch and spring to those found on sailboats.

————

When BMW considered sites for the new Rolls facility, it was established from the start that it should be in Great Britain. Said BMW chairman Helmut Panke: "It would have been cheaper to do something in Spartanburg [BMW's U.S. plant, which builds the Z4 roadster and the X5 SUV], but the brand demands that it is built in Britain, crafted by British artisans. This was clearly a case where build origin was critical to the brand. This isn't so any more for BMW, because we build in the U.S. and South Africa and the vehicles that come from both places are 100 percent BMW and no one seems to think anything's been lost. But this was different."

Besides cost and brand, a number of other factors were taken into account. The site had to be large enough, with good transport links, access to a test track, and proximity to a skilled workforce. Also, as many Rolls-Royce customers would wish to visit the plant, it was important that it should be in an attractive part of the country. To visit Chichester, England, is to know that it is a place practically created for would-be Rolls-Royce buyers. The southern coast of England is nearby, with its posh hotels, estates, yacht moorings, and yacht-building shops. It's the ideal place for an immersion in British history, culture, and luxury. There is an airfield and helipad for the wealthy car aficionados to land alongside the estate. Golf courses are in close proximity and orchestral concerts are performed in the plant's courtyard on summer evenings. The new plant, visitor's center, and museum constitute a must-visit destination for the nearly 200,000 car enthusiasts who visit Goodwood in July and September for the annual Festival of Speed and Goodwood Revival. Both events celebrate automotive history and the history of racing, and draw thousands of "the right sort" of people who have bank accounts flush enough for a $350,000 Roller.

To say that the Rolls-Royce Phantom is being built in Goodwood is an exaggeration. The engines and bodies of the new car are delivered complete to Goodwood, where the cars are painted in a state-of-the-art paint shop and assembled by a workforce of 350. Wood and leather trim are manufactured at Goodwood from scratch—the leather, woods, cashmere, and chrome bits are all crafted and applied at the estate factory. The Spirit of Ecstasy hood ornament is cast down the road from the state, at Polycast in Southampton. Each Rolls requires 2,600 labor-hours to complete, about 10 times what it takes to assemble an average Ford when every component is taken into account. The production goal is to have three Phantoms exit the line each day. The aluminum body of the Phantom is built in BMW's Dingolfing, Germany, factory. The 6.75-liter V12 engine is designed and built by BMW. It is not the same engine that it is in the BMW 7 Series. BMW felt that any sort of "badge" engineered Rolls-Royce would be a death knell for the brand. The engine was designed specifically for the Phantom, though it will certainly be used in future Rollers as well.

Still, it seems to be enough English craftsmanship to suit the anglophiles who want a Roller. In fact, it wouldn't surprise Gott and Mosher if there are more people who will now consider a Rolls *because* of the BMW engineering under the hood and beneath the floorboards than there are people who won't because of the German parentage.

There is, of course, the question of whether people will, in the long run, accept a German-built Rolls-Royce that has a BMW engine under the bonnet. And this Rolls-Royce Phantom, while looked after by British engineers flying back and forth between Heathrow and Munich, was actually designed by a Yugoslavian designer whose boss is American.

As with any good design, there are passionate arguments on both sides about whether BMW got it right. Says Richard Gibbon, motoring correspondent for the Rolls-Royce Enthusiast Club in southcentral England: "Sure, it's made in Germany and the enormous body shell is shipped to the Goodwood Estate for assembly but the car is about as British as you can get. And it attracts enormous attention—the A27 (a British highway) had seen nothing the like of it when I headed off to Portsmouth in the Phantom. Dozens gawped, waved, gave the thumbs-up and we even raised a huge smile from a smart driver who succeeded in overtaking us, punching his fist through the roof as he went past!"

On the other hand, shortly after it was unveiled in January 2003 and driven by journalists a month later, Great Britain's *Auto Express* magazine reported its mailbox jammed with letters about the new Rolls Phantom, with emotions running ten-to-one against the BMW design. "The front end has all the architectural flair of a fortified concrete bunker and boasts what appear to be Ford Granada headlamps," complained Tony Gondby, an *Auto Express* reader. "All the beauty of the curvaceous lines of its Silver Cloud forebears has been lost in a clumsy, bulky mass of straight-edged metal, upright glass and weird lights," wrote reader Richard Usher to *Autocar,* another car magazine.

The Phantom is a difficult car to judge at first, because it is designed to appeal to such a small number of buyers. That said, Tony Gott admits that for the Phantom to be a success, and for any BMW-designed Rolls-Royce to be a success, the brand depends on a majority of the masses of people who will never contemplate buying one admiring the car, and therefore the brand. "Many a multi-millionaire isn't going to want to own one if he thinks most of the people who see him in it think he's got bad taste or spent his money foolishly," says Gott. "When people buy a new Rolls-Royce, they are buying a product which is like no other motor car, from its basic concept right through to its design. This will be obvious to people as soon as they see it," added Gott.

Some marketing experts around Great Britain, the ones who should know best if the Rolls marque is beyond saving, say BMW is giving the brand its best chance of reasserting itself. And they only look to the example of the Mini to prove the point that BMW has some deft hands when it comes to handling iconic British brands. Says Britisher Ali Large, a veteran of the marketing wars in Britain, who has been in the employ of both British and American advertising agencies: "It has been the epitome, almost the definition, of quality and luxury for almost a century and it is still the brand name that most people reach for when looking for the best product in its field (e.g., such and such is the Rolls-Royce of . . .). Originally it also stood for that quintessentially British thing, 'class.' But that was before the brand got hijacked by footballers and gangsters and became the preserve of those lacking taste at one extreme and dowagers at the other. In contemporary Britain, 'style' has mostly replaced 'class' as a desirable attribute and the ostentatious and sumptuous imagery associated with Rolls Royce is a long way from a contemporary view of stylishness. So far not so good for a RR revival! But I believe Rolls-Royce is in brilliant hands at BMW. There are real parallels between Rolls-Royce and the Mini: both iconic, British brands built on the back of a groundbreaking product that people took to their hearts but which we in Britain (along with a litany of other great automotive brands) have failed to 'move on' and keep relevant in the competitive market. By contrast, BMW (and Mercedes) have successfully managed the image of its brand long term to keep them prestigious, desirable and contemporary—both in their home market and overseas."

———

Is the BMW Rolls any good? There is nothing so subjective as taste in wine, political candidates, and automobiles. When I first met the 2003 Phantom, I thought it reminded me of something, but I couldn't recall what. The mass of the vehicle is disarming. The underpinnings consist of a hefty aluminum space frame that supports body panels fabricated from aluminum and composites. The job of the aluminum was to bring down the weight of the 19-foot-plus vehicle. But at 5,600 pounds, the Phantom is beef on the bone. It's longer on its 140.6-inch wheelbase than the largest SUV in the market, the Ford Excursion. It's not the heaviest Rolls sedan on record, but it's the biggest.

Mechanically speaking, the Phantom uses an unequal-length control-arm front suspension and a multilink design at the rear of the car based somewhat on the BMW 7 Series. "Ah ha!" say those ready to bash the Phantom as a kaiser in the kings's clothing. But they should relax. The 2002 7 Series is a world-class driving machine, and it would be silly not to share at least some design and mechanical bits. Both the 7 Series and the Phantom are bolted to steel subframes, and there are air springs at all four corners, with automatic load leveling and computer-controlled dampers. All that weight and mass is moved by a 453-hp direct-injection DOHC 48-valve aluminum V12 engine mated to a ZF six-speed automatic gearbox, which is also borrowed from the 7 Series. The V12 was expanded to 6.7 liters, with a long intake manifold to enhance torque. Peak torque—531 pound-feet—comes on at 3,500 rpm, but 75 percent of it is on tap at just 1,000 rpm. That torque keeps the car from behaving like a beached sea lion when it comes to getting away from the curb.

The tendency when looking at the Phantom, or any Rolls-Royce, is to assume that most owners ride in the backseat. Tony Gott says that's a myth and that 90 percent of the owners do their own driving. But there are some design attributes clearly meant for the "Jeeves and Wooster" set. The rear-hinged doors, called "coach" doors rather than "suicide" doors, make getting into and out of the roomy rear cabin a lot easier than negotiating conventional portals, posh or otherwise. The commands for the sound and navigation systems are handled by BMW's iDrive-style controller—excoriated in the 2002 7 Series because so many techno-challenged owners hated it—but the basic and old-fashioned audio controls are in plain sight and operable with elegant "violin key" switches. The climate-control air vents are controlled by push-pull organ stops. One switch allows the driver to make the hood ornament disappear into the grille shell when the car is parked. This is an obvious nod to the fact that some Rolls buyers will occasionally venture into neighborhoods where people would be tempted to purloin the flying lady and plunk her down on a Hyundai hood.

BMW clearly has been torn between the need to make the Phantom a technological and mechanical paragon and at the same time give it that cigar-smoke-and-sherry feeling of a Yorkshire country estate library. The iDrive is the first nod to this battle, but the Phantom version is not as advanced as the 7 Series, and it's easier to bypass it if its suits the owner. The delicate electronic gear shifter from the 7 Series seems puny and touchy for such a massive, hulking vehicle, like using a pull-string to turn on a lighthouse. The power reserve gauge, which tells the driver how effortlessly the V12 handles its workload, is one of those nods to the German engineering "look what I can do" modus operandi that seems like overkill. Less clutter and more beautiful wood please! The dashboard also had an aluminum-finish panel that was a magnet for unsightly fingerprints—"Jeeves, it's time to Windex the dash again." Must even the passengers wear driving gloves? Two of the most endearing gimmicks: the umbrella that slips into the innards of the rear door for easy storage, with a vented slot so the water on the umbrella wicks away with the motion of the car and the wheel covers that keep the interlocking "RR" logo always upright and readable, even as the tires rotate. *Cool.*

After driving the Rolls for a day, I found myself staring at it when it was at rest. What was it? What *is* my problem with this car besides the fact that it costs more than my house? Some of my fellow journalists harped on the too-small headlamps and the too-big grille, charging that it gave the front of the car the look of a Freightliner truck wearing tiny art-house spectacles. What kept nagging at me, though, was the chunkiness of the vehicle. Old classic Rollers like the Phantom II and Silver Cloud had elegant, if costumed, lines that made me think of elegantly tailored morning suits—too dressy for most occasions but beautiful for the right affairs. This Phantom reminded me of the front of the Twentieth Century Limited locomotive—powerful, massive, and arguably attractive for its scale—but arguable, yes, always arguable. Debating design is like debating politics. Half the people in the room are always bound to be right.

American-born Chris Bangle is the head of design at BMW, and his lieutenant in charge of Rolls design is the British born Ian Cameron. Under Cameron is Belgrade, Yugoslavia–born Marek Djordjevic, whose design for the Phantom was chosen over others. Djordjevic's job was to create a design that was unmistakably Rolls-Royce, the flagship for BMW's new brand. No pressure. This former Yugoslavian soldier only had to draw on nearly 100 years of British tradition.

Djordjevic said the job was challenging because the designs of the Rolls-Royce in the last 35 years were disappointments to most fans of the cars and the brand. Said Djordjevic: "The designs we had been living with were victims of neglect and were not up to the brand, so we didn't look to make the Phantom any kind of logical progression from the recent cars. We had to go back. It's like when art restorers work to pick and peel away what has been added after the original artist is done with it. Da Vinci's *The Last Supper,* for example. They have been working to restore that, removing attempts by later artists to retouch or paint over what Leonardo did, and also the grime and mold that had collected on the painting to get back to what the fresco was. That's what we tried to do. Take the brand back to what it was, but in a totally modern execution."

When Djordjevic began working on it, he was 30 years old and threw himself into the task of creating an elegant British motorcar by cutting his shoulder-length hair in favor of a short-cropped look. "I think I dressed better while I was working on it, too," he said. Djordjevic knows that his work is being closely scrutinized because he is playing against Rolls-Royce's own history more than he is playing against competition from Volkswagen's Bentley and Mercedes-Benz's Maybach. He turns his hands and eyes to the roofline of the grand saloon to show how it increases in depth as it nears the rear of the car, bending into a strong C-pillar designed to shelter rear-seat occupants from view. The downward curve of the roofline is mirrored by a subtle upward curve, running from front to back, along the bottom. Said Djordjevic: "The Rolls-Royce sensibility is in many ways the opposite of the BMW sensibility. With BMW's, you expect the cars to be angled downward like it's eating up the road. The Phantom, I felt, should look like it is gliding forward and up as if it might take flight. I like the line of the sill, gently rising toward the front of the car."

Chris Bangle: "The car is very *mighty*. We aren't used to cars like this today. We aren't used to cars that exude that much confidence. Our world is no longer full of things that define elegance. Audrey Hepburn *Breakfast at Tiffany's* elegance is not the same sort of elegance found in the QE2 or massive multi-ton sailing ships that have elegance and delicate lines. How often do we confront such elegance? We rarely confront things that have that much size and confidence. The history of the Rolls-Royce marque, though, demands that it be elegant. There is a grace of movement of the car. We tried to put a kind of power-yacht movement into the shape and lines."

BMW went to a lot of trouble to disconnect the people who worked on the Phantom from the rest of the BMW operation. And Bangle says, "We weren't bashful about telling people, 'hands off' unless you understand this. Because our first obligation was to protect Rolls-Royce *from* BMW."

The question of whether BMW succeeded will take at least 5 to 10 years to decide. Only half of the question is whether BMW's interpretation of Rolls-Royce is correct. The other half of the question is whether the market is still there for a $350,000 luxury car. If Rolls-Royce was the only one playing in the category, the answer would be a simple yes. But Bentley is aiming to ratchet up its production of a family of Bentleys ranging from $150,000 or so to $350,000 to perhaps 5,000 to 6,000 a year. Mercedes-Benz wants to sell several hundred Maybach luxury saloons a year, directly competing against Rolls's Phantom.

In 2003, the year the world saw the Concorde superfast airplane fly its last trip across the Atlantic, in part because the market for $9,000 plane tickets was simply not there in sufficient numbers, it's worth asking how many $350,000 cars will be gobbled up by even the wealthiest people who own more than five cars. Is it a coincidence that the Concorde was powered by Rolls-Royce aero engines?

The Ultimate Hydrogen Future

EIGHT

Nothing to fear. . . . Yes, my friends, I believe that water will one day be employed as fuel, that hydrogen and oxygen which constitute it, used singly or together, will furnish an inexhaustible source of heat and light. . . . I believe then that when the deposits of coal are exhausted, we shall heat and warm ourselves with water. Water will be the coal of the future.

—JULES VERNE, THE MYSTERIOUS ISLAND

There is, at first look, perhaps no bigger threat to BMW's brand—to its reason for existing and being viewed as special and distinct from other, more humdrum brands—than the coming hydrogen age. Though the debate over the precise future of hydrogen as fuel for powering automobiles still rages among scientists, engineers, industrialists, regulators, and lawmakers, there is broad-based belief that hydrogen, over the next 100 years, figures to gradually replace fossil fuels like coal, oil, and natural gas as humanity's primary source of light, heat, and mobility. But anyone who has ever driven a hydrogen fuel cell car knows that the technology doesn't yet fulfill the desire to hear an engine rev and roar, nor does it deliver the same performance, feel, and feedback from machine to driver.

BMW knows this, and it is proceeding boldly. While General Motors, DaimlerChrysler, and many other car companies are pursuing a strategy of electric cars powered by hydrogen fuel cells—electric batteries powered by hydrogen—that can be recharged quickly, BMW is exclusively pursuing a strategy of perpetuating the internal combustion engine (ICE), but using a bi-fuel engine fed either by gasoline/diesel or by liquid hydrogen. Decades down the line BMW sees its internal combustion engine fueled by hydrogen alone. But until a hydrogen infrastructure of service stations is built for consumers to conveniently use, BMW will market bi-fuel vehicles—in small batches—starting around 2005 or 2006.

Just one company so far in 2003, Ford, is pursuing both fuel cells and liquid hydrogen internal combustion. Like GM, Ford was pursuing a hydrogen fuel cell–only strategy until former BMW product chief Wolfgang Reitzle and BMW engineer Gerhard Schmidt arrived in 1999 and brought their hydrogen ICE know-how. "At this stage [in 2003] it is very worthwhile to pursue both technologies—fuel-cells *and* hydrogen IC engines—but I feel that the IC engine will ultimately be the most desirable from a driver's perspective," said Schmidt, introducing Ford's liquid hydrogen/gasoline hybrid concept car at the 2003 North American International Auto Show. Ford's decision to pursue hydrogen ICE technology on Schmidt's say-so reflects BMW's influence in the global automotive marketplace.

By 2003 BMW had built fifteen 7 Series prototype IC cars powered by liquid hydrogen, and it plans to have dozens more, perhaps between 100 and 200, running around Germany and possibly other European countries by mid-decade as it monitors and studies real-life usage of the cars: how much people enjoy living with them; whether people consider them legitimate and authentic BMWs; whether they hold up well; whether customers are satisfied and comfortable with hydrogen filling stations. By 2003, BMW road tested fifteen 750hL liquid hydrogen–powered sedans, logging over 170,000 kilometers. The vehicles were used as shuttle cars at the World Expo in Hannover, Germany, in 2000 and as part of BMW's CleanEnergy project in Munich. No mechanical problems or mishaps were recorded. BMW followed the 750hL with the 745h, a concept based on the current-generation 2002 7 Series and the basis for the production hydrogen/gasoline hybrid car BMW will sell to the public.

BMW is intent on fulfilling its liquid hydrogen IC strategy to the exclusion of fuel cells (though it is deploying fuel cells as a replacement for conventional wet-cell batteries to power the vehicle's electrical system but not to drive the vehicle power train) because the company is determined that its customers shouldn't feel they have compromised any of the driving enjoyment found in a BMW if they *have* to live with hydrogen. "The research vehicles have been very comparable in performance to the gasoline driven 7 Series, and it looks very promising to have a good number in customers' hands by 2005 or 2006," according to Manfred Heller, BMW's director for environmental protection. Though rivals like GM and DaimlerChrysler believe BMW's hydrogen IC strategy is not as wise as their fuel cell plan, it's not difficult to understand BMW's reasoning. The sound of GM's fuel cell Hy-wire concept car, for example, is closer to that of a golf cart than that of a performance car despite the car's acceleration properties, which are comparable to many of GM's gasoline-fed cars. Says Dr. Burkhard Goeschel, head of BMW product development, "We are relying on the combustion engine because we are convinced that our customers will continue to value dynamics, comfort and range in the future just as they do today." Adds Anton Reisinger, head of marketing for BMW's CleanEnergy program, "Our future hydrogen cars will be *real* BMWs. They have to be!"

BMW likes the idea of having both gasoline and hydrogen fuels aboard its so-called CleanEnergy cars, believing it's the ideal transition strategy between a gasoline-fed auto world and one driven by hydrogen. As hydrogen refueling stations multiply, owners of hydrogen cars will undoubtedly fill up their tanks with hydrogen as often as possible, even if they already have half a tank. It's only natural that those early adopters who embrace hydrogen technology from the outset would be willing to go out of their way at times to fill up. Their behavior will help drive the business case for oil companies and utility companies to outfit more filling stations with hydrogen pumps. But in the event a hydrogen station can't be found, gasoline will see the driver through. Onboard electronics take care of preparing the engine to receive the two different fuels, though a flip of a switch or push of a button will change over the fuel supply. As with all new technology, BMW is starting hydrogen use with the priciest model range, the 7 Series. By starting with the model that delivers the greatest profit margin, BMW can recoup its investment in hydrogen technology faster than if it started with the lower-priced 3 Series. Also, people shopping the 7 Series model range aren't as price sensitive as people shopping the 5 Series or 3 Series. Buyers of 7 Series cars, the thinking goes, will be willing to pay even thousands more for a hybrid hydrogen-powered version of the car. Then, after acceptance is achieved, the company plans to cascade the technology through its other products—provided, of course, the hydrogen infrastructure continues to develop. Too, automakers like BMW and General Motors are hoping that China embraces hydrogen as a source of energy more quickly than the United States, thus accelerating demand so the per-unit cost of the technology decreases faster than if they had to just rely on adoption of hydrogen by the West.

The biggest hurdles to overcome are the storage of hydrogen aboard the vehicle and the infrastructure to support the use of hydrogen. BMW, GM, and other car companies don't seem to have any trouble designing vehicles that will run on hydrogen. The real challenge is coming up with a system to store the hydrogen, either in liquid or in gas form, on board the vehicle at a price that won't add $50,000 to the cost of each vehicle and in sufficient quantity so a driving range of at least 300 miles between fill-ups is achieved. Convincing oil companies to invest in supplying hydrogen as readily as they do gasoline is an even bigger challenge. How much of an investment is this for oil companies and utilities? BMW's Christoph Huss estimates the required investment in Germany alone to be $100 billion to cover the cost of filling stations, trucks, storage containers, and production facilities. *Ouch!*

The size and cost of the tanks to store hydrogen on board BMW's cars are formidable problems. Cooling hydrogen to −253°C is necessary to keep it from evaporating or "boiling off." Hydrogen is compressed to one-thousandth of its original volume in order to fit enough in a tank to power a driving range of at least 300 miles. It takes 70 layers of aluminum and fiberglass sheets between the exterior and the interior vehicle walls of the storage tank to ensure that the liquid hydrogen stays at the extremely low temperature. If the temperature of the hydrogen rises, it dissipates. If this isn't prevented, a car's fuel supply would go down, even when the car sits idle in the garage. That's not going to make the owner of a hydrogen vehicle too happy. Debate continues about whether it's best to have technology in place at service stations that will enable the creation of liquid and compressed hydrogen at the station so that the only storage link in the chain is in the car. This is one of the biggest questions yet to be answered by the auto and fuel industries. Will hydrogen tanker trucks be needed in large numbers to take hydrogen to filling stations to be stored again in holding tanks, or will filling stations be equipped with reformers on-site that create the hydrogen by electrolyzing water or stripping the hydrogen out of gasoline, methanol, and natural gas? GM favors the creation of hydrogen at stations, while BMW believes it will be better to have liquid hydrogen trucked to stations.

In 1999 BMW, working with Aral Corp., established the first liquid hydrogen filling station where liquid hydrogen is dispersed from the gasoline pump at Munich Airport. That hydrogen is trucked in.

Why hydrogen?

Hydrogen makes up about 75 percent of the known universe. It is not an energy source, though, like fossil fuels or wind or solar power, but an energy *carrier*. It's not thought of exactly as an energy source because it's never found by itself in usable form. It can't be dug or pumped out of the ground. Hydrogen must be split away from other compounds, such as water and fossil fuels like coal or natural gas. Indeed, two-thirds of the atoms burned from fossil fuels are hydrogen atoms. Because we have long known about the harmful results of burning the other one-third—carbon—scientists have believed for more than a century that we ought to find a way to get by with just the hydrogen atoms.

The U.S. Environmental Protection Agency released a report in 2003 showing that despite attempts for 25 years to make substantial headway in achieving greater fuel efficiency in gasoline-powered vehicles, the average fuel economy of the nation's new-vehicle fleet was going in the other direction. It stood at 20.4 miles to the gallon for the average vehicle, worse than the previous year, which was worse than the year before that. It's not that the auto industry has been getting dumber or lazier; it's that consumers are demanding larger and more powerful vehicles, especially sport utility vehicles, which offer much less fuel economy than cars. In fact, auto companies had become pretty good at improving fuel efficiency by 2003, holding the fuel consumption of most models in check or improving fuel economy every time they developed a new vehicle. But increased weight from the extra equipment and structure demanded by new safety regulations and the extra space demanded by consumers outran the engineers' ability to achieve much in the way of net gains in fuel economy. The 2004 Ford F150 pickup truck, for example, gets roughly the same mileage as its predecessor, despite the fact that it weighs almost 500 pounds more than the old model. The added weight came mostly from size and extra features that added to crash safety. Ford's engineers achieved greater fuel *efficiency* but did not actually add to the truck's fuel *economy*. BMW has been a bit more clever. The 2002 7 Series, while larger than its predecessor, is 60 pounds lighter than the old 7 Series thanks to the use of lighter-weight materials in certain areas of the car, and it is 15 percent more fuel efficient, thus eliminating the gas guzzler tax that the old 7 Series was subject to.

According to the Natural Resources Defense Council in Washington, D.C., the average car on the road today consumes 600 gallons of gasoline and produces six tons of carbon dioxide per year. The United States consumes approximately 2.2 billion barrels of oil every year. Supplementing the total vehicle fleet with hydrogen could reduce the U.S. trade deficit, by $60 billion a year with small hydrogen penetration, according to some estimates. But even those figures don't take into account all the money the United States spends maintaining the military or protecting investments in the Middle East. What would the United States and other industrialized nations spend in the Middle East oil region if their home economies didn't need Middle East oil?

When it comes to pollution and emissions, hydrogen offers an amazing alternative to fossil fuels. Molecular hydrogen, H_2, is the lightest of all the known elements—eight times lighter than natural gas and 64 percent lighter than gasoline. About 2.2 pounds of hydrogen packs the same energy as one gallon, or 6.2 pounds, of gasoline. Most of the general public doesn't realize the extent to which hydrogen can go to help solve the problems of pollution and global warming. The air that comes out of the exhaust pipe of an IC engine running off hydrogen, like BMW's, is cleaner than it was when it went in; this is called *minus emissions*. And engine oil remains clean for an extended period of time because there are no sulfur or carbon compounds to degrade the oil.

Gasoline-powered vehicles emit a quarter of the world's carbon dioxide, contributing to what the United Nations Environment Program sees as a dire problem of global warming. Hydrogen cars, by contrast, emit water vapor instead of CO_2. Estimates vary regarding how soon the earth will exhaust the supply of fossil fuel. Whether sub-scribing to a date of 2080, 2100, or 2150, most sane scientists and industrialists agree that the auto industry and oil companies would be criminal to plan to exhaust the supply of fossil fuels before getting seri-ous about hydrogen as an alternative.

As the most common element in the universe, hydrogen is seen as the best solution to ending the world's dependence on fossil fuels. Besides being a component of water, hydrogen is produced as a by-product in many industrial processes, including, ironically, crude oil refining. It can also be "cracked" out of gasoline by way of a chemical reforming process. It might sound silly to consider refining gasoline only to then employ technology to crack the hydrogen out of it; how-ever, this approach is discussed only as a means of leveraging the mas-sive gasoline infrastructure that is already in place—refineries, service stations, pipelines, and trucks—while the industrial world transitions to hydrogen. It's impossible to think that the oil companies are going to allow a rapid overhaul and obsolescence of the gasoline infrastruc-ture. These companies, arguably the most politically and economically powerful in the world, have hundreds of billions of dollars invested in refineries, oil rigs, and oil exploration. They will need decades more to realize their return on investments in all that infrastructure as they slowly turn their dials toward hydrogen power.

Hydrogen currently costs much more to create and store than refin-ing and storing gasoline, but that is partly due to its limited production mostly for specialty applications. The more hydrogen that is created, the more its costs can be spread across a greater number of users. Annual worldwide production of hydrogen for widespread industrial use stood at 54 million metric tons in 2002. Hydrogen has been used for various applications such as fuel cells that power rockets for the U.S. space program and for powering up office buildings that have adopted fuel cells to defray electricity costs and provide critical backup power during power outages. The National Aeronautics and Space Agency (NASA) has used hydrogen as a rocket fuel since the 1940s. During a shuttle liftoff, onlookers can see that the orbiter's three main engines produce a light blue flame. These are the onboard hydrogen rockets. NASA also uses hydrogen for its primary fuel while moving in space and for making drinking water. One pound of hydrogen combined with oxygen will make nine pounds of pure distilled drinking water. A significant amount of electricity is created as a by-product. The U.S. Navy, too, has long used electrolyzers for its submarines to make oxygen for long missions. The submarines run on diesel engines but are able to turn the seawater into hydrogen and oxygen. At least three times the current levels of hydrogen produced, or about 150 million metric tons, would be needed to power 500 million cars if they were all running on hydrogen, according to some estimates.

The most common process for producing hydrogen is through electrolysis—the electrification of water—in which the electricity is supplied from natural gas, coal, gasoline, or diesel fuel. Obviously, using fossil fuels to create hydrogen is not desirable in the long term because that process still produces CO_2. The electricity for the electrolysis must eventually come, at least in part, from nonpolluting energy like wind or solar power if the world is to be able to sustain a viable hydrogen future. Some of the electricity might also be generated from biomass (agricultural waste).

BMW executives say the best method of creating liquid hydrogen for its IC engines (although it is also presently the most expensive way) is by taking electricity generated from solar power to split water into its separate oxygen and hydrogen components through electrolysis. With this method, the oxygen is released into the atmosphere, while the hydrogen is liquefied and stored at the very low temperature ($-253°C$) needed to keep it intact and usable to power a vehicle. During internal combustion, the liquid hydrogen combines with oxygen. The energy resulting from the recombination drives the vehicle much the way gasoline that is burned drives an engine. Solar panels to collect energy from the sun, like the ones envisioned by BMW, are already being deployed in the Mojave Desert in California and in Saudi Arabia as well as in other desert locales. The areas of the earth located around 40 degrees of latitude are ideal for solar power stations. Europe is looking to solar-produced hydrogen supplied from North Africa, the nearest desert locale, combined with hydrogen produced from biomass in local markets to prevent a hydrogen version of the Organization of the Petroleum Exporting Countries (OPEC) from developing.

Wind power as a means of supplying hydrogen is not to be cast aside either. While Great Britain, for example, is a poor place to build a solar energy collection station—foggy London—the British Isles is an excellent place for wind farms, provided the real estate is available.

And some countries where real estate is scarce are placing wind farms at sea, off the coastline. Says Karl-Heinz Kalbfell, senior vice president of group marketing at BMW, "There are countries that can be considered more sun-drenched than the British Isles, and the same can be said of many other places, but the conditions for wind power are excellent. Britain is one of the countries that has the potential of producing a large share of the entire hydrogen demand regeneratively. That is why hydrogen is so promising." Adds BMW's product development chief Goeschel, "Each region of the world enjoys a local potential all its own, which must be intelligently utilized—that is, water power in Scandinavia or Canada, wind energy at high-altitude locations or along the coasts, and sunlight and warmth in the equatorial regions. There is no single answer for every region as far as how to get to a hydrogen economy, but I have no doubt that we must all get there." Of course, another obstacle to widespread wind power is the not-in-my-backyard syndrome, in which people don't want to see coastal areas, rich with wind, heavily dotted with industrial windmills. They spoil the view.

Oil companies want to control the transition to a hydrogen economy as best they can, but they do seem to accept the eventuality of a hydrogen economy. A 2001 report by Royal Dutch Shell projected that industrialization of China would, if it were smart, largely leapfrog fossil fuels to hydrogen-based power, which is already under way, and that 25 percent of the world's new-vehicle sales (motorcycles not included) would be powered by hydrogen by 2025. That estimate may be generous, but it's interesting that an *oil* company would overshoot the estimate.

———

Hydrogen as fuel is not a new idea. Hydrogen was discovered and defined as an element in 1766 by Henry Cavendish in London, England. The hydrogen fuel cell was conceived by a brilliant English lawyer turned scientist, William Grove, in 1839. Grove, a close associate of renowned British physicist Michael Faraday, thought if it was possible to break water down into its component elements of oxygen and hydrogen using electric current, it might also be possible to do the reverse. He built a device that produced a small electric current by combining hydrogen and oxygen across a pair of platinum electrodes and then boosted the available current in later experiments by making several such devices and connecting them.

Author Jules Verne, well aware of Grove's work, incorporated hydrogen power into his novel *The Mysterious Island*. In the story, a group of Union officers from the Northern army in the U.S. Civil War of the 1860s escape by hot-air balloon from a prison only to crash-land on a deserted island in the Pacific Ocean. The officers discuss at length the army's problem of being too dependent on coal, which is in short supply. One officer in the band says, "Nothing to fear. . . . Yes, my friends, I believe that water will one day be employed as fuel, that hydrogen and oxygen which constitute it, used singly or together, will furnish an inexhaustible source of heat and light. . . . I believe then that when the deposits of coal are exhausted, we shall heat and warm ourselves with water. Water will be the coal of the future." "I should like to see that," one of the officers chimes in.

There were few applications of Grove's discovery until the 1960s when General Electric built hydrogen fuel cells to power the Gemini space flights for NASA. Fuel cells today are found on space shuttle vehicles, as well as in industrial plants and as a power source for cell phone towers and large office buildings. In 2003, as interest in hydrogen fuel cells was mounting, driven primarily by the hype surrounding fuel cell vehicles and the increasing interest in finding credible alternative power sources, computer companies and cell phone producers were moving to introduce small hydrogen fuel cells to replace dry-cell batteries. Toshiba, for one, announced it would sell a fuel cell for laptop computers by 2004. Motorola was working on the same for video cameras and phones.

Is hydrogen safe as a fuel and for the public to handle? Most of the public associates hydrogen with one major if misleading event, and this doesn't spell good news for easy consumer acceptance. That event is the fiery crash of the *Hindenburg,* a German zeppelin, over Lakehurst, New Jersey in 1937, an event that has been replayed on television and in newsreels almost as often as Charles Lindbergh's arrival in Paris in 1927 after his first nonstop transatlantic flight. In fact, hydrogen played no part in the *Hindenburg* accident. The cause was an onboard wire that became hot and set ablaze the highly flammable aluminum-threaded cloth covering on the zeppelin.

The truth is, however, that the systems being designed around hydrogen as a fuel are highly secure. A Munich filling station for BMW's prototype hydrogen cars, for example, is equipped with robotic arms that fasten a filler hose to the side of the car, lock the seal so no hydrogen escapes, and close the filler neck. The driver never gets out of the car. In a paper titled "Twenty Myths About Hydrogen," physicist Amory Lovins, CEO of the Rocky Mountain Institute, argued that hydrogen is "at least as safe as natural gas or liquid petroleum gas and arguably inherently safer than gasoline."[1] Environmentalists endorse hydrogen cars. Lovins makes the point that hydrogen is 14 times more buoyant than air and 12 times more diffusive than gasoline fumes. This means that leaking hydrogen evaporates much more quickly than gasoline fumes or even natural gas. Burning hydrogen produces only 30 percent as much radiant heat as carbon-based combustion. (Firefighters dislike hydrogen fires because of the special viewing apparatus needed to see the flames. Yet it takes a highly concentrated hydrogen flame to burn someone.) Further adding to its safety, says Lovins, hydrogen, unlike natural gas, is far more likely to just burn rather than explode because it burns at a far lower concentration than its explosion threshold. And in the rare cases where it does explode, it still does so with 22 times less force than the comparable gasoline vapor.

BMW has done extensive crash testing to prove the safety of its hydrogen vehicles. The company tested its hydrogen tanks in a series of accident simulations that included collision and fire and tank ruptures, and in all cases the hydrogen cars fared better than the gasoline vehicles. In one series of tests, tanks full of hydrogen with their safety valves disabled were destroyed under high pressure; the tank's design yielded a safe, steady discharge of the hydrogen into the atmosphere. In fire tests, tanks carrying liquid hydrogen were engulfed in fierce flames for more than an hour; the hydrogen escaped through the safety valves without incident. Additionally, tanks filled with liquid hydrogen were severely damaged in simulated worst-case crashes without a single explosion. BMW also replicated the government and insurance tests in the 7 Series hydrogen cars, for instance, by crashing them in the front at a speed of 56 km/h, as well as from the rear and side. Side crash tests hit the car at its most vulnerable point: the filler neck of the hydrogen tank. No fires or explosions were recorded, demonstrating that the hydrogen vehicles are at least as safe as their gasoline counterparts.

Ignorance, though, still prevails among much of the public and even some lawmakers and officials. In 2002, the deputy mayor of Los Angeles, Brian Williams, fanned public fears by comparing driving a fuel cell car to piloting the *Hindenburg*—this despite speaking at a media event introducing Honda's fuel cell cars to Los Angeles. Onlooking Honda representatives winced visibly, knowing that such a remark by an official can have more impact on public perception than tens of millions of dollars' worth of advertising.

——

While BMW envisions a hydrogen future in internal combustion engines, its strategy differs markedly from that of General Motors, its research partner in hydrogen filling stations and infrastructure. The case can certainly be made for hydrogen fuel cells that drive electric motors rather than a hydrogen IC engine—a case that varies a lot depending on who's making it. Fuel cell proponents such as General Motors' research and development chief Larry Burns argue that fuel cells have twice the energy efficiency of liquid hydrogen IC engines, plus sprightly acceleration at low speeds. But GM, it's worth noting, is not overly dependent on customers who *love* to drive or on drivers willing to pay top dollar for the sort of unique driving experience created by Bavarian engineers. "A fuel-cell car sounds like a vacuum cleaner, and that's not what our customers are looking for," says BMW's Heller. GM sells vehicles to the masses, and it endeavors to make their Cadillacs, Saturns, Hummers, Saabs, Opels, and Pontiacs as interesting and pleasurable to drive as possible. But a Saturn minivan doesn't have to be as much fun to drive as a BMW 3 Series in order to be successful in the marketplace.

GM's Burns believes there will be at least a million fuel cell vehicles on the road worldwide by 2010. But there are doubters. Volkswagen AG research chief Ulrich Eichhorn notes former DaimlerChrysler chairman Jürgen Schrempp's prediction of a zero-fuel-consumption car by 2004. But, says Eichhorn, "How will they generate the hydrogen? How will they solve the question of hydrogen storage? When he [Schrempp] answers these, ask how the car starts when the temperature drops below freezing. Then, how much the car is going to cost and where it will be refueled. I think they are getting desperate, trying to live up to their promises."[2] Former BMW chairman and current chairman of VW AG Bernd Pischetsrieder is also skeptical, despite having supported BMW's liquid hydrogen strategy before his 1999 ouster. His skepticism, though, seems to reflect some Volkswagen-specific practical concerns rather than the technology's potential. "I have four more product cycles at least to worry about before hydrogen is any issue at all," Pischetsrieder said over dinner at the 2002 Paris Auto Show. When asked about Volkswagen's hydrogen strategy, Pischetsrieder said simply, "We do not have one." He added that VW will probably be content to buy hydrogen technology off the shelf as it develops rather than spending big to help pioneer it. It's not difficult to understand Pischetsrieder's position. With fat profit margins, BMW is a tightly focused company with an equally focused brand image that it fiercely protects. But VW is more akin to General Motors: a mass marketer of several brands that it must sell to a far more diverse customer base than BMW's. When Pischetsrieder took over VW in 2002, the company labored under the weight of worsening quality, falling profits, and a muddled product portfolio left to him by his predecessor, Ferdinand Piech. He simply has numerous and more immediate fires to douse than any fueled by hydrogen.

GM's Burns brushes off Volkswagen's hydrogen reticence and says the cold-start problem, for example, is already solved at GM. He thinks hydrogen can and will be generated from a variety of sources including gasoline, methanol, natural gas, wind, solar energy, and biomass. Moving to hydrogen is not an overnight, all-or-nothing transformation like a country changing from driving on the left to driving on the right. It's going to be a slow, gradual "walk to hydrogen," says Burns. "GM and BMW have chosen to be leaders in hydrogen technology along with Honda and Toyota." He adds that "Volkswagen would feel differently if they had chosen to be a leader in this revolution. GM is too big, and we have too much at stake to let others lead on this. BMW is much smaller in sales than GM, but it has a culture of leadership."

———

I haven't had the opportunity to drive BMW's gasoline/hydrogen car as of late 2003. No journalist I could find has had the pleasure. But we have had the chance to drive GM's, Ford's, Chrysler's, Honda's, and

Toyota's fuel cell vehicles. Driving GM's Hy-wire fuel cell test car is disorienting at first. I drove it at GM's proving ground in Milford, Michigan. Drivers can sit in either the left seat or the right, having their legs level with their hips rather than being bent as normal. The steering wheel is like an airplane's, with handles on either side of a center console that has an electronic screen display. Feet are not a factor; everything that controls the movement of the car is on that wheel. The throttle and braking are controlled by hand, and the wheel turns only 20 degrees in either direction to maneuver the car. Given the projected rollout of 2015 or beyond, the Hy-wire's handling—the hand-eye coordination required—unsurprisingly enough, seems more closely related to that of a video game than to any car I've driven. GM has clearly designed it for people born after 1980 who are used to control by hand with no foot pedals. The car goes *whirrrrrrr* rather than *vroom*. GM product boss Bob Lutz, who test-drove the Hy-wire for the first time the same day I did, wonders whether digitally produced, virtual engine sounds could be programmed into the vehicle's computer and audio system to mimic the sound of gasoline-fed cars, especially performance cars with growling engines. "But it's hard to know how much people will miss engine sounds. I know I would, but I'll be 90 or more [Lutz was 71 at the time] before we have to worry about really marketing hydrogen cars to consumers," said Lutz. Hy-wire accelerates well with no real loss of power or acceleration compared with a Chevy Impala or Cadillac CTS.

———

GM does not feel compelled to pursue hydrogen fuel cells because oil will eventually run out. Rather, GM and BMW want to *lead* the transition to hydrogen, positioning their cars in the forefront where they are seen as advantageous to own. "The idea is to make these cars desirable when they hit the market, not something to settle for," says GM's Burns. BMW's Huss agrees. BMW advertises its all-wheel-drive system this way: "The difference between our all-wheel-drive system and our competitors' is ours comes with a BMW attached." The same strategy is envisioned for selling BMW hydrogen vehicles. "Hydrogen: the BMW way."

Hydrogen fuel cell vehicles—more so than BMW's proposed hydrogen IC vehicles—figure to usher in a revolution in manufacturing and design. GM, for example, proposes to have perhaps only three sizes of

HyWire chassis for all its cars and trucks. The vision consists of modular bodies that get plunked down on the basic hydrogen electric engineering platform. Taken to visionary extremes, Burns says he can see people trading in a sedan body for a minivan body while keeping the same chassis—or even owning two bodies and just one chassis, and having a lift in the garage to switch bodies as needed. Going to church? Lower the four-door sedan body. Going to the lumberyard? Lower the pickup body. Because the chassis has so few moving parts and isn't subjected to the same heat and friction generated by combustion engines, a fuel cell chassis could last much longer than a gasoline one. On an ever more crowded planet, that has tremendous implications for future car scrappage rates.

In 2003, the two biggest hurdles for hydrogen vehicles were the delivery infrastructure and cost. That year, Hy-wire's power train cost 10 times more than that required for an internal combustion engine—$45,000 or so compared with $4,500. That doesn't deter Burns: "Look how fast the computer industry brought costs down, from $15,000 computers to $1,500 computers."

———

BMW has spent about $1 billion over 20 years developing its hydrogen future—a fraction of its eventual cost. Everyone in the hydrogen loop will have to spend hundreds of billions more. BMW's Huss says the biggest challenge is managing the timing of the spending. Said Huss, "You can't change the energy system from one day to the next. It will take step after step after step to accomplish it. And we constantly face the chicken and egg argument. Auto companies have to spend on product in a cadence with the developing infrastructure, and the companies involved in the infrastructure are spending as they look at our progress with the cars. The breadth of companies that are and will be involved is enormous. And capital spending is a very important function of the development, but it is also a function of each company's bottom line quarter to quarter and year to year. Each company in the loop has to be careful about how much it spends and *when* it spends it because it will be years before profits are realized from hydrogen vehicles. It's a huge issue. The development of transmissions, gearboxes, engines. It's an amazing challenge of balance. The right speed of investment is critical. It can't be jumps. It has to be a walk."

Both GM and BMW have traveled the world with their hydrogen vehicles and technology, garnering interest from governments, the media, and the public. But as of 2003, neither had sold any certified hydrogen vehicles to customers. Honda was the first to sell government-certified hydrogen fuel cell cars, albeit in very small numbers, in Japan and California. Just as Toyota and Honda were first to market with gasoline/electric hybrids, they hope to seize leadership in the hydrogen arena as well. GM's Burns says being first with such technology pays some public relations dividends, but is well beside the point of what is a "monumental" transition. "We're not that interested in being the first with certification for the sake of being first, whether it's the first fuel cell car certified for public use or the first fuel cell car to travel across country on a gallon of water. We are only interested in leading the transition to hydrogen *profitably*." Both Burns and Huss have pondered the Japanese companies' launch of gas/electric hybrid vehicles, such as Toyota's Prius and Honda's Insight. According to Burns, despite big subsidies to those companies by the Japanese government to develop the cars for the home market, Toyota and Honda sold these cars at a tremendous loss per vehicle for the first few years, and the vehicles themselves—bought by curious early adopters—were small and in the least-profitable category: subcompacts. "Will we be out later than Toyota and Honda with hybrids? Yes, but we'll quickly pass them in total sales volume and we will do it profitably. . . . It's important for companies making these transitions to do it profitably, and it's also important to be able to offer the technology in vehicle packages that are attractive," says Burns. BMW, with fewer products and much smaller total sales volume than GM and Toyota, hadn't announced any plans by the end of 2003 to even enter the gas/electric hybrid category, preferring to concentrate on its hydrogen/gasoline hybrid strategy.

Huss says that despite BMW's drive to the hydrogen age with an internal combustion engine instead of a fuel cell, the company is pursuing using either compressed hydrogen or liquid to power the IC engine. Compressed and liquid hydrogen alike will power both a hydrogen IC engine and a fuel cell vehicle, with the main difference being in the onboard storage tank as well as some other components. But it's a certainty that eventually both types of power trains will run on either form of hydrogen. "It would be mismanagement if we didn't pursue both fuel forms, so we will be ready if the infrastructure favors compressed hydrogen over liquid. . . . Our cars will run on either form," says Huss.

The storage question is vital to the development of both the vehicle and the supporting infrastructure. And because most companies see storage as a commodity business, the auto and oil companies are pushing ahead together in league with companies like Ballard Power Systems and Linde AG to goose development as much as possible.

———

Two hydrogen versions of BMW's 7 Series already exist, leading up to production of hydrogen/gasoline hybrids for the 2005 model year: the 745h and the faster, more powerful 750hL. The BMW 745h is powered by a 4.4-liter V8, featuring variable valve timing, Valvetronic variable intake runners, and a fully variable intake manifold. Running on hydrogen, the 745h produces 184 horsepower with a top speed of 215 km/h (133 mph) and a cruising range of 310 kilometers (190 miles) that compares with 325 horsepower for a gasoline-fueled 745. Added on to the 640-kilometer (400-mile) range of the gasoline fuel tank, the 745h can go 950 kilometers (600 miles) between fill-ups.

"It feels like a normal car. It can be operated like a normal car. And so the feeling for our customers will be: They have a high-powered car, a normal car with clean emissions," comments Klaus Pehr, head of concept cars for BMW. A number of design features distinguish the prototype BMW 745h from its conventional, gas-fed siblings. One is the transparent filler flap where the fuel is pumped into the car, redolent of pure water and BMW's CleanEnergy theme. In fact, Clean-Energy branding symbols could be a feature of the production cars. The car comes with an auxiliary power unit (APU), generating electricity for the car's various power-consuming items such as the air conditioner. While conventional batteries have to be charged by an alternator, this system based on a PEM (polymer electrolyte membrane) fuel cell, operates independently of the engine and is fed with hydrogen straight from the tank. This means you can use power-consuming items such as the air conditioner, heat, or a 12-volt power outlet even if the engine isn't running. BMW claims that its fuel cell generates three times as much power as a traditional alternator; it's more efficient because it provides electric power only when needed by specific power-consuming items. An alternator, on the other hand, is always working, though not always required. Applying this more economical mode of operation to a conventional engine running on gasoline, BMW says that this results in a saving of one liter of fuel for every 100 kilometers in city traffic. It adds up.

The heart of the 750hL is a hybrid, 12-cylinder combustion engine with two independent electronically controlled fuel induction systems, which allows the 750hL, like the 745h, to run on either gasoline or hydrogen. The 5.4-liter engine offers excellent torque and acceleration, while the specially insulated 140-liter tank for the liquid hydrogen provides a range of 400 kilometers. The 750hL, the fifth-generation hydrogen vehicle BMW has developed since the late 1970s, generates the equivalent of 204 hp, accelerating from zero to 100 km/h in 9.6 seconds and reaching a top speed of 226 km/h.

The 7 Series is not BMW's only hydrogen experiment. A hydrogen-powered Mini concept was unveiled at the 2001 Frankfurt Motor Show. Running solely on hydrogen, it demonstrates the advantages of a virtually zero-emission vehicle that still offers outstanding performance in an affordable package. The hydrogen-powered Mini features a new injection process in which supercooled liquid hydrogen is injected into the intake ducts, where it mixes with air before entering the cylinders for ignition. Previously, the liquid hydrogen was heated to ambient temperature before combustion. This supercooled mixture increases the cylinder charge, boosting both engine output and efficiency. It offers a hydrogen engine with the potential to match a modern gasoline engine in every respect. The car also features a breakthrough in alternative fuel packaging, in that its fuel tank takes up the same space as a conventional fuel tank.

While BMW favors the hydrogen IC engine, it does, as stated previously, use a hydrogen fuel cell to run the electrical system. This autonomous use of the fuel cell enables some new features: the windows can be defrosted while the driver sips coffee in the kitchen, and the seats and steering wheel can be warmed. The air-conditioning can be operated optimally regardless of the engine speed. With existing fuel cell technology, air-conditioning the car with the engine off can already be carried out using a quarter of the energy required today from a gasoline-only power train and wet-cell battery. Future "by-wire" systems, such as electrically operated steering or brakes, will require greater amounts of electrical energy, which can be provided by the fuel cell far more efficiently than by a conventional wet-cell battery. And various Internet and online services in the car—the evolving mobile office—are greatly facilitated by the fuel cell.

BMW has a glorious history of engineering cars to be chock-full of fun and excitement. That journalists haven't yet driven the 745h and 750hL implies that the company wasn't quite ready to let drivers outside the BMW family put foot to a prototype pedal in advance of the production cars. BMW says journalists haven't driven the cars because it requires a special license. Whatever the reason, journalists are anxious to see whether BMW has managed to create the ultimate hydrogen machine.

———

Though BMW and General Motors are cooperating on research while pursuing different strategies, consumers will play a major role in deciding which hydrogen cars are desirable and which are mere appliances. As BMW CleanEnergy project manager Bernd Gebler puts it, "It is the customer who will decide whether an electric vehicle with a fuel-cell is preferable to a dynamic car with a combustion engine." In 2003, though the BMW hydrogen prototype was not equal in total performance to a gasoline-fed Bimmer, it was more powerful than the fuel cell vehicles produced by GM, Honda, and DaimlerChrysler. Again, BMW is counting on its own hybrid strategy to see it through, whereby 7 Series hydrogen/gas hybrid drivers use hydrogen when they want, such as in city driving, while switching over to gasoline if they wish on the autobahn. On paper, it seems like the best of both the old world and the new.

The world's previous conversions to new energy sources—from wood to coal, from coal to oil, and from oil to natural gas—have shown that it takes 50 to 70 years to achieve even 50 percent market penetration. BMW's Huss says that if the industrialized world wishes to prepare for the end of the oil age, then it must begin introducing new sources of energy *today*. But since the construction of hydrogen infrastructure makes sense only with enough hydrogen-driven vehicles to make it worthwhile, someone must dare to take the first step. Says Huss, "That's just what we are doing."

The Ultimate Outlook

E P I L O G U E

The most admired car company in the world? Given the controversy surrounding BMW's latest designs, there are many who agreed with this book's premise a few years ago, but are now having doubts.

In the past, BMW typically introduced one new car a year. But 2003 and 2004 will tax BMW's resources like never before. Going back to late summer of 2003 when the company launched its all-new 5 Series and continuing into 2004 with a new 6 Series, 1 Series, and X3 Sports Activity Vehicle, BMW is trying to prove that it can grow rapidly without acquiring another car company. Perhaps more important, it is out to prove that it can grow the BMW business profitably without being acquired. Its goal is to increase sales from 2003 to 2008 by 40 percent, reaching $1.4 million in sales.

Though the 3 Series is BMW's most important vehicle because of its sales volume, the two vehicles being watched most closely are the 1 Series and the X3. The idea of the 1 Series is to launch a credible entry-level (for BMW) car, with prices starting in the range of $20,000 to $25,000, that is a legitimate BMW. Many industry pundits and competitors do not believe BMW can do it. They don't believe the car can

achieve the "carved out of stone" feeling in the suspension for which
BMW is known, or in a short-wheel-base rear-drive car. Critics will be
ruthless in their attempts to discover where the company scrimped in
order to preserve a decent profit in a lower-priced vehicle. Will the mere
existence of a 1 Series—if it's not seen as a "legit" BMW—cheapen the
image of the 3 Series? This is what has happened to Mercedes-Benz. As
DaimlerChrysler launched cheap versions of the Mercedes C Class and
an A Class, fewer people started aspiring to be Mercedes owners. Automotive research firm AutoPacific says that in its studies of buyer intentions the number of car shoppers who would like to buy a Lexus or a
BMW was growing in 2003 twice as fast as those who would like to buy
a Mercedes.

As BMW has taken its brand into niches previously shunned, such
as sport utility vehicles, critics say the brand is being diluted. Already in
late 2003, writers exposed to the X3 were charging BMW with water-
ing down its brand for the sake of sales volume. Canadian auto writer
Jim Kenzie said, ". . . But the simple facts are that the 3 Series wagon
with four-wheel-drive does just about everything the X3 can do, only
better. It's lighter, so it's faster and more fuel-efficient. It rides better.
Handles better. Stops better." The motivation for adding an X3 seems
to be simply to give BMW buyers a new package choice, whether it
makes sense from a BMW handling and performance standpoint or
not. Even if the 3 Series all-wheel-drive wagon does darn near anything an X3 can and does it better on the road, the company still feels
obliged to have one in the showroom for those who, presumably for
reasons of great insecurity, must have an elevated seating position
from which to look down their noses at drivers of genuine cars. Chairman Helmut Panke says simply, "We have to keep filling the niches."
More distressing to BMW than Kenzie's jabs was the review by *Car and
Driver* in its January 2004 issue. *Car and Driver* historically leans heavily
toward endorsing BMWs, but not this time. Wrote reviewer Aaron
Robinson, "The X3's flaws are glaring, especially from a company
known for clipping the perfection apex tighter than most. . . . If the X3
never rose up from the paper, we'd be quaffing schnapps in its
honor. . . . The X3's ride is hard-edged, concussive, and insufferable.
Hit a craggy, undulating section of road, and the X3 bucks like a mare
with Little Richard's pinky ring stuck under the saddle. Do it at speed,
and the X3 is almost as good as a guillotine for testing your neck

joints. . . . The ceaseless shuddering of our test vehicle did its best to separate interior panels from the walls and the seats from their mounts. A few squeaks and rattles took carcinogenic root and were spreading." *Car and Driver* colleague Patrick Bedard piled on, "This BMW X3 is the 21st-century record holder [for silly cars]. Especially with the sport-suspension option and six-speed box, BMW seems to have combined the worst features of sports cars and SUVs—the jarring ride, fast-wearing tires, and dinky cargo area of the former with the excessive weight and precious pricing of the latter. For $41,000 you get a sports car on stilts. Mondo silly."

Launching new vehicles successfully is not an easy task. It's expensive because of the start-up costs at the factories and the marketing expenditures. It requires multiple parts of the company and dealer body to be singing the same song at the same time. Launches are easy to blunder. BMW is not used to such a busy schedule. And when an organization suddenly finds itself doing three things at once instead of one, mistakes happen. There is an oft-cited saying in the car business: "You only get to launch once." And the launch of a car, a period of three months, can color the image of a vehicle for its entire seven-year life. Despite robust sales for the 2002 7 Series, its difficult and heavily criticized launch still permeates the car's image as BMW's "problem child."

Still, actual signs of weakness creeping into BMWs appear mostly on the margins. An *Automobile* magazine article in 2002 rated an Infiniti G35 as a legitimate threat to the vaunted 3 Series. A 2003 *Car and Driver* comparison rated the Honda S2000 ahead of the BMW Z4. But as long as it maintains something close to its historic net profit margins of 8 to 10 percent, there is plenty of room for a few swerves as long as it doesn't leave the road altogether in a crash.

Though BMW's middle name is "Motoren" (Motor), the company has long used "The Mobility Company" as a kind of slogan. Given its history in aero engines, motorcycles, cars, and all-activity vehicles, it is a fitting idea for a company that seems to relentlessly pursue the goal of making basic mobility as fun and interesting as possible.

Notes

Introduction

1. Dan Neil, "Behind the Wheel/2004 Acura TSX—A Sedan So Complete Only Its Soul Is Missing," *New York Times*, May 11, 2003.
2. Nigel Holloway, "The Best Driven Brand," *Forbes*, July 22, 2002.

Chapter 1

1. "Ten Best," *Car and Driver*, January 2002.
2. 2003 5 Series Review, www.consumerreports.org.
3. March Cranswick, *BMW 5 Series*, Motorbooks International, 2002.
4. Ibid.
5. Ibid.
6. Ibid.
7. Ibid.
8. Interview by author at 2002 North American International Auto Show.
9. James Taylor, *BMW 5 Series: The Complete Story*, Crowood Press, 1999.
10. Martin Buckley, *BMW Cars*, Motorbooks International, 2001.
11. Taylor, *BMW 5 Series*.
12. Martin Brickman interviewed by Elaine Catton.
13. *Bimmer*, July 2003
14. Ibid.
15. Ibid.
16. Anton Ruf interviewed by Elaine Catton.

17. Matthias Hoffman interviewed by Elaine Catton.
18. Catton, Ruf interview.
19. Ibid.
20. www.consumerreports.com.
21. Jan P. Norbye, *BMW: Bavaria's Driving Machines,* Publications International, 1984.
22. Steven Cole Smith, "Road Test," *Car and Driver,* April 2000.
23. Ibid.
24. Ibid.
25. Alan Henry, *BMW M Series: The Complete Story,* Crowood Press, 1998.
26. Ibid.
27. Ibid.
28. Ibid.
29. Csaba Csere, "Battle of the Best," *Car and Driver,* March 2000.
30. Ibid.

Chapter 2

1. Horst Monnich, *The BMW Story: A Company in Its Time,* BMW AG, 1991.
2. Ibid.
3. Ibid.
4. Mick Walker, *BMW Twins: The Complete Story,* Crowood Press, 1998.
5. Ibid.
6. Halwart Schrader, *BMW: A History,* Princeton Publishing, 1979.
7. Monnich, *The BMW Story.*
8. www.cooper.edu/humanities/core/hss3/nuremberg.html.
9. Lawrence Meredith, *Essential BMW Roadsters & Cabriolets: The Cars and Their Story from 328 to Z3,* Motorbooks, 1992.
10. Jan P. Norbye, *BMW: Bavaria's Driving Machines,* Publications International, 1984.
11. Ibid.
12. Monnich, *BMW.*
13. Ibid.
14. Ibid.
15. Norbye, *BMW.*
16. Monnich, *BMW.*
17. Ibid.
18. Ibid.
19. Ibid.
20. Ibid.
21. Ibid.
22. Ibid.
23. "Turn Your Hymnals to 2002," *Car and Driver,* 1968. Article accessed on http://www.francisscott.com/~bmw2002/indexa.htm.
24. Ibid.

Chapter 3

1. Rudiger Jungbluth, *Die Quandts*, Campus Verlag, 2002.
2. Ibid.
3. Anna Maria Sigmund, *Women of the Third Reich*, NDE Publishing, 2000.
4. Ibid.
5. David Irving, *Goebbels: Mastermind of the Third Reich*, St. Martin's Press, 1996.
6. Jungbluth, *Die Quandts*.
7. Sigmund, *Women of the Third Reich*.
8. Ibid.
9. Jungbluth, *Die Quandts*.
10. Irving, *Goebbels*.
11. Jungbluth, *Die Quandts*.
12. Irving, *Goebbels*.
13. Jungbluth, *Die Quandts*.
14. Ibid.
15. Ibid.
16. Irving, *Goebbels*.
17. Jungbluth, *Die Quandts*.
18. Ibid.
19. Ibid.
20. Horst Monnich, *The BMW Story: A Company in Its Time*, BMW AG, 1991.
21. Jungbluth, *Die Quandts*.

Chapter 4

1. Nigel Holloway, "Best Driven Brand," *Forbes*, July 22, 2002.
2. "2003 Global Most Admired Companies," www.fortune.com.
3. Douglas Brinkley, *Wheels for the World*, Viking Press, 2003.
4. Horst Monnich, *The BMW Story: A Company in Its Time*, BMW AG, 1991.
5. Martin Buckley, *BMW Cars*, Motorbooks International, 2001.
6. http://eightiesclub.tripod.com/id230.htm.
7. Ibid.
8. Ibid.
9. Ibid.
10. Ibid.
11. Richard Corliss, "Log On a Drive-In Movie: Top Directors Make Spiffy Films for the Internet—And the Real Hero Is a German Luxury Sedan," *Time*, May 7, 2001.
12. Ibid.
13. Elvis Mitchell, "Critic's Notebook: Honk If You've Seen These Online Films; BMW Hopes That Its Mini-Movies by Master Filmmakers Will Sell Cars," *New York Times*, June 26, 2001.
14. Amy Taubin, *Village Voice*, June 20, 2001.

15. "BMW Films," Harvard Business School Case Study, January 11, 2002.
16. "BMW Touts Z4's Testosterone," *Automotive News*, November 11, 2002.
17. Barbara Lippert column, *Adweek*, October 28, 2002.

Chapter 5

1. Chris Bangle, BMW Global Design, Bruno Alfieri, Robert Cumberford, Valentina Lovetti, *Automobilia*, 2000.
2. Ibid.
3. Bill Breen, "BMW: Driven by Design," *Fast Company*, September 2002.
4. *Automotive News*, September 21, 2001.
5. Alex Taylor III, "Do You Think This Car Is Ugly," *Fortune*, November 29, 2001.
6. *Automotive News*, December 3, 2001.
7. Ibid.
8. Taylor, *Fortune*, November 29, 2001.
9. Bill Breen, "BMW: Driven by Design."
10. Mark Gillies, "The New BMW Z4 Is Wonderful to Drive, but About That Styling," *Automobile*, December 2002.
11. James Healey, "BMW Z4: Howling Good Fun That'll Scare You, *USA Today*, January 31, 2003.
12. Mark Vaughn, "Z Best Yet," *Autoweek*, November 11, 2002.
13. Chris Bangle, "How BMW Turns Art into Profit," *Harvard Business Review*, January 2001.
14. Interview with Boyka Boyer conducted by Elaine Catton.
15. Danny Hakim, "BMW Design Chief Sees Art on Wheels; Some Just See Ugly," *New York Times*, November 21, 2002.
16. James Taylor, *BMW Z Cars*, Veloce Publishing, 2001.
17. Ibid.
18. Ibid.
19. James Taylor, *BMW 3 Series*, Crowood Press, 2000.
20. Ibid.
21. Wolfgang Reitzle, "Luxus schafft Wohlstand. Die Zukunft der globalen Wirtschaft," *Erscheinungsdatum*, July 2001.
22. Ibid.
23. Interview by author with Gary Cowger, September 2003.
24. Reitzle, "Luxus."
25. *Car and Driver*, January 2003.

Chapter 6

1. McKinsey & Co. Report prepared for BMW in 1996.
2. Andrew Lorenz and Chris Brady, "End of the Road: BMW and Rover, A Brand Too Far," *Financial Times*, Prentice Hall, 2000.
3. Ibid.

Chapter 7

1. Anders Ditlev Clausager, *Essential Mini Cooper*, Bay View Books-MBI Publishing, 1997.
2. Ibid.
3. Ibid.
4. Graham Robson, *New Mini*, Haynes Publishing, 2002.
5. Ibid.
6. Ibid.
7. Daniel Pund, "Der Mini," *Car and Driver*, August 2001.
8. Richard Feast, *Kidnap of the Flying Lady: How Germany Captured Both Rolls-Royce and Bentley*, Motorbooks International, 2003.
9. Ibid.
10. Jonathan Wood, *Rolls-Royce*, Great Marques Series, Book Sales, 1989.

Chapter 8

1. Amory Lovins, "Twenty Myths About Hydrogen," Rocky Mountain Institute, June 2003.
2. Drew Winter, with Peter Robinson, Eric Mayne, and Herb Shuldiner, "Behind the Fuel Cell Hype," *Ward's Auto World*, August 1, 2002.

Index

Active Steering, 18–21
Acura. *See* Honda
Advertising, BMW:
   1960s–1970s, 110–117
   1980s–1990s, 127–137
   2000s, 137–149
   Ammirati & Puris, 113–117, 128
   brand image, 107–110, 117–127
   Fallon McElligott, 135–136, 140–148
   Hire, The (BMW films), 143–148
   Internet films, 140–149, 248–249
   Mini brand, 239–240, 245–250
   Mullen Agency, 134–135, 136
   "New Class," 75–76, 107, 124, 128
   product placement in Bond films,
      136, 141–142, 147, 248
   product placement in TV series, 237
   "Ultimate Driving Machine," 115,
      123, 125, 134–135, 139, 181
Adweek, 147–148
AFA (batteries), 86, 93–94, 98–99, 100
Aircraft engines:
   BMW, 47–48, 50, 52–55
   Rolls-Royce, 258, 260
Albrecht, Theo, 82

Alchemy (venture capital), 225–228
Altana AG, 84–85
American Demographics, 129
Ammirati, Ralph, 113–114, 134
Ammirati & Puris, 113–117, 128, 130–134
Antilock braking system (ABS). *See*
   Braking systems
Arlosoroff, Chaim, 89, 90
Art Cars, BMW, 176–177
Audi, 17–18, 44, 137, 188
Austin (British automaker), 47, 51–52, 58
Austin, Herbert, 50–51
Auto, Motor und Sport, 185
Autocar and Motor, 40–41, 185
Autocar magazine, 11, 43, 267
Auto Express magazine, 267
Automobile magazine, 9, 167, 193, 295
Automotive News, 110, 147, 163
AutoPacific (consultants), 33, 75, 178, 294
Autoweek magazine, 167

Bangle, Chris:
   background of, 153–161
   as BMW designer, 30, 86, 193

Bangle, Chris *(Continued)*:
  on BMW logo, 120
  criticism of, 2, 9–10, 25, 34, 173
  design of 6 Series, 26, 28
  design of 7 Series, 9–10, 163–166
  design philosophy, 168–179
  and Mini brand, 243
  Rolls-Royce design, 270–271
  and Wolfgang Reitzle, 151–153
Bangle, Edward, 155–156
Bangle, Lura, 156
Barker, Michael, 62
Barlow, Jason, 261–262
Bauer (German automaker), 40, 183
Bavaria, and BMW culture, 117–122
Bedard, Patrick, 295
Behrend, Auguste, 88–89
Bentley, 253–256, 259, 260–261, 272
Bez, Ulrich, 184
Bildstein, Bruce, 137, 148
Bimmer magazine, 21
Birkman, Martin, 18–19
Birmingham (England) *Post and Mail,* 213
BMW. *See also* BMW products
  versus competition, 1–6
  corporate culture, 105, 117–122, 127,
    190
  customer profile, 108–110, 128–130,
    138–140
  future of, 293–295
  logo, 8, 55, 59, 64, 117, 120, 124
  naming system, 16–17
  post-WWII era, 64–79
  pre-WWII history, 47–60
  product development, 22–26, 29–30
  WWII activities, 60–64
BMW products. *See also* Mini
  1 Series, 293–294
  3 Series, 127–128, 185–187, 293–294
  5 Series, 8–18, 127, 188–189
  6 Series, 26–29
  7 Series, 9, 22–26, 162–166, 189,
    274–276, 289–291
  Art Cars, 176–177
  craftsmanship of, 7–8
  design specs, 18–21
  Dixi, 47–50, 52, 58–59

under Helmut Panke, 30–35
hydrogen-powered, 273–277, 284–291
Isetta, 47, 66, 76, 156, 238
M Series, 39–45, 126
pre-WWII, 47–60
X Series, 23, 35–39, 36–39, 104,
    170–171, 192, 294–295
Z Series, 9, 27–28, 32
BMW Story, The (Monnnich), 121–122
Bobos in Paradise (Brooks), 191
Bohn, Arno, 199
Bomhard, Helmut, 121
Boston Consulting, 83
Bourne Identity, The, 248
Boyer, Boyke, 159, 174
Bracq, Paul:
  BMW 5 Series, 17
  BMW 6 Series, 26, 169
  BMW GT show car, 183
  BMW Turbo, 40, 41, 169
Braking systems, 13, 20
Brand image. *See* Advertising
Brandt, Arthur J., 51
Brandweek, 139
Brany, Chris, 229
Braun, Eva, 88, 92
Braun, Hans, 157
British Motor Corp. (BMC), 236,
    238–239, 260
British Rover Group. *See* Rover Group
Brooks, David, 191
Bruhn, Wolfgang, 82
Buckley, Martin, 17, 123
Buick, 7–8, 108, 146
Burns, Larry, 284–285, 286–288
Business Week, 233, 246

Cadillac:
  versus BMW, 6, 11, 24
  brand image, 107–108, 115, 136
Cameron, Ian, 270
Car and Driver:
  on BMW 5 Series, 11
  on BMW 1500, 68, 69–70, 73
  on BMW 2002, 78, 111
  on BMW Mini, 250–251

on BMW M Series, 44
on BMW X Series, 37–38
comparative ratings, 12
criticism of BMW, 294–295
as fan of BMW, 114, 186
Car magazine, 210
Castiglioni, Camillo, 54–58
Catton, Elaine, 45
Cavendish, Henry, 281
Celebration (BMW publication), 41
Chevrolet, 42, 108
Chicago Tribune, 129
Chung, Hennie, 147
Clausager, Anders Ditlev, 237, 239
Connery, Sean, 142
Consumer Guide, 18
Consumer Reports, 11, 25–26, 37–38
Cooper, John, 236
Corliss, Richard, 145
Cowger, Gary, 192
Cranswick, Marc, 11
Crispin-Porter & Bogusky, 246
Csere, Csaba, 11, 44
Cumberford, Robert, 193

Daimler-Benz. *See also* Mercedes-Benz
   as BMW rival, 65–67, 78, 119
   Quandt family involvement, 100–103
DaimlerChrysler, 30, 36, 127, 275
Datacard, 83
Datsun, 51
Davis, David E., Jr., 78–79, 111
Day, Graham, 207
Der Spiegel, 73, 77–78
Designworks, 161, 165, 241
Detroit Motor Show:
   1990, 158
   2002, 240
   2003, 171, 252
Djordjevic, Marek, 270–271
Dodge, 42
Donath, Kurt, 64–65
Doolan, Victor, 110, 131–134
Doppelfeld, Volker, 200, 204, 217, 222
Draeger, Hedwig, 86
Dymock, Eric, 41

Edmunds, Henry, 256–257
Ehrhardt, Heinrich, 48–49
Eichhorn, Ulrich, 284
End of the Road (Brany and Lorenz), 229
Engine design, BMW:
   airplanes, 63–64
   in BMW 5 Series, 14–18
   in-line, 72–73, 126
   marketing, 123
   Mini brand, 244–245
   motorcycles, 56–57
   power-to-weight ratio, 12–13
English, Andrew, 251–252
European Car, 45
Ewald, Antonie, 86–87

Fallon, Pat, 135
Fallon McElligott, 135–136, 140–148
Fane, A. F. P., 39
Feast, Richard, 261, 262
Ferrari, 114, 137
Ferrari, Enzo, 114
Films, BMW. *See* Advertising
Financial Times (London), 221
Fincher, David, 141
Flesher, Carl, 158, 178
Forbes, 6
Ford:
   acquisition of Jaguar, 137, 211
   acquisition of Land Rover, 36, 228,
      229
   versus BMW, 17, 69, 127, 247, 262–263
   brand image, 108–109
   car designs, 15, 52, 74, 235
   courtship of BMW, 104
   high-performance cars, 42, 71
   hydrogen-powered cars, 274
   SUVs, 192
Fortune magazine, 109, 125, 163
Frankenheimer, John, 141
Frankfurt Motor Show:
   1950s, 65, 66, 71
   1960s, 67, 72, 125
   1987, 185
   1999, 27
   2001, 9, 155, 161, 233, 290

Friz, Max, 55, 57, 59–61
Fuel technology. *See* Hydrogen-powered
    cars

Ganal, Michael, 25
Gaul, Richard, 32, 215, 253
Gebler, Bernd, 291
General Electric, 282
General Motors:
    versus BMW, 9, 35, 42, 127
    Bob Lutz at, 2, 124
    brand image, 108–109
    Chris Bangle at, 155, 157
    hydrogen-powered cars, 275–277,
        284–288, 291
    model updates, 74, 169–170
    Opel brand, 15, 69
    SUVs, 192
Geneva Motor Show:
    1955, 29
    1970s, 26, 188
    1990s, 244, 261
Gerlinger, Karl, 133, 158
Gibbon, Richard, 266
Gilles, Mark, 167
Glas (German manufacturer), 14, 74, 76
Goebbels, Joseph, 88–92, 97–98, 100
Goebbels, Magda, 88–92, 97
Goebbels: Mastermind of the Third Reich
    (Irving), 88
Goeschel, Burkhard:
    background of, 29–30, 120
    as BMW product boss, 153, 154, 193
    design issues, 10, 20–21, 25, 36–39,
        165
    and hydrogen power, 275, 281
Goldeneye (movie), 136, 141–142, 147
Gott, Tony, 252, 261, 264, 266–267, 269
Gould, Stephen Jay, 178
Graham-White, Montague, 257
Grove, William, 281–282

Hahnemann, Paul, 39–40, 73–78, 122
Hakim, Danny, 178
Halem, Hans-Hilman von, 103
Hall, Jim, 33, 75, 124, 174, 178

Hampton, Peter, 138–139
Harbour, Ron, 3, 162
Harriman, George, 236
Hasselkus, Walter, 216, 219
Healey, James, 167, 250
Heller, Manfred, 275, 284
Henne, Ernst, 39
Henry, Alan, 39
Hess, Rudolf, 96
Hildebrand, Gert, 242
Hindenburg disaster, 282, 284
Hire, The, BMW films, 143–148
Hitler, Adolf:
    Günther Quandt and, 95–100
    and Magda Goebbels, 88, 90–92
    Volksauto concept, 58, 60–63
Hoffman, Max, 65–66, 71, 77
Hoffmann, Matthias, 22
Hofmeister, Wilhelm, 69, 188
Honda:
    Acura brand, 5, 11, 13, 158
    versus BMW, 44, 195, 219–220, 295
    brand image, 4–5, 108, 133
    hydrogen-powered cars, 284, 285, 288
    Rover involvement, 202–203
Hooydonk, Adrian van, 28, 165–166
Hughes, Charlie, 16
Huss, Christoph, 276, 286–289, 291
Hydrogen-powered cars:
    advantages of, 277–281
    BMW development of, 287–291
    history of, 281–282
    safety of, 282–284
    technology issues, 273–277, 284–287

iDrive, 9, 24–26, 161–165, 269
Iñárritu, Alejandro González, 141, 144
Infiniti (by Nissan):
    versus BMW, 11, 31, 137, 158
    brand image, 133
    SUVs, 38
Internet, BMW films, 140–149,
    248–249
Irving, David, 88
Issigonis, Alexander, 211, 235–236, 238,
    243
Italian Job, The, 248

Jaguar, 27, 28, 44, 137, 211
J.D. Power and Associates, 24, 37–38,
     158, 209, 214, 250
Jeep Grand Cherokee, 36–37
Jidosha Seizo Co., 51
Johnson, Claude, 257–259
Jungbluth, Rudiger, 85, 94, 103

Kalbfell, Karl-Heinz, 264, 281
Kamm, Wunibold, 57–58
Kampfer, Ernst, 101
Karl Rapp Motorwerke, 54
Kawamoto, Nobuhiko, 202
Keene, Dennis, 236, 239
Kenzie, Jim, 294
Kidnap of The Flying Lady (Feast), 261
Kissel, Wilhelm, 61
Klatten, Jan, 84
Klatten, Susanne (Quandt), 81–86,
     104–105, 215, 222–225
Kuah, Ian, 21

Lamborghini, 40, 183
Land Rover. See Rover Group
Lange, Hans-Peter, 217
Large, Ali, 267
Lee, Ang, 141, 143
Lee, Chris, 241, 243
Letsch, Gabriel, 53
Leverton, Tim, 263–264
Lewis, E. W., 206
Lexus. See Toyota
Liechtenstein, Roy, 176
Linde, 152, 289
Lippert, Barbara, 147–148
Lord, Leonard, 238–239
Lorenz, Andrew, 229
Lovins, Amory, 283
Lubars, David, 148–149
Luderitz, Hagen, 203–204, 225–226, 253
Ludvigsen, Karl, 109
Lummert, Fritz, 75
Luthe, Claus, 157–158, 186, 188–189
Lutz, Bob:
  at BMW, 113–116, 183
  at Chrysler, 244

  at GM, 2, 16, 25, 170
  on hydrogen power, 286
  as marketing guru, 40, 123–124
  on Wolfgang Reitzle, 152
  Luxury Creates Prosperity (Reitzle), 179

Mays, J, 152, 154
Mazda, 42, 147, 185
McCarthy, Mike, 145
McDowell, Jim, 128, 135–148
McElligott, Tom, 135
McGurn, Tom, 133
McKinsey & Co.:
  as BMW consultant, 198
  Helmut Panke at, 3, 31
  Rover report, 208, 213–215
Mercedes-Benz:
  against BMW 3 Series, 128
  against BMW 5 Series, 15
  against BMW 6 Series, 27
  against BMW 7 Series, 189
  against BMW X Series, 37
  against BMW Z Series, 147, 185
  brand image, 74–75, 108, 114, 115,
     136
  Internet films, 146–147
  model names, 14, 16
  rivalry with BMW, 60–61, 63, 69,
     77–78, 124, 137, 181, 190
  as threat to BMW, 47, 66–67, 101–102,
     119
Meredith, Lawrence, 62
Milberg, Joachim:
  as BMW chairman, 8, 29, 32, 34, 105
  and Rover disaster, 222, 224–226
Mini, BMW. See also Rover Group
  as acquisition target, 198, 200–201
  BMW's redesign of, 240–245
  brand image, 231–234, 239
  fuel economy, 226
  history of, 234–240
  hydrogen-powered, 290
  marketing of, 110, 245–251
  McKinsey report, 214
Mitchell, Elvis, 145
Mitter, Gerhard, 39
Molnar, Imre, 162

Monnich, Horst, 70, 71, 121
Morris (British automaker), 51–52
Mosher, Howard, 262–263, 266
Motorcycles, BMW, 39, 47, 56–59, 156
Motor magazine, 231, 237–238
Motor Sport magazine, 41–42
Motorsports, BMW, 39–45, 183
Moulton, Alex, 238
Mullen, Jim, 134–135
Mullen Agency, 134–135, 136
Munstermann, Ursel, 94–95

Nallinger, Fritz, 101
Neerpasch, Jochen, Motorsport chief, 40
Neil, Dan, 5
Newsweek, 129
New York Times:
  on Acura versus BMW, 5
  on BMW films, 145, 149
  on Chris Bangle, 178
Nissan, 51, 146, 195. *See also* Infiniti
Norbye, Jan P., 57
Nordhoff, Heinz, 65

Onassis, Jacqueline Kennedy, 16
Opel. *See* General Motors
Otto, Gustav, 47, 52–54
Otto, Nikolaus August, 52

Panke, Helmut:
  on Art Cars, 177
  background of, 30–35
  as BMW chairman, 8, 86, 294
  and BMW culture, 119–120
  on BMW 7 Series, 163–164
  on BMW X Series, 38
  branding issues, 3, 109–110, 133
  design issues, 25
  on Mini brand, 232, 234, 240
  on Rolls-Royce brand, 252, 264, 265
  and Rover disaster, 211, 225–227
Paris Motor Show:
  1904, 257
  1923, 57
  2002, 9, 155, 166, 256

Pavel, Horst, 98
Pehr, Klaus, 289
Pelly, Charles, 161
Piech, Ferdinand:
  at Audi, 188
  as Porsche board member, 201
  and Rolls-Royce brand, 252–256
  as VW chairman, 30, 104, 218
Pischetsrieder, Bernd:
  at BMW, 30–33, 160
  on BMW culture, 119
  design issues, 24–25, 161
  on hydrogen power, 285
  and Mini brand, 243
  ouster of, 8, 32, 104–105, 117
  related to Alec Issigonis, 211, 238
  and Rolls-Royce brand, 252–256
  and Rover disaster, 174, 200–206,
    208–225, 229
  at VW, 227
Pitney, Jack, 232, 237, 245–249
Plasto, David, 199–200, 201
Popp, Franz Josef, 54–56, 58, 60–64
Porsche, 127, 137, 197, 199
Porsche, Ferdinand, 57–61, 65, 188, 253
Poulain, Hervé, 176
Power, Dave, 158
Power-to-weight ratio, 12–13
Puris, Martin, 113–115, 131–132, 134
Purves, Tom, 251

Quandt, Antonie, 86–87
Quandt, Ello, 90
Quandt, Emil, 86
Quandt, Günther, 67, 84, 86–89, 93–94,
    95–100
Quandt, Harald, 67–68, 87, 89–92, 100,
    102–103, 125
Quandt, Helmuth, 87–88, 89, 93
Quandt, Herbert:
  at AFA, 98–99, 100
  background of, 87, 93–95
  as business titan, 100–104
  control of BMW, 8, 47, 67–68, 124
  estate of, 84, 102
  marriage to Johanna, 81–83
Quandt, Inge, 102–103

Quandt, Johanna, 81–83, 85, 102–104
Quandt, Lieselotte Blobelt, 82
Quandt, Magda, 87–93
Quandt, Silvia, 102
Quandt, Stefan, 81–86, 104–105, 215, 218, 222–225
Quandt, Susanne, 81–86. *See also* Klatten, Susanne (Quandt)
Quandt, Sven, 102
Quandt, Ursel, 94–95
Quandt, Werner, 90
Quandt family:
   contrasted to Ford family, 6
   history of, 61, 67, 86–105, 119
   and Pischetsrieder's ouster, 32
   and Rover disaster, 215, 218, 220–225
Quandts, The (Jungbluth), 85

Range Rover, 192, 198, 207
Rapp, Karl, 54
Rechtin, Mark, 163
Reisinger, Anton, 275
Reitsch, Hanna, 92
Reitzle, Wolfgang:
   background of, 179–190
   and BMW branding, 119, 123, 126, 190–193
   on BMW engines, 17–18
   as BMW product chief, 35, 105, 209
   and Chris Bangle, 2, 151–153, 159–160
   compared with Burkhard Goeschel, 29–30
   contrasted to Helmut Panke, 33, 34
   design issues, 24–25, 161–162, 175
   and hydrogen power, 274
   and Mini brand, 236–237, 241–244
   ouster, 8
   Rover disaster, 174, 204–205, 212–213, 222–224, 229–230
Renault, 109
Richter, Gerhard, M Series, 42–43
Richtofen, Manfred von, 55
Riefenstahl, Leni, 90
Ritchie, Guy, 141, 144
Ritschel, Magda, 87–93
Ritschel, Oskar, 87, 89
Road & Track, 12, 15–16, 17, 26

Robins, Ralph, 254–255
Robinson, Aaron, 294
Rolls, Charles Stewart, 256–259
Rolls, John Allan, 256
Rolls-Royce:
   acquisition by BMW, 231–232, 251–256
   as BMW acquisition target, 196–200, 217
   brand image, 108, 262–268
   design issues, 268–272
   history of, 256–262
Rosche, Paul, 39, 71
Rover Group:
   as BMW albatross, 6, 86, 110, 127
   BMW's acquisition of, 36, 50, 104, 195–206, 234
   BMW's divestiture of, 30, 104, 225–230
   Chris Bangle on, 173
   history of, 206–207
   Land Rover, 36, 198, 200–201, 214, 227–228
   Pischetsrieder's undoing, 32, 208–225
   Reitzle's role, 195–201
   von Kuenheim's role, 195–201
Royce, Frederick Henry, 256–259
Ruf, Anton, on design issues, 22–25

Saab, 1, 35, 137
Scarlett, Michael, 43
Scheele, Nick, 205–206
Schmidt, Gerhard, 274
Schrader, Halwart, 57
Schrempp, Jürgen, 30, 284
Schroer, Jim, 2–3
Seck, Willy, 49
*Secret Agent (*TV series), 237
Senn, Fred, 146
Shapiro, Jakob, 50, 52, 58
Sidgreaves, Arthur, 259
Sigmund, Anna Maria, 90
Simpson, George, 201–204
Slaven, John, 131
Sport Activity Vehicles (SAVs), 23, 35–39, 170–171
Stahmer, Michael, 28

Steering mechanisms. *See* Active
    Steering
Stephenson, Frank, 240, 242–243
Suddeutsche Zeitung, 71
SUVs, BMW. *See* Sport Activity Vehicles
Sykes, Charles, 258

Taylor, Telford, 60
Telegraph Motoring, 251–252, 261
Time magazine, on BMW films, 145
Tjaarda, Tom, 162
Towers, John, 216, 228
Toyota:
    versus BMW, 5, 127, 195
    brand image, 108–109, 133
    hydrogen-powered cars, 285–286, 288
    Lexus brand, 24, 31, 37, 133, 158
Triumph (British automaker), 51

USA Today, 145, 167, 250

Vaughn, Mark, 167
Vickers plc, 197–200, 253–254, 261
Village Voice, 145
Vivian, David, 40–41
Volkswagen:
    Beetle, 52, 76, 112, 235–237, 240
    Bentley acquisition, 232, 253–254,
        265
    versus BMW, 2, 17, 65, 112, 114,
        127
    brand image, 107, 109, 112, 123
    courtship of BMW, 104
    as cultural icon, 77, 112, 235
    global branding, 23
    and hydrogen power, 284–285
    U.S. market, 112–113, 158
Volvo, 114, 137
von der Goltz, Hans Graf, 200
von Falkenhausen, Alex, 68–71, 77,
    123

von Kuenheim, Eberhard:
    background of, 122–125
    and BMW branding, 116, 131–132
    as BMW chairman, 103–106, 125
    and BMW culture, 117, 119, 127
    contrasted to Helmut Panke, 30,
        32–33
    design philosophy, 181–183, 188–189
    Rolls-Royce acquisition, 253–255
    Rover disaster, 195–201, 220–224
Vorstand (BMW management board):
    design approval, 135, 153–154, 189
    effect of Rover disaster, 174, 204, 224
    expansion issues, 182, 200
    makeup of, 10, 25, 29, 30–31, 34, 190

Warhol, Andy, 176–177
Web films, BMW, 140–149
Welch, David, 233, 246
Werner, Helmut, 77
Wilcke, Gerhard, 125
Williams, Brian, 284
Willows, Chris, 255–256
Women of the Third Reich, The
    (Sigmund), 90
Woo, John, 143, 146
World War I:
    aircraft engine production, 54–55, 207
    effect on auto market, 48–49
World War II:
    effect on BMW, 64–65
    Rolls-Royce aircraft engines, 260

Young & Rubicam, 84

Ziebart, Wolfgang, 29, 153, 227
Z Series roadsters:
    in BMW films, 146–147
    design, 9, 153, 166–168, 184–185
    in *Goldeneye* movie, 136, 141–142, 147
    U.S.-built, 32, 104, 136